ARCHAEOLOGY
97/98

Third Edition

Editor
Linda L. Hasten

Linda Hasten received both her B.A. and M.A. from the University of California, Los Angeles.
Her background is in archaeology and she has done fieldwork in several areas, including
California, the southwest United States, Peru, Europe, Mexico, and British Columbia. She
formerly taught anthropology and archaeology full-time, as a professor at Pasadena City College
from 1971 to 1992. She has also taught experimental anthropology classes to children at UCLA.
Currently, she is continuing her career as the author of both fictional and nonfictional works.
Ms. Hasten is a member of the American Anthropology Association and the Author's Guild of
America.

A Library of Information from the Public Press
Dushkin/McGraw·Hill
Sluice Dock, Guilford, Connecticut 06437

Visit us on the Internet—http://www.dushkin.com

The Annual Editions Series

ANNUAL EDITIONS is a series of over 65 volumes designed to provide the reader with convenient, low-cost access to a wide range of current, carefully selected articles from some of the most important magazines, newspapers, and journals published today. ANNUAL EDITIONS are updated on an annual basis through a continuous monitoring of over 300 periodical sources. All ANNUAL EDITIONS have a number of features that are designed to make them particularly useful, including topic guides, annotated tables of contents, unit overviews, and indexes. For the teacher using ANNUAL EDITIONS in the classroom, an Instructor's Resource Guide with test questions is available for each volume.

VOLUMES AVAILABLE

Abnormal Psychology
Adolescent Psychology
Africa
Aging
American Foreign Policy
American Government
American History, Pre-Civil War
American History, Post-Civil War
American Public Policy
Anthropology
Archaeology
Biopsychology
Business Ethics
Child Growth and Development
China
Comparative Politics
Computers in Education
Computers in Society
Criminal Justice
Criminology
Developing World
Deviant Behavior
Drugs, Society, and Behavior
Dying, Death, and Bereavement

Early Childhood Education
Economics
Educating Exceptional Children
Education
Educational Psychology
Environment
Geography
Global Issues
Health
Human Development
Human Resources
Human Sexuality
India and South Asia
International Business
Japan and the Pacific Rim
Latin America
Life Management
Macroeconomics
Management
Marketing
Marriage and Family
Mass Media
Microeconomics

Middle East and the
    Islamic World
Multicultural Education
Nutrition
Personal Growth and Behavior
Physical Anthropology
Psychology
Public Administration
Race and Ethnic Relations
Russia, the Eurasian Republics,
    and Central/Eastern Europe
Social Problems
Social Psychology
Sociology
State and Local Government
Urban Society
Western Civilization,
    Pre-Reformation
Western Civilization,
    Post-Reformation
Western Europe
World History, Pre-Modern
World History, Modern
World Politics

Cataloging in Publication Data
Main entry under title: Annual Editions: Archaeology. 1997/98.
    1. Archaeology—Periodicals. I. Hasten, Linda L., *comp*. II. Title: Archaeology.
ISBN 0–697–37206–5   930.1'05

Third Edition

On the cover: Tomb of Hatshepsut at the Valley of the Kings, Egypt. Photo by Phillip Rizzo/Anthro-Photo.

Printed in the United States of America   Printed on Recycled Paper

Editors/Advisory Board

Members of the Advisory Board are instrumental in the final selection of articles for each edition of ANNUAL EDITIONS. Their review of articles for content, level, currentness, and appropriateness provides critical direction to the editor and staff. We think that you will find their careful consideration well reflected in this volume.

EDITOR

Linda L. Hasten

ADVISORY BOARD

Staff

Ian A. Nielsen, Publisher

To the Reader

In publishing ANNUAL EDITIONS we recognize the enormous role played by the magazines, newspapers, and journals of the *public press* in providing current, first-rate educational information in a broad spectrum of interest areas. Many of these articles are appropriate for students, researchers, and professionals seeking accurate, current material to help bridge the gap between principles and theories and the real world. These articles, however, become more useful for study when those of lasting value are carefully *collected, organized, indexed,* and *reproduced* in a *low-cost format,* which provides easy and permanent access when the material is needed. That is the role played by ANNUAL EDITIONS. Under the direction of each volume's *academic editor,* who is an expert in the subject area, and with the guidance of an *Advisory Board,* each year we seek to provide in each ANNUAL EDITION a current, well-balanced, carefully selected collection of the best of the public press for your study and enjoyment. We think that you will find this volume useful, and we hope that you will take a moment to let us know what you think.

This third edition of *Annual Editions: Archaeology 97/98* consists of a number of readings specifically selected to present a lively overview of the field of archaeology as it is practiced today. Each article was chosen to make the old bones, shards of pottery, and stone tools pop into the living cultural context in which they once existed. The pop or sensuality of doing a thing is not to be found in the typical archaeology textbook.

The guiding concept behind this book is to present a approach in which archaeologists can speak for themselves of their own special experiences. The student will be exposed to a holistic perspective about archaeology as a living and applied science. In good writing, an author does not say Darwin was a very tall man but rather that Darwin had to duck his head to walk through his seven-foot-high library door. The *show me* literature here will energize the necessary basics and enable the student to transform passive learning into active learning, so that information is both conceptualized and perceptualized. In other words, the light bulb goes on when a student reads these selections.

This book is organized into six units, each of which contains several articles on various aspects of practicing archaeology. At the beginning of the book a *table of contents* provides a short synopsis of each article. This is followed by a *topic guide* that cross-references general areas of interest as they appear in the different articles. At the end of the book is a comprehensive *index.* Each unit is introduced by an overview that provides both commentary on the unit topic and *challenge questions* to provoke thought and discussion. It is highly recommended that the students read these *unit overviews.*

The organization of this book is both suggestive and subjective. The articles may be assigned or read in any fashion that is deemed desirable. Each reading stands on its own and may be assigned in conjunction with or in contrast to any other reading. For introductory archaeology courses, this anthology may serve as a supplement to a standard textbook, or it may be used with other books to replace the standard textbook altogether. It may also be used as supplementary reading in general courses, upper division courses, or graduate seminars in anthropology/archaeology. Additionally, it is useful to an interested lay public.

Unlike most academic texts, this book will be updated annually to keep pace with its rapidly changing subject matter and to allow for greater exposure to the vast literature available in the field of archaeology. Those involved in the production of this volume wish to make each edition a valuable and provocative teaching tool. We welcome your criticisms, advice, and suggestions in order to carefully hone each edition into a finer artifact of education. Please use the postage-paid form at the end of the book for your comments. Each year these comments are read by me and the advisory board in shaping the next year's edition.

It is humbling to realize that today is tomorrow's past and that evidence abounds of truths whose questions we have not yet asked.

Linda L. Hasten
Editor

Contents

UNIT 1

About Archaeology

Nine articles present overviews of the history and definition of archaeology and how archaeologists view themselves and each other.

The concepts in bold italics are developed in the article. For further expansion please refer to the Topic Guide and the Index.

UNIT 2

Problem-Oriented Archaeology

Nine articles examine the contemporary goal of archaeology, which is to solve problems rather than to make discoveries. Problems range from the discovery of art by prehistoric human beings to general issues when earliest peoples first migrated to the New World.

The concepts in bold italics are developed in the article. For further expansion please refer to the Topic Guide and the Index.

UNIT 3

Experimental Archaeology

Five selections demonstrate how modern archaeologists purposely set up experiments to reenact past events. Whatever the experiments, a whole new body of fundamental information about archaeological processes is generated.

The concepts in bold italics are developed in the article. For further expansion please refer to the Topic Guide and the Index.

UNIT 4

History and Ethno-archaeology

Six articles consider the use of the studies of contemporary societies, including but not limited to primitive societies, to extrapolate back to the past in order to re-create a kind of living social archaeology.

UNIT 5

The New Politics of Archaeology: A Trowel for Your Thoughts

Eight selections examine who has what rights and responsibilities with respect to archaeological sites. Nationalistic politics as well as local politics come into play in attempting to meet these various and often conflicting demands.

The concepts in bold italics are developed in the article. For further expansion please refer to the Topic Guide and the Index.

UNIT 6

Contemporary Archaeology

Eight articles explore the expanding roles of archaeologists as they move into the areas of salvage, private business, cultural resource management, preservation of sites, and public archaeology, all underscored by significantly reduced funding.

The concepts in bold italics are developed in the article. For further expansion please refer to the Topic Guide and the Index.

The concepts in bold italics are developed in the article. For further expansion please refer to the Topic Guide and the Index.

Topic Guide

This topic guide suggests how the selections in this book relate to topics of traditional concern to students and professionals involved with the study of archaeology. It can be very useful for locating articles that relate to each other for reading and research. The guide is arranged alphabetically according to topic. Articles may, of course, treat topics that do not appear in the topic guide. In turn, entries in the topic guide do not necessarily constitute a comprehensive listing of all the contents of each selection.

TOPIC AREA	TREATED IN	TOPIC AREA	TREATED IN
African-American Archaeology	24. Earth Is Their Witness 25. Legacy of Fort Mose	**Cultural Resource Management (CRM) and Preservation (continued)**	41. Damming the Past 42. Before the Deluge 44. Maya Resurrection 45. Boom in Volunteer Archaeology
Antiquities, Antiquarians, and Amateur Archaeologists	1. Quest for the Past 2. Enlightened Archaeologist 31. Antiquities Market 32. Who Owns the Spoils of War? 33. Troy's Prodigious Ruin 45. Boom in Volunteer Archaeology	**Epistemology**	2. Enlightened Archaeologist 3. How Archaeology Works 4. Golden Marshalltown 5. Epistemology 6. Archaeology 8. History Unearthed
Art and Religion	12. Rhinos and Lions and Bears (Oh My!) 13. Ancient Odysseys 14. Toward Decolonizing Gender 17. Find Suggests Weaving Preceded Settled Life 18. Thailand's Good Mound 20. Moving the Moai 22. Paleolithic Paint Job 28. Colorful Cotton! 31. Antiquities Market 32. Who Owns the Spoils of War? 33. Troy's Prodigious Ruin 43. Tales from a Peruvian Crypt 44. Maya Resurrection	**Ethics and Laws**	4. Golden Marshalltown 7. Surrogate Stone 26. Guns of Palo Alto 29. Murders from the Past 30. Anthropological Culture Shift 31. Antiquities Market 32. Who Owns the Spoils of War? 33. Troy's Prodigious Ruin 34. Lure of the Deep 35. 35,000-Year-Old Artifacts Repatriated in Tasmania 36. Beruit Digs Out 37. Past as Propaganda 38. Preservation of Past 39. Saving Our World's Heritage 40. Largest Pueblo Ruin to Be Saved 41. Damming the Past 42. Before the Deluge 43. Tales from a Peruvian Crypt 44. Maya Resurrection
Burials, Reburials, and Human Remains	1. Quest for the Past 2. Enlightened Archaeologist 9. Hard Times at Lizard Man 18. Tailand's Good Mound 24. Earth Is Their Witness 27. Living through the Donner Party 29. Murders from the Past 30. Anthropological Culture Shift 31. Antiquities Market 33. Troy's Prodigious Ruin 34. Lure of the Deep 38. Preservation of Past 43. Tales from a Peruvian Crypt	**Ethnographic Analogy and Ethnoarchaeology**	24. Earth Is Their Witness 25. Legacy of Fort Mose 26. Guns of Palo Alto 27. Living through the Donner Party 28. Colorful Cotton! 29. Murders from the Past 37. Past as Propaganda
Contract Archaeology	16. Denizens of the Desert 24. Earth Is Their Witness 25. Legacy of Fort Mose 34. Lure of the Deep 35. 35,000-Year-Old Artifacts Repatriated in Tasmania 36. Beirut Digs Out 39. Saving Our World's Heritage 40. Largest Pueblo Ruin to Be Saved 44. Maya Resurrection	**Experimental Archaeology**	19. Yes, Wonderful Things 20. Moving the Moai 21. Ice Age Lamps 22. Paleolithic Paint Job 23. Bushmen 28. Colorful Cotton!
		Forensic Archaeology	9. Hard Times at Lizard Man 29. Murders from the Past
Cultural Resource Management (CRM) and Preservation	12. Rhinos and Lions and Bears (Oh My!) 16. Denizens of the Desert 20. Moving the Moai 22. Paleolithic Paint Job 25. Legacy of Fort Mose 33. Troy's Prodigious Ruin 34. Lure of the Deep 36. Beirut Digs Out 38. Preservation of Past 39. Saving Our World's Heritage 40. Largest Pueblo Ruin to Be Saved	**Frauds**	5. Epistemology 7. Surrogate Stone 37. Past as Propaganda
		Garbology	1. Quest for the Past 19. Yes, Wonderful Things
		Gender and Sex Roles	1. Quest for the Past 14. Toward Decolonizing Gender 15. Lithic Technology and the Hunter-Gatherer Sexual Division of Labor

TOPIC AREA	TREATED IN	TOPIC AREA	TREATED IN
History and Historical Archaeology	1. Quest for the Past 2. Enlightened Archaeologist 19. Yes, Wonderful Things	**Politics in Archaeology**	16. Denizens of the Desert 26. Guns of Palo Alto 30. Anthropological Culture Shift 31. Antiquities Market 32. Who Owns the Spoils of War? 35. 35,000-Year-Old Artifacts Repatriated in Tasmania 36. Beirut Digs Out 37. Past as Propaganda 38. Preservation of Past 39. Saving Our World's Heritage 40. Largest Pueblo Ruin to Be Saved 41. Daming the Past 42. Before the Deluge 44. Maya Resurrection
Hunter-Collectors	9. Hard Times at Lizard Man 10. Coming to America 11. First Americans 12. Rhinos and Lions and Bears (Oh My!) 14. Toward Decolonizing Gender 15. Lithic Technology and the Hunter-Gatherer Sexual Division of Labor 17. Find Suggests Weaving Preceded Settled Life 21. Ice Age Lamps 22. Paleolithic Paint Job 23. Bushmen 31. Antiquities Market 35. 35,000-Year-Old Artifacts Repatriated in Tasmania 41. Damming the Past	**Public Archaeology**	2. Enlightened Archaeologist 28. Colorful Cotton! 31. Antiquities Market 32. Who Owns the Spoils of War? 33. Troy's Prodigious Ruin 38. Preservation of Past 40. Largest Pueblo Ruin to Be Saved 45. Boom in Volunteer Archaeology
Looters, Grave Robbers, and Pot Hunters	1. Quest for the Past 20. Moving the Moai 31. Antiquities Market 32. Who Owns the Spoils of War? 33. Troy's Prodigious Ruin 34. Lure of the Deep 38. Preservation of Past 39. Saving Our World's Heritage 40. Largest Pueblo Ruin to Be Saved 43. Tales from a Peruvian Crypt 44. Maya Resurrection	**Repatriation**	16. Denizens of the Desert 30. Anthropological Culture Shift 31. Antiquities Market 32. Who Owns the Spoils of War? 33. Troy's Prodigious Ruin 34. Lure of the Deep 35. 35,000-Year-Old Artifacts Repatriated in Tasmania 36. Beirut Digs Out 40. Largest Pueblo Ruin to Be Saved 44. Maya Resurrection
Migration	10. Coming to America 11. First Americans 17. Find Suggests Weaving Preceded Settled Life 18. Thailand's Good Mound 23. Bushmen 25. Legacy of Fort Mose	**Ritual and Myth**	7. Surrogate Stone 12. Rhinos and Lions and Bears (Oh My!) 16. Denizens of the Desert 20. Moving the Moai 27. Living through the Donner Party 33. Troy's Prodigious Ruin 43. Tales from a Peruvian Crypt 44. Maya Resurrection
New World	2. Enlightened Archaeologist 9. Hard Times at Lizard Man 10. Coming to America 11. First Americans 19. Yes, Wonderful Things	**Salvage Archaeology**	2. Enlightened Archaeologist 16. Denizens of the Desert 34. Lure of the Deep 35. 35,000-Year-Old Artifacts Repatriated in Tasmania 36. Beirut Digs Out 38. Preservation of Past 39. Saving Our World's Heritage 40. Largest Pueblo Ruin to Be Saved 41. Damming the Past 42. Before the Deluge 43. Tales from a Peruvian Crypt 44. Maya Resurrection
Old World	7. Surrogate Stone 8. History Unearthed 12. Rhinos and Lions and Bears (Oh My!) 14. Toward Decolonizing Gender 15. Lithic Technology and the Hunter-Gatherer Sexual Division of Labor 16. Denizens of the Desert 17. Find Suggests Weaving Preceded Settled Life 18. Thailand's Good Mound 21. Ice Age Lamps 22. Paleolithic Paint Job 23. Bushmen 32. Who Owns the Spoils of War? 33. Troy's Prodigious Ruin 36. Beirut Digs Out 37. Past as Propaganda 42. Before the Deluge	**Scientific Method**	*See* Epistomology
		Subterranean Dwellings	9. Hard Times at Lizard Man 16. Denizens of the Desert
Paleolithic Archaeology	7. Surrogate Stone 10. Coming to America 13. Ancient Odysseys 14. Toward Decolonizing Gender 15. Lithic Technology and the Hunter-Gatherer Sexual Division of Labor 17. Find Suggests Weaving Preceded Settled Life 21. Ice Age Lamps 22. Paleolithic Paint Job	**Underwater Archaeology**	34. Lure of the Deep

About Archaeology

What is the difference between archaeology and anthropology? Would the archaeologists or anthropologists who have been asked this question please stand up and be counted!

If human behavior were a baseball game, the anthropologist would be in the broadcaster's booth. But long before the game was over, in a seeming paradox, the anthropologist would run into the stands to be a spectator, chow down on a good mustard-covered hot dog, and then rush onto the field to be a player and catch a high fly to right field. This is the eccentric nature of anthropology. This is why anthropologists are so interesting.

If one compares anthropology, psychology, sociology, and history as four disciplines that study humankind, anthropology is the one that takes the biggest step back and uses a panoramic camera that gives a 360-degree view. The psychologist stands nose to nose with the individual person, the sociologist steps back for the group shot, and the historian steps back in time as well as space. However, the anthropologist does all these things, standing well behind the others, watching and measuring, in a sense using the data of all these disciplines but weaving them into the uniqueness of the anthropological perspective.

Anthropology is the science of human behavior that studies all humankind, starting with our biological and evolutionary origins as cultural beings and continuing with the diversification of our cultural selves. Humankind is the single species that has evolved culture as a unique way of adapting to the world.

Academically, anthropology is divided into the two major fields of physical and cultural anthropology. Cultural anthropologists hold a generally shared concept of cul-ture. The basic question that cultural anthropologists address is how to explain the differences and similarities between cultures. In order to achieve this, cultural anthropologists view people with a cross-cultural perspective. This encompasses comparing all cultures, present and past, with each other. A grand task, indeed.

What is culture? Culture is the unique way in which our species adapts to its total environment. Total environment includes everything that affects human beings—the physical environment, plants, animals, the weather, beliefs, values, a passing insult, or an opportunistic virus. Everything! Human beings are both created by culture and creators of culture.

Culture is the human adaptive system in which all people live in groups defined by time, space, and place, pass on shared values and beliefs through a common language(s), and manipulate things in the environment through tool use and tool making. Cultures change and evolve through time. And perhaps most enigmatic, cultures, all cultures, whether they are high civilizations or small tribes, eventually cease to exist.

It is archaeology as a subfield of cultural anthropology that studies these extinct cultures. Archaeologists dig up the physical remains, the tools, the houses, the rubbish, of once-living cultures. From this spare database, archaeologists try to reconstruct these past cultures. Is this important to anthropology? Yes, because these once-living cultures represent approximately 98 percent of all cultures that have ever existed. They tell us where we have been, when we are there again, and where we might go in the future.

How do archaeologists do this? Today the media is the major source of the epistemology in the modern world and thus underscores cultural values as well as creating the necessary cultural myths by which all humans must live. The media is as much a response to our demands as we are to its manipulations. But the media-mind is characterized by *fuzzy thinking*. The secret of archaeology is scientific thinking. If minds are trained to be articulate, speech and actions will follow suit. Scientific thinking involves a very strict set of unchanging rules and regulations that test the veracity of conclusions. A kind of operationalized language emerges, somewhat codified like mathematics, that allows apples to be compared to apples. Postmodernists may argue that knowledge is only knowable in a relative sense. But we know what we know in a very real and pragmatic sense because we are, after all, human—the cultural animals. It is our way of knowing.

Let us proceed now to see how archaeologists ply their magical trade.

Looking Ahead: Challenge Questions

What is the general relationship between anthropology and archaeology?

What does it mean to say that archaeology started as an "underground" science?

When was archaeology recognized as a science? Why?

Describe how archaeology raises questions of ethics.

What is the range of variation in the scale of archaeological digs? Give some examples.

What is a hypothesis? How is it different from a theory? Give an example of each.

What are the four rules of science? Do they change? Does luck ever play a role in practicing archaeology?

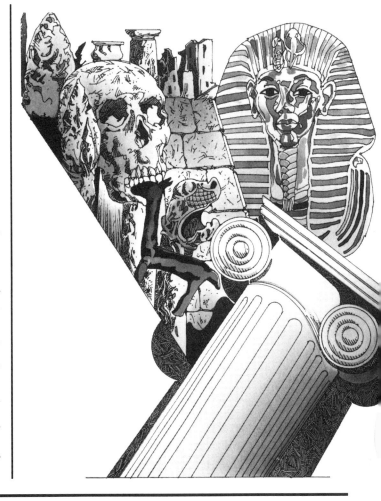

The Quest for the Past

Brian M. Fagan

Archaeologists are commonly thought to be eccentric people who wear rumpled khaki shorts and sun helmets and spend their lives unearthing crumbling ruins in the shadow of mighty pyramids. They live in a world of lost civilizations and buried treasure, deep mysteries and unexplained phenomena. The archaeologist of novel and television seems to be continually off on a "dig," searching for missing links and unwrapping innumerable Ancient Egyptian mummies. Sometimes, too, the angry mummies chase the unfortunate archaeologists, intoning dreadful curses that lead to their premature deaths. Many of us, at one time or another, have dreamed of pursuing such a romantic—if, in fact, mythical—career.

This is . . . about actual archaeological discoveries, about remarkable archaeologists whose explorations have dramatically expanded our understanding of human history. It is . . . about the excitement of archaeological discovery, about a scientific world that many consider to be one of the most engrossing frontiers of science. Its heroes are archaeologists of extraordinary ability who have made fascinating discoveries, often after years of patient effort. Each was a pioneer who pursued a dream, a conviction that spectacular archaeological finds awaited his or her spade.

The face of archaeology has changed considerably in recent years. Archaeologists of the 1840s, and even as late as the 1930s, could hope to uncover hitherto unknown civilizations: the Assyrians and Sumerians of Mesopotamia surfaced in the mid-nineteenth century, the Maya of Mexico in the 1840s, the Mycenaeans of Greece in the 1870s, the Shang civilization of China in the late 1920s. All of these discoveries captured the public imagination, for they were made under conditions of great difficulty, conditions that often required near-heroic efforts, The early archaeologists had few resources and no advanced excavation techniques. By constant improvisation, by drawing on their own wealth, and by acute political maneuvering, they frequently achieved miracles. They learned digging the hard way, made brilliant finds, and, regrettably, sometimes irreparably damaged vital clues to the past.

Some of our archaeologists belong to this heroic era, others to our own generation, where there are simply no lost civilizations left to find. But today's archaeologists still make remarkable discoveries, often as a result of applying such advanced tools as the computer to archaeological data. Modern archaeology is big business; thousands of people all over the world are currently involved in digging up the past. Practically every nation now employs a few archaeologists—as museum curators, university professors, or conservators of national culture. All of these archaeologists use excavation techniques that have evolved over generations of archaeological discovery. The newer techniques enable them to tackle problems that would have boggled the mind even a few years ago.

One of Mexico's earliest cities, Teotihuacán, is a case in point. Early archaeologists could only gasp at the size of Teotihuacán, sample a portion of a pyramid or a few houses, then turn away in despair. They simply did not have the technology needed to carry their explorations further. It has taken a team of modern archaeologists over a decade to map the entire twelve-and-a-half square miles of Mexico's largest prehistoric city. Their task would have been impossible without a mosaic of air photographs and highly sophisticated computer programs that enabled them to store inventories of archaeological finds and millions of other items of information on computer tape. When the time came to put the data together, the archaeologists could recall and classify thousands of data items in a few seconds. The result: a whole new picture of Teotihuacán.

How do archaeologists dig up the past? What makes archaeological excavation different from ditch digging or the treasure-hunting activities of our mythical, sun-helmeted archaeologist? To get some idea of just how far the field of archaeology has progressed, let's look back over its colorful history.

Archaeology has a long and disreputable line of descent: its ancestors were, quite literally, grave robbers and adventurers. A century and a half ago, even serious archaeological excavation was little more than licensed treasure hunting. Everyone, whether archaeologist or treasure hunter, had the same objective—to recover as many valuable objects as possible in the shortest time. Serious archaeologists would not hesitate to use gunpowder to blast their way into a burial chamber or a pyramid. Everything was cast aside in a frantic search for the valuable and spectacular. As a result, most excavations resembled untidy vegetable gardens.

Mummy hunters in Egypt literally waded through piles of discarded coffins to reach their prey. The famous Italian collector Giovanni Belzoni, who worked in Egypt from 1817 to 1820, would crawl hundreds of yards into the rocky hillsides behind Thebes in search of mummies and papyri. Exhausted, he would perch in the darkness for a few minutes on a convenient mummy. Once his perch collapsed in a cloud of smelly dust. "I sank altogether among the broken mummies, with a crash of bones, rags, and wooden cases," he remembered. It was a good quarter of an hour before Belzoni could extricate himself.

Belzoni and his contemporaries were quite open about their efforts to "rob the Egyptians of their papyri." No one thought this either eccentric or wrong. Rather, Belzoni's audiences would be agog as he related his eerie experiences in the dark burial chambers, where, in the flickering lamplight, the mummies seemed almost to converse with one another and the naked Arab workmen, coated in layers of dust, resembled mummies themselves. The audiences would gasp as Belzoni produced pieces of desiccated ancient Egyptians, remarking casually that "mummies are rather unpleasant to swallow."

In general, the nineteenth century was a time of frantic search for ancient sculptures and fine artifacts, whether from Egypt, Greece, Mesopotamia, or the Americas. Everyone wanted items for their collections and no one had any scruples about the means used to dig up their pet acquisitions. All too often we read in their early reports that such and such a find "crumbled to dust" on discovery or that exposure to the open air caused the finds to "dissolve before our very eyes."

One cannot entirely blame Belzoni and his successors. Basically, they were ignorant. No one had ever tried to dig a large archaeological site at all systematically. Even today, the technology of conservation is in relative infancy and modern archaeologists are still at a loss as to how to preserve

many delicate finds satisfactorily. Considering the state of the art, it's a miracle that so much is preserved from early excavations. But the archaeological price of filling the British Museum, the Louvre, and other great museums was simply enormous: witness Austen Henry Layard's excavations in Mesopotamia at ancient Nineveh and Nimrud from 1845 to 1851.

Layard started digging Nimrud with precious little money and absolutely no archaeological experience. He simply tunneled into the huge mounds reputed to be the remains of these ancient cities and went on digging until he hit a fine sculpture or a stone-walled palace room. At Nimrud he was lucky enough to find two palaces. But, as he dug through mud-brick walls and houses, he failed to recognize invaluable inscribed tablets of unbaked clay. To his unskilled eyes, the bricks and tablets were indistinguishable from the brown soil of the mound. Later excavators recovered thousands of these tablets from areas of Nimrud that Layard left untouched. They had developed the skills and techniques to find them.

The deep tunnels that Layard dug along walls or lines of sculptured slabs at least sheltered him from the merciless sun and sweeping winds of the open plains. He would shovel out the contents of each room with dispatch, then sit down to record the intricate details of prancing horsemen and fighting warriors that flickered in the somber shadows. When his trenches were open to the elements, clouds of blinding dust stirred by savage gale-force winds would bombard the workmen. Layard himself would take refuge behind a giant sculpture until the sandstorm subsided. Under the circumstances, it is remarkable that he succeeded in excavating at all.

Austen Henry Layard shifted thousands of tons of soil, discovered nearly two miles of bas-reliefs, and cleared seventy rooms in the Palace of Sennacherib at Kuyunjik alone. Although he did keep some records, he more or less shoveled his way into the past. He tore Nimrud and Nineveh apart and, in the process, wiped out priceless archaeological information—data on

daily life and ancient diet, details of houses and storerooms, and, above all, the complex sequence of layers that made up the occupation mounds.

Every Mesopotamian city mound was formed over centuries of occupation through complex processes of rebuilding houses, dumping garbage, and the natural actions of rain and wind. Many years before Layard came to Nineveh, geologists studying railway cuttings and canal excavations in Europe and America had observed the layered strata of the earth and established the classic principle of superposition. Very simply stated, this means that the lower levels of a succession of geological horizons were laid down earlier than the higher levels. The law of superposition had obvious applications to great city mounds like Nimrud or Nineveh, for every site started as a small settlement on a low ridge. The first occupation levels were soon covered by later settlements built in the same place. A thousand years later, the same city could look down from the top of a high mound of age-old occupation debris. The archaeologist wishing to understand the history of the city would have to dissect this mound layer by layer.

Layard himself was well aware that his mounds had gone through many changes. He knew that many kings had ruled his cities. But his excavation methods were simply too crude to permit him to dig the mounds period by period. One cannot blame Layard. If anything, he was more conscientious than his contemporaries, for he at least wrote popular accounts of his findings.

Many excavations of Layard's time were little more than picnic parties. Wealthy country gentlemen would open Indian burial mounds or Bronze Age earthworks for the sheer fun of it. When the English antiquarian Thomas Wright attended the opening of an ancient burial mound in 1844, he found a large party of interested gentry assembled for the sport. While the workmen opened eight burial mounds, the ladies and gentlemen "continued to spend [their] time, at intervals between digging and picnicking, in games of various descriptions . . . and in other amusements. The weather was fortunately exquisitely fine." When a sudden shower threatened to drench the party, they took refuge in the trench under a shield of umbrellas. The burial mounds contained "skeletons, more or less entire, with the remains of weapons in iron, bosses of shields, urns, beads, armlets, and occasionally more vessels." All of these finds vanished into the landowner's private collection, which the party inspected after partaking of a "sumptuous repast." This burial-mound dig was in no way exceptional; rather, it was typical of thousands.

The techniques of excavation were still in their infancy when Heinrich Schliemann began work on the great Hissarlik mound, site of ancient Troy. Schliemann, a millionaire, attacked archaeological problems with the same single-minded intensity he applied to business ventures. His wealth gave him the means to work on a truly grand scale, with resident experts and hundreds of workmen. He arrived on the site in 1871 with the vague notion that the mound contained many different settlements. So he set out to dig to bedrock, on a scale that almost beggars description. In 1872, for example, he borrowed a railroad engineer and employed three overseers to direct over a hundred men. They sliced into Hissarlik with a cutting over 230 feet wide that eventually penetrated over 40 feet into the huge mound. The city walls found in the upper-most strata were ruthlessly cleared away as Schliemann dug his way down through the centuries, toward his Homeric city.

Eventually, Schliemann identified the remains of seven cities, one above the other. His excavations exhibited a notable lack of finesse. In his books, he refers to the clearance of entire ancient streets, to the removal of "older walls which I am also having broken through," and to thousands upon thousands of potsherds, ornaments, and other small finds that were shoveled out as thousands of tons of soil were dug out of Hissarlik. At one point, he boasted that he had removed 325,000 cubic yards of soil from ancient Troy.

Schliemann's motto was speed, more speed, and yet still more. When he dug, he cleared an entire landscape. Every day he described his findings in a comprehensive diary, which he eventually published. Unlike many of his contemporaries, Schliemann kept his finds and recorded all of them, not just the spectacular pieces. And, although he has been castigated as little more than a treasure hunter, he in fact undertook the first large-scale dissection of a city mound where, unlike the situation at Nineveh or Nimrud, there were no sculptures to guide the way to ancient structures. As his digging experience increased, Schliemann began to rely more heavily on expert diggers, who were able to refine his methods drastically.

While Schliemann was working at Troy, German archaeologists had begun a quiet revolution in excavation methods that was to affect both the Troy excavations and many other digs as well. The Austrian archaeologist Alexander Conze dug at the site of Samothrace in Greece between 1873 and 1875. He dug with the help of architects and a photographer, who recorded the progress of the excavations. The Samothrace report was a beautiful production, the first to be illustrated with photographs. Conze's example was not lost on the German Archaeological Institute, which started work at Olympia in 1875. For six winters, Ernst Curtius directed a brilliant campaign of excavations on the site of the original Olympic Games. The Kaiser himself paid for part of the dig. Every find was carefully preserved and housed in a special museum built at the site. No artifacts were exported. Curtius and Wilhelm Dörpfeld worked out every detail of the stratigraphy at Olympia with the aid of new and very precise record-keeping methods. The Olympia excavations set new standards that the ever-energetic Dörpfeld took with him to Troy. In his later years at Hissarlik, Schliemann became what one authority has called "a constitutional monarch among expert ministers." Dörpfeld refined Schliemann's seven cities into the complex history of a mound that, he said, flourished from

about 3000–700 B.C., the Homeric city dating from 1500–1000 B.C.

Curtius and Dörpfeld were concerned with the trivial as well as the spectacular. Their excavations were far more meticulous than those of their predecessors, although still crude by modern standards. A retired British general named Augustus Pitt-Rivers revolutionized the art of excavation even further. The general, a formidable personality, spent much of his military career working on the development of army rifles. His experimental research involved him in the history of firearms and the study of different types of primitive artifacts from all over the world. Pitt-Rivers was deeply interested in the evolution of human technology. He became an avid collector of artifacts of all types—masks, shields, weapons, even canoes. His collections became so large that he donated them to Oxford University, where they are to this day.

In 1880, Pitt-Rivers inherited an enormous estate in southern England, an estate littered with ancient burial sites and earthworks. The general decided to devote the rest of his life to investigation of the sites on his property. He did so with ruthless efficiency, diverting enormous sums from his fortune into leisured excavations that lasted twenty years, until his death in 1901. Pitt-Rivers had a mania for records and detail. "Every detail should be recorded in the manner most conducive to facility of reference," he wrote. "I have endeavored to record the results of these excavations in such a way that the whole of the evidence may be available for those who are concerned to go into it." He had realized a cardinal point: all archaeological excavation is permanent destruction and all objects found in a site have a vital context in time and space that is just as important a piece of information as the find itself.

The learned general was far ahead of his time. He trained archaeological assistants, had "before" and "after" models of his sites constructed, built a special museum to display his finds, and even marked his filled-in trenches with special medallions that said, in effect, "Pitt-Rivers was here." His ideas were revolutionary. Consider some of his basic principles of digging: "No excavation ought to ever be permitted except under the immediate eye of a responsible and trustworthy superintendent." "Superfluous precision may be regarded as a fault on the right side." "Tedious as it may appear to some to dwell on the discovery of odds and ends that have, no doubt, been thrown away by the owners as rubbish . . . yet it is by the study of such trivial details that archaeology is mainly dependent for determining the date of earthworks."

Hundreds of man-hours went into each of Pitt-Rivers's sumptuous reports. Each was published privately, complete with detailed plans, accurate measurements of every artifact, and precise information on every aspect of the site from pottery to hut foundations, stratigraphy to animal bones. It was to be years before anyone would equal or surpass Pitt-Rivers's painstaking work. He deplored the destruction of earthworks by plowing, laid out picnic grounds for people visiting his museum, and urged his fellow landowners to follow his example. The general was not a particularly endearing gentleman, but his legacy to archaeology is unquestioned. An interesting glimpse into the man comes from a photograph of the excavations which is tersely captioned: "The figure standing at attention in the foreground gives the scale." Evidently Pitt-Rivers was a military man, as well as an archaeologist, to the very end.

Few people followed Pitt-Rivers's example. One could still become an excavator without any training at all, although well-known archaeologists like Wilhelm Dörpfeld and the immortal Egyptologist Flinders Petrie were busy training students to follow in their footsteps. Petrie begged his colleagues to be quit of "the brandy-and-soda young man . . . of the adventurous speculator. Without the ideal of solid continuous work, certain, accurate, and permanent, archaeology is as futile as any other pursuit." He went on to urge informal attire: "To attempt serious work in pretty suits, shiny leggings or starched collars, would be like mountaineering in evening dress." "It is sickening to see the rate at which everything is being destroyed," he once remarked, "and the little regard paid to preservation."

Some of the better digging that stemmed from Pitt-Rivers's work took place on Roman sites in Britain. Still, to modern eyes, the efforts appear to have been terribly amateurish and the excavators incredibly ill-equipped. Young Leonard Woolley, for example, later to become famous for his skilled excavations of royal graves at Ur-of-the-Chaldees in Mesopotamia, found himself in charge of a major Roman excavation without any experience at all or the least idea of how to survey a site or make plans.

The early part of this century also seems to have been a difficult period for female archaeologists. When a little-known archaeologist named J. P. Droop wrote a small manual on excavation in 1915, he spent a lot of time worrying about male/female roles. "I have never seen a trained lady excavator at work," he admitted. "Of a mixed dig, however, I have seen something, and it is an experiment that I would be reluctant to try again." His reasons were twofold. "In the first place, there are the proprieties." Excavators should respect the etiquette and mores of the countries they are working in. Droop's other reasons were more personal. It seems that, in his experience, the "charm" of ladies vanishes during an excavation, for the dig lays on its mixed participants "a bond of closer daily intercourse than is conceivable." Droop found this irritating. "The ordinary male at least cannot stand it," he added. He cited the strain of "self-restraint in moments of stress, moments that will occur on the best regulated dig, when you want to say just what you think without translation, which before ladies, whatever their feelings about it, cannot be done." Droop was never to know of the key roles played by twentieth-century women in major archaeological excavations the world over.

Nevertheless, there were a handful of women who carried out important work in the field long before female excavators became Commonplace. One pioneer was the English novelist Amelia Edwards, a Victorian lady in the classic sense of the word, who embarked on a two-month journey up the Nile in 1874. She traveled in genteel company aboard a sailing ship complete with upright piano and proper chaperones. Edwards was horrified by the looting and destruction of Ancient Egyptian sites on every side, at the blatant forgery of antiquities, and the "black-robed, grave men, who always lay in wait ready to sell you anything." Nevertheless, she was entranced by the Pyramids, the Temple of Karnak, and Abu Simbel, by the columns of ancient temples which she compared to groves of redwood trees. Her *Thousand Miles Up the Nile* (1877) is one of the classics of early archaeological travel and still bears reading today. Edwards devoted the rest of her life to lecturing and writing about the destruction in Egypt and was instrumental in the founding of the Egypt Exploration Society, which works in the Nile Valley to this day.

Harriet Boyd Hawes, a Smith graduate who met Amelia Edwards while in college, was even more remarkable. In 1897, she traveled to Athens to study archaeology, one of the first women to do so. Archaeology soon took a back seat to nursing when Turkey declared war on Greece. For months, Hawes cared for wounded Greek soldiers within sound of artillery barrages, developing a passion for humanitarian causes that guided much of her life. Much to her surprise, she won a fellowship at the American School in Athens from Yale University, but was not allowed to excavate, this being considered a male domain. The British were more encouraging and she went over to Crete, where she combed the countryside for archaeological sites on the back of a mule. Her persistence was rewarded and she became the first woman to excavate a Minoan town. Hawes's monograph on Gournia is one of the classics of early Mediterranean archaeology. Not that Harriet did much more fieldwork, for she threw herself into humanitarian work among Serb soldiers in Corfu and served as a ward aid in American hospitals in France during World War I. But she opened doors into the narrow archaeological world for many talented women that followed in her footsteps.

There were other talented women pioneers, too, among them the redoubtable Gertrude Bell, who became an expert desert traveler and founded the Iraq Museum; Gertrude Caton-Thompson, who discovered what were then the earliest farmers in the world in Egypt's Fayum in the 1920s; and Dorothy Garrod, the first woman Professor of Archaeology anywhere in Europe, who excavated the Stone Age caves on Mount Carmel in the Levant in the 1930s. For the most part, they worked on shoestring budgets and often with few companions. But the discoveries they made contributed to the revolution in archaeological methods that took hold after World War I, in the hands of several capable excavators. Indeed the lax standards of Pitt-Rivers's contemporaries and successors were assaulted by archaeologists of the 1920s and 1930s. "There is no right way of digging but there are many wrong ones," wrote one of Pitt-Rivers's most avid disciples—Mortimer Wheeler. Wheeler, who was ten years old when Pitt-Rivers died, came to archaeology through the good offices of Arthur Evans, discoverer of the ancient palace of King Minos on Crete. Wheeler spent his lifetime digging large sites with meticulous precision and training new generations of archaeologists in methods that owed their inspiration to the Victorian general.

Wheeler worked first on Roman forts, then on the famous Iron Age fortress at Maiden Castle in southern Britain. From archaeological evidence, he was able to reconstruct a blow-by-blow account of the Roman storming of that fort. After a distinguished military career in World War II, Wheeler was asked to head up the Archaeological Survey of India. With characteristic and flamboyant energy, he took up the task of organizing archaeology out of chaos. He found Roman imported pottery in southern India and dug deeply into the ancient city mounds of Harappa and Mohenjo-daro in the In-

dus Valley. There he sketched a fascinating picture of a long-extinct Indian civilization that had traded with Mesopotamia and developed its own distinctive, and still undeciphered, script. Mortimer Wheeler's excavations were, quite simply, meticulous, and the results remarkable. Most modern excavations build on the basic principles that he and Pitt-Rivers, as well as a handful of other pioneers, set out.

"The archaeologist is not digging up things, he is digging up people," Wheeler would begin. Good excavation takes imagination, an ability to understand what one is digging up. According to Wheeler, people who do not have this kind of imagination should collect bus tickets instead of digging. He believed the key to excavation was accurate observation and recording of occupation levels and architectural features, of the layout of burials and minute artifacts. The relationship between different objects in the ground can tell one much about the behavior of their makers, he taught his students. Wheeler's excavations were models of tidiness, with straight walls and carefully swept trenches to make the tasks of observation and discovery more precise. The observation of superimposed layers and the features and artifacts in them would give one an accurate chronology to work with, an essential framework for studying the numerous pot fragments and other finds from the dig. He pointed out how buildings should be dissected with great care, so that the foundations could be related to the underlying, dated strata and the contents isolated from those in other parts of the site. The burials Wheeler found were exposed bone by bone and carefully photographed in position before removal.

All of Wheeler's excavations were carefully designed not only to find artifacts but to answer specific questions about chronology or other matters. These questions were formulated in advance or as the dig was in progress. The staff of the excavation was organized into a hierarchy of specialists, led by the director himself, whose task was to "cultivate a scrupulous accuracy and completeness in the observation

and record of his factual evidence." Wheeler's ideal director had "the combined virtues of the scholar and the man of action," an ability to achieve accuracy "not for accuracy's sake, but as a basis for using his imagination to interpret his finds." "Archaeology," wrote Wheeler, "is primarily a fact-finding discipline." But, he would always add, we have to dig sites as a means to an end, the end being the understanding of humanity's complex and changing relationship with its environment.

Schliemann dug up the past of Troy. He and many other early archaeologists taught us that archaeological sites contain many treasures. Curtius, Dörpfeld, Pitt-Rivers, and Wheeler developed techniques for recording the contents of each site in meticulous detail. And Wheeler himself threw down the gauntlet to his successors—he challenged them to apply these recording methods to such complex problems as "estimating the density and social structure of populations." His words were prophetic, for that is what leading archaeologists are now trying to achieve.

Mortimer Wheeler died in 1976 after witnessing a revolution in digging methods all over the world, a revolution whose impact is still being felt. His students and their students, as well as those of other pioneering archaeologists, have refined his methods even further. Some idea of the complexity of a modern excavation can be gained by a brief look at the investigation of an ancient site at Olduvai Gorge in Tanzania. The site dates to about 1.75 million years ago.

"Archaeology," wrote British archaeologist Stuart Piggott some years ago, "is the science of rubbish." And rubbish is precisely what Louis and Mary Leakey had to dissect when they excavated the scatters of bones and stone artifacts in the lowest levels of Olduvai Gorge. All that remained were small scatters of discarded animal bones, stone tools, and waste chips, lying in irregular concentrations on the very land surfaces ancient people once trod. Often the scatter of artifacts and bones was only a few inches thick and was sealed under dozens of feet of sterile sand and lake clay. How old were these scatters? What activities took place there? Could any information on prehistoric diet and food-getting methods be obtained from the scatters? These and many other questions came to mind as the Leakeys began clearing these small but complicated sites. They had no doubt as to the importance of their excavations: these were probably among the earliest traces of human behavior in the world. To avoid damaging any human fossils and to prevent disturbance of the artifacts from their original positions, only the most delicate methods could be used.

Each scatter lay within a major geological horizon of Olduvai Gorge, one that the Leakeys knew dated to the earliest millennia of the human experience. But dating samples had to be obtained, that is, lumps of lava that could be dated by laboratory tests for their radioactive content. These samples had to come from the scatters themselves, from lava fragments that had actually been carried to the site by those who had lived there. The Leakeys had no choice: they knew they must excavate each entire site, plot all the objects on them, and obtain dating samples from among the finds in the scatter.

One site yielded the famous skull of *Zinjanthropus* in 1959. . . . Mary Leakey originally found a portion of the fossil outcropping from the lower lake beds of the Gorge. A small excavation was immediately undertaken at the site of this discovery to aid both in the removal of the precious skull and in establishing the exact level from which the fossil came. The immediate surroundings of the skull were sifted carefully in case additional fragments had already fallen down the slope on which it was found. The trial excavation yielded broken animal bones, some rodent fragments, and a few stone tools that lay in place near the skull. There seemed a strong possibility that the skull was directly associated with the tools—indeed, its owner might have made them.

It was seven months before Mary Leakey could return to the site, for the skull had been found at the very end of the 1959 season. When the time came for larger-scale excavations, she did not attack the site at once. Her task was to establish the precise position of the artifact scatter in the Olduvai geological strata. To determine this, she dug a six-foot trial trench in steps through the entire forty feet of the geological bed the skull had come from, right down to bedrock. She found that the scatter was halfway up the bed.

Once the stratigraphical position of the fossil skull was established, Mary Leakey set out to determine the extent of the scatter itself. The workmen removed the sterile over-burden of lake bed from the area around the trial trench. This unproductive soil was removed with picks and shovels in rough levels. When they reached a whitish-yellow volcanic-ash zone that Mary Leakey knew directly overlay the precious scatter, they stepped aside. The trench was now divided into four-foot-wide strips that were worked one by one with great care. Skilled workers carefully pared away the volcanic ash to within a few inches of the underlying artifacts and bones. Sometimes bones and other finds protruded through into the ash. So dry was the soil that the excavators had to dampen it before removal to guard against damaging valuable fossils underneath.

The scatter proved to be about a foot thick. With great care, Mary Leakey worked each strip of the trench from one side of the floor to the other. Whenever possible, every find was cleared from the surrounding soil with dental probes and small paintbrushes. Every find of any size, whether a stone tool or an animal bone, was marked with black or white ink and plotted on the floor plan before being lifted. A complete photographic record of the site was maintained as well. Once the larger finds had been removed, the soil was wet- or dry-sifted through one-sixteenth-inch screens so that even the tiniest stone chips and bone fragments were recovered for laboratory analysis. As a result of this painstaking excavation, the position of every significant find on the site was known to within an inch or less. What a contrast

to Belzoni's burial chambers or Layard's palaces!

The man-hours expended on the *Zinjanthropus* site were well worth the expense. The amount of detail about early human lifeways that came from the *Zinjanthropus* floor was truly astonishing, all of it the result of meticulous excavation. In addition to the dating samples gathered—which proved the site to be 1.75 million years old—the Leakeys obtained data on the dimensions and layout of one of the earliest archaeological sites in the world. Mary Leakey found and took apart a concentration of stone tools and flakes and over a thousand broken bone fragments covering an area twenty-one feet by fifteen feet near the spot where *Zinjanthropus* was found. This central zone was separated from another concentration of bones by a less densely covered area that she felt might have been the site of a crude shelter. We know that the inhabitants used crude stone choppers and many flakes in the preparation of food and the butchering of small animals. They smashed the limb bones of antelope and zebra and broke open the skulls to remove the brain. But large scavengers like hyenas visited the site as well and chewed up some of the freshly broken bones—presumably after the inhabitants left. None of this information could have been obtained without rigorous excavation techniques. The Leakeys literally drained the site of information. . . .

Archaeology has come a long way since Leonard Woolley performed miracles with plaster at Ur. Today, it is a sophisticated science that calls on experts from dozens of academic disciplines. It owes much to the natural and physical sciences, to revolutionary dating techniques . . . that enable us to date 2.5-million-year-old archaeological sites or tiny fragments of a wooden spear shaft extracted from the socket of a bronze spearhead used three thousand years ago. Computers enable archaeologists to manipulate vast data bases of artifacts and food remains, to plot intricate jigsaw puzzles of water-logged timbers that once formed a prehistoric house. We can trace the

1. ABOUT ARCHAEOLOGY

sources of volcanic rock used to make mirrors in three-thousand-year-old Mexican villages, establish whether stone workers making tools in a Belgian hunting camp ten thousand years ago were left- or right-handed. Using minute pollen grains, we can reconstruct the landscape around twenty-thousand-year-old Stone Age winter camps. Thousands of bison bones from an ancient mass kill on the American Plains can be reassembled so precisely that we know exactly how bison hunters of eight thousand years ago butchered their prey.

But the greatest advances of all have not been in the field or the laboratory, where all the hi-tech wizardry of archaeology comes into play. They have been in the ways in which we think of archaeology and plan our research. Much early archaeology was designed to recover as many spectacular objects as possible. This is what Layard strove for at Nimrud and Nineveh, and Schliemann at Hissarlik. Today's archaeology has three much more sophisticated goals: to construct the culture history of the past, to reconstruct ancient lifeways, the ways in which people made their living, and, most important of all, to explain how and why ancient human cultures changed through prehistoric times. This is where the most important advances in archaeology have been made—in seeking to explain why humans took up farming and aban-

doned hunting and gathering, or what caused people to congregate in cities, develop writing, and establish a literate civilization. Studying such topics has involved the development of sophisticated theoretical models for explaining and interpreting the past, models that owe much to evolutionary and ecological theory. Science now realizes that archaeology is about the only discipline that enables us to study human biological and cultural evolution over long periods of time. The development of the tools to do so ranks among the greatest scientific triumphs of this century. Not that archaeology is confined to such topics, for in recent years there has been an explosion of interest in such issues as gender roles in ancient societies, and in such fascinating problems as social inequality in the past. One of the great fascinations of modern archaeology is its sheer range and diversity that accommodates archaeologists who study everything from foraging camps that are millions of years old to Mayan cities and abandoned railroad stations from the Industrial Revolution.

. . . there is a tremendous satisfaction and excitement in searching out the past. Even today, most talented archaeologists, at one time or another, feel they are in touch with the people they are studying. They seem to have an instinct for discovery, to know where to search and dig, and a sense of

identity with their subjects. This sense seems to have been highly developed in Louis Leakey, Heinrich Schliemann, and Howard Carter. Carter experienced an almost eerie bond with Tutankhamun. He summed it up well when he wrote: "I stood in the presence of a king who reigned three thousand years ago." One suspects Carter was not speaking strictly figuratively: he felt he *really had*. Sometimes, as I have stood gazing over a long-deserted prehistoric settlement, silent on a cool evening as the sun casts long shadows over earthworks and eroding occupation deposits, I have experienced a sudden collapse of time. The site comes to life: thatched huts rise from the ground, scented wood smoke ascends in the evening still, dogs bark and children laugh in play. Outside their huts, old men sit and gossip quietly for a brief evening hour. Then, just as quickly, the image recedes and the village once again becomes a deserted archive of archaeological information, a silent complex of mud-hut foundations, dusty pot fragments, and broken food bones. For a moment, the ancient inhabitants of that village sprang to life, shedding their cloaks of anonymity to reach out across the millennia. Heady emotions, perhaps, but, for a moment, one understands why archaeology is so much more than just a set of techniques and tools for digging up the past.

The Enlightened Archaeologist

Thomas Jefferson's exploration of an Indian burial mound was, for its time, an extraordinary achievement. Recent excavations in Virginia offer new insights into his goals and interpretations.

Jeffrey L. Hantman and Gary Dunham

Jeffrey L. Hantman, an associate professor of anthropology at the University of Virginia, has conducted research on the prehistory of the Pueblo Southwest and the late prehistoric and contact periods in Virginia. He is currently writing a book on Monacan archaeology and ethnohistory.
Gary Dunham, a doctoral candidate in anthropology at the University of Virginia, directed the excavations at the Rapidan Mound.

Thomas Jefferson's excavation of an Indian burial mound near Charlottesville, Virginia, has earned him the title "Father of American Archaeology." Jefferson described his dig on the South Fork of the Rivanna River in his book, *Notes on the State of Virginia*. He also reported that "many [mounds] are to be found all over this country [though] cleared of their trees and put under cultivation [they] are much reduced in their height, and spread in width, by the plough, and will probably disappear in time." In fact, the mound excavated by Jefferson has disappeared from view, despite several attempts to locate it earlier in this century. Jefferson's description of it remains the sole documentation that it existed at all.

In 1988, an opportunity arose to study a burial mound quite similar to the one dug by Jefferson. Known as the Rapidan Mound, it is located just 14 miles from the one Jefferson excavated. It had been placed on the endangered sites list of the Virginia Department of Historic Resources, and money was available to help excavate and preserve the remaining portions of it. Once prominent in the middle of a floodplain, it had been steadily eroded by the shifting course and destructive flooding of the Rapidan River. Early nineteenth-century accounts of the Rapidan Mound suggest it was then a 12- to 15-foot-high conical mound with a diameter of some 50 feet. In 1892, the Smithsonian's Gerard Fowke, who had been an assistant to Cyrus Thomas on the great mound surveys of the late nineteenth century, recorded the mound as being reduced to six feet in height, though the width had remained stable. Fowke dug a large trench through the mound, even then severely eroded by the river and partially leveled by farmers. In 1979, Archaeological Society of Virginia members Charlton G. Holland, Sandra Spieden, and David van Roijen opened two small excavation units on the river's edge and described apparently random deposits of human bone and a submound pit. By 1988 those units had been washed away, and only a small fragment of the mound's south edge remained. The rate of destruction had quickened even in the past few years, and there was no way possible to secure the site without flooding farm fields downstream.

On a cold spring day, we met with archaeologists Keith Egloff, David Hazzard, Randy Turner, and Catherine Slusser from the Virginia Department of Historic Resources and discussed the possibility of salvaging the site. Because preservation was simply not possible, we decided to record what was left of the mound, in accordance with Virginia's new burial laws that include a commitment to rebury human remains.

Initially we were skeptical that there would be anything left within the mound to record. Although respectfully protected in recent years by the family that owned the land on which it was located, the mound's condition was rapidly deteriorating. Recent floods had eroded the north face exposed to the river; a few abandoned cars buried off the south edge of the mound acted as a makeshift flood wall. Despite the erosion, we felt a season of testing was worth the effort. Funds from the Virginia Department of Historic Resources provided for a professional staff to oversee the excavation; students from the University of Virginia's summer field school joined in the dig after receiving extensive training at nearby sites. It would be three years before we finished our work.

Most of our first season was spent clinging to the riverbank, our feet in small rests cut into the submound soils, cleaning off flood debris and roots to reveal the mound's inner levels. We could see the clear outline of the trench that Fowke had made. Having located the old trench, we could focus our attention on undisturbed areas. What we discovered was an astonishing similarity between the profiles of our mound and the one excavated by Jefferson—layers of dark stained soil with bone in it, interrupted by lighter colored soils brought to the site. Where Jefferson had seen seven such levels near the center of his mound, we could see three.

Jefferson had actually employed two excavation strategies. One was trenching, which allowed him to look at the internal structure of the mound and its stratigraphy. In this he was about 100 years ahead of his time. But he also wrote: "I first dug superficially in several parts of it, and came to collections of human bones, at different depths, from six inches to three feet below the surface. These were lying in the utmost confusion, some vertical, some oblique, some horizontal, and directed to every point of the compass, entangled, and held together in clusters by the earth. Bones of the most distant part were found together. . . ." What Jefferson could not see or fully appreciate with his narrow trenching and random digging was the internal structure of each of the separate burial features he had carefully identified.

In 1989 and 1990 we excavated the Rapidan River mound by exposing broad horizontal areas in an effort to study the spatial relationships among the mound's burial features, as well as the internal configuration of each burial. We were able to identify six burial features, three of which we excavated completely. We found that the bones were not "lying in utmost confusion," as Jefferson described them, nor were they random placements as posited by later excavators. Instead, the bones, after an initial burial or exposure of the body to remove the flesh, had been recovered and reburied as part of a mortuary ritual. The skulls had been placed in concentric circles with long bones distributed around them in linear arrangements. Our excavations also revealed a pattern of change in burial practice over time from earlier individual or small multiple burials in pits, to later secondary

burials containing up to 20 individuals. Jefferson did not record any submound pits, although they are common in most Virginia mounds, and we, as well as Fowke, found them at Rapidan Mound. Like the careful arrangement of bones, Jefferson probably missed them because he dug only narrow trenches and excavation pits.

We estimate that between 1,000 and 1,500 people were buried in the Rapidan Mound. Remarkably, with considerably less information in hand, Jefferson wrote of the Rivanna River mound, "I conjectured that in this barrow might have been a thousand skeletons." Based on our study of the Rapidan Mound, we now have good reason to believe his conjecture was accurate. The central Virginia mounds may not be extraordinary in terms of size, but the number of burials they contained and the generations it took for them to accumulate, is quite extraordinary.

A page from Jefferson's personal copy of the 1787 edition of Notes on the State of Virginia *includes comments in his own hand, mostly in Greek, which he hoped to include in a new edition to be published in his lifetime. They stress his interest in the similarities in Greek, Roman, and Native American burial practices.*

Detail from John Smith's 1612 map of Virginia shows the location of Monacan Indian towns, including the village of Monasukapanough, top right corner, which may have been across the river from the mound excavated by Jefferson.

Analysis of bones from Rapidan Mound has provided interesting new insights. Sandra Olsen, an archaeologist at the Carnegie Museum of Natural History, who was then on the staff of the Virginia Museum of Natural History, performed a scanning electron microscope analysis of five detached skull caps and two skulls missing caps that were found in a single burial feature. Separating skulls from skull caps, presumably with a sharp instrument, was a practice described in local histories relating to the treatment of an enemy prisoner after death. Of further interest was an intact cranium that had an unusual depressed fracture and V-shaped linear groove indicating a blow to the head with a sharp weapon. We inferred from this that some of those buried in the mound may have been killed in warfare. Such evidence, though tentative, contrasts with Jefferson's finding that "no holes were discovered in any of them, as if made by bullets, arrows or other weapons." In the absence of scanning electron microscopy, Jefferson may well have missed some tell-tale signs of violent death.

On so many other points, however, it is quite remarkable how well Jefferson's interpretations hold up in the late twentieth century. His reading of the stratigraphy of the mound has been well supported by excavations at other mounds in Virginia. Our own work also sheds light on the question of why Jefferson didn't mention any artifacts, and didn't appear to keep any from his excavation. At Rapidan Mound we found very little in the way of artifacts. Using screens and flotation, we did find small potsherds that appear to have been intentionally broken into small pieces as part of the burial ritual, and some stone tools including triangular projectile points. It is not likely that a trenching operation like Jefferson's, without screening, would have turned up such inconspicuous items.

2. Enlightened Archaeologist

Jefferson accurately described the variety of mounds in central Virginia, noting how they were of different sizes, some built of loose earth and others of stone. More than many twentieth-century archaeologists, he was aware of how the mound he was excavating fit into a regional archaeological perspective. He was also fairly accurate in describing the function of the mounds as community burial places, and the development of the mounds over an unstated period of time. He wrote: "Appearances certainly indicate that [the mound] has derived both origin and growth from the accustomary collection of bones, and deposition of them together; that the first collection had been deposited on the common surface of the earth, a few stones put over it, and then a covering of earth, that the second had been laid on this, had covered more or less of it in proportion to the numbers of bones, and was then also covered with earth, and so on."

To what extent did Jefferson's excavation contribute to an understanding of Native American history? The area in which his mound was located was the territory of the Monacan Indians. He noted that the mound was located across the river from an Indian town, most likely the Monacan town of Monasukapanough, or any one of a number of Late Woodland and possibly early contact period villages identified in archaeological surveys along the Rivanna. But of the Monacans, Jefferson only wrote that he thought they had merged with the Tuscarora and were now part of the Iroquois Confederacy to the north. He did not connect the mound to local Indian history. In fact, in his description of the excavation in *Notes,* Jefferson did not use archaeology to comment on Indian history at all. His focus was not on time, or cultural history, but on the inner construction of an odd feature on the landscape.

Why did he describe the mound at all? Because he was asked to do so. In 1780, a French diplomat in Philadelphia, François Marbois, circulated a letter to representatives of all the newly formed states requesting information on 22 separate topics such as their natural history, resources, population, climate, Indian population, etc. Jefferson was the Virginian who elected to answer this questionnaire, and his response became *Notes on the State of Virginia.* When Jefferson wrote *Notes,* he abbreviated the Indian question put to him by the Frenchman as: "A description of the Indians established in that state." In fact, Marbois' letter had requested: "A description of the Indians established in the state before the European settlements and of those who are still remaining. An indication of the Indian Monuments in that state."

Jefferson's chapter on Indians in *Notes,* titled "Aborigines," is in answer to these three questions posed by Marbois. First, he described the Indians established in the state before the Europeans, but he based this discussion entirely on his reading of colonist John Smith's account of Indians in the Jamestown area at the beginning of the seventeenth century—not on archaeological evidence. He then described the current distribution of the Indian tribes in Virginia, but argued that most had moved away, been greatly reduced in number or now "have more negro than Indian blood in them." Then he added, "I know of no such thing existing as an Indian monument for I would not honour with that name arrow points, stone hatchets, stone pipes, and halfshapen images." Jefferson then described his mound excavation. His archaeology was done in response to the request for information on Indian monuments, and was not undertaken as a matter of historical interest. In fact, in the section on Indian history in *Notes* he did not even mention the mounds. Jefferson concluded, however, with a moving personal memory that must have dated to his childhood: "But on whatever occasion they may have been

made, they are of considerable notoriety among the Indians: for a party passing, about thirty years ago, through the part of the country where this barrow is, went through the woods directly to it, without any instructions or inquiry, and having staid about it some time, with expressions of sorrow, they returned to the high road, which they had left about half a dozen miles to pay this visit, and pursued their journey."

There is little reason to doubt the veracity of this account. We know that Indians were still living in central Virginia into the eighteenth century, even if they had relocated away from the Charlottesville area. The moundbuilder myth that would soon sweep the country and which denied any tie between ancient mounds and contemporary Indians was apparently not a temptation to Jefferson. Such myths are often attributed to the period of American expansion and the pushing west of American Indians, and Jefferson was, as governor of Virginia and later president, a prominent agent in such forced relocation. In 1781, the very year he wrote *Notes,* he was also authorizing and closely monitoring the removal of the Cherokees from the western part of Virginia. Difficult as it is to comprehend such contradictory sides of Jefferson, we simply note here that he apparently did not rationalize his actions by manipulating his archaeological writing as some nineteenth-century scholars did.

At the time he wrote *Notes,* Jefferson did not see archaeological research as the key to understanding Native American origins. In *Notes* he followed the description of his archaeological excavation with a consideration of Indian origins based on linguistics, and suggested a close tie between Asians and Indians. However, seven years after publishing *Notes,* he wrote in a

letter to a colleague that he would be interested in hearing more of his colleague's linguistic theory of the descent of the Creek Indians from the Carthaginians, noting that he "saw nothing impossible in this conjecture." Clearly, his archaeological excavations had not dissuaded him from considering rather spectacular theories of Indian origins. But his opinions were subject to change. By 1813, in a lengthy letter to John Adams, he dismissed as "really amusing" notions of Indian origins in a distant Trojan or Hebrew past, concluding that "the question of origins was so unresolved that it could not be deciphered; Thus it was not a very practical question to ask."

Jefferson's excavation stands as one of many original scientific achievements in a lifetime of remarkable achievements. That it was intended to answer a particular question, not merely to collect relics, is notable, although Jefferson *was* a notable relic collector. And the publication of his excavation strategy, hypotheses, observations, and conclusions was extraordinary for his time. In moving from speculation to empirical observation, his concern was with the inner construction of a man-made phenomenon. In this regard, as in his interest in architecture, landscape, and so much else, Jefferson was particularly concerned with form and function rather than history. Yet, in his sympathetic depiction of the mound visit by Indians, he hinted at a continuity between present and past Indian cultures. And his description of the mound excavation preserved information that would otherwise have been lost, and provides a comparative base for our own excavations and interpretations of the prehistoric and early historic period in Virginia.

How Archaeology Works

Wendy Ashmore and Robert J. Sharer

... We examine the information archaeologists work with and the ways it is acquired. You may have read about archaeologists "piecing together the past" by studying ancient pottery, "arrowheads," or other artifacts found by excavation. However, these artifacts represent only one of several categories of evidence with which archaeologists work, and excavation is only one of several means of collecting information about the past.

ARCHAEOLOGICAL DATA

The material remains of past human activity, from the microscopic debris produced by chipping stone tools to the most massive architectural construction, become *data* when the archaeologist recognizes their significance as evidence and collects and records them. The collection and recording of these material remains constitutes the acquisition of archaeological data. Here we are concerned with the three basic classes of data—artifacts, features, and ecofacts—and how they cluster into larger units. These categories are not inflexible. There is some overlap among them, but they illustrate the variety and range of information available.

Artifacts

Artifacts are portable objects whose form is modified or wholly created by human activity (Fig. 3.1). Stone hammers or fired clay vessels are artifacts because they are either natural objects modified for or by human use, such as a hammer-stone, or new objects formed completely by human action, such as a pottery vessel. The shape and other traits of artifacts are not altered by removal from their place of discovery; both the hammerstone and the vessel retain their form and appearance after the archaeologist takes them from the ground.

Features

Features are nonportable artifacts that cannot be removed from their place of discovery without altering or destroying their original form (Fig. 3.2). Some common examples of features

Figure 3.1

Artifacts are portable objects whose form is modified or wholly created by human activity, while ecofacts are nonartifactual remains that nonetheless have cultural relevance. Here a projectile point (an artifact) lies embedded among the bones (ecofacts) of an extinct form of bison at Folsom, New Mexico. (All rights reserved. Photo Archives, Denver Museum of Natural History.)

From *Discovering Our Past: A Brief Introduction to Archaeology* by Wendy Ashmore and Robert J. Sharer, 1988, pp. 30-54. © 1988 by Mayfield Publishing Company. Reprinted by permission.

Figure 3.2

Features are artifacts that cannot be recovered intact, in this case a partially excavated cremation burial pit.

are hearths, burials, storage pits, and roads. It is useful to distinguish between these simple features and composite features such as buildings and other multiple component remains. It is also useful to differentiate features that have been deliberately constructed from others, such as trash heaps, that have grown by simple accumulation. Features usually define an area where one or more activities once took place.

Ecofacts
Ecofacts are nonartifactual natural remains that nonetheless have cultural relevance (Fig. 3.1). Although they are neither directly created nor significantly modified by human activity, ecofacts provide information about past human behavior. Examples include remnants of both wild and domesticated animal and plant species (bones, seeds, pollen, and so forth). These and other ecofacts such as soils contribute to our understanding of the past because they reflect ancient environmental conditions, diet, and resource exploitation.

Sometimes the line between ecofacts and artifacts is blurred. For example, bones with cut marks from butchering might be considered arti-

facts (reflecting human technology) as well as ecofacts (yielding clues to the ancient environment).

Sites
Sites are spatial clusters of artifacts, features, and/or ecofacts. A site may consist of only one form of archaeological data—a surface scatter of artifacts, for example—or of any combination of the three different forms. Site boundaries are sometimes well defined, especially if features such as walls or moats are present. Usually, however, a decline in density or frequency of the material remains is all that marks the limits of a site. However boundaries are defined, the archaeological site is usually a basic working unit of archaeological investigation.

Sites can be described and categorized in a variety of ways, depending on the characteristics one wants to note. For instance, location—sites in open valley positions, cave sites, coastal sites, mountaintop sites, and so forth—may reflect past environmental conditions, concern for defense, or relative values placed on natural resources located in different areas. Sites

may be distinguished by one or more functions they served in the past. For example, one can speak of habitation sites, trading centers, hunting (or kill) sites, ceremonial centers, burial areas, and so on. Sites may also be described in terms of their age and/or cultural affiliation. For example, a Near Eastern site may be described as belonging to the Bronze Age, or a Mexican site may be described as Aztec.

The nature and depth of cultural deposits at a site can reveal the time span of activities: whether occupation was brief or extended. At some sites occupation (and deposition of artifacts) may have been continuous. Other sites may have had multiple occupations with periods of abandonment marked by naturally deposited (nonartifactual or "sterile") layers. Depth of accumulation is not an automatic indicator of length of occupation; at one spot a great deal of material can be deposited very rapidly, while elsewhere a relatively thin deposit of trash might represent layers laid down intermittently over hundreds of thousands of years. Whether thick or thin, the remains of sites may be visible on the ground surface or completely buried and invisible to the naked eye.

Some "buried" sites lie not underground but underwater, the most common being sunken ships. However, sites that were once on dry land may also become submerged because of changes in water level (sometimes resulting from human activity such as dam building) or land subsidence. A famous example of the latter is Port Royal, Jamaica, a coastal city that sank beneath the sea after an earthquake in 1692.

Regions
Regions are the largest and most flexible spatial clusters of archaeological data. The region is basically a geographic concept: a definable area bounded by topographic features such as mountains and bodies of water (Fig. 3.3). But the definition of an archaeological region may also consider ecological and cultural factors. For instance, a region may be defined as the area

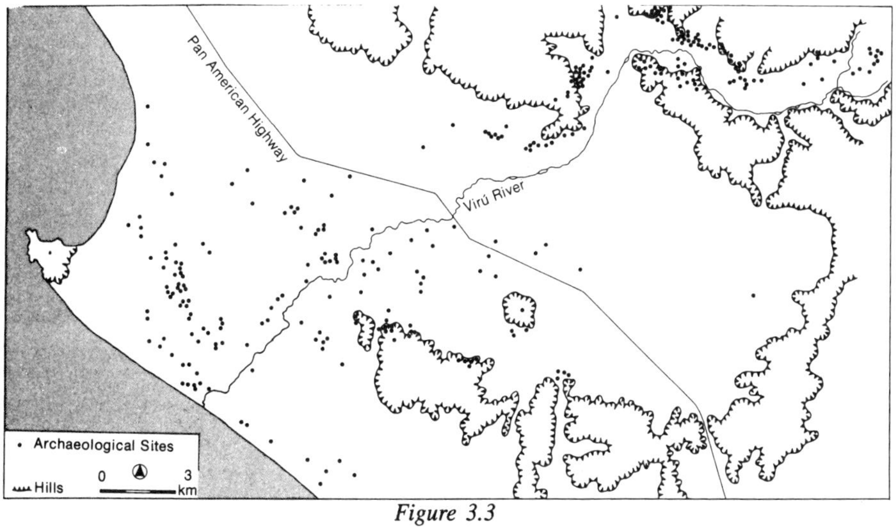

Figure 3.3

An archaeological region is often defined by topographic features: In this case, hilly areas and seacoast define the limits of the Virú Valley, Peru, (After Willey 1953.)

used by a prehistoric population to provide its food and water. By considering whole regions the archaeologist can reconstruct aspects of prehistoric society that may not be well represented by a single site.

Obviously, the nature and scope of an archaeological region vary according to the complexity of the prehistoric society and its means of subsistence. Part of the archaeologist's task is to identify the factors that define a particular region under study, as well as to show how these factors changed through time. In other words, the archaeologist usually works within a convenient natural region defined by geographical boundaries and seeks to determine that region's ancient ecological and cultural boundaries as well.

DEPOSITION AND TRANSFORMATION

Archaeological data are the result of two factors: behavioral processes and transformational processes. We will describe them in the order of their involvement with archaeological data.

All archaeological sites represent the products of human activity. While some human behavior, such as storytelling, leaves no tangible trace, many activities produce material remains. The activities responsible for

these remains are *behavioral processes* comprising four consecutive stages: acquisition, manufacture, use, and disposal or deposition (Fig. 3.4). Artifacts such as tools are made from acquired raw materials, used for one or more specific purposes, and then discarded when broken or worn. Features such as houses are built from gathered materials, occupied, and then abandoned and destroyed or left to ruin. Ecofacts such as meat animals are hunted, butchered, cooked, eaten, and passed as waste products. The complex aggregate of these activities delineates the same stages in the life span of the site as a whole.

Thus the archaeologist can use all forms of archaeological data to reconstruct the acquisition, manufacture, use, and disposal stages of ancient

behavior. Clues to all four kinds of ancient behavior may be found in characteristics of the data themselves and in the circumstances of their deposition (Fig. 3.5).

These behavioral processes represent the first stage in the formation of archaeological data. The second step consists of *tranformational processes*. These processes include all conditions and events that affect material remains from the time ancient use stops (at any point in the behavioral process) to the time the archaeologist recognizes and acquires them as data. When the specific materials under study are plants or animals, the archaeologist draws on the field of *taphonomy*: the study of what happens to remains of plants and animals after they die. One important book on taphonomy is appropriately titled *Fossils in the Making*.

The tangible products of ancient human behavior are never completely indestructible, but some survive better than others. As a result the data recovered by the archaeologist always present a picture of the past that is biased by the effects of transformational processes (see Fig. 3.5). To gauge bias it is crucial to determine the processes that have been at work in each archaeological situation. Both natural and human events act either to accelerate or to retard destruction. Natural agents of transformation include climatic factors, which are usually the most basic influences acting on the preservation of archaeological evidence. Temperature and humidity are generally the most critical: Extremely dry, wet, or cold conditions preserve fragile or-

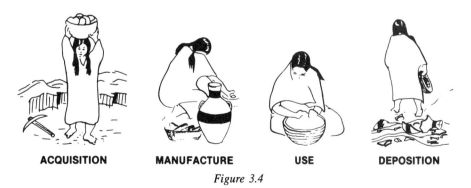

ACQUISITION **MANUFACTURE** **USE** **DEPOSITION**

Figure 3.4

Archaeological data represent at least one behavioral cycle of acquisition, manufacture, use and deposition.

ganic materials such as textiles and wooden tools, as well as bulkier perishable items such as human corpses. Organic remains have been preserved under these circumstances along the dry coast of Peru, in the wet bogs of Scandinavia, and in the frozen steppes of Siberia.

Natural destructive processes such as oxidation and decay and catastrophic events such as earthquakes and volcanic eruptions also have profound effects on the remains of the past. Underwater remains may be broken up and scattered by tidal action, currents, or waves. Catastrophes such as volcanic eruptions may either preserve or destroy archaeological sites; often the same event may have a multitude of effects. For example, around 1500 B.C. both an earthquake and a volcanic eruption struck the island of Thera in the Aegean Sea near Greece. Part of the island blew up; another part collapsed inward and was filled by the inrushing sea; and still other areas were immediately buried under a blanket of ash. The population abandoned the island, but the remains of its settlements were sealed beneath the ash. Recent excavations have disclosed well-preserved buildings, some intact to the third story—a rarity in more-exposed sites—as well as beautiful wall paintings and traces of fragile baskets.

One of the most decisive factors in the transformation process is subsequent human activity. Reoccupation of an archaeological site may destroy all traces of previous occupation. Earlier buildings are often leveled to make way for new construction or to provide construction materials. In other cases, however, later activity may preserve older sites by building over and thus sealing the earlier remains (see Fig. 3.5). Of course, large-scale human events such as war usually have destructive consequences for archaeological preservation, as does a flourishing market in antiquities, which encourages the looting and consequent destruction of archaeological sites.

In summary, archaeologists must determine what conditions and events have transformed the site before they

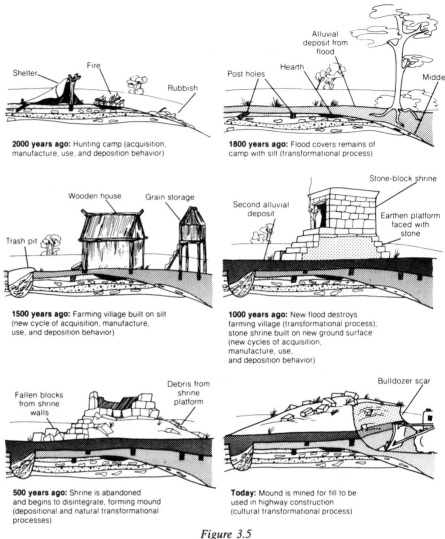

Figure 3.5

The characteristics of archaeological data and their deposition reflect both behavioral and transformational processes.

can consider reconstructing past human behavior. Obviously, the behavioral and transformational processes are specific to each site, so each must be evaluated individually. Archaeologists begin to reconstruct these processes from the circumstances under which the data are recovered, including their matrix, provenience, and association.

Matrix refers to the physical medium that surrounds, holds, and supports other archaeological data (Fig. 3.6). Most frequently it consists of combinations of soil, sand, gravel, or rock. The nature of a matrix is usually an important clue to understanding the artifacts, features, or ecofacts it contains. For instance, artifacts recovered from an alluvial matrix (deposited by

running water) may have been deposited by the natural action of a river. A matrix may also be produced by human activity, such as the deposition of immense amounts of soil in order to construct an earthen platform. In this case, the soil is not only a matrix for any artifacts or ecofacts contained in it and for other features constructed on it, but also a constructed feature.

Provenience simply refers to a three-dimensional location of any kind of archaeological data on or within the matrix. Horizontal provenience is usually recorded relative to a geographical grid system using known reference points. Vertical provenience is usually recorded as elevation above or below sea level. Provenience information allows the archaeologist to record (and

Figure 3.6

In this photograph, a human burial has been excavated from most of its matrix, but the relationship of the remains to the matrix is readily apparent. (Courtesy of the Ban Chiang Project, Thai Fine Arts Department/University Museum.)

later to reconstruct) association and context.

Association refers to two or more artifacts (or any other kind of data) occurring together in the same matrix (Fig. 3.7). The associations of various kinds of data are often crucial to the interpretation of past events. For instance, the artifacts found in association with a human burial, such as hunting weapons, may be clues to the individual's sex and livelihood.

Context is a summary evaluation of the significance of the provenience, association, and matrix for a given artifact or other bit of evidence, in light of effects of both behavioral and transformational processes. In other words, context is an assessment of where the evidence is, how it got there, and what has happened to it in the meantime.

There are two basic kinds of archaeological contexts: primary and secondary. Each of these may be divided into two further categories.

Primary context refers to conditions in which both provenience and matrix have been undisturbed since original deposition. Intact archaeological features are always in primary context, although later disturbance can remove portions of such features from primary context. There are two kinds of primary contexts:

1. *Use-related primary context* results from deposition in the place where the artifact was acquired, made, or used. The occurrence of two or more associated artifacts in use-related primary context ideally means that they were used and deposited at the same time. Such an occurrence allows the archaeologist to reconstruct the activity of which the artifacts were a part. Truly undisturbed archaeological contexts, however, are rare, the best examples being burials and tombs. Most contexts have been altered to some degree by transformational processes.

2. *Transposed primary context* is a more specific category since it results from behavior concerned with disposal of refuse (formation of trash heaps or *middens*). In other words, it is the product of the final stage in the behavioral cycle. The association of two or more artifacts in transposed primary context does not allow direct inferences about any ancient behavior other than waste disposal. However, association in transposed primary context does support the conclusion that the artifacts were made and used during the same general period. It can be seen, therefore, that use-related primary context represents a wider range of ancient activities, but archaeological data in primary contexts

Figure 3.7

A group of pottery vessels found in association as a result of intentional ritual deposition (primary context). This indicates there were used together as part of an ancient ceremony (ca. first century A.D., El Porton, Guatemala).

are more commonly found in transposed situations.

Secondary context refers to a condition in which provenience, association, and matrix have been wholly or partially altered by processes of transformation. There are two kinds of secondary contexts:

1. *Use-related secondary context* results from disturbances by subsequent human activity, ancient or modern.
2. *Natural secondary context* results from disturbance by a variety of nonhuman agents, such as burrowing animals, tree roots, erosion, decay, volcanic eruptions, or earthquakes.

The differences among the types of archaeological context and the significance of accurately determining context, can be illustrated by several examples. In the first place, any artifact may be modified to be reused for different purposes over its use span. Thus a pottery vessel may be manufactured for the transport of water but later modified to use as a container for food or other substances and then (when inverted) as a mold for the shaping of new pottery vessels. If this vessel were abandoned during, or immediately after, any of these activities—say its use as a pottery mold—and remained in an undisturbed matrix with its associated artifacts, ecofacts, and features, its archaeological context upon discovery would be primary (undisturbed) and use-related (as part of pottery making activity). Knowing the provenience, associations, and context (in this case reflected in the finding of an inverted vessel surrounded by other vessels in various stages of manufacture, along with clay-working tools and so forth), the archaeologist would be able to reconstruct both the type of activity and many specific techniques used in this instance of pottery making. Any prior uses, however, would not be directly detected.

As already noted, the survival of use-related primary contexts is relatively rare and depends on both the circumstances of the original behavior and transformation processes that ten-

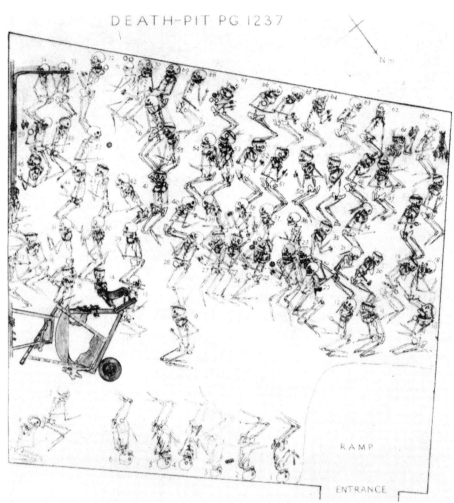

DEATH-PIT PG 1237

Figure 3.8

This plan shows positions of bodies in the "Great Death-Pit" adjacent to the royal tombs at Ur. (From Woolley 1934; by permission of the University Museum, University of Pennsylvania.)

ded to preserve rather than destroy. Discoveries of chipped stone projectile points in clear association with bones of animals have been important keys to the reconstruction of early human activities in the New World. In the mid-1920s, discoveries at Folsom, New Mexico, revealed such points in undisturbed use-related contexts associated with bones of a species of bison that has been extinct for at least 10,000 years (Fig. 3.1). The dates have been supplied by paleontological study, but archaeological association and context were critical in establishing the cultural meaning of these finds.

Many kinds of activity can disturb or erase earlier use-related primary contexts. In some cases, however, subsequent human activity can preserve them—as in the building of a new

structure over the recently abandoned pottery workshop described above. In other cases the manner of original deposition may tend to secure use-related primary contexts from disturbance. One of the best examples of such deposition is provided by the preparation of burials and tombs. In many areas of the world ancient people developed elaborate funerary customs. When found undisturbed the resultant tombs provide opportunities to reconstruct ancient ritual activity and belief systems.

A good illustration of this reconstruction can be seen in the Royal Tombs of Ur, an ancient Mesopotamian site in Iraq, excavated by Sir Leonard Woolley in the late 1920s (Fig. 3.8). Careful recording of provenience and associations enabled Woolley to reconstruct a nearly complete funerary scene, including elaborate grave goods and sacrificed victims. From the reconstructions Woolley was able to infer a great deal about royal customs of the time, as well as specific details such as court costume. Only the chamber of the king himself, which had been looted, could not be reconstructed; the rest had been protected and preserved by interment.

Other examples of use-related primary context have been preserved by natural events. The deposition of soil by wind and water has buried countless sites under deep layers of earth; a famous example of a buried site is the ancient Roman city of Pompeii, which was covered by volcanic ash from the eruption of Mount Vesuvius in A.D. 79.

Not all primary contexts are use related, however. People in most societies discard items after they are damaged, broken, or no longer useful. Middens are specialized areas for rubbish disposal; they contain artifacts that are usually undisturbed from the moment of their deposition. Furthermore, if used over long periods of time, middens may become stratified or layered, with each layer corresponding to a period of rubbish deposition. Middens are thus in primary context, but because of the nature of their deposition, the only past behavior directly reflected by this context is the general practice of rubbish accumulation and disposal. For this reason, material recovered from middens is in *transposed primary context*. If a midden is used over a long period of time, relative position within the deposit (or within a particular layer of the midden) can be used to assess relative chronological position (Fig. 3.9).

The identification of use-related secondary context can often help the archaeologist understand how artifacts came to be associated. Of course, if the disturbed context is not recognized as such, the interpretation can be badly in error. For example, the contents of a heavily disturbed tomb might include not only some portion of the original furnishings, but also materials such as tools and containers that were brought

in and left behind by the looters. During the excavation of the tomb of the Egyptian Pharaoh Tut-ankh-amun, ancient looting was recognized by evidence of two openings and reclosings of the entry; the final sealings of the disturbed areas were marked by different motifs from those on the undisturbed portions. If the disturbance had not been recognized, the associations and arrangements of recovered artifacts might be wrongly interpreted as representing burial ritual behavior.

Natural secondary context, which might occur, for example, when burrowing animals have placed later artifacts in apparent association with earlier features, can also make interpretation difficult. At Ban Chiang, a site in northern Thailand, ancient burials are juxtaposed in a very complex fashion, with later pits intruding into or overlapping earlier ones. The job of segregating distinct units was made even more difficult by the numerous animal burrows, including those of worms, crisscrossing the units, so that tracing pit lines and other surfaces was exacting and intricate work.

The archaeologist uses the foregoing kinds of information along with the products of past behavior—archaeological data—to reconstruct both the behaviors and the cultural systems by

which they were produced. As the first step in linking the data to a past cultural system, the archaeologist must assess the effects on the data of the processes we have discussed: the kinds of ancient behavior that produced the evidence (behavioral processes), and the natural or human events that have affected the evidence from the time of deposition to the moment of archaeological recovery (transformational processes).

A point to be emphasized is that any kind of excavation—by archaeologists or anyone else—*destroys* matrix, association, and context. The only way to preserve the information these factors convey is in drawings, photographs, and written records. Without them, even the most painstakingly controlled excavation is no more justifiable or useful than a looter's pit.

ACQUIRING DATA

Archaeologists are concerned with gathering evidence of past human behavior as a first step toward understanding that ancient behavior and toward meeting both the specific objectives of their research and the general goals of archaeology. Realizing these objectives requires discovery of

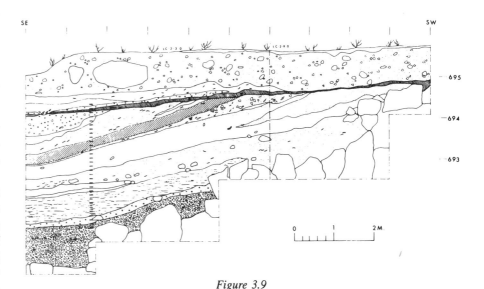

Figure 3.9

Cross-section drawing of a stratified midden representing nearly 2000 years of accumulation at Chalchuapa, El Salvador. One of the characteristics of transposed primary context, such as this midden, is that the artifacts from a given layer are contemporaneous but cannot be assumed to represent the same set of ancient activities.

1. ABOUT ARCHAEOLOGY

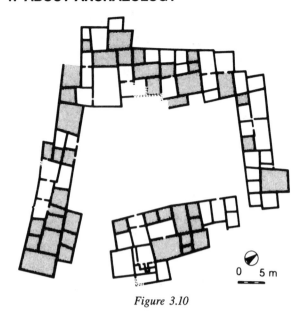

Figure 3.10

A universe with nonarbitrary units: In this case, rooms in a prehistoric Southwestern pueblo. The shaded rooms were the ones excavated. (By permission from Broken K Pueblo, Prehistoric Social Organization in the American Southwest, *by James N. Hill, University of Arizona Anthropological Paper #18, Tucson: University of Arizona Press, copyright 1970.)*

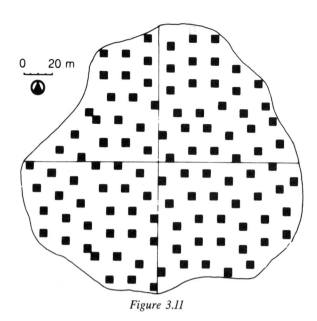

Figure 3.11

A universe with arbitrary units at Girik-i-Haciyan, Turkey: the black areas were the units investigated. (After Redman and Watson, reproduced by permission of The Society for American Archaeology, adapted from American Antiquity 35: 281–282, 1970.)*

as much as possible about the characteristics of the data. Ideally archaeologists seek to recover the full range of variation in the archaeological data relevant to their research questions. What was the range of activities carried on at a site? What was the range of places chosen for location and settlement? What was the range of forms and styles of artifacts? To the extent that such variation existed but is not known, the picture of ancient life is unnecessarily incomplete and any inferences drawn may be wrong. In a sense archaeological data are always unrepresentative; not all behavior produces tangible evidence, and not all the evidence will survive. The ideal goal is seldom realized, but understanding the processes that affected the production and preservation of the evidence can compensate to some extent for the unevenness in the availability of data. At this point we need to consider how the archaeologist chooses data acquisition strategies to maximize the usefulness of the evidence that *is* available.

The first step in data acquisition is to define the limits of the region under investigation. This will impose a practical limit on the amount of evidence to be collected. A bounded research area may be referred to as a *data universe*. An archaeological data universe is bounded both in time and geographical space. An investigator may define a data universe as a single site or even a portion of site. In a regional situation the research area corresponds to a much larger universe, such as an entire valley or a coastal area containing many sites. The archaeologist may also draw temporal boundaries to seek data corresponding to a relatively short era, such as the Pueblo II period of the American Southwest (ca. A.D. 900–1100), or a much longer span, such as a period of several thousand years corresponding to an entire interglacial period of the Pleistocene (Ice Age).

Once defined, the data universe is subdivided into *sample units*. A sample unit is the unit of investigation; it may be defined by either arbitrary or nonarbitrary criteria. *Nonarbitrary sample units* correspond either to natural areas, such as microenvironments, or to cultural entities, such as rooms,

houses, or sites (Fig 3.10). *Arbitrary sample units* are spatial divisions with no inherent natural or cultural relevance (Fig. 3.11). Examples of the latter include sample units defined by a grid system (equal-sized squares). *Sample units should not be confused with data:* If an archaeologist is looking for sites, the sample units will be geographical areas where sites might be located. If sites are the sample units, the data to be gathered will be artifacts, ecofacts, and features within the site.

The choice between arbitrary and nonarbitrary sample units is made by the investigator; it reflects the specific objectives of the study and the nature of the data (see below). But in any case all sample units are (or are assumed to be) comparable. That is, nonarbitrarily defined units are assumed to yield similar or complementary information about ancient behavior. For example, if sites are the sample units, one "cemetery" site will give information similar to that from another cemetery site and complementary to information from "habitation" sites and other sample units within the data population. Arbitrarily defined units, on the other hand, are comparable because they are always regular in size and/or shape.

The aggregate of all sample units is the *population*. Note that when the universe is a region and the sample units correspond to all the known sites, the population will not include unknown sites or locations in the region without sites, even though these areas are part of the universe. Nevertheless, conclusions drawn about the population are often inferred to be "true" of the research universe as well.

Total data acquisition involves investigation of all the units in the population. Of course the archaeologist never succeeds in gathering every shred of evidence from a given data universe; we are constantly developing new techniques of recovery and analysis that broaden the very definition of archaeological data. A change in the research problem also alters the definition of what materials and relationships are considered appropriate data. It is nonetheless important to distinguish between investigations that attempt to collect all available evidence (by investigation of all sample units) and those that set out to collect only a portion of the available data. Something approaching total data acquisition is often attempted in salvage situations, as when a site or region is threatened with immediate destruction by construction of a new highway or dam.

Sample data acquisition refers to situations in which only a portion or sample of the data can be collected from a given archaeological data pool. The limits of the sample recovered are often influenced by economic constraints: The archaeologist seldom has the funds to study all potential units. Nor is research time unlimited; seasonal weather conditions, scheduling commitments, and other factors often determine the time available to gather evidence. Access to archaeological data may be restricted by natural barriers, lack of roads or lack of permission from property owners. Even when there are no restrictions to access, however, it is still desirable to collect only

part of the available archaeological data. Except in situations of threatened site destruction, most archaeologists recommend that a portion of every site be left untouched to allow future scientists a chance to work with intact sources of archaeological evidence using techniques more sophisticated than today's. In this way future research can check and refine the results obtained with present methods.

RESEARCH DESIGN

Whether total or sample coverage is used, research must be planned to ensure that its goals will be addressed and met. Traditionally, archaeological research has been "site-oriented." The major goal was to excavate a particular site and, in many cases, collect spectacular remains. With the emergence of archaeology as a scientific discipline, more systematic approaches have become the rule. Today, regional and problem-oriented investigations are increasingly the norm. This kind of research aims at solving specific problems or testing one or more hypotheses by using controlled and representative samples of data.

Archaeological research design refers to a sequence of stages that guides the conduct of investigation (Fig. 3.12) to ensure the validity of results and make efficient use of time, money, and effort. Each stage has one or more specific purposes. Although the stages may be ideally portrayed as a series of steps, the process is flexible in practice. Aspects of two or more stages may be carried out simultaneously, or the stages may be accomplished in a different order, depending on circumstances. Furthermore, since each research situation is unique, this generalized research design must be capable of adapting to a wide variety of specific applications.

Formulation involves definition of the research problem, background investigations, and feasibility studies. Decisions regarding the problem to be investigated and the geographical area of study both limit and guide further work. Once these choices are made,

the archaeologist conducts background research to locate and study any previous work that may be relevant to the investigation. Useful information at this point may include geographical, geological, climatological, ecological, and anthropological studies, when available. Such data may be found in publications, archives, laboratories, and so on and through consultations with individual experts. Because archaeological research usually requires fieldwork, the archaeologist must usually do a feasibility study involving a trip to the region or sites to be investigated to evaluate the archaeological situation and local conditions such as accessibility, availability of supplies, and so forth.

Thorough background investigations facilitate the actual research by refining the problem under investigation and defining specific research goals. The goals of most archaeological research include testing one or more specific hypotheses. Some of these may come from previously proposed models, while others may arise during the formulation of the basic research problem. As the research progresses, of course, new hypotheses may be generated and tested. It is important to remember, however, that the initial formulation of research problem(s) leads the archaeologist to look for particular kinds of data and thus sets the course for the entire study.

Implementation involves completing all the arrangements necessary for the success of the planned fieldwork. These arrangements may be complex, especially if the research is to be done in a foreign country. The first step in implementing a study may be to secure the necessary permits for conducting research, usually from government agencies responsible for overseeing archaeological work. The owners of the land on which the work will take place must also grant permission before investigations can proceed. The laws governing archaeological work vary from country to country and from state to state within the United States, so the archaeologist must be aware of the relevant regulations and customs within the area being investigated.

1. ABOUT ARCHAEOLOGY

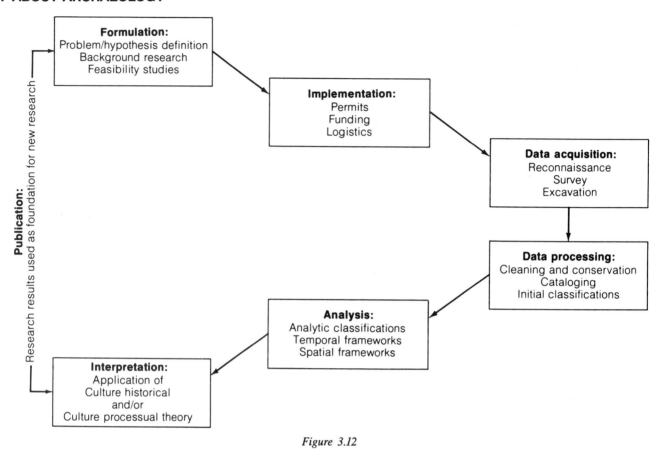

Figure 3.12

Diagram of stages of archaeological research.

At some point the archaeologist must find funds to finance the research. In some cases this involves submitting a research proposal to private or governmental agencies that fund archaeological investigations. In many CRM situations the agency issuing the contract provides the funding for the research.

When funding and permit have been secured, the archaeologist can turn to making logistic arrangements. Research equipment and supplies must be acquired. In most cases field facilities must be rented or built for safekeeping of the equipment and for laboratory processing and storage of artifacts and field records. Many projects require a staff that must be recruited, transported, housed, and fed, and these arrangements must be completed before the work can begin.

Acquisition involves three basic procedures for the collection of data: reconnaissance, survey, and excavation. . . . Reconnaissance is the means for identifying and locating archae-

ological sites, accomplished by on-the-scene visual search and by remote sensors. Survey is undertaken to record as much as possible about archaeological sites without excavation, through photography, mapping, remote sensors, and collection of surface artifacts. Excavation is undertaken to expose the buried characteristics of archaeological sites, using a variety of techniques to retrieve and record the data revealed.

Data processing refers to the manipulation of raw data (artifacts and ecofacts) and the creation and manipulation of records. Portable remains are usually processed in a field laboratory to insure that they are recorded, preserved, and stored to be available for further analysis. Records referring to these data (descriptions, photographs, and scaled drawings) are also completed and filed to be accessible for later use.

Analysis provides a variety of information useful for archaeological interpretations. For artifacts these studies

include classification, determination of age, and various technical analyses designed to identify sources of raw materials, methods of manufacture, and uses. Some of these procedures can be done in the field laboratory, but the more technical or complex analyses are usually undertaken at specially equipped permanent scientific facilities.

Interpretation involves the synthesis of all the results of data collection, processing, and analysis as a means of answering the original goals of the investigation. The use of the scientific method in these procedures is an important characteristic of modern professional archaeology. A variety of models are used in the interpretive process, including both specific and general historical and anthropological frameworks.

Publication completes the research cycle and makes the findings fully accessible so that the results can be used and retested by fellow archaeologists and any other interested individuals. This ensures that any research contributes to the broadest objectives of archaeology and of science in general.

ARCHAEOLOGICAL RESEARCH PROJECTS

Scientific archaeology demands a broad range of expertise. Today's archaeologist must be a theoretical scientist, a methodologist, a technician, an administrator, and more. In reality, of course, it is nearly impossible for one individual to do everything necessary for a particular project; usually the archaeologist must bring together specialists from a wide variety of disciplines. Doing so requires an interdisciplinary approach and coordination of the efforts of many scientists, each of whom focuses on a particular aspect of the research. Scientific teams—usually led by an archaeologist but including botanists, ecologists, geologists, and other specialists—are often created to conduct thorough fieldwork on a research question. Only by depending on others can the archaeologist ensure that the data collected are used to the maximum degree possible. In some cases the archaeologist may find most of the required support specialists housed under one roof, as in the larger museums and research institutions in many parts of the world. In the United States, the Smithsonian Institution provides one of the most complete support facilities for archaeology.

The size and duration of archaeological research projects depend on the scale of the problems being investigated. A few months' work by a single individual may be all that is required to plan and conduct the data-gathering stages of the research. But even the single individual will need some form of assistance from outside specialists in processing and analyzing the results. Archaeological research concerned with complex civilizations, such as the work being done at large urban sites in the Near East and Mexico, usually calls for a large archaeological staff and a huge labor force (Fig. 3.13). Projects in these and simi-

Figure 3.13

The modern large-scale archaeological excavation at Quiriguá, Guatemala, involved over 100 people and continued over a six-year period. (Quiriguá Project, University Museum, University of Pennsylvania.)

lar areas have employed teams of on-site specialists in research extending over many years.

Like most activities, archaeological research is limited by the availability of time and money. A far greater problem, however, is one that threatens the very existence of archaeological research: the increasing destruction wrought by our rapidly expanding world. The destruction of archaeological remains has reached such proportions that we may well ask, "Does the past have a future?"

SUMMARY

The material remains from the past become archaeological data once they are recognized, collected, and recorded. The direct products of past human activity are either artifacts (portable) or features (nonportable). Indirect products of past human activity are called ecofacts. Archaeologists usually examine distributions of data within sites (clusters of data), or, as is increasingly common today, within re-

gions (clusters of sites). Further information is gleaned from recording the specific location (provenience), associations, and matrix (surroundings) of data. The context of data—their behavioral significance—is revealed by evaluation of all these factors. The understanding of context, with care to discriminate among the various kinds of context, is the crucial link that allows the archaeologist to reconstruct the kinds of ancient behavior the recovered data represent.

The material record ideally reflects four major categories of human activity—acquisition, manufacture, use, and deposition—which together constitute behavioral processes. But archaeologists can never recover data representing all kinds of past behavior. Some activity leaves no tangible trace, and the evidence of other kinds of ancient behavior may be altered over time by human and natural transformational processes. These processes act selectively either to preserve or to destroy archaeological evidence. Thus the data available to the archaeologist constitute a sample determined first by ancient human activity (behavioral processes) and then by human or natural forces acting after the remains are deposited (transformational processes).

The resulting data form the base that the archaeologist attempts to recover, either totally (by collection of all available evidence) or by sampling methods. Whatever collection method is used, the archaeologist seeks data that represent, as much as possible, the full range of ancient human activity. With very few exceptions (such as when a site is about to be destroyed), it is generally practical and desirable to collect only a sample of the data.

Archaeological research is usually aimed at solving specific problems or testing specific hypotheses. To guide such investigations, most archaeologists follow a similar research design that begins with formulation of the problem, based on background and feasibility studies, followed by implementation, which includes fund-raising, securing permits, and making logistical arrangements. The next stage is data acquisition, which often includes reconnaissance (locating unknown sites), survey (mapping and collecting surface data), and excavation (removal of matrix to reveal buried data). This is followed by data processing and analysis, leading to interpretation (reconstruction of the past to address the specific research goals) and publication of the research.

To be a successful researcher, today's archaeologist must command a broad range of expertise. He or she must have knowledge of field methods, theory, administration, and a range of technical skills. Seldom can one individual perform all the tasks demanded by the complexity of archaeological investigation, so in almost all cases the archaeologist calls on a variety of specialists for assistance.

The scale of archaeological research ranges from the study conducted by a single person in a few weeks to the work of large research teams over several years or decades. The practical limits to such research are usually determined by time and money, but the severest threat to our understanding of the past is posed by our expanding world's destruction of archaeological data.

The Golden Marshalltown:
A Parable for the Archeology
of the 1980s

Kent V. Flannery

Kent V. Flannery is Professor of Anthropology and Curator of Environmental Archeology, Museum of Anthropology, University of Michigan, Ann Arbor, MI 48109. He presented the Distinguished Lecture to the American Anthropological Association at the national meetings in Los Angeles on December 5, 1981.

I am happily too busy *doing* science to have time to worry about philosophizing about it. [Arno Penzias, Nobel Laureate, 1978]

This is a story about archeological goals and rewards, and no one should look for anything too profound in it. It's really just the story of a ride I took on an airplane from San Diego to Detroit. That may not sound very exciting to those of you who fly a lot, but this particular trip was memorable for me. For one thing, it was my first time on a 747. For another, I met someone on the plane who became one of the most unforgettable characters I've ever run across.

The flight was taking me home to Ann Arbor after the Society for American Archaeology meetings in May of 1981. I was leaving San Diego a day early because I had endured all the physical stress I could stand. I didn't particularly feel like watching the

movie, so as soon as the plane was airborne and the seat belt sign had been turned off, I went forward to the lounge area of the plane. There were only two people there, both archeologists, and both recognized me from the meetings. So I had no choice but to sit down and have a beer with them.

I want to begin by telling you a little about my two companions, but you have to understand, I'm not going to give their actual names. Besides, their real identities aren't important, because each considers himself the spokesman for a large group of people.

The first guy, I suppose, came out of graduate school in the late 1960s, and he teaches now at a major department in the western United States. He began as a traditional archeologist, interested in Pueblo ruins and Southwestern prehistory, and he went on digs and surveys like the rest of us. Unlike the rest of us, he saw those digs and surveys not as an end in themselves, but as a means to an end, and a means that proved to be too slow. After a few years of dusty holes in hot, dreary valleys he was no closer to the top than when he had started, and in fact, he was showing signs of lamentable fallibility. In 50 tries at laying out a 5-ft square, he had never come closer than 4 ft 10 in by 5 ft 3 in, and he'd missed more floors than the elevator in the World Trade Center. And then, just when all seemed darkest, he discov-

ered Philosophy of Science, and was born again.

Suddenly he found the world would beat a path to his door if he criticized everyone else's epistemology. Suddenly he discovered that so long as his research design was superb, he never had to do the research; just publish the design, and it would be held up as a model, a brass ring hanging unattainable beyond the clumsy fingers of those who actually survey and dig. No more dust, no more heat, no more 5-ft squares. He worked in an office now, generating hypotheses and laws and models which an endless stream of graduate students was sent out to test; for he himself no longer did any fieldwork.

And it was just as well, for as one of his former professors had said, "That poor wimp couldn't dig his way out of a kitty litter box."

In all fairness to the Born-Again Philosopher, he was in large measure a product of the 1960s, and there are lots more like him where he came from. And let us not judge him too harshly until we have examined my other companion in the lounge, a young man whose degree came not from 1968, but from 1978. I will refer to him simply as the Child of the Seventies.

Like so many of his academic generation, the Child of the Seventies had but one outstanding characteristic: blind ambition. He had neither the commitment to culture history of my generation nor the devotion to theory of the generation of the 1960s. His goals were simple: to be famous, to be well paid, to be stroked, and to receive immediate gratification. How he got there did not matter. Who he stepped on along the way did not matter. Indeed, the data of prehistory did not matter. For him, archeology was only a vehicle—one carefully selected, because he had discovered early that people will put up with almost anything in the guise of archeology.

As a graduate student, the Child of the Seventies had taken a course in introductory archeology from a man I will simply refer to as Professor H. Professor H. worked very hard on the course, synthesizing the literature, adding original ideas and a lot of his own unpublished data. The Child of the Seventies took copious notes. Sometimes he asked questions to draw the instructor out, and sometimes he asked if he could copy Professor H.'s slides. When the professor used handouts, he bound them in his notebook.

At graduation, the Child of the Seventies went off to his first job at Springboard University. The day he arrived, he went directly to Springboard University Press and asked if they would like a textbook on introductory archeology. Of course they did. The Child polished his notes from Professor H.'s course and submitted them as a book. It was published to rave reviews. Today it is the only textbook on the subject that Professor H. really likes, and he requires it in his course. The faculty at Springboard U overwhelmingly voted the Child of the Seventies tenure. Professor H., on the other hand, has been held back because he hasn't published enough. "He's a great teacher," his colleagues say. "If only he could write more. Like that student of his at Springboard U."

To his credit as an anthropologist, the child had merely discerned that our subculture not only tolerates this sort of behavior, it *rewards* people for it. But the story doesn't end there.

The Child of the Seventies had written a six-chapter doctoral dissertation. Now he xeroxed each chapter and provided it with an introduction and con-

clusion, making it a separate article. Each was submitted to a different journal, and all were published within a year. He then persuaded Springboard University Press to publish a reader composed of his six reprinted works. In that reader, the chapters of his dissertation were at last reunited between hard covers. He added an overview, recounting the ways his perspective had changed as he looked back over the full sweep of his 18 months as a professional archeologist.

His publisher asked him to do another reader. This time, he invited six colleagues to write the various chapters. Some were flattered. Some were desperate. All accepted. He wrote a three-page introduction and put his name on the cover as editor. The book sold. And suddenly, his path to the top was clear; he could turn out a book a year, using the original ideas of others, without ever having an original idea himself. And in the long run, he would be better known and better paid than any of his contributors, even though they worked twice as hard.

I ordered a Michelob, and paid my buck-fifty a can, and sat wondering exactly what I could say to these two guys. It isn't easy when you know that one will criticize any idea you put forth, and the other will incorporate it into his next book. Fortunately I never had to say anything, for it was at exactly that moment that the third, and most important, character of this story entered the lounge.

He stood for a moment with his battered carryon bag in his hand, looking down at the three of us. He was an Old Timer—no question about that—but how old would have been anybody's guess. When you're that tanned and weather-beaten you could be 50, or 60, or even 70, and no one could really tell. His jeans had been through the mud and the barbed-wire fences of countless field seasons, his hat had faded in the prairie sun, and his eyes had the kind of crow's feet known locally as the High Plains squint. I could tell he was an archeologist by his boots, and I could tell he was still a good archeologist by the muscle tone in his legs.

(You see, I have a colleague at Michigan—an ethnologist—who claims that since archeologists have strong backs and weak minds, when an archeologist starts to fade, it's the legs that go first. On the other hand, his wife informs me that when an ethnologist starts to fade, the first thing to go is not his legs.)

The Old Timer settled into the seat next to me, stowed his carryon bag, and turned to introduce himself. I failed to catch his name because the stewardess, somewhat out of breath, caught up with him at that moment and pressed a bourbon and water into his hand. "Thank you, ma'am," he said, sipping it down; and he stared for a moment, and said, "I needed that. And that's the God's truth."

"I know what you mean," I said, "The meetings can do that to you. Six hundred people crammed into the lobby of a hotel. Two hundred are talking down to you as if you're an idiot. Two hundred are sucking up to you as if you're a movie star. Two hundred are telling you lies, and all the while they're looking over your shoulder, hoping they'll meet somebody more important."

"This year it was worse than that, son. Last night my department retired me. Turned me out to pasture."

"I wouldn't have guessed you were retirement age," I lied.

"I'm not. I had two years to go. But they retired me early. Mostly because of an article in the *New York Times Sunday Magazine* by an ethnologist, Eric Wold. You remember that one?"

"I read it," I said, "but I don't remember him calling for your retirement."

The Old Timer reached into his pocket, past a half-empty pouch of Bull Durham, and brought out a yellowed clipping from the Sunday *Times* of November 30, 1980. I caught a glimpse of Wolf's byline, and below it, several paragraphs outlined in red ink. "See what he says here," said the Old Timer.

An earlier anthropology had achieved unity under the aegis of the culture concept. It was culture, in the view of anthropologists, that distinguished humankind from all the rest of the universe, and it was the possession of varying cultures that differentiated one society from another. . . . The past quarter-century has undermined this intellectual sense of security. The relatively inchoate concept of "culture" was attacked from several theoretical directions. As the social sciences transformed themselves into "behavioral" sciences, explanations for behavior were no longer traced to culture; behavior was to be understood in terms of psychological encounters, strategies of economic choice, strivings for payoffs in games of power. Culture, once extended to all acts and ideas employed in social life, was now relegated to the margins as "world view" or "values." [Wolf 1980]

"Isn't that something?" said the Old Timer. "The day that came out my department called me in. The chairman says, 'It has come to our attention that you still believe in culture as the central paradigm in archeology.' I told him yes, I supposed I did. Then he says, 'We've talked about it, and we all think you ought to take early retirement.' "

"But that's terrible. You should have fought it."

"I *did* fight it," he said. "But they got my file together and sent it out for an outside review. Lord, they sent it to all these distinguished anthropologists. Marvin Harris. Clifford Geertz. And aren't there a couple of guys at Harvard with hyphenated names?"

"At least a couple." I assured him.

"Well, they sent my file to one of them. And to some Big Honcho social anthropologist at the University of Chicago. And the letters started coming back.

"Harris said he was shocked to see that in spite of the fact that I was an archeologist, I had paid so little attention to the techno-eco-demo-environmental variables. Geertz said as far as he could tell, all I was doing was Thick Description. The guy from Harvard said he wasn't sure he could evaluate me, because he'd never even heard of our department."

"And how about the guy from Chicago?"

"He said that he felt archeology could best be handled by one of the local trade schools."

There was a moment of silence while we all contemplated the heartbreak of an archeologist forced into early retirement by his belief in culture. In the background we could hear our pilot announcing that the Salton Sea was visible off to the right of the aircraft.

"They sure gave me a nice retirement party, though," said the Old Timer. "Rented a whole suite at the hotel. And I want to show you what they gave me as a going-away present."

His hand groped for a moment in the depths of his battle-scarred overnight bag, and suddenly he produced a trowel. A trowel such as no one had ever seen. A trowel that turned to yellow flame in the rays of the setting sun as he held it up to the window of the 747.

"This was my first Marshalltown trowel," he said. "You know what an archeologist's first Marshalltown is like? Like a major leaguer's first Wilson glove. I dug at Pecos with this trowel, under A. V. Kidder. And at Aztec Ruin with Earl Morris. And at Kincaid with Fay-Cooper Cole. And at Lindenmeier with Frank Roberts. Son, this trowel's been at Snaketown, and Angel Mound, and at the Dalles of the Columbia with Luther Cressman.

"And then one night, these guys from my department broke into my office and borrowed it, so to speak. And the next time I saw it, they'd had that sucker plated in 24-karat gold.

"It sure is pretty now. And that's the God's truth."

The trowel passed from hand to hand around our little group before returning to the depths of the Old Timer's bag. And for each of us, I suppose, it made that unimaginably far-off day of retirement just a little bit less remote.

"What do you think you'll do now?" asked the Child of the Seventies, for whom retirement would not come until the year 2018.

"Well," said the Old Timer, "so far the only thing that's opened up for me are some offers to do contract archeology."

The Born-Again Philosopher snickered condescendingly.

"I take it," said the Old Timer, "you have some reservations about contract archeology."

"Oh, it's all right, I suppose," said the Philosopher. "I just don't think it has much of a contribution to make to *my* field."

"And what would that field be?"

"Method and theory."

"No particular region or time period?"

"No. I wouldn't want to be tied down to a specific region. I work on a higher level of abstraction."

"I'll bet you do," said the Old Timer. "Well, son, there are some things about contract archeology I don't like either. Occasional compromises between scientific goals and industrial goals. Too many reports that get mimeographed for the president of some construction company, rather than being published where archeologists can read them. But in all fairness, most of the contract archeologists I know express just as strong an interest in method and theory as you do."

"But they're law *consumers,*" said the Philosopher. "I'm committed to being a law *producer.*"

The Old Timer took a thoughtful drag on his bourbon. "Son," he said, "I admire a man who dispenses with false modesty. But you've overlooked what I see as one of the strengths of contract archeologists: they still deal directly with what happened in prehistory. If I want to know what happened in Glen Canyon, or when agriculture reached the Missouri Basin, or how long the mammoth hunters lasted in Pennsylvania, often as not I need to talk to a contract archeologist. Because the answers to the cultural-historical questions don't always lie on a 'higher level of abstraction.' "

"No," said the Born-Again Philosopher. "Only the *important* questions lie on that level."

"There was an interruption as the stewardess reappeared before us, pushing an aluminum beverage cart. We ordered another round of beer, and she picked up our empty cans, depositing them in a plastic trash bag attached to the cart.

1. ABOUT ARCHAEOLOGY

"I'd like to ask a favor," said the Born-Again Philosopher. "Before our 10-minute stopover in Tucson, I'd like to examine the contents of that bag."

"Now I've heard everything," said the stewardess.

"No, it's not a come-on," said the Philosopher. "It's a favor for a friend. I have a colleague, Bill Rathje, who's doing a study of garbage disposal patterns in the city of Tucson [Rathje 1974]. He's got the internal system pretty well mapped out, but he realizes that Tucson is not a closed system: garbage enters and leaves via planes, cars, and backpacks. I promised him if I were ever on a plane landing or taking off from Tucson, I'd sample the refuse on board."

The stewardess struggled to remove all trace of emotion from her face. "Well," she said, "I suppose if you clean up everything when you're done—."

"I'll be checking the refuse in the tourist-class cabin," said the Philosopher, "while my friend here" (indicating the Child of the Seventies) "will be checking the first-class cabin, and coauthoring the paper with me."

"And what do you call your profession?" she asked.

"Archeology."

"You guys are weird," she called over her shoulder as she and the cart disappeared down the aisle.

The Born-Again Philosopher settled back in his seat with a pleased smile on his face. "Now there's a perfect example of why archeologists should not restrict themselves to the study of ancient objects lying on the surface or underneath the ground. If we're to develop a truly universal set of covering laws, we must be free to derive them from any source we can.

"In my opinion," he said, "the greatest legacy we can leave the next generation is a body of robust archeological theory."

"Well, son, I'll give you my opinion," said the Old Timer. "I don't believe there's any such thing as 'archeological theory.' For me there's only *anthropological* theory. Archeologists have their own methodology, and ethnologists have theirs; but when it comes to theory, we all ought to sound like anthropologists."

"My God, are you out of it!" said the Born-Again Philosopher. "For ten years we've been building up a body of purely archeological laws. I myself have contributed 10 or 20."

"I'd love to hear a few," I said. And I could see I was not the only one: the Child of the Seventies was getting ready to write them down unobtrusively on his cocktail napkin.

"Number One," said the Philosopher: "Prehistoric people did not leave behind in the site examples of everything they made. Number Two: Some of the things they did leave behind disintegrated, and cannot be found by archeologists."

"I don't want to sound unappreciative," I said, "but I believe Schliemann already knew that when he was digging at Troy."

"If he did," and the B.A.P. ," he never made it *explicit*. I have made it *explicit*."

"Son," said the Old Timer, "I guess we can all sleep easier tonight because of that."

"I also came up with the following," the Philosopher went on. "Number Three: Objects left on a sloping archeological site wash downhill. Number Four: Lighter objects wash downhill farther than heavy objects."

"Hold it right there, son," said the Old Timer, "because you've just illustrated a point I was hoping to make. So often these things you fellows call archeological laws turn out not to be laws of human behavior, but examples of the physical processes involved in the formation of sites. And son, those are no more than the products of *geological* laws."

The Born-Again Philosopher's face lit up in a triumphant smile. "That objection has been raised many times before," he said, "and it was disposed of definitively by Richard Watson, who is both a geologist and a philosopher. In his 1976 *American Antiquity* article, Watson (1976:65) makes it clear (and here I am paraphrasing) that even when hypotheses are directly dependent on laws of geology, they are specifically archeological *when they pertain to archeological materials*."

Now it was the Old Timer's turn to smile "Oh. Well. That's different," he said. "In that case, I guess, archeology just barely missed out on a major law."

"How's that?" asked the Child of the Seventies earnestly, his pencil at the ready.

"Well, following your argument, the Law of Uniform Acceleration could have been an archeological law if only Galileo had dropped a metate and mano from the Leaning Tower of Pisa."

"I don't think you're taking this seriously," the Born-Again Philosopher complained.

"Son," said the Old Timer. "I'm taking it fully as seriously as it deserves to be taken. And as far as I'm concerned, so far the only legitimate archeological law I know of is the Moss-Bennett Bill."

The Born-Again Philosopher drew himself erect. "I think I'd better go back and start my inventory of the tourist-class trash," he said, and he began working his way down the aisle toward the galley.

"You're being awfully hard on him," said the Child of the Seventies. "You have to remember that he's the spokesman for a large number of theoretical archeologists who hope to increase archeology's contribution to science and philosophy."

The Old Timer took a long, slow pull on his bourbon. "Son, do you watch Monday Night Football?" he asked.

"Occasionally," said the Child. "When I'm not correcting page proofs."

"I have a reason for asking." said the Old Timer. "I just want to try out an analogy on you.

"During Monday Night Football there are 22 players on the field, 2 coaches on the sidelines, and 3 people in the broadcast booth. Two of the people in the booth are former players who can no longer play. One of the people in the booth never played a lick in his life. And who do you suppose talks the loudest and is the most critical of the players on the field?"

"The guy who never played a lick," I interrupted. "And the guys with him, the former players, are always saying things like, 'Well, it's easy to criticize from up here, but it's different when you're down on the field.' "

"Well said, son," the Old Timer chuckled. "And I want you to consider the symbolism for a moment. The field is lower than everything else; it's physical, it's sweaty, it's a place where people follow orders. The press box is high, detached, Olympian, cerebral. And it's verbal. Lord, is it verbal.

"Now football is a game of strategy, of game plans (or 'research designs,' if you will), and what are called differing philosophies. In our lifetime we've witnessed great innovations in strategy: the nickel defense, the flex, the shotgun, the wishbone—and the list goes on. How many of them were created in the press box?"

"None," I said. "They were created by coaches."

"By coaches, many of them former players, who are still personally involved in the game, and who diligently study their own mistakes, create new strategies, and return to the field to test them in combat," said the Old Timer.

"I think I see what you're driving at," said the Child of the Seventies, but we knew he was lying.

"There are estimated to be more than 4,000 practicing archeologists in the United States," said the Old Timer. "Most of them are players. Sure, many of us are second- or third-string, but when we're called upon to go in, we do the best we can. And we rely on the advice and strategy of a fair number of archeological 'coaches'—veterans, people we respect because they've paid their dues the same as we have.

"What's happening now is that we're getting a new breed of archeologist. A kind of archeological Howard Cosell. He sits in a booth high above the field, and cites Hempel and Kuhn and Karl Popper. He second-guesses our strategy, and tells us when we don't live up to his expectations. 'Lew Binford,' he says, 'once the fastest mind in the field, but frankly, this season he may have lost a step or two.' Or, 'It's shocking to see a veteran like Struever make a rookie mistake like that.'

"What I worry about, son, is that every year there'll be fewer people down on the field and more up in the booth. There's a great living to be made in the booth, but it's a place that breeds a great deal of arrogance. No one in the booth ever fumbles a punt or, for that matter, misclassifies a potsherd or screws up a profile drawing. They pass judgment on others, but never expose themselves to criticism. The guys in the booth get a lot of exposure, and some even achieve celebrity status. What rarely gets pointed out is that the guys in the booth have had little if any strategic and theoretical impact on the game, because they're far removed from the field of play.

"But the players know that. Especially the contract archeologists, and those of us who perennially work in the field. Because we have the feeling the guys in the booth look down on us as a bunch of dumb, sweaty jocks. And we're damn sick of it, son, and that's the God's truth."

"But you surely don't deny the importance of theory in archeology," said the Child of the Seventies. "I'm sure you've used what Binford [1977] calls middle-range theory in your own work."

"Of course," said the Old Timer. "I've used it to organize and make sense out of my data. Which is, when you stop to think about it, one of the main purposes for theory. The problem came when the guys in the booth began to think of 'archeological theory' as a subdiscipline in its own right—a higher and more prestigious calling than the pursuit of data on prehistory, which they see as a form of manual labor. As if that weren't bad enough, some of them are now beginning to think of themselves as philosophers of science."

"I find that exciting," said the Child of the Seventies.

"Son," said the Old Timer, "it would be exciting, if they were any good at it. Unfortunately, in most cases, it's the only thing they're worse at than field archeology."

"But some are establishing a dialogue with philosophers," said the Child.

"That's right," said the Old Timer. "Now we're going to have philosophers who don't know anything about archeology, advising archeologists who don't know anything about philosophy."

"They want archeology to make a contribution to philosophy," said the Child.

"I'll tell you what," said the Old Timer. "I'd settle for making a contribution to *archeology*. I guess I'd rather be a second-rate archeologist than a third-rate philosopher."

"But doesn't archeology have more to offer the world than that?"

The Old Timer leaned back in his seat and sipped at his bourbon. "That's a good question," he said. "We hear a lot about archeology's relevance to anthropology in general. To the social sciences. To the world. And of course, we're all waiting for our recently departed friend to come up with his first Great Law. But I'd like to turn the question around and ask What does the world really want from archeology?

"If I turn on television, or walk through a paperback bookstore, I'll tell you what I see. I see that what the world wants is for archeology to teach it something about humanity's past. The world doesn't want epistemology from us. They want to hear about Olduvai Gorge, and Stonehenge, and Macchu Picchu. People are gradually becoming aware that their first three million years took place before written history, and they look at archeology as the only science—the *only one*—with the power to uncover the past.

"I remember Bill Sanders telling me once that the only legitimate reason to do archeology was to satisfy your intellectual curiosity. And I suspect that if we just try to do a good job at that, the more general contributions will follow naturally. I don't think Isaac Newton or Gregor Mendel ran around saying 'I'm a law producer.' Their laws grew unself-consciously out of their efforts to satisfy their own curiosity.

"Son, if the world wants philosophy, it will surely turn to philosophers, not archeologists, to get it. I'd hate to see us get so confused about what the world wants from archeology that we turn our backs on what we do best. In my opinion, our major responsibility to the rest of the world is to do good, basic archaeological research."

1. ABOUT ARCHAEOLOGY

"You know," said the Child of the Seventies, "as I listen to you talk, I'm thinking how nice it would be to have you write an overview for the book I'm editing right now. A book on future directions in archeology."

"I'm not sure how excited I am about some of the future directions," said the Old Timer.

That's why your overview would give us needed balance," said the Child. "Why, you're our link with the past. You've stepped right out of the pages of archeology's rich, much maligned empiricist tradition."

"You overestimate me, son."

"No. You're too modest," said the Child, who was not used to being turned down. "I feel that you may well be the most significant figure of your generation, and I'd consider myself deeply honored to have your overview in my book."

"Horsefeathers," said the Old Timer.

The Child of the Seventies stood up with a gesture of frustration. "I've got to inventory the trash in the first-class cabin, or I won't get to coauthor that article," he said. "But think over what I said. And don't say anything important until I get back."

We watched him disappear through the curtain into the first-class section.

"You must have been inoculated against soft soap." I told the Old Timer.

"Son," he said, "if that young fellow's nose were any browner, we'd need a Munsell Soil Color Chart to classify it."

"If you think he's at all atypical," I suggested, "take a good look around you at the next archeology meeting."

"And you know," said the Old Timer, "we're partly to blame for that. All of us in academic departments.

"We hire a young guy, right out of graduate school, and we give him all our introductory courses to teach. Then we tell him it's publish or perish. His only choices are to write something half-baked, or make an article out of an attack on some already established figure. You take those two kinds of papers out of *American Antiquity*, and you got nothing left but the book review.

"What we *ought* to do, if we really want these young people to grow, is give them their first year off, so they can go collect their own data and make their own positive contribution. How can we give them eight courses to teach and then put pressure on them to publish?"

"You're right," I said. "But our two friends here have discovered how to beat the system. One has created a specialty that never requires him to leave his office, and the other has figured out how to get other people to write his books for him. And we reward both of them for it."

"But not without some reservations," said the Old Timer. "You know, archeologists don't really like having a colleague who's so ambitious he'd kick his own grandmother's teeth in to get ahead. Businessmen, or perhaps show-business people, will tolerate it. They'll say, 'He's a real S.O.B., but he gets things done.' But archeologists don't want a colleague who's a real S.O.B. They're funny that way."

The stewardess with the beverage cart paused by our seats for a moment to see if we needed a refill. We did. And I took that opportunity to ask how our friends were coming with their inventory of her garbage.

"The one in the aft cabin seems to have hit a snag," she said thoughtfully. "I think he ran into a couple of airsickness bags."

"Well," said the Old Timer, "nobody said fieldwork was easy."

"What are those guys trying to find out, anyway?" she asked.

"As I understand it," I said, "they're trying to provide us with a better basis for archeological interpretation. Since archeologists study the garbage of ancient peoples, they hope to discover principles of garbage discard that will guide us in our work."

The Old Timer's eyes followed the stewardess as she passed through the curtain into the next cabin.

"Son," he said, "I want to hit you with a hypothetical question. Let's say you're working on a 16th-century Arikara site in South Dakota. There's lots of garbage—bison scapula hoes, Catlinite pipes, Bijou Hills quartzite, cord-marked pottery—you know the kind of stuff. You got to interpret it. You got an 18th-century French account of the Arikara, and you got a report on Tucson's garbage in 1981. Which would you use?"

"I think you already know the answer to that one," I smiled.

"Then why do I have the distinct impression that these two kids would use the report on Tucson's garbage?" he demanded.

"Because *you* still believe in *culture*," I said, "and these kids are only concerned with *behavior*."

"I guess that's right," he said thoughtfully. "I guess I believe in something called 'Arikara culture,' and I think you ought to know something about it if you work on Arikara sites."

"But suppose, as Eric Wolf suggests in that *Times* article, you're one of those people who no longer looks to culture as an explanation for behavior," I suggested. "Suppose you believe that behavior is explained by universal laws, or psychological encounters, or strategies of economic choice. Then it really doesn't matter whether your interpretive framework comes from tribal ethnohistory or 20th-century industrial America, does it?"

"Nope. And that's sure going to simplify archeology," said the Old Timer. "For one thing, we can forget about having to master the anthropological literature."

He fell silent as the Born-Again Philosopher and the Child of the Seventies returned to their seats, their notebooks filled with behavioral data and their faces flushed with success.

"Did we miss much?" asked the Child.

"Not much," said the Old Timer. "I was just fixing to ask my friend here where he thinks anthropology will go next, now that it no longer has culture as its central paradigm."

"I'm kind of worried about it," I admitted. "Right now I have the impression that anthropology is sort of drifting, like a rudderless ship. I have the feeling it could fragment into a dozen lesser disciplines, with everybody going his own way. Somehow it's not as exciting as it used to be. Enroll-

34

ments are down all over the country. The job market sucks. I suspect one reason is that anthropology is so lacking in consensus as to what it has to offer, it just can't sell itself compared to more unified and aggressive fields."

"Doesn't Wolf tell you in his *Times* article what the next central paradigm will be?" asked the Child of the Seventies. He was hoping for a title for his next book.

"No," said the Old Timer. "He mentions other things people have tried, like cultural materialism, cultural ecology, French structuralism, cognitive and symbolic anthropology, and so on. But you know, none of those approaches involves more than a fraction of the people in the field."

"But it's useful to have all those approaches," I suggested.

"That's the God's truth," he agreed. "But what holds us all together? What keeps us all from pursuing those things until each becomes a separate field in its own right? What is it that makes a guy who works on Maori creation myths continue to talk to a guy who works mainly on Paleoindian stone tools?"

"In my department," I said, "they *don't* talk any more."

"Nor in mine," he said. "But they used to. And they *used* to talk because however obscure their specialties, they all believe in that 'integrated whole,' that 'body of shared customs, beliefs, and values' that we called culture."

"That's right," I said. "But now the Paleoindian archeologist would tell you his stone tools were best explained by Optimal Foraging Strategy. And the Maori ethnologist would tell you his creation myths are the expression of a universal logic inside his informants' heads."

"You know," said the Old Timer, "we've got an ethnologist like that on our faculty. He told me once, 'I'm not interested in anything you can feel, smell, taste, weigh, measure, or count. None of that is real. What's real is in my head.' Kept talking and talking about how what was in his head was what was important. For a long time, I couldn't figure it out.

"Then one day he published his ethnography, and I understood why what was in his head was so important. He'd made up all his data."

The Born-Again Philosopher stirred restlessly in his seat. "It's incredible to me," he said, "that you people haven't realized that for more than a decade now the new paradigm has been Logical Positivism. It's hard to see how you can do problem-oriented archeology without it."

Slowly the Old Timer rolled himself a cigarette. The Child of the Seventies sat up momentarily, leaned forward to watch, then slumped back in his seat with disappointment when he realized it was only Bull Durham.

"Have you considered," said the Old Timer deliberately, "the implications of doing problem-oriented archeology without the concept of culture?"

"Now you're putting us on," said the Philosopher.

For just a moment, the Old Timer allowed himself a smile. "Consider this," he said. "An ethnologist can say, 'I'm only interested in myth and symbolism, and I'm not going to collect data on subsistence.' He can go to a village in the Philippines and ignore the terraced hillsides and the rice paddies and the tilapia ponds, and just ask people about their dreams and the spirits of their ancestors. Whatever he does, however selective he is in what he collects, when he leaves the village, it's still there. And next year, if a Hal Conklin or an Aram Yengoyan comes along, those terraces and paddies and fish ponds will still be there to study.

"But suppose an archeologist were to say, 'I'm only interested in Anasazi myth and symbolism, and I'm not going to collect data on subsistence.' Off he goes to a prehistoric cliff dwelling and begins to dig. He goes for the pictographs, and figurines, and ceremonial staffs, and wooden bird effigies. What, then, does he do with all the digging sticks, and tumplines, and deer bones that he finds while he's digging for all the other stuff? Does he ignore them because they don't relate to his 'research problem?' Does he shovel them onto the dump? Or does he pack them up and put them in dead storage, in the hope that he can farm them out to a student some day to ease

his conscience? Because, unlike the situation in ethnology, no archeologist will be able to come along later and find that stuff in its original context. It's *gone,* son."

"It's as if—well, as if your Philippine ethnologist were to interview an informant on religion, and then kill him so no one could ever interview him on agriculture," I ventured.

"Exactly, son," he said. "Archeology is the only branch of anthropology where we kill our informants in the process of studying them."

"Except for a few careless physical anthropologists," I said.

"Well, yes, except for that."

"But hasn't that always been the conflict between 'problem-oriented' archeology and traditional archeology?" asked the Born-Again Philosopher. "Surely you have to have a specific hypothesis to test, and stick pretty much to the data relevant to that hypothesis, rather than trying to record everything."

"And what about other archeologists with other hypotheses." I asked. "Don't you feel a little uncomfortable destroying data relevant to their problem while you're solving yours?"

"Well, *I* don't, because I really don't do any digging now," said the Philosopher. "I see my role as providing the hypotheses that will direct the research efforts of others. There are lots of archeologists around who can't do anything *but* dig. Let *them* do the digging.

"Look," he said, "I can't say it any better than Schiffer [1978:247] said it in Dick Gould's 1978 volume on ethnoarchaeology. To paraphrase him: I feel free to pursue the study of laws wherever it leads. I do *not* feel the need to break the soil periodically in order to reaffirm my status as archeologist."

"Son," said the Old Timer, "I think I just heard 10,000 archeological sites breathe a sigh of relief."

There was a moment of air turbulence, and we all reached for our drinks. The sleek ribbon of the Colorado River shimmered below us, and over the audio system we could hear the captain advise us to keep our seat belts loosely fastened. Hunched in his seat, reflective, perhaps just a little sad, the Old Timer whispered in my ear: "That's what the ethnologists will never understand, son. There's a basic conflict between problem-oriented archeology and archeological ethics. Problem orientation tells you to pick a specific topic to investigate. Archeological ethics tell you you *must* record everything, because no one will ever see it in context again. The problem is that except for certain extraordinary sites, archeological data don't come packaged as 'cognitive' or 'religious' or 'environmental' or 'economic.' They're all together in the ground— integrated in complex ways, perhaps, but integrated. That's why the old concept of culture made sense as a paradigm for archeology. And it still does, son. That's the God's truth."

I wish I could tell you how the rest of the conversation went, but at this point I could no longer keep my eyes open. After all, you wear a guy out at the meetings, and then give him six beers and start talking archeological theory, and that guy's going to fall asleep. So I slept even through those bumpy landings in the desert where the Child of the Seventies and the Born-Again Philosopher retired to their respective universities, and then somewhere between St. Louis and Detroit, I started to dream.

Now, I don't know whether it was because of the beer or the heated discussion we'd had, but my dream was a nightmare. I don't really know what it means, but my friends who work with the Walbiri and the Pitjandjara tell me that Dream Time is when you get your most important messages. So let me talk about it for a minute.

In this dream, I'd been released by the University of Michigan—whether for moral turpitude or believing in culture is really not clear. No job had opened up anywhere, and the only work I could find was with Bill Rathje's Garbage Project in Tucson. And not as a supervisor, just as a debagger. Sorting through the refuse of a thousand nameless homes, Anglo and Chicano, Pima and Papago, hoping against hope for that discarded wallet or diamond ring that could underwrite my retirement program.

And then, one day, I'm standing on the loading dock with my gauze mask on, and my pink rubber gloves, and my white lab coat with "Le Projet du Garbage" embroidered on the pocket, and this *huge* garbage truck pulls up to the dock and unloads a 30-gallon Hefty Bag. The thing is heavy as the dickens, and I wrestle it onto a dolly, and wheel it inside the lab; and we dump it onto the lab table, where the thing splits under its own weight and its contents come out all over the place.

And you know what's in it?

Reprints.

Reprints of *my* articles. Every single reprint I ever mailed out. All of them. And I'm not just talking reprints; I'm talking *autographed* reprints. The kind where I'd written something in the upper right-hand corner like, "Dear Dr. Willey, I hope you find this of interest."

You know, you can mail 'em out, but you never know whether they *keep* 'em or not.

And I suddenly realize that my whole career—my entire professional output—is in that Hefty Bag. Along with a couple of disposable diapers, and a pair of pantyhose, and a copy of *Penthouse* with the Jerry Falwell interview torn out.

But that's not the worst part.

The worst part is that the form Rathje's people fill out doesn't have a space for "discarded reprints." So my whole career, my entire professional output, simply has to be recorded as "other."

And that's where the nightmare ended, and I woke up on the runway at Detroit. I was grabbing my carryon bag as I bumped into the stewardess on her way down the aisle. "The Old Timer who was sitting next to me," I said. "What stop did he get off at?"

"What Old Timer?" she asked.

"The old guy in the boots and the faded hat with the rattlesnake hatband."

"I didn't see anybody like that," she said. "The only 'old guy' in the lounge was you."

"Have a nice day," I said sweetly. And I caught the limousine to Ann Arbor, and all the way home to my front door I kept wondering whether I had dreamed the whole thing.

Now I'll bet some of you don't think this all really happened. And I was beginning to doubt it myself until I started to unpack my carryon bag, and I was almost blinded by a gleam. A 24-karat gleam.

And there, hastily stuffed into my bag with a note wrapped around the handle, was the golden Marshalltown.

And the note read: "Son, where I'm going, I won't be needing this. I know you and I see eye to eye on a lot of things, so I'm going to ask a favor. I want you to save it for—well, just the right person.

"First off, I don't see any paradigm out there right now that's going to replace culture as a unifying theme in archeology. If some ethnologists want to go their separate ways—into sociobiology, or applied semeiotics, or social psychology—well, fine, they can call themselves something else, and let *us* be the anthropologists. I sort of felt that the concept of culture was what distinguished us from those other fields and kept us all from drifting apart for good.

"Because of the way our data come packaged in the ground, we pretty much have to deal with all of them to deal with any of them. It's harder for us to abandon the traditional concerns of anthropology, and we can't afford sudden fads, or quixotic changes in what's 'in' this year. We need long-term stability. And because we kill our informants as we question them, we have to question them in ways that are less idiosyncratic and more universally interpretable. And we have to share data in ways they don't.

"Because of that, we have to have a kind of integrity most fields don't need. I need your data, and you need mine, and we have to be able to trust each other on some basic level. There can't be any backstabbing, or working in total isolation, or any of this sitting on a rock in the forest interpreting culture in ways no colleague can duplicate.

"That's why we can't afford too many S.O.B.s. We can't afford guys whose lives are spent sitting in a press box criticizing other people's contributions. Son, all of prehistory is hidden in a vast darkness, and my generation was taught that it was better to light one tiny candle than curse the darkness. Never did I dream we'd have people whose whole career was based on cursing our *candles*.

"In the old days we mainly had one kind of archeologist: a guy who scratched around for a grant, went to the field, surveyed or excavated to the best of his ability, and published the results. Some guys labored patiently, in obscurity, for years. And one day, their colleagues would look up and say, 'You know, old Harry's doing good, solid work. Nothing spectacular, mind you, but you know—I'd trust him to dig on my site.' I believe that's the highest compliment one archeologist can pay another. And that's the God's truth.

"Now that doesn't sound like much, son, but today we got archeologists that can't even do that. What's more, they're too damn ambitious to labor in obscurity. So they've decided to create a whole new set of specialties around the margins of the field. Each defines himself (or herself) as the founder of that specialty, and then sets out to con the rest of us into believing that's where all the action is.

"And because archeologists will believe *anything,* pretty soon you've got a mass migration to the margins of the field. And pretty soon that's where the greatest noise is coming from.

"Now, don't get me wrong. A lot of these kids are shrewd and savvy, and they'll make a contribution one way or another. But that's one out of ten. The other nine are at the margins because things weren't moving fast enough for them in the main stream. You know, some of these kids think archeology is a 100-meter dash, and they're shocked and angry when no one pins a medal on them after the first 100 meters. But I'll tell you a secret: archeology is a marathon, and you don't win marathons with speed. You win them with character.

"Son, after our talk this afternoon, I got to wondering about what archeology needed the most.

"I decided there probably isn't an urgent need for one more young person who makes a living editing other people's original ideas. I decided there probably wasn't an urgent need for one more kid who criticizes everyone else's research design while he or she never goes to the field. And I decided we probably didn't need a lot more of our archeological flat tires recapped as philosophers. There seem to be enough around to handle the available work.

"What I don't see enough of son, is first-rate archeology.

"Now that's sad, because after all, archeology is fun. Hell, I don't break the soil periodically to 'reaffirm my status.' I do it because archeology is still the most fun you can have with your pants on.

"You know, there are a lot of awards in archeology. The Viking Fund Medal, the Kidder Medal, the Aztec Eagle, the Order of the Quetzal. But those awards are for intellectual contributions. I'd like to establish an award just for commitment to plain, old-fashioned basic research and professional ethics. And that's what this trowel is for.

"So, son, some day when you meet a kid who still believes in culture, and in hard work, and in the history of humanity; a kid who's in the field because he or she loves it, and not because they want to be famous; a kid who'd never fatten up on somebody else's data, or cut down a colleague just to get ahead; a kid who knows the literature, and respects the generations who went before—you give the kid this golden Marshalltown."

And the note ended there, with no signature, no address, and no reply required.

So that, I guess, is what I'm really here for tonight: to announce an award for someone who may not exist. But if any of you out there know of such a kid coming along—a kid who still depends on his own guts and brains instead of everyone else's—a kid who can stand on the shoulders of giants, and not be tempted to relieve himself on their heads—have *I* got an award for *him.*

And that's the God's truth.

REFERENCES CITED

Binford, Lewis R., 1977. General Introduction. *In* For Theory Building in Archeology: Essays on Faunal Remains, Aquatic Resources, Spatial Analysis, and Systemic Modeling. Lewis R. Binford, ed. pp. 1–10. New York: Academic Press.

Rathje, William L., 1974. The Garbage Project: A New Way of Looking at the Problems of Archaeology. Archaeology 27:236–241.

Schiffer, Michael B., 1978. Methodological Issues in Ethnoarchaeology. *In* Explorations in Ethnoarchaeology. Richard A. Gould, ed. pp. 229–247. Albuquerque: University of New Mexico Press (for the School of American Research).

Watson, Richard A., 1976. Inference in Archaeology. American Antiquity 41(1):58–66.

Wolf, Eric, 1980. They Divide and Subdivide, and Call It Anthropology. The New York Times Sunday Magazine, Nov. 30, 1980.

Epistemology: How You Know What You Know

Kenneth L. Feder

KNOWING THINGS

The word *epistemology* means the study of knowledge—how you know what you know. Think about it. How does anybody know anything to be actual, truthful, or real? How do we differentiate the reasonable from the unreasonable, the meaningful from the meaningless—in archaeology or in any other field of knowledge? Everybody knows things, but how do we really know these things?

I know that there is a mountain in a place called Tibet. I know that the mountain is called Everest, and I know that it is the tallest land mountain in the world (there are some a bit taller under the ocean). I even know that it is precisely 29,028 feet high. But I have never measured it; I've never even been to Tibet. Beyond this, I have not measured all of the other mountains in the world to compare them to Everest. Yet I am quite confident that Everest is the world's tallest peak. But how do I know that?

On the subject of mountains, there is a run-down stone monument on the top of Bear Mountain in the northwestern corner of Connecticut. The monument was built toward the end of the nineteenth century and marks the "highest ground" in Connecticut. When the monument was built to memorialize this most lofty and auspicious of peaks—the mountain is all of 2,316 feet high—people knew that it was the highest point in the state and wanted to recognize this fact with the monument.

There is only one problem. In recent times, with more accurate, sophisticated measuring equipment, it has been determined that Bear Mountain is not the highest point in Connecticut. The slope of Frissell Mountain, which actually peaks in Massachusetts, reaches a height of 2,380 feet on the Connecticut side of the border, eclipsing Bear Mountain by about 64 feet.

So, people in the late 1800s and early 1900s "knew" that Bear Mountain was the highest point in Connecticut. Today we *know* that they really did not "know" that, because it really was not true—even though they thought it was and built a monument saying so.

Now, suppose that I read in a newspaper, hear on the radio, or see on television a claim that another mountain has been found that is actually ten (or fifty, or ten thousand) feet higher than Mount Everest. Indeed, recently, new satellite data convinced a few, just for a while, that a peak neighboring Everest was, in actuality, slightly higher. You and I have never been to Tibet. How do we know if these reports are true? What criteria can we use to decide if the information is correct or not? It all comes back to epistemology. How indeed do we know what we think we "know"?

Collecting Information: Seeing Isn't Necessarily Believing

In general, people collect information in two ways:

1. Directly through their own experiences

2. Indirectly through specific information sources like friends, teachers, parents, books, TV, etc.

People tend to think that number 1—obtaining firsthand information, the stuff they see or experience themselves—is always the best way. This is unfortunately a false assumption because most people are poor observers.

For example, the list of animals alleged to have been observed by people that turn out to be figments of their imaginations is staggering. It is fascinating to read Pliny, a first-century thinker, or Topsell, who wrote in the seventeenth century, and see detailed accounts of the nature and habits of dragons, griffins, unicorns, mermaids, and so on (Byrne 1979). People claimed to have seen these animals, gave detailed descriptions, and even drew pictures of them. Many folks read their books and believed them.

Some of the first European explorers of Africa, Asia, and the New World could not decide if some of the native people they encountered were human beings or animals. They sometimes depicted them with hair all over their bodies and even as having tails.

Neither are untrained observers very good at identifying known, living animals. A red or "lesser" panda escaped from the zoo in Rotterdam, Holland, in December 1978. Red pandas are very rare animals and are indigenous to India, not Holland. They are distinctive in appearance and cannot be readily mistaken for any other sort of animal. The zoo informed the press that the panda was missing, hoping the

From *Frauds, Myths, and Mysteries* by Kenneth L. Feder, 1990, Chapter 2, pp. 9-26. © 1990 by Mayfield Publishing Company. Reprinted by permission.

publicity would alert people in the area of the zoo and aid in its return. Just when the newspapers came out with the panda story, it was found, quite dead, along some railroad tracks adjacent to the zoo. Nevertheless, over one hundred sightings of the panda *alive* were reported to the zoo from all over the Netherlands *after* the animal was obviously already dead. These reports did not stop until several days after the newspapers announced the discovery of the dead panda (van Kampen 1979). So much for the absolute reliability of firsthand observation.

Collecting Information: Relying on Others

When we explore the problems of secondhand information, we run into even more complications. Now we are not in place to observe something firsthand; we are forced to rely on the quality of someone else's observations, interpretations, and reports—as with the question of the height of Mount Everest. How do we know what to believe? This is a crucial question that all rational people must ask themselves, whether talking about medicine, religion, archaeology, or anything else. Again, it comes back around to epistemology; how do we know what we think we know, and how do we know what or whom to believe?

Science: Playing by the Rules

There are ways to knowledge that are both dependable and reliable. We might not be able to get to absolute truths about the meaning of existence, but we can figure out quite a bit about our world—about chemistry and biology, psychology and sociology, physics and history, and even prehistory. The techniques we are talking about to get at knowledge that we can feel confident in—knowledge that is reliable, truthful, and factual—are referred to as *science*.

In large part, science is a series of techniques used to maximize the probability that what we think we know really reflects the way things are, were, or will be. Science makes no claim to have all the answers or even to

be right all of the time. On the contrary, during the process of the growth of knowledge and understanding, science is often wrong. The only claim that we do make in science is that if we honestly, consistently, and vigorously pursue knowledge using some basic techniques and principles, the truth will eventually surface and we can truly know things about the nature of the world in which we find ourselves.

The question then is, What exactly is science? If you believe Hollywood, science is a mysterious enterprise wherein old, white-haired, rather eccentric bearded gentlemen labor feverishly in white lab coats, mix assorted chemicals, invent mysterious compounds, and attempt to reanimate dead tissue. So much for Hollywood. Scientists don't have to look like anything in particular. We are just people trying to arrive at some truths about how the world and universe work. While the application of science can be a slow, frustrating, all-consuming enterprise, the basic assumptions we scientists hold are really very simple. Whether we are physicists, biologists, or archaeologists, we all work under four underlying principles. These principles are quite straightforward, but equally quite crucial.

1. There is a real and knowable universe.
2. The universe (which includes stars, planets, animals, and rocks, as well as people, their cultures, and their histories) operates according to certain understandable rules or laws.
3. These laws are immutable—that means they do not, in general, change depending on where you are or "when" you are.
4. These laws can be discerned, studied, and understood by people through careful observation, experimentation, and research.

Let's look at these assumptions one at a time.

There Is a Real and Knowable Universe

In science we have to agree that there is a real universe out there for us to

study—a universe full of stars, animals, human history, and prehistory that exists whether we are happy with that reality or not.

The Universe Operates According to Understandable Laws

In essence, what this means is that there are rules by which the universe works: stars produce heat and light according to the laws of nuclear physics; nothing can go faster than the speed of light; all matter in the universe is attracted to all other matter (the law of gravity).

Even human history is not random but can be seen as following certain patterns of human cultural evolution. For example, the development of complex civilizations in Egypt, China, India/Pakistan, Mesopotamia, Mexico, and Peru was not based on random processes (Lamberg-Karlovsky and Sabloff 1979; Haas 1982). Their evolution seems to reflect similar general patterns. This is not to say that all of these civilizations were identical, any more than we would say that all stars are identical. On the contrary, they existed in different physical and cultural environments, and so we should expect that they be different. However, in each case the rise to civilization was preceded by the development of an agricultural economy. In each case, civilization was also preceded by some degree of overall population increase as well as increased population density in some areas (in other words, the development of cities). Again, in each case we find monumental works (pyramids, temples), evidence of long-distance trade, and the development of mathematics, astronomy, and methods of record keeping (usually, but not always, in the form of writing). The cultures in which civilization developed, though some were unrelated and independent, shared these factors because of the nonrandom patterns of cultural evolution.

The point is that everything operates according to rules. In science we believe that, by understanding these rules or laws, we can understand stars, organisms, and even ourselves.

1. ABOUT ARCHAEOLOGY

THE LAWS ARE IMMUTABLE

That the laws do not change under ordinary conditions is a crucial concept in science. A law that works here, works there. A law that worked in the past will work today and will work in the future.

For example, if I go to the top of the Leaning Tower of Pisa today and simultaneously drop two balls of unequal mass, they will fall at the same rate and reach the ground at the same time, just as they did when Galileo performed a similar experiment in the seventeenth century. If I do it today, they will. Tomorrow, the same. If I perform the same experiment countless times, the same thing will occur because the laws of the universe (in this case, the law of gravity) do not change through time. They also do not change depending on where you are. Go anywhere on the earth and perform the same experiment—you will get the same results (try not to hit any pedestrians or you will see some other "laws" in operation). This experiment was even performed by U.S. astronauts on the moon. A hammer and a feather were dropped from the same height, and they hit the surface at precisely the same instant (the only reason this will not work on earth is because the feather is caught by the air and the hammer, obviously, is not). We have no reason to believe that the results would be different anywhere, or "anywhen" else.

If this assumption of science, that the laws do not change through time, were false, many of the so-called historical sciences, including prehistoric archaeology, could not exist.

For example, a major principle in the field of historical geology is that of *uniformitarianism*. It can be summarized in the phrase, "the present is the key to the past." Historical geologists are interested in knowing how the various landforms we see today came into being. They recognize that they cannot go back in time to see how the Grand Canyon was formed. However, since the laws of geology that governed the development of the Grand Canyon have not changed through time, and

since these laws are still in operation, they do not need to. Historical geologists can study the formation of geological features today and apply what they learn to the past. The same laws they can directly study operating in the present were operating in the past when geological features that interested them first formed.

The present that we can observe is indeed the "key" to the past that we cannot. This is true because the laws or rules that govern the universe are constant—those that operate today operated in the past. This is why science does not limit itself to the present, but makes inferences about the past and even predictions about the future (just listen to the weather report for an example of this). We can do so because we can study modern, ongoing phenomena that work under the same laws that existed in the past and will exist in the future.

This is where science and theology are often forced to part company and respectfully disagree. Remember, science depends on the constancy of the laws that we can discern. On the other hand, advocates of many religions, though they might believe that there are laws that govern things (and which, according to them, were established by a Creator), usually (but not always believe that these laws can be changed at any time by their God. In other words, if God does not want the apple to fall to the ground, but instead, to hover, violating the law of gravity, that is precisely what will happen. As a more concrete example, scientists know that the heat and light given off by a fire results from the transformation of mass (of the wood) to energy. Physical laws control this process. A theologian, however, might agree with this ordinarily, but feel that if God wants to create a fire that does not consume any mass (like the "burning bush" of the Old Testament), then this is exactly what will occur. Most scientists simply do not accept this assertion. The rules are the rules. They do not change, even though we might sometimes wish that they would.

The Laws Can Be Understood
This may be the single most important principle in science. The universe is knowable. It may be complicated, and it may take years and years to understand even apparently simple phenomena. However, little by little, bit by bit, we expand our knowledge. Through careful observation and objective research and experimentation, we can indeed know things.

So, our assumptions are simple enough. We accept the existence of a reality independent of our own minds, and we accept that this reality works according to a series of unchanging laws or rules. We also claim that we can recognize and understand these laws or at least recognize the patterns that result from these universal rules. The question remains then: how do we do science—how do we explore the nature of the universe, whether our interest is planets, stars, atoms, or human prehistory?

THE WORKINGS OF SCIENCE

We can know things by employing the rules of logic and rational thought. Scientists—archaeologists or otherwise—usually work through a combination of the logical processes known as *induction* and *deduction*. The dictionary definition of induction is "arguing from specifics to generalities," while deduction is defined as the reverse, arguing from generalities to specifics.

What is essential to good science is objective, unbiased observations—of planets, molecules, rock formations, archaeological sites, and so on. Often, on the basis of these specific observations, we induce explanations called *hypotheses* for how these things work.

For example, we may study the planets Mercury, Venus, Earth, and Mars (each one presents specific bits of information). We then induce general rules about how we think these inner planets in our solar system were formed. Or, we might study a whole series of different kinds of molecules and then induce general rules about how all molecules interact chemically. We may study different rock formations and make general conclusions about their origin. We can study a number of specific prehistoric sites and make generalizations about how cultures evolved.

Notice that we cannot directly observe planets forming, the rules of molecular interaction, rocks being made, or prehistoric cultures evolving. Instead, we are inducing general conclusions and principles concerning our data that seem to follow logically from what we have been able to observe.

This process of induction, though crucial to science, is not enough. We need to go beyond our induced hypotheses by testing them. If our induced hypotheses are indeed valid—that is, if they really represent the actual rules according to which some aspect of the universe (planets, molecules, rocks, ancient societies) works—they should be able to hold up under the rigors of scientific hypothesis testing.

Observation and suggestion of hypotheses, therefore, are only the first steps in a scientific investigation. In science we always need to go beyond observation and hypothesizing. We need to set up a series of "if . . . then" statements; "if" our hypothesis is true "then" the following deduced "facts" will also be true. Our results are not always precise and clear-cut, especially in a science like archaeology, but this much should be clear—scientists are not just out there collecting a bunch of interesting facts. Facts are always collected within the context of trying to explain something or in trying to test a hypothesis.

As an example of this logical process, consider the health effects of smoking. How can scientists be sure that smoking is bad for you? After all, it's pretty rare that someone takes a puff on a cigarette and immediately drops dead. The certainty comes from a combination of induction and deduction. Observers have noticed for about three hundred years that people who smoked seemed to be more likely than people who did not to get certain diseases. As long ago as the seventeenth century, people noticed that habitual pipe smokers were subject to tumor growths on their lips and in their

mouths. From such observations we can reasonably, though tentatively, induce a hypothesis of the unhealthfulness of smoking, but we still need to test such a hypothesis. We need to set up "if . . . then" statements. If, in fact, smoking is a hazard to your health (the hypothesis we have induced based on our observations), then we should be able to deduce some predictions that must also be true. Sure enough, when we test specific, deduced predictions like

1. Smokers will have a higher incidence than nonsmokers of lung cancer
2. Smokers will have a higher incidence of emphysema
3. Smokers will take more sick days from work
4. Smokers will get more upper respiratory infections
5. Smokers will have diminished lung capacity
6. Smokers will have a shorter life expectancy

we see that our original, induced hypothesis—cigarette smoking is hazardous to your health—is upheld.

That was easy, but also obvious. How about an example with more mystery to it, one in which scientists acting in the way of detectives had to solve a puzzle in order to save lives? Carl Hempel (1966), a philosopher of science, provided the following example in his book *The Philosophy of Natural Science*.

THE CASE OF CHILDBED FEVER

In the 1840s things were not going well at the Vienna General Hospital, particularly in Ward 1 of the Maternity Division. In War 1 more than one in ten of the women brought in to give birth died soon after of a terrible disease called "childbed fever." This was a high death rate even for the 1840s. In one year 11.4 percent of the women who gave birth in Ward 1 died of this disease. It was a horrible situation and truly mystifying when you consider the fact that in Ward 2, another maternity

division in the *same* hospital at the *same* time, only about one in fifty of the women (2 percent) died from this disease.

Plenty of people had tried their hand at inducing some possible explanations or hypotheses to explain these facts. It was suggested that more women were dying in Ward 1 due to "atmospheric disturbances," or perhaps it was "cosmic forces." However, no one had really sat down and considered the deductive implications of the various hypotheses—those things that would necessarily have been true if the proposed, induced explanation were in fact true. No one, that is, until a Hungarian doctor, Ignaz Semmelweis, attacked the problem in 1848.

Semmelweis made some observations in the maternity wards at the hospital. He noted some differences between Wards 1 and 2 and induced a series of possible explanations for the drastic difference in the mortality rates. Semmelweis suggested:

1. Ward 1 tended to be more crowded than Ward 2. The overcrowding in Ward 1 was the cause of the higher mortality rate there.
2. Women in Ward 1 were from a lower socioeconomic class and tended to give birth lying on their backs, while in Ward 2 the predominate position was on the side. Birth position was the cause of the higher mortality rate.
3. There was a psychological factor involved; the hospital priest had to walk through Ward 1 to administer the last rites to dying patients in other wards. This sight so upset some women already weakened by the ordeal of childbirth that it contributed to their deaths.
4. There were more student doctors in Ward 1. Students were rougher than experienced physicians in their treatment of the women, unintentionally harming them and contributing to their deaths.

These induced hypotheses all sounded good. Each marked a genuine difference between Wards 1 and 2 that might have caused the difference in the death rate. Semmelweis was doing what most scientists do in such a situation; he was relaying on creativity and imagination in seeking out an explanation.

Creativity and imagination are just as important to science as good observation. But being creative and imaginative was not enough. It did not help the women who were still dying at an alarming rate. Semmelweis had to go beyond producing possible explanations; he had to test each one of them. So, he deduced the necessary implications of each:

1. If hypothesis 1 were correct, then cutting down the crowding in Ward 1 should cut down the mortality rate. Semmelweis tried precisely that. The result: no change. So the first hypothesis was rejected. It had failed the scientific test; it simply could not be correct.
2. Semmelweis went on to test hypothesis 2 by changing the birth positions of the women in Ward 1 to match those of the women in Ward 2. Again, there was no change, and another hypothesis was rejected.
3. Next, to test hypothesis 3, Semmelweis rerouted the priest. Again, women in Ward 1 continued to die of childbed fever at about five times the rate of those in Ward 2.
4. Finally, to test hypothesis 4 Semmelweis made a special effort to get the student doctors to be more gentle in their birth assistance to the women in Ward 1. The result was the same; 10 or 11 percent of the women in Ward 1 died compared to about 2 percent in Ward 2.

Then, as so often happens in science, Semmelweis had a stroke of luck. A doctor friend of his died, and the way he died provided Semmelweis with another possible explanation for the problem in Ward 1. Though Semmelweis's friend was not a woman who had recently given birth, he did have precisely the same symptoms as did the women who were dying of childbed fever. Most importantly, this doctor had died of a disease just like childbed

fever soon after accidentally cutting himself during an autopsy.

Viruses and bacteria were unknown in the 1840s. Surgical instruments were not sterilized, no special effort was made to clean the hands, and doctors did not wear gloves during operations and autopsies. Semmelweis had another hypothesis; perhaps the greater number of medical students in Ward 1 was at the root of the mystery, but not because of their inexperience. Instead, these students, as part of their training, were much more likely than experienced doctors to be performing autopsies. Supposing that there was something bad in dead bodies and this something had entered Semmelweis's friend's system through his wound—could the same bad "stuff" (Semmelweis called it "cadaveric material") get onto the hands of the student doctors, who then might, without washing, go on to help a woman give birth? Then, if this "cadaveric material" were transmitted into the woman's body during the birth of her baby, this material might lead to her death. It was a simple enough hypothesis to test. Semmelweis simply had the student doctors carefully wash their hands after performing autopsies. The women stopped dying in Ward 1. Semmelweis had solved the mystery.

SCIENCE AND NONSCIENCE: THE ESSENTIAL DIFFERENCES

Through objective observation and analysis, a scientist, whether a physicist, chemist, biologist, psychologist, or archaeologist, sees things that need explaining. Through creativity and imagination, the scientist suggests possible hypotheses to explain these "mysteries." The scientist then sets up a rigorous method through experimentation or subsequent research to deductively test the validity of a given hypothesis. If the implications of a hypothesis are shown not to be true, the hypothesis must be rejected and then it's back to the drawing board. If the implications are found to be true, we can uphold or support our hypothesis.

A number of other points should be made here. The first is that in order for a hypothesis, whether it turns out to be upheld or not, to be scientific in the first place, it must be testable. In other words, there must be clear, deduced implications that can be drawn from the hypothesis and then tested. Remember the hypotheses of "cosmic influences" and "atmospheric disturbances"? How can you test these? What are the necessary implications that can be deduced from the hypothesis, "More women died in Ward 1 due to atmospheric disturbances"? There really aren't any, and therefore such a hypothesis is not scientific—it cannot be tested. Remember, in the methodology of science, we ordinarily need to:

1. Observe
2. Induce general hypotheses or possible explanations for what we have observed.
3. Deduce specific things that must also be true if our hypothesis is true
4. Test the hypothesis by checking out the deduced implications

If there are no specific implications of a hypothesis that can then be analyzed as a test of the validity or usefulness of that hypothesis, then you simply are not doing and cannot do "science."

For example, suppose you observe a person who appears to be able to "guess" the value of a playing card picked from a deck. Next, assume that someone hypothesizes that "psychic" ability is involved. Finally, suppose the claim is made that the "psychic" ability goes away as soon as you try to test it (actually named the "shyness effect" by some researchers of the paranormal). Such a claim is not itself testable and therefore not scientific.

Beyond the issue of testability, another lesson is involved in determining whether an approach to a problem is scientific. Semmelweis induced four different hypotheses to explain the difference in mortality rates between Wards 1 and 2. These "competing" explanations are called *multiple working hypotheses*. Notice that Semmelweis did not simply proceed by a process of elimination. He did not, for example, test the first three hypotheses and—after finding them invalid—declare that the fourth was necessarily correct since it was the only one left that he had thought of.

Some people try to work that way. A light is seen in the sky. Someone hypothesizes it was a meteor. We find out that it was not. Someone else hypothesizes that it was a military rocket. Again this turns out to be incorrect. Someone else suggests that it was the Goodyear Blimp, but that turns out to have been somewhere else. Finally, someone suggests that it was the spacecraft of people from another planet. Some will say that this must be correct, since none of the other explanations panned out. This is nonsense. There are plenty of other possible explanations. Eliminating all of the explanations *we* have been able to think of except one (which, perhaps, has no testable implications) in no way allows us to uphold that final hypothesis. . . .

It's like seeing a card trick. You are mystified by it. You have a few possible explanations: the magician did it with mirrors, there was a helper in the audience, the cards were marked. But when you approach the magician and ask which it was, he assures you that none of your hypotheses is correct. Do you then decide that what you saw was an example of genuine, supernatural magic? Of course not! Simply because you or I cannot come up with the right explanation does not mean that the trick has a supernatural explanation. We simply admit that we do not have the expertise to suggest a more reasonable hypothesis.

Finally, there is another rule to hypothesis making and testing. It is called *Occam's Razor* or *Occam's Rule*. In essence it says that when a number of hypotheses are proposed through induction to explain a given set of observations, the simplest hypothesis is probably the best.

Take this actual example. During the eighteenth and nineteenth centuries, huge, buried, fossilized bones were found throughout North America and Europe. One hypothesis, the simplest, was that the bones were the remains of animals that no longer existed. This hypothesis simply relied on the assumption that bones do not come into existence by themselves, but always serve as the skeletons of animals. Therefore, when you find bones, there must have been animals who used those bones. However, another hypothesis was suggested: the bones were deposited by the Devil to fool us into thinking that such animals existed (Howard 1975). This hypothesis demanded many more assumptions about the universe than did the first: there is a Devil, that Devil is interested in human affairs, he wants to fool us, he has the ability to make bones of animals that never existed, and he has the ability to hide them under the ground and inside solid rock. That is quite a number of unproven (and largely untestable) claims to swallow. Thus, Occam's Razor says the simpler hypothesis, that these great bones are evidence of the existence of animals that no longer exist—in other words, dinosaurs—is better. The other one simply raises more questions than it answers.

THE ART OF SCIENCE

Don't get the impression that science is a mechanical enterprise. Science is at least partially an art. It is much more than just observing the results of experiments.

It takes great creativity to recognize a "mystery" in the first place. In the apocryphal story, countless apples had fallen from countless trees and undoubtedly conked the noggins of multitudes of stunned individuals who never thought much about it. It took a fabulously creative individual, Isaac Newton, to even recognize that herein lay a mystery. Why did the apple fall? No one had ever articulated the possibility that the apple could have hovered in midair. It could have moved off in any of the cardinal directions. It could have gone straight up and out of sight. But it did not. It fell to the ground as it always had, in all places, and as it always would. It took great imagination to recognize that in this simple observation (and in a bump on the head) rested the eloquence of a fundamental law of the universe.

Further, it takes great skill and imagination to invent a hypothesis in this attempt to understand why things seem to work the way they do. Remember, Ward 1 at the Vienna General Hospital did not have written over its doors, OVERCROWDED WARD or WARD WITH STUDENT DOCTORS WHO DON'T WASH THEIR HANDS AFTER AUTOPSIES. It took imagination first to recognize that there were differences between the wards and, quite importantly, that some of the differences might logically be at the root of the mystery. After all, there were in all likelihood many, many differences between the wards: their compass orientations, the names of the nurses, the precise alignment of the windows, the astrological signs of the doctors who worked in the wards, and so on. If a scientist were to attempt to test all of these differences as hypothetical causes of a mystery, nothing would ever be solved. Occam's Razor must be applied. We need to focus our intellectual energies on those possible explanations that require few other assumptions. Only after all of these have been eliminated, can we legitimately consider others. As summarized by that great fictional detective, Sherlock Holmes:

> It is of the highest importance in the art of detection to be able to recognize, out of a number of facts, which are incidental and which are vital. Otherwise, your energy and attention must be dissipated instead of being concentrated.

Semmelweis concentrated his attention on first four, then a fifth possible explanation. Like all good scientists he had to use some amount of what we can call "intuition" to sort out the potentially vital from the probably incidental. Even in the initial sorting we may be wrong. Overcrowding seemed a very plausible explanation to Semmelweis, but it was wrong nonetheless.

Finally, it takes skill and inventiveness to suggest ways for testing the hypothesis in question. We must, out of our own heads, be able to invent the "then" part of our "if . . . then" statements. We need to be able to suggest those things that must be true if our hypothesis is to be supported. There really is an art to that. Anyone can claim there was a Lost Continent of Atlantis, but often it takes a truly inventive mind to suggest precisely what archaeologists must find if the hypothesis of its existence were indeed to be valid.

Semmelweis tested his hypotheses and solved the mystery of childbed fever by changing conditions in Ward 1 to see if the death rate would change. In essence, the testing of each hypothesis was an experiment. In archaeology, the testing of hypotheses often must be done in a different manner. There is a branch of archaeology called, appropriately enough, "experimental archaeology" that involves the experimental replication and utilization of prehistoric artifacts in an attempt to figure out how they were made and used. In general, however, archaeology is largely not an experimental science. Archaeologists more often need to create "models" of some aspect of cultural adaptation and change. These models are simplified, manipulable versions of cultural phenomena.

For example, James Mosimann and Paul Martin (1975) created a computer program that simulated or modeled the first human migration into America some 12,000 years ago. By varying the size of the initial human population and their rate of growth and expansion, as well as the size of the big-game animal herds in the New World, Mosimann and Martin were able to test their hypothesis that these human settlers caused the extinction of many species of game animals. The implications of their mathematical modeling can be tested against actual archaeological and paleontological data.

Ultimately, whether a science is experimentally based or not makes little logical difference in the testing of hypotheses. Instead of predicting what the results of a given experiment must be if our induced hypothesis is useful or valid, we predict what new data we must be able to find if a given hypothesis is correct.

For instance, we may hypothesize that long-distance trade is a key ele-ment in the development of civilization based upon our analysis of the ancient Maya. We deduce that if this is correct—if this is, in fact, a general rule of cultural evolution—we must find large quantities of trade items in other parts of the world where civilization also developed. We might further deduce that these items should be found in contexts that denote their value and importance to the society (for example, in the burials of leaders). We must then determine the validity of our predictions and, indirectly, our hypothesis by going out and conducting more research. We need to excavate sites belonging to other ancient civilizations and see if they followed the same pattern as seen for the Maya relative to the importance of trade.

Testing a hypothesis certainly is not easy. Sometimes errors in testing can lead to incorrectly validating or rejecting a hypothesis. Some of you may have already caught a potential problem in Semmelweis's application of the scientific method. Remember hypothesis 4? It was initially suggested that the student doctors were at the root of the higher death rate in Ward 1, because they were not as gentle in assisting in birthing as were the more experienced doctors. This hypothesis was not borne out by testing. Retraining the students had no effect on the mortality rate in Ward 1. But suppose that Semmelweis had tested this hypothesis instead by removing the students altogether prior to their retraining. From what we now know, the death rate would have indeed declined, and Semmelweis would have concluded incorrectly that the hypothesis was correct. We can assume that once the retrained students were returned to the ward (gentler, perhaps, but with their hands still dirty) the death rate would have jumped up again since the students were indeed at the heart of the matter, but not because of their presumed rough handling of the maternity patients.

This should point out that our testing of hypotheses takes a great deal of thought and that we can be wrong. We must remember: we have a hypothesis, we have the deduced implications, and we have the test. We can make errors at any place within this process—the hypothesis may be incorrect, the implications may be wrong, or the way we test them may be incorrect. Certainty in science is a scarce commodity. There are always new hypotheses, alternative explanations, and more deductive implications to test. Nothing is ever finished, nothing is set in concrete, nothing is ever defined or raised to the level of religious truth.

Beyond this, it must be admitted that scientists are, after all, ordinary human beings. They are not isolated from the cultures and times in which they live. They share many of the same prejudices and biases of other members of their societies. Scientists learn from mentors at universities and often inherit their perspectives. It often is quite difficult to go against the scientific grain, to question accumulated wisdom, and to suggest a new approach or perspective.

For example, when German meteorologist Alfred Wegener hypothesized in 1912 that the present configuration of the continents resulted from the breakup of a single inclusive landmass and that the separate continents had "drifted" into their current positions (a process called *continental drift*), most rejected the suggestion outright. Yet today, Wegener's general perspective is accepted and incorporated into the general theory of *plate tectonics*.

Philosopher of science Thomas Kuhn (1970) has suggested that the growth of scientific knowledge is not neatly linear, with knowledge simply building on knowledge. He maintains that science remains relatively static for periods and that most thinkers work under the same set of assumptions—the same *paradigm*. New ideas or perspectives, like those of Wegener or Einstein, that challenge the existing orthodoxy, are usually initially rejected. Only once scientists get over the shock of the new ideas and start testing the new frameworks suggested by these new paradigms are great jumps in knowledge made.

That is why in science we propose, test, tentatively accept, but never prove a hypothesis. We keep only those hypotheses that cannot be disproved. As long as an hypothesis holds up under the scrutiny of additional testing through experiment and/or is not contradicted by new data, we accept it as the best explanation so far. Some hypotheses sound good, pass the rigors of initial testing, but are later shown to be inadequate or invalid. Others—for example, the hypothesis of biological evolution—have held up so well (all new data either were or could have been deduced from it) that they will probably always be upheld. We usually call these very well supported hypotheses *theories*. However, it is in the nature of science that no matter how well an explanation of some aspect of reality has held up, we must always be prepared to consider new tests and better explanations.

We are interested in knowledge and explanations of the universe that work. As long as these explanations work, we keep them. As soon as they cease being effective because new data and tests show them to be incomplete or misguided, we discard them and seek new ones. In one sense, Semmelweis was wrong after all, though his explanation worked at the time—he did save lives through its application. We now know that there is nothing inherently bad in "cadaveric material." Dead bodies are not the cause of childbed fever. Today we realize that it is a bacteria that can grow in the flesh of a dead body that can get on a doctor's hands, infect a pregnant woman, and cause her death. Semmelweis worked in a time before the existence of such things was known. Science in this way always grows, expands, and evolves.

SCIENCE AND ARCHAEOLOGY

The study of the human past is a science and relies on the same general logical processes that all sciences do. Unfortunately, perhaps as a result of its popularity, the data of archaeology have often been used by people to attempt to prove some idea or claim. Too often, these attempts have been bereft of science.

Archaeology has attracted frauds and fakes. Myths about the human past have been created and popularized. Misunderstandings of how archaeologists go about their tasks and what we have discovered about the human story have too often been promulgated. As I stated . . . my purpose is to describe the misuse of archaeology and the nonscientific application of the data from this field. . . .

Archaeology: Integrating the Sciences and the Humanities

Robert Ehrenreich

It seems that the big argument these days in meetings, Internet discussions and now newsletters is what archaeology and anthropology "must" be if they are to be anything. I have heard that "archaeology must be anthropology, or it is nothing." I have heard that "archaeology

---

The dilemma within archaeology occurs once the artifacts have been catalogued and the original excavation objectives have been met.

---

must be science, or it is nothing." I have heard that archaeology must be history

(or humanities), or it is nothing." The dilemma lies not in whether archaeology belongs in the sciences or the humanities but in an apparent disagreement over our ability to interpret the archaeological record and the value of data recovered from such softer sources as ethnographics and oral traditions.

Archaeologists are adept at analyzing site layouts and formulating excavation strategies. We scrutinize topographies, environmental conditions and prehistoric and historic trends; employ advanced remote sensing techniques; and identify the tools, site crews and schedules that are required to excavate sites and ensure that the maximum amount of information is obtained. Archaeologists are also experts at determining the basic structure and subsistence of an excavated site by the analysis of its construction, site plan and artifact assemblages. We take all the finds recovered, translate them using a range of scientific and

archaeometric techniques into a variety of data sets that can be statistically analyzed and build hypotheses about how the inhabitants of a site survived: for example, what they ate, what they made, when they made it and how they obtained their tools and weapons. Archaeologists then test these hypotheses by comparing them with the results of other sites. I would find it difficult for anyone to argue that these technical and methodological underpinnings of archaeology are not science.

The dilemma within archaeology occurs once the artifacts have been catalogued and the original excavation objectives have been met. Every object can stimulate an incredible wealth of interpretation about the original population, but to what extent can we vouchsafe these interpretations? After all, did we get into this field just to find out what people ate? The diet of populations alone has much larger implications. Did diets remain constant, or did they change with seasons and time? Were new foods introduced that permitted the population to increase, or were they a response to some external stress and adopted out of necessity? Who obtained and prepared the food? Were there rituals associated with both the food and its preparation? What do these data tell us about the inhabitants' subsistence strategies, societal organization and personal beliefs? Is there anything that we can learn from these data that could help us better understand our own societies? These questions form a logical progression that moves archaeology from its scientific to its humanistic underpinnings.

Many archaeologists believe that the only way to raise the stature of the field within academia and in public opinion is to increase the amount of scientifically oriented research.

The more scientifically oriented archaeologists believe that you cannot and should not carry interpretations too far from excavation data and thus into the humanistic component. A simplified form of the argument is that only hard data allow credible hypotheses to be built, tested and correlated with theories about other sites, regions and time periods to determine underlying patterns. Overinterpretation of the data produces a series of anecdotes about specific groups of people that cannot be cross-correlated, that are based purely on personal biases and

perspectives and that can only be supported by personal charisma or bullying. Many archaeologists also believe that the only way to raise the stature of the field within academia and in public opinion is to increase the amount of scientifically oriented research. This opinion is reinforced by advances in archaeometry, which have allowed archaeologists to steadily increase the quantity of hard data used in their work and the level and credibility of their interpretations.

The more humanistically oriented archaeologists believe that far higher levels of interpretation are possible, that additional, complementary data can be acquired in a scientific manner from such "softer" sources as ethnographies and oral traditions and that biases and prejudices can never be truly eradicated even in interpretation of so-called hard data. The simplified form of this argument is that the restriction solely to digitized excavation data will never permit archaeologists to truly understand the societal organization or belief systems of the individuals who inhabited the sites. For instance, how can we determine by statistical analysis the personal and societal motivations behind the production and decoration of a bowl by a potter? The more humanistically oriented archaeologists also question whether the interpretation of any data can be entirely divorced from the ideologies and biases of the researcher. Even physicists have begun to debate the objectivity of scientific research and the importance of context in the history and development of their discipline. They have come to realize that the prevailing theories and laboratory equipment of any time period will affect the hypotheses developed, the experiments constructed and the results interpreted. Thus, the more humanistically oriented archaeologists see advantages in producing detailed descriptions that supplement excavation results with data from ethnographies and oral traditions. Such research permits new levels of understanding to be attained about the sociocultural complexities of the people being studied and clearly

exhibit the interpretive context within which the research was performed.

This distinction between the sciences and the humanities within archaeology should become less defined as more archaeologists realize the strengths of the 2 approaches, borrow components from each other's work and collaborate to identify and accumulate the data required to support higher levels of interpretation.

As opposed to seeing the problem presented above negatively as one side versus the other, it should be viewed as a positive dialogue between 2 symbiotic approaches. Few fields straddle the sciences and the humanities so intrinsically as does archaeology, and it is the combination of these 2 components that keeps the field moving forward and keeps both sides honest. The increasing reliance on scientific data will force more humanistically derived hypotheses to the test of systematic research and credible arguments. The humanistic aspects of the field will ensure that the more scientifically oriented research does not lose sight of the fact that interpretation of data depends on the understanding of the interpreter. This distinction between the sciences and the humanities within archaeology should become less defined as more archaeologists realize the strengths of the 2 approaches, borrow components from each other's work and collaborate to identify and accumulate the data required to support higher levels of interpretation. While this argument rages, a large number of archaeologists are trying to build just these bridges.

The true danger to archaeology is that this argument will so divide the field that both components will end up engaging in bad research and open the field to less qualified individuals and charlatans. In an attempt to make the discipline more quantitative, archaeologists and pseudoarchaeologists could begin accumulating inordinate quantities of irrelevant data and submitting them to advanced statistical analyses without properly formulating the research objectives or completely understanding the biases and limitations of the analytical techniques and statistical packages. Conversely, in an attempt to make the discipline more humanistic, excavation data could be increasingly marginalized in favor of interpretations relying on personal experience and pseudoscience. At best, such results would be irrelevant and ignored. At worst, they could be spurious, inflammatory and destructive to both archaeology and society.

Since archaeology straddles both the sciences and the humanities, archaeologists must learn to bridge these distinctions through understanding and collaboration. The key is for archaeologists to produce a new systemic approach that provides the right admixture of humanities and scientific ingredients necessary to extract an optimal amount of credible information and support new levels of shared interpretation. In this way, all archaeologists would work together toward a united goal and toward advancing the field.

Surrogate Stone

David and Noelle Soren

David Soren is a professor of classical archaeology at the University of Arizona. Noelle Soren is the director of photography for excavations at Lugnano and Chianciano, Italy.

In the rolling hills of southeastern Portugal lies the picturesque town of Santiago do Cacem, a friendly village of whitewashed cottages with red tile roofs and the home of the best bacalhau ao Brás (salt cod and eggs) in all of Portugal. In Roman times and in the pre-Roman Iron Age under the Celtic name of Mirobriga it was a place of considerable importance. It marked the start of the major inland road to ancient Emerita Augusta (Merida), capital of the Roman province of Lusitania, and it was a key town along the westernmost road of the Roman Empire, which linked Lacobriga (modern Lagos) in the south to Bracara Augusta (Braga) in the north.

The site of Mirobriga has striking ruins that include a large circus, houses, a bridge, and a taverna or roadside inn. Though the area has been studied since at least the sixteenth century, the first major excavation occurred between 1959 and 1979, when archaeologist Fernando de Almeida dug and restored the site. De Almeida concentrated his efforts on an extensive forum complex anchored along its northwestern side by a temple that he believed enclosed a sanctuary dedicated to the healer god Aesculapius. The restored Temple of Aesculapius, as it soon became known, was notable for its stately entrance columns and a plaster copy of a marble dedicatory inscription nailed to its cella wall. Santiago do Cacem's delighted townsfolk immediately embraced the temple as the village symbol, featuring it on T-shirts, ashtrays, and party napkins.

In 1979 de Almeida died, and in 1981 we began our own excavations as part of a team from the University of Missouri. We soon realized that the temple was really a sacred house of cards. There were traces of foundations beneath the walls but no evidence to merit de Almeida's extensive and meticulous restoration. Molded cornices on benches that he placed in front of the temple had been borrowed from a nearby chapel building, probably of medieval date, that served as our excavation field house. We even found the workman who had moved them. Worse still, the temple's famous columns had once graced the baths located below the forum.

Furthermore, while the inscription hanging on the cella wall was indeed a copy of an ancient marble panel that had hung at the old hospital in Santiago do Cacem since at least 1603, its provenance remains unknown, and there is absolutely no evidence that it came from Mirobriga. Before de Almeida's excavations it had never been associated with the site, much less with the temple. In fact, the inscription refers to Gaius Attius Januarius, a doctor of ancient Pax Julia, a town some 70 miles from Mirobriga, who had erected a monument there to honor a group of senators for arranging a festival known as the Quinquatrus. Neither Mirobriga nor Aesculapius is mentioned in the inscription.

It is now clear that the temple was not built in the third or fourth century A.D., as de Almeida had claimed. Evidence suggests that its entire superstructure was constructed in 1966 on foundations dating to the mid-first century A.D. But the damage was done. By 1981 the temple was thoroughly a part of the local popular culture and an item in the national and international guidebooks to Portugal. Even such distinguished scholars as Jorge Alarcão of Portugal's University of Coimbra and Paul Mackendrick of the University of Wisconsin cited the Temple of Aesculapius at Mirobriga as a great regional pilgrimage center of the late Roman period. Our own excavations showed that the forum, along with a temple, was more likely built about A.D. 50 or 60 under Claudius or Nero, and that Mirobriga was probably a provincial Roman town that had gained its livelihood from its position at the crossroads of two major arteries, not from its fame as a pilgrimage center.

So who was Fernando de Almeida, and what inspired him to concoct such an elaborate fiction? He was a professor or archaeology and the director of the National Museum of Archaeology and Ethnology in Lisbon. But he started his professional life as a gynecologist and harbored an abiding fascination for the healer god Aesculapius. The temptation to honor his favorite divinity had clearly been impossible to resist.

History Unearthed

When we think about great discoveries, we may conjure up the image of a lone, bleary-eyed researcher in a lab coat hovering over test tubes late into the night. Or of a team of obsessed scientists crouched behind gigantic spark- and smoke-emitting contraptions that could blow up any second, risking their lives to advance human knowledge a few millimeters.

In reality, however, lots of times big breakthroughs are, like so much in life, simply the result of unexpectedly good luck. Take the case of the archaeological team that found the long-lost site of a once-important 4,000-year-old city—while looking for a place to picnic.

The team, headed by UCLA archaeologist Giorgio Buccellati and his wife, Marilyn Kelly-Buccellati of California State University, Los Angeles, had been searching throughout northeastern Syria trying to identify relics of Hurrian civilization. Despite references in the Old Testament and the existence of a few texts suggesting Hurrian prominence in the Near East around the time of 1400 B.C., little is known about the people—certainly significantly less than about the Sumerians and the Semites, who lived contemporaneously with the Hurrians. The lost city of Urkesh, assumed to have been the political and religious hub of earliest Hurrian civilization—and known in mythology as the home of a primordial god—was believed to have been destroyed without a trace millennia ago.

Having completed work at one excavation, Buccellati and his team were in search of a new site. One nearby possibility caught their eye: a mound in the distance, less than a mile from the main road in the modern village of Tell Mozan. The hill—covering roughly the same area as the UCLA campus—was located where mythology placed Urkesh. Moreover, the researchers knew that two bronze lions with "Urkesh" in-

(ILLUSTRATION: GREG CLARKE)

scribed on them had been unearthed there some 40 years earlier. However, Agatha Christie and her archaeologist husband had excavated the hill back in the '30s and declared it to be Roman. So these researchers, like other Hurrian sleuths who preceded them, rejected the site as unpromising.

Until one day, when it was time for lunch, the group noticed that the mound was appealingly shaded from the midday sun. They hiked over and took a break. "As long as we were there, we thought we would at least look at the pottery," recalls Buccellati. Four senior members of the team went off in different directions to look for surface pottery shards, which could help determine the age of the site.

They soon returned, astonished. "There was absolutely nothing there that was Roman," Buccellati says. "It was all 3rd millennium B.C.—precisely the period we were interested in." Buccellati's team hypothesized that they were standing on Urkesh. They instituted a dig in

1984. Last November, after years of analyzing more than 600 seal impressions left on clay and mud found scattered on the floor of a room in a royal storehouse buried just under Tell Mozan, Buccellati announced they had indeed found the first Hurrian city ever to be identified. The researchers knew the city was abandoned around 1500 B.C., so everything found under the hill's surface could be linked with Urkesh. It was a monumental discovery.

In finally locating Urkesh, Buccellati's team has uncovered an ancient model of urban development—a model developed at a turbulent time when writing, bronze weaponry, slavery and economic stratification were taking root. And the archaeologists only scratched the surface—literally. "People will be excavating this site long after we're gone," says Buccellati.

Who knows? One day ancient Hurrian picnic tables may even be unearthed there.

—*Dan Gordon '85*

Hard Times at Lizard Man

John Whittaker

John Whittaker is an assistant professor in the anthropology department at Grinnell College, Iowa. As well as working in the Southwest, he experiments with prehistoric stone and metal technology, and is interested in how our visions of prehistory interact with modern life.

Few of us would bother with archaeology if we weren't emotionally involved with the past. We don't dig for dry bones and dusty potsherds, but for people. My wife Kathy and I lead a field school at Lizard Man Village, near Flagstaff, Arizona. Lizard Man was a small Sinagua community occupied sporadically between A.D. 1060 and 1260. There were never more than a few families there, living in semisubterranean pit houses and small stone pueblos. They made their living by farming and hunting and gathering—we have found ample remains of corn and other crops, and the bones of the animals they hunted. Such a small village must have been part of a larger community of villages. We have found shell or-

naments and other artifacts, presumably imported from considerable distances, so we know that they did not live in isolation. We can be very confident about this kind of inference, and from what we know of pre-industrial villages elsewhere in the world, we can guess at a lot more.

Although we can put together a good picture of how the Sinagua lived, most of us would like to know what it was like to *be* a Sinagua. Few of us would spend summers sweating in the sun, getting dirty in excavations and scrabbling up cliffs to explore the land, or suffer the academic year sorting potsherds and reading technical articles while trying to instill in our students some enthusiasm for prehistory if we did not care about trying to understand people. As a result, most of us, even the most detached, develop a strong feeling for "our" site, "our" people.

I admire the Sinagua, who made a living in a difficult land. I have tried to plant a garden as they would have, and have watched the corn shrivel during a drought almost before the blisters from the digging-stick healed on my hands. I

have made stone tools, and exulted when I could surpass the knappers at Lizard Man, and I have tried to reproduce the smooth symmetry of their pots and have failed miserably. I have explored their land in great detail. But I can never come close to knowing what it was like to *be* a Sinagua.

It always pains me when I realize that. Even though I don't think I want to be a Sinagua, I want to understand them. I admire them, and I love the land in which they lived. I like to sleep on the site, and, ignoring the rumble of traffic and an occasional train, I smell the trees and hear the wind. I think of the homey chatter of a small village, a few families living in peace; sturdy, active people who hope the gods will be good and bring the rain, look forward to seeing a friend from a nearby village, and plan the next day's work. I like to think of happy Sinagua, living the kind of lives I would wish on my own friends.

But life was not all so idyllic. In 1989 I worked with two experts, Marc Krouse, a forensic pathologist for a country coroner's office, and Marcia Regan, a physical anthropologist. With their special skills, we examined the burials from Lizard Man, and I received some shocks. Some of what we found fit my preconceptions. There were no signs of violence and intentional injury. The small scattered villages of this time seem to have lived in peace, in contrast to the later larger sites where human remains show some evidence of wounds and scalping. The Sinagua bones were large and robust, often with heavy muscle markings. These would have been strong, tough people, as you would expect from their life in the wilderness, and as I like to picture them. But they

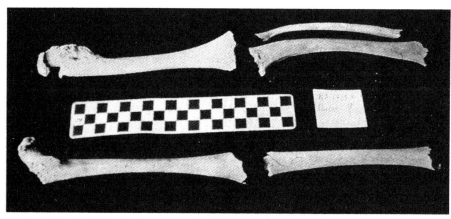

A crippled child's leg bones reveal a healed fracture of the right femur and bowing of the right tibia and fibula, top. Left femur and tibia were normal.

Lavish grave goods including characteristic Sinagua pottery were placed alongside the skeleton of a crippled child at Lizard Man Village. A necklace made of olive shells and a frog-shaped shell pendant also accompanied the burial.

were not healthy people, and their lives were probably much harder than I had imagined.

Most of them died young. First, there was heavy infant mortality. Many babies died soon after birth, and even older children were at risk because there were periodic shortages of food. The teeth of the survivors usually show bands of discoloration, resulting from periods when growth was interrupted by sickness or malnutrition. The bones of children are generally shorter than they should have been. I was not the only one whose corn failed, but if it was a disappointment for me, it was fatal for some Sinagua. Our burials probably come from the later occupation of the site in the 1200s, when agricultural conditions seem to have been deteriorating; by A.D. 1300 or so, the area was abandoned and scarcely occupied for the next 600 years.

Once a Sinagua had survived six or eight years, he or she was probably accustomed to many of the common diseases, and used to going without food from time to time. Nonetheless, the chances of reaching what we consider old age were slim. Pregnancy and childbearing were times of stress for women. Even most men died before they were 40, often earlier.

Life was not only short, it must often have been full of pain. Arthritis in many joints attests the heavy labor endured by the Sinagua. There was little they could do for injuries and infections. The Sinagua diet probably included plenty of corn, at least in good years. Sticky carbohydrates promoted cavities, and the grit from grinding stones wore the enamel off their teeth. Those who managed to live to "old age" had lost at least half their teeth, usually years before they

died. Almost everyone had cavities, receding gums, and plaque, as well as active and probably painful abscesses, some of which may have caused fatal infections.

Most of the time archaeologists make fairly general conclusions about the way groups of people lived at a particular time. Archaeologists are fascinated with burials because they bring us as close as we can come to actually seeing people, reconstructing what they looked like, and learning some of the history of individual lives. At Lizard Man, for instance, one burial contained the remains of a Sinagua child. At five or six, it is hard to tell the sex from a skeleton, so we don't know whether it was a boy or a girl, but I can imagine the child's life with painful clarity. About a year before death, the child's right leg had been broken, probably in a fall. Healing was al-

Tooth loss and abscesses apparent in this skull of a Sinagua woman in her twenties reflect the hard life at Lizard Man. Flattening of the back of the skull resulted from the use of a cradleboard during childhood.

most complete, but the upper leg had been shortened somewhat. During the period of inactivity while the leg healed, the muscles and bones of the lower leg had atrophied, and when the child began to walk again, the bones warped. By age six the child had several cavities and had lost one tooth to an abscess that was still festering. Tiny pores in the eye sockets indicate the child had an anemic condition, probably from malnutrition, and the child was very small for the age indicated by its teeth.

My students called the child "Tiny Tim," not just because of the leg injury but because he or she was probably a valued person in the village, loved and cared for. There were more artifacts in the grave than in any other at the site. Around its neck was a string of shell beads, imported from the coast, with a pendant in the form of a frog. The neck-lace was valuable jewelry in its day. There were several locally made pots, some shapely and finely polished, and three that were small and crude, probably a child's work. Most touching was a pair of pots in the shape of shells, nested together. One was very finely made, the other thick and lumpy, and I cannot resist the image of a child sitting in the shade of a wall, its mother watching proudly as small hands try to imitate her work. I know that someone wailed as they put a small still body into a grave, and laid its toys beside it.

I am dealing, of course, in speculation. I cannot prove that the crude shell pot was a copy of the other, or that the child in the grave made it, or even that it was not made by a clumsy adult. But it is a reasonable speculation, because people are that way. I think of my own nine-year-old daughter and share the joy and the sorrow of a parent dead for 700 years. The power of such images in my mind tells me something. It tells me why I do archaeology, and why archaeology interests the public.

It pains me to learn that the Sinagua were probably not as happy as I would like them to have been, although I know that is irrational. I still admire their skills and knowledge, even though they probably didn't bathe and had rotten teeth that stank. I'm sure that like the rest of us they could be mean and stupid, loving and kind. And I am quite certain that I would like to meet them and talk to them, touch their battered, calloused hands. God forbid that I should ever have to live their life, but the Sinagua are real people to me, and I care about them and want to tell their story.

Problem-Oriented Archaeology

What are the goals of archaeology? What kinds of things motivate well-educated people to go out and dig square holes in the ground and sift through their diggings like flour for a cake? How do they know where to dig? What are they looking for? What do they do with the things they find? Let us drop in on an archaeology class at Big City University.

"Good afternoon, class, I'm Dr. Penny Pittmeyer. Welcome to Introductory Archaeology. Excuse me, young lady. Yes, you in the back, wearing the pith helmet. I don't think you'll need to bring that shovel to class this semester. We aren't going to be doing any digging."

A moan like that of an audience that had just heard a bad pun sounded throughout the classroom. Eyes bugged out, foreheads receded, and mouths formed into alphabet-soup at this pronouncement.

"That's right, no digging. You are here to learn about archaeology."

"But archaeology *is* digging. What are we going to do all semester?" protested a thin young man with scratched granny glasses and a scraggly beard, wearing a mail-order safari suit with a trowel tucked firmly into his belt.

Dr. Pittmeyer calmly surveyed the class and quietly repeated, "You are here to learn about archaeology." In a husky but compelling voice, she went on. "Archaeology is not digging, nor is it just about Egyptian pyramids or lost civilizations. It's a science. First you have to learn the basics of that science. Digging is just a technique. Digging comes later. Digging comes after you know *why* you are going to dig."

"No Egyptian pyramids," a plaintive echo resonated through the still classroom. "You can have your pyramids later. Take a class in Egyptian archaeology, fine! If you want ancient civilizations, take a course in world prehistory. But this class is the prerequisite to all those other classes. I hate to be the one to tell you this, people, but there ain't no Indiana Jones!" Dr. Pittmeyer said this with a slightly lopsided smile. But a veiled look in her light eyes sent an "uh-oh" that the students felt somewhere deep in their guts. They knew that the woman had something to teach them. And teach them, she would!

Dr. Pittmeyer half sat on the old desk at the front of the classroom, leaning one elbow on the podium to her right, picked up a tall, red, opaque glass, and took a long and greedy drink from it. Behind her large-framed black glasses, her eyes watered noticeably. She wiped away an invisible mustache from her upper lip and settled onto the desk, holding the red glass in her left hand and letting it sway slightly as she unhurriedly looked over the students. Her left eyebrow rose unconsciously and made a few of the more imaginative students think that she looked like Scarlet O'Hara in glasses. The quiet lengthened so that the students filling out the bright-orange drop cards stopped writing, conscious of the now-loud silence in the room.

"O.K! Let's go!" Dr. Pittmeyer said with a snap in her voice, as if the class were going to run a relay. The startled students went straight-backed in unison.

"Archaeology is a science, ladies and gentlemen. It's part of the larger science of anthropology. The goals of both are to understand and predict human behavior. Let's start by looking at an area or subfield of archaeology that we may designate as problem-oriented archaeology. Humans evolved in Africa, Asia, and Europe, or what we refer to as the Old World."

Dr. Pittmeyer simultaneously turned out the lights and clicked on an overhead projector and was writing rapidly with a harshly bright purple pen in a hieroglyphic scrawl. Dangling from her neck she had a microphone that was plugged into a speaker that was then plugged back into the same cart where the overhead projector was, which in turn was plugged into an old, cracked, wall socket. It was the only electric outlet in the large, old high-ceilinged room, whose floor tiles were made of asbestos and whose ceiling was insulated with the same poisonous stuff.

Doubtful students suddenly felt compelled to take notes in the dim light provided by the irregularities of old-fashioned thick blinds that did not quite close completely.

"In the New World, in the Americas, from Alaska down to the tip of Tierra del Fuego, people did not live until about 13,000 years ago. Whereas people have been living in the Old World for 100,000 years or more. People in the sense of *Homo sapiens*."

"So what took them so long to get here?" a perplexed female voice asked.

"The continents were not always connected. But let's leave the geology until later. Let me point out that your question contains a very telling assumption. You said what took them so long to get *here*. The question is moot because these early peoples were not trying to get here. We're talking about the Paleolithic. People were migratory. They hunted and collected their food every day. Some of them may have followed the migrations of big game animals. So it is a nonquestion. Let me explain, please.

"In archaeology, you have to ask the right questions before you can get any useful answers. That is why archaeologists dig—not to make discoveries, but to answer questions. Now here's what I want you to do. Go home and try to think yourself back into the Paleolithic. It's 35,000 years ago, and mostly you hang out with your

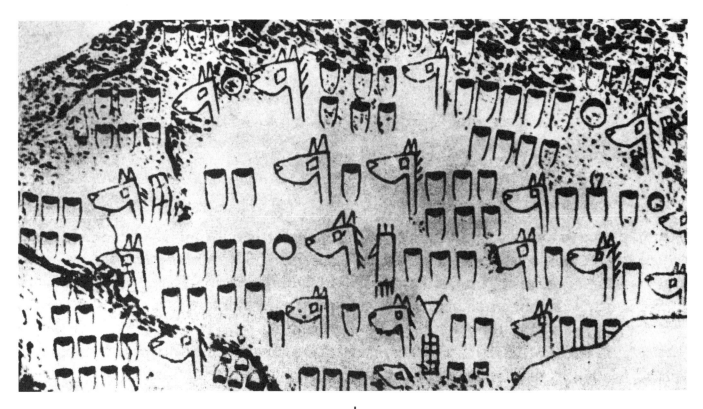

family and other close relatives. You get your food and shelter on a daily basis, and you have a lot of free time. Everyone cooperates to survive. The point is that wherever you are, you are *there*. There is no place to try to get to. There is no notion of private property or ownership of land. Nobody needs to conquer anybody. There are no cities, no freeways, no clocks, no rush. Think about it. It's a concept of time without measurements or urgencies."

"But they must have been pretty stupid back that long ago!" the young man with the trowel protested.

"Please think about that assumption! No, these were people just like you and me. If they were here today, they probably could program their VCRs. These were people with many skills and accomplishments. They met their needs as we meet ours. But they had something we might envy. They were already there no matter where they were! There's a lot to be learned from our prehistoric ancestors. But tomorrow's another day."

Alone in the classroom, Dr. Penny Pittmeyer finished her soda and allowed her eyes to glaze over as the bright orange drop cards fluttered to the floor. She stared far back in time where she saw intelligent people living a simple life in peace . . . or so she hoped.

Looking Ahead: Challenge Questions

How long ago did modern humans migrate to the New World? How do we know this? What is the importance of the Clovis point as a time marker?

What are some suggested hypotheses as to how the Paleoindians may have used different survival techniques in different regions?

When did humans first start expressing themselves through art?

What is a new interpretation of some Paleolithic cave paintings?

What new hypothesis is presented to explain the so-called Venus figurines of the Upper Paleolithic?

How does the consideration of gender affect the interpretation of stone tool technologies through time?

What new hypothesis is proffered to explain why people living 6,000 years ago in a Near Eastern desert area choose to make subterranean settlements?

What new evidence suggests a greater cultural complexity for preagricultural hunters and gatherers?

What can mortuary analysis tell us about ancient economies? About ancient religions? Give examples.

Coming to America

When did humans arrive here? Was it the long-accepted date of 11,200 years ago, or 10,000 years earlier? A remarkably detailed site in Chile may finally give us the answer.

David J. Meltzer

David J. Meltzer is an archeologist at Southern Methodist University in Dallas, a frequent contributor to New Scientist, *and the author of* Search for the First Americans.

The Southern High Plains were dusted with snow, and from 30,000 feet they appeared to be a vast marble slab. Since the flight from San Francisco to Dallas wasn't full, I slipped back and forth across the aisle, peering out the windows, hoping to spot a landmark. There aren't many on this flat, featureless terrain. I was looking, in vain, for a sign that we were passing over Clovis, New Mexico, home of the archeological site that's given its name to the people who first set foot in America. That is supposed to have been about 11,200 years ago.

I'd been thinking about Clovis since we took off from San Francisco that morning last December, mostly because I'd heard so much about it the day before, at the American Anthropological Association's annual meeting. There molecular biologists who use human DNA as a "clock" to date population migrations gave a message to us hands-in-the-dirt archeologists: the Clovis-based arrival date is wrong. Very wrong.

The messenger was molecular anthropologist Tad Schurr, representing the Emory University laboratory of geneticist Douglas Wallace. Schurr and Wallace had examined the mitochondrial DNA of various Native American peoples. This DNA exists in little organelles—mitochondria—outside a cell's nucleus, and you inherit it solely from your mother. Because it doesn't get mixed up with DNA from your father, any changes in the molecule as it moves from generation to generation are a result only of random mutations. These, it turns out, happen at the conveniently steady rate of 2 to 4 percent per million years. That makes mitochondrial DNA a genetic clock.

Schurr and Wallace found that the Native Americans belong to four distinct lineages. The Emory researchers then counted the mitochondrial DNA mutations in each lineage, figured out how much time was needed for them to occur, and deduced when these lineages were last together—that is, when they first diverged from a common maternal ancestor. That ancestor was someone who walked across the land bridge that once connected Siberia with Alaska, and the genetic clock started ticking when her descendants then spread across the New World. According to the biologists, that ancestor took her stroll long before Clovis time. "Upwards of 21,000 to 42,000 years ago," Schurr told us, without batting an eye.

That's hearsay testimony, of course: genes cannot be directly dated. Still, the news caused something of a buzz, and not just because modern genetics was failing to uphold a cherished tenet of old-fashioned archeology. What got people talking was that Schurr's date provided support, from an unexpected quarter, for one of the most talked-about archeological finds of the last decade. From 1978 to 1985, researchers working in southern Chile excavated a site they claim was occupied earlier than Clovis times—some 2,000 years earlier, in fact. Ever since the news began spreading, that site, called Monte Verde, has received a lot of attention from archeologists seeking traces of a pre-Clovis human presence in the Americas. Schurr's date fits beautifully with the Monte Verde evidence, and together they may revolutionize our views on the peopling of the Americas.

That won't come as much of a surprise to those of us who were at another meeting, three years earlier, on the Orono campus of the University of Maine. A couple hundred archeologists had assembled to wrangle over the origin and antiquity of the first Americans. We were there for three long days and three very long nights, and by the last afternoon session I was—all of us were, I suppose—tired, hungry for dinner, and ready to go home. The *New York Times* reporter had already left: no more news fit to print.

And then Tom Dillehay of the University of Kentucky, the final speaker, began to tell us about Monte Verde.

Ten minutes into the talk, the fellow sitting next to me whistled softly in astonishment, then asked aloud of no one in particular, "What planet is this stuff from?" I was wondering that my-

Reed and Cane

A LOOP OF REED ONCE
BOUND TOGETHER
TIMBERS OF A HUT. THE
PIECE OF CANE WAS
PART OF A HANDLE ON
A TOOL OR WEAPON.

self. The evidence from Monte Verde was unlike anything most of us—who early in our careers learned to be thankful just for stone tools and scraps of bone—had ever encountered before in our archeological earth. When Dillehay finished 45 minutes later, the hall erupted in applause. I forgot about dinner.

That day in Maine many of us saw for the first time pictures of the extraordinary archeological treasures of Monte Verde: artifacts of stone and bone, of course, but also of wood and ivory; freshly preserved leftovers from meals of leaves, fruits, nuts, and seeds; the remains of crayfish and paleocamel; the torn flesh of an extinct mastodon; even the footprint of a child.

Those are hardly the usual contents of an archeological site. They are unheard of for one in the Americas dating to some 13,000 years before the present. The pros in the hall that afternoon

knew exactly what *that* meant: the Clovis-first barrier to the peopling of the Americas, standing strong at 11,200 years, was threatened.

Established in the 1930s with the discovery of the Clovis site, and buttressed with radiocarbon dating in the 1950s, the idea that Clovis people were the first Americans once made perfect sense. As envisioned, they came out of northeast Asia across the Bering land bridge (Beringia) to Alaska, then headed south. Their migration was thought to be timed to the rhythm of glaciers. By 25,000 years ago those vast ice sheets had frozen 5 percent of the oceans' water on land, plunging global sea levels and uncovering the land bridge. But 20,000 years ago the glaciers had grown so much that they blocked the routes south from Alaska. Only around 12,000 years ago, once the glaciers had melted back and the terrain dried and was reforested,

did a passable southern route reopen, roughly along the present border of Alberta and British Columbia.

The first Americans must have headed south soon thereafter, and fast, for by 11,200 years ago groups were camping at a freshwater pond at Clovis, and by 11,000 years ago they had reached Tierra del Fuego, at the southern tip of South America. One can recognize traces of the Clovis people in the fluted stone spear points they left behind—a design first noted at the New Mexico pond. The explosive move to the south corresponded neatly with the extinction of over 150 million mammoths, mastodons, ground sloths, and other giant Ice Age mammals. To some that was no coincidence: these rapacious hunters, encountering big game that had never before peered down the shaft of a spear, would have had easy pickings and been spurred onward by visions of still more prey.

Not a bad model, all things considered, and for six decades it held up well while pretenders came and went. But the Clovis-first model has problems, and one of them is enormous: How and why, did people race from Alaska—where archeologists have found Clovis-like traces in sites about 11,300 years old—down to Tierra del Fuego, *nearly 10,000 miles away,* in scarcely 300 years?

Granted, that's only 33 miles a year, unbearably slow by today's standards; many of us have longer daily commutes. Yet it's a breakneck pace for hunter-gatherers, easily four times faster than the current world record for prehistoric colonization of an empty area, set by ancestral Thule Eskimos. In just a couple of centuries around A.D. 1000, the Thule flashed from Alaska to Greenland. But they had it easy, following a familiar corridor of animals they had lived with for millennia. The corridor had just stretched thousands of miles eastward following a long period of warmer-than-average temperatures.

The first Americans had no such advantage. They were pioneering an infinitely trackless, ever changing, and (to former Siberians) ecologically exotic realm, from high mountains to high plains, and near-polar deserts to tropical forests. They were slowed each time they entered a new habitat and had to find plants, animals, water, stone, and other resources vital to their survival. Sadly, the romantic vision of fast-moving, mammoth-chasing hunters has no archeological reality. They were slowed by obstacles along the way, such as rivers swollen by glacial melt-water, mountains shrouded in ice, and freshly deglaciated barren landscapes. They were also slowed by the demands of keeping contact with kin, finding mates, and raising families. (Ever try to go *anywhere* fast with kids?)

But if the first Americans didn't race through the continent, why do Clovis sites suddenly spring like dragon's teeth from the ground in the centuries around 11,000 years ago? Maybe Schurr and his colleagues have the answer. Assume for the moment that the Americas were peopled 21,000 to 42,000 years ago, and then around 11,200 years ago someone invented the

Clovis point—a handy, versatile tool useful in dozens of applications. How fast might such a good invention travel among groups?

Of course, if Schurr's group is right, then we ought to find lots of pre-Clovis archeological sites. Some pre-Clovis proponents say we already have, pointing to sites throughout the hemisphere that brandish dates of 13,000, 33,000, and even 200,000 years ago.

But these sites have few believers—and for good reason. Of the scores of pre-Clovis archeological finds made in the last 60 years, none so far has withstood the harsh glare of critical scrutiny. Either their ages were inflated, their artifacts proved of natural and not human origin, or they hid some other fatal flaw. Exposing these flaws usually takes less than a decade, and then the site is tossed on the archeological scrap heap. Archeologists have long memories—it's part of the job, after all—and in the face of many

false alarms over the years, they have grown deeply skeptical of any and all pre-Clovis claims. The first site to topple the Clovis barrier will have to have undeniable artifacts in an undisturbed setting accompanied by unimpeachable dates, and it will have to win over the severest pre-Clovis critics: the Jackie Robinson rule, my colleague Mott Davis calls it.

That's why Monte Verde rivets our attention. It may well be archeology's Jackie Robinson.

Monte Verde sits along a small tributary creek of the Rio Maullín, some 30 miles inland from the Pacific Ocean. This is a region shrouded in mist and clouds and a thick, verdant cover of forest and marsh that softens and rounds the landscape. At the site itself the land opens into a grassy plain about the size of a football field, through which shallow Chinchihuapi Creek slowly meanders. The sharp, snow-capped spine of the

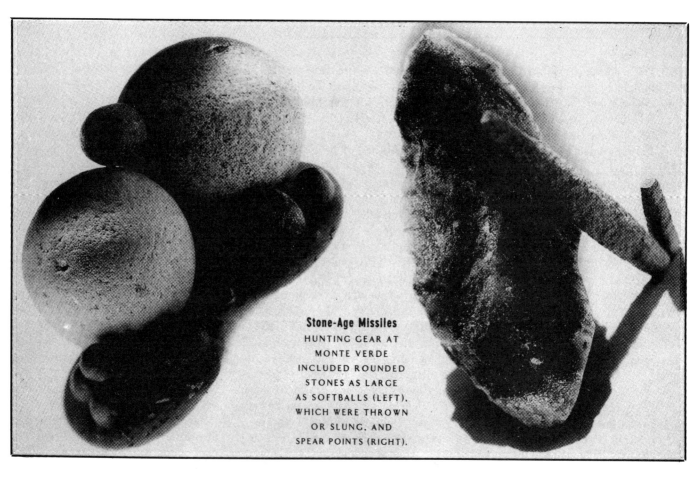

Stone-Age Missiles
HUNTING GEAR AT
MONTE VERDE
INCLUDED ROUNDED
STONES AS LARGE
AS SOFTBALLS (LEFT),
WHICH WERE THROWN
OR SLUNG, AND
SPEAR POINTS (RIGHT).

Andes looms to the east, but only on a clear summer's day can you see the steam and smoke rising from its active volcanoes. And those days are rare enough in this damp and chilly climate.

But it's the damp climate that makes the site special. The archeological debris that Dillehay told us about in Maine rests on a sandy bank, which, soon after the residents departed, was blanketed by water-saturated, grass-matted, oxygen-deprived peat. Beneath this anaerobic quilt the normal decay of organic materials was checked, preserving the site. Monte Verde came to light only in the mid-1970s, when local woodsmen, cutting back the banks of the creek to widen trails for their oxcarts, dislodged some buried wood and mastodon bones from their resting place.

Dillehay's subsequent excavation showed that the bank was littered with the roots, stems, fruits, and nuts of nearly 70 species of plants, and even 3 types of marine algae. That's many more plant species than might be expected in a comparable-size *natural* deposit. We know that because Dillehay's excavators hiked about a mile upstream from Monte Verde to dig where there was no hint of any human presence, just to see what was deposited naturally on surfaces of the same age. Such preemptive shoveling helps muffle critics who argue that the plants could as easily have been left at the site by flood-waters, for instance, as by people.

If nature was responsible for depositing the plants on the site, then nature is awfully hardworking—and more than a little bit devious. More than a third of the plants were imports, brought from their native habitats on the Pacific coast, high in the Andes, or from grasslands and other settings 30 to 250 miles distant. Coincidence or not, 42 of the species found on the sandy bank are still used by contemporary native Mapuche for food, drink, or medicine. Only the usable parts of many of those plants made it to Monte Verde and were found burned in some food pits, on the floors of what once were huts, and in shallow hearths. Even more unusual was the discovery of several plugs of chewed boldo leaves—prehistoric chaw, they'd call that here in Texas—mixed with what appears to be seaweed and a third, as yet unidentified, plant. Boldo leaves are still used today to cure stomach ills and relieve colds and congestion.

The chaw was lying on a wishbone-shaped foundation of sand and gravel, which appeared to be glued together by animal fat. Along the foundation's edges were vertical wood stubs and scraps of animal skin, the remnants of a hide-draped frame hut that once stood there. Fronting the structure was a small cache of salt crystals, plant remains, mastodon bones, a chunk of animal meat (which, based on preliminary DNA analysis, most likely belonged to a mastodon), hearths, and stone tools.

Tools of the Trade
FROM THESE STONE CORES (LEFT), MONTE VERDEANS STRUCK OFF SHARP FLAKES. THE MASTODON TUSKS (RIGHT) MAY HAVE BEEN USED AS GOUGES.

Monte Verde's stone artifact inventory, now 700 pieces strong, includes finely crafted spear points, a slender and polished basalt drill, and cores, choppers, and flakes, several dozen of which are made of rock quarried many miles from the site. One can imagine that with these tools the Monte Verdeans worked, ate, and took cures in the wishbone structure. Most of them, however, lived 40 yards away in a group of 12 rectangular huts, each some 45 feet square. Nine of these huts were arranged in two rows, like row houses, lined by log planks staked together, framed by poles, and draped with a common roof of mastodon hide. Their floors were of sediments high in nitrogen and phosphate—a sure chemical sign of human waste—and littered with ash and grit. The huts surrounded two large communal hearths, two dozen smaller hearths (the child's footprint alongside one of them), and more tools: digging sticks, mastodon-tusk gouges, grinding slabs, knives, spear points, and bola stones (rounded, grooved stones; when sinew is wrapped around the groove, the stone can be whirled and flung). Some of the artifacts were still speckled with the tar that bound them to their wooden or bone handles. In the huts were still more traces of the Monte Verdeans' meals: plant remains, animal remains large and small (mastodon and camel bones, as well as a bird's charred feathers, eggshells, and bone), and even a few human coprolites (the politely scientific word for fossilized excrement).

The age of Monte Verde is anchored by a chain of radiocarbon dates run on artifacts and samples of different materials, including charcoal, wood, bone, and ivory. The dates range in age from 11,790 to 13,565 years ago. Dillehay thinks the oldest one, from charcoal that was sealed and preserved in a clay-lined hole, best represents the age of the site, making it a good 2,000 years older than Clovis times.

But there the skeptics pounce. University of Massachusetts archeologist Dena Dincauze, for example, accuses Dillehay of "uncritical use" of the radiocarbon ages. A better approach, she argues, is to discard the oldest date, then look at the time ranges for each radiocarbon date and use their overlap as the best age for the site. In response, Dillehay suggests dropping the younger dates on bone and ivory (which are more susceptible to contamination) and averaging the dates run on charcoal and wood. Doing so, he says, puts the occupation at around 12,250 years ago, which, as retired archeologist Tom Lynch happily observes, lies "at the very margin of Paleo-Indian time."

Of course, the passage south from Alaska didn't open up for another 250 years, making the trip to Monte Verde an unlikely matter of time travel. But let's assume there's some slop in both dates, and that both the passage and the site appear a little before 12,000 years

---

If the first Americans left Siberia soon after 21,000 years ago, they could have moved south before ice became an obstacle and been at Monte Verde exactly on time.

---

ago, with the passage opening first. Monte Verde is still 6,000 miles farther south than Clovis. To reach the Chilean site on time, these first Americans had to have left Alaska immediately after the passage opened up—giving them maybe 200 or 300 years to make the trip (our record-setting Thule could never have kept up). Leaving Alaska before the glaciers advanced 20,000 years ago, or earlier, seems a little more plausible.

So is Monte Verde just another Paleo-Indian site, albeit slightly older than most? Lynch growls that we cannot be sure, since so few of the artifacts have been illustrated or described in print. Dillehay's first published volume on Monte Verde said next to nothing about the site's artifacts or architecture, saving them for the (yet unpublished) second volume. This was a novel gambit on Dillehay's part to convince his readers, solely on the testimony of the

nonarchaeological remains, that Monte Verde was a genuine archeological site. It caused a fair amount of grumbling, but he nearly pulled it off. Lynch, for example, admits the plant remains didn't get to the site by chance—he's just not willing to have them be there as early as Dillehay is.

Ultimately, making the case for Monte Verde—as Dillehay knows—will require more detailed descriptions and photographs of the artifacts. It will require precise maps of the layout of the huts and hearths, showing why these features are demonstrably of human origin. And it will require showing the distribution of the artifacts, organic remains, and dated samples within these features. Jackie Robinson didn't have it easy his first few years in the majors, either.

But will the publication of Dillehay's second volume be all that's needed to reach consensus on this site, and perhaps break the Clovis barrier? I put the question to University of Arizona archeologist Vance Haynes, the dean of the skeptics:

"No."

"But why not?"

"Have you ever visited a site," Haynes asked me, "that looked just the way you thought it would, based on what you'd read of it beforehand?" I had to admit I hadn't (truth is, sometimes I have trouble recognizing sites I've dug from descriptions I've written of them). In archeology, what one reads and what one sees are often very different. Archeology is like that: unlike researchers in the experimental sciences, we cannot replicate a crucial study in our own labs nor fully recreate a site's evidence in words and pictures. Having Haynes visit Monte Verde for a guided tour of the site and an explanation of its history would be the best way for Dillehay to dispose of any lingering doubts the hard-boiled skeptics might have.

"The next book's important," Haynes said, "but one day on the site of Monte Verde would be worth all the words they could write."

Dillehay's response: "Fine. I've been inviting people since 1979 to come to the site. Let's go look at it."

So the wrangling over Monte Verde will last several more years, while we wait for Dillehay and his team of specialists to wrap up volume two, and for Haynes and the other skeptics to hustle funds for the plane tickets to Chile. In the meantime, though, Emory's molecule hunters are doing their part to hasten the end of the Clovis hegemony.

Wallace and his colleagues inaugurated their mitochondrial DNA studies among Native Americans in the mid-1980s, just about the time excavations at Monte Verde were winding down. Almost immediately their results were extraordinarily encouraging. In analyzing mitochondrial DNA from Arizona's native Pima, Wallace's group spotted a mutation that occurs in 1 to 2 percent of Asian people (*Hinc*II morph 6 at bp 13259, in the alphabet-soup idiom of genetics). Among the Pima, however, the mutation's incidence was 20 times higher. That telltale clue does more than affirm the Pima's shared ancestry with Asians. The mutation is so frequent among them that the Pima must have descended from a small number of Asian immigrants, nearly all of whom carried that mutation in their genetic baggage.

Half a dozen years and a couple of hundred more samples later (including mitochondrial DNA samples from Navajo and Apache in North America, Yucatán Maya in Central America and Ticuna in South America), Wallace's team was able to show that all native peoples throughout the Americas share four mitochondrial DNA founding lineages. That's powerful evidence that the very first Americans were few in number. Genetically speaking, they left their Siberian sisters carrying but a fraction of the mitochondrial DNA gene pool.

If Wallace's group is right, the genetic clock started ticking the moment those first Americans left Siberia, at least 21,000 years ago by mitochondrial DNA reckoning. As it happens, the first Siberians appear archeologically

Marching to the New World
MONTE VERDE LIES 30 MILES INLAND FROM THE PACIFIC—AND OVER 9,000 MILES FROM SIBERIA, WHERE ITS SETTLERS CAME FROM.

about then. If they left Siberia soon thereafter, they could have crossed Beringia, moved south before glacial ice became an obstacle, and been at Monte Verde exactly on time (and without having to break any hunter-gatherer speed records).

Of course, Wallace's group may not be right. There are biologists who think the genetic clock was already ticking back in Siberia—long before the future first Americans departed—and some of those naysayers were at the San Francisco meeting to say so. Ryk Ward, of the University of Utah, and Svante Pääbo, of the University of Munich, have also analyzed mitochondrial DNA variation among Native Americans—in their case, the Nuu-Chah-Nulth of Vancouver Island. Of the 63 individuals they studied, they found 28 separate molecular variants. That's an astonishingly high rate of molecular diversity in just one tribe. Measured by the mitochondrial DNA clock, the Nuu-Chah-Nulth's ancestors had to have left Siberia up to 78,000 years ago.

That startling number implies one of two things: either that Americans are

of an antiquity inconceivable to all but the most passionate pre-Clovis crusaders—a humbling prospect for archeologists, because it means people were here for tens of thousands of years before Clovis and we've utterly failed to detect them—or that the Emory group is dead wrong about how the Americas were colonized.

Ward thinks the latter. The genetic diversity evident in the Nuu-Chah-Nulth, he believes, cannot have evolved in America, at least not until archeologists find some evidence of a 70,000-year-old occupation. Therefore, it must have originated in Asia long before the first Americans left Siberia. In other words, the first emigrants were already genetically diverse at departure, and the mitochondrial DNA clock says nothing about when the populations departed for America. "Even if we are able to use molecular data to define the divergence times of a set of lineages," Ward told his Bay Area audience, "we cannot state at what time the representative populations themselves split."

But Wallace's group isn't giving an inch. "We're looking at the genetic tree very differently," Schurr says. For the Emory researchers, the separate branches on which Asians and Native Americans perch are so genetically distinct that there must have been a branching event somewhere near Siberia. But for Ward, the twigs on the American branch are too numerous for the branching to have happened only here.

Are we back where we started? Not entirely—the archeology is proceeding apace. Dillehay expects to complete the second volume on Monte Verde next year, and he, Haynes, and others are planning to visit the site together. If the skeptics leave converted, then the biologists will have a reason to pick one molecular-clock scenario over another. And the rest of us will have a much clearer picture of the hardy pioneers who long ago slipped across the unmarked border between Siberia and Alaska and found a truly new world.

First Americans: Not Mammoth Hunters, But Forest Dwellers?

For archaeologists on the trail of the first Americans, fluted points found near the town of Clovis, New Mexico, in 1932 have been sharp indicators of the pioneers' identity. The points—10,900 to 11,200 years old and long accepted as the continent's oldest known human artifacts—were found among the bones of mammoths, leading to the conclusion that their makers were big-game hunters. Similar points have turned up since, helping to fill in a picture of these "Clovis people" as intrepid hunters who crossed a land bridge over the Bering Strait to Alaska, then swept rapidly across North America and into South America in pursuit of wide-ranging mammoths, mastodons, bison, camels, and other giant mammals.

But recently, evidence has been accumulating that the Clovis people may have shared the Americas with a different culture, one based on gathering fruits and nuts, fishing, and hunting small animals rather than felling mammoths. And a new excavation of a Brazilian cave provides some of the strongest evidence yet for that notion. The new findings indicate that early Paleoindians were living in the Amazon jungle of South America at the same time as the Clovis people, 11,000 years ago, or shortly thereafter. Stone tools, lumps of paint, and the remains of their meals—including fruits, nuts, and bones—indicate these cave dwellers foraged for food in the forest and river basin, had their own distinct tool kits, and painted art on their cave walls.

"We found strong evidence that a culture quite distinct from the North American Paleoindian culture, but more or less contemporary with it, existed more than 5000 miles south, in this humid, tropical

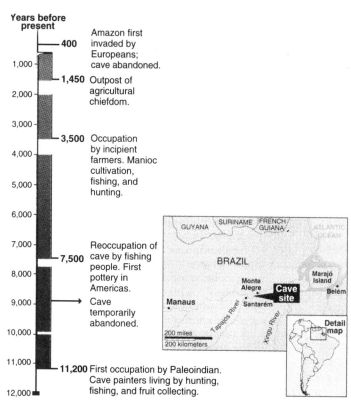

Early arrivals. Radiocarbon dates from a cave in Brazil indicate it was occupied from 11,200 years ago by people who gathered nuts, fished, and painted figures on cave walls.

habitat," says Anna Roosevelt, an archaeologist at the Field Museum and the University of Illinois, Chicago, and lead author on the article.

These discoveries are surprising for another reason: Many archaeologists had assumed that tropical forests didn't provide enough food to support people until the advent of slash-and-burn cultivation, thousands of years later. But while questions have been raised about the dating of older sites in South America, such as Monte Verde in Chile and Pedra Furada in Brazil, most researchers agree that the dating of Roosevelt's site is

solid enough to challenge this view. "It means you have people roaming around the Amazon very early," says University of Arizona geoarchaeologist C. Vance Haynes, an expert on Clovis. "It does suggest that something different is going on in the Amazon from what is going on with Paleoindians in the U.S." And some scientists say the differences mean that the Amazonians' ancestors may have arrived separately in a different migration over the Bering Strait—and perhaps they came over even before the Clovis people. "This suggests you could have had an earlier wave of people," says Ken Tankersley, an archaeological geologist at Kent State University in Ohio.

Roosevelt and her colleagues have been excavating a warren of caves on a high plain 10 kilometers west of the lower Amazon River, in the sandstone hills of Monte Alegre—which means Happy Mountain in Portuguese—since 1991. A local school teacher led them to the most intriguing cave, Caverna de Pedra Pintada, where they found sandstone walls covered with red and yellow handprints and paintings of humanlike figures, animals, and geometric shapes. Excavating layer after layer from the floor of the cave, they found burned food remains and stone tools.

In the deepest—and oldest—layers of the cave, the researchers found that the earliest cave dwellers left behind 30,000 stone chips and 24 stone tools, including two-sided projectile points, some of which had stems that probably were used on the tips of spears, darts, or harpoons—all sealed under a sterile layer of sand. The earliest inhabitants also left carbonized wood in hearths, and the remains of what they ate—thousands of fruits, seeds, and small and large fish and animals.

Fifty-six radiocarbon dates on the wood and carbonized plants put humans at the site for a 1200-year span between 11,200 and 10,000 years ago. Two other dating techniques also support the antiquity of the site. Researchers at the University of Washington, Seattle, used optically stimulated luminescence (OSL) on quartz grains from the sandy cave floor, and investigators at the Centre des Faibles Radioactivites in France used thermoluminescence (TL) on quartz in the burned stone tools. Both methods count the number of electrons trapped in physical defects within the quartz crystals: The electrons get trapped at a regular rate, forming the basis for a clock. In OSL, scientists release—and count—the trapped electrons by shining a bright light on the quartz; in TL, heat does the trick. Those methods usually produce older dates with wider ranges than radiocarbon dating produces. Indeed, they yield a spread of dates for the earliest cave layer that extend from 11,300 to 16,000 years ago, and Roosevelt argues that this bolsters the oldest of the radiocarbon dates.

Not everyone agrees with her on that point, however. There is a dispute about the accuracy of the dates at the older end of the radiocarbon range. Although Roosevelt argues for the first human occupation at 11,200 years ago, Haynes and some others feel 10,500 is safer. He and Tankersley say that any single radiocarbon date from a layer of soil is subject to error (the number of carbon-14 atoms emitted during each test can vary), so archaeologists usually take several dates from a soil layer and average them, giving more weight to the dates with the least amount of error. When Haynes averages the 14 earliest dates, for example, he gets a date of about 10,500. University of Massachusetts, Amherst, archaeologist Dena Dincauze agrees that the more recent dates are more reliable, noting that the earlier ones have larger error bars.

Roosevelt argues, however, that averaging is inappropriate for a cave floor that was repeatedly occupied for 1200 years, as it wouldn't point to the beginning of the occupation, but the middle. The average date also ignores the stratigraphy at the site, says Roosevelt. The oldest dates came from stone tools and burned seeds at the bottom of the earliest layer of the floor, while more recent dates came from artifacts just above them. And the oldest seeds produced a cluster of six dates contemporary with Clovis, with standard deviations ranging from 135 years to 300 years, which is less than the error bars on many dates from Clovis sites.

An argument over a rough 700-year spread may seem like splitting hairs, but that split is the difference between saying the people of Monte Alegre were among the first Americans themselves or descendants of the Clovis people. Haynes says: "My bias is they are descendants of Clovis." Those centuries may have been enough time for the Clovis settlers to move south, changing their tool kits and diet as they adapted to new terrain, he says. And there is archaeological evidence that people who made points similar to Clovis made it as far south as Panama, perhaps as early as 11,000 years ago, says Temple University archaeologist Anthony Ranere.

Other archaeologists, however, think that Haynes is cutting things too close.

Even though Tankersley supports the younger dates for Monte Alegre, he says that Roosevelt's site is the latest in a series that shows humans using diverse tools and displaying diverse behavior at too early a time to be derived from the Clovis tradition. New technologies, he says, take more time to develop. Differences in tool kits found at sites in North and South America—including Hell Gap, Wyoming, Mill Iron, Montana, and Monte Verde, Chile—support the idea that there was more than one group of Paleoindians in America during this general period and that their ancestors may have come over in a different wave from that of the first Clovis people. Roosevelt agrees: "This is not Clovis. We haven't got the whole story. Something else was going on."

Although archaeologists may disagree about the initial occupation of Monte Alegre, they do concur that the cave adds other important details to the prehistory of the Americas. "This shows there were people living in the tropical rain forest before agriculture," says Gustavo Politis, an archaeologist at the University of La Plata and the University del Centro de la Provincia de Buenos Aires. For decades, many scientists thought no one could live in the jungle before agriculture because there wasn't enough starch in the plants to give them the calories they needed to survive. But the site shows that the people of Monte Alegre had a rich and varied diet from gathering fruit and nuts, fishing, and hunting animals in the forest. And over time, their descendants became increasingly sophisticated at surviving in the forest, setting up fishing villages on the shores of the river, developing pottery, and cultivating trees and crops on the uplands.

This cultivation, over thousands of years, has had an effect on the forest itself. "What's exciting about this is that it shows humans have been changing the forest from early on," says Dincauze. The clustering of plants, such as cashews, Brazil nuts, and certain palms, in parts of the forest today may be the result of prehistoric human activity, says Tulane University anthropologist William Balée. The so-called "virgin" forests of Amazonia may, in part, be the product of human hands. —**Ann Gibbons**

Rhinos and Lions and Bears (Oh, My!)

An archeologist explores the newly discovered Chauvet Cave

Jean Clottes

Jean Clottes is scientific adviser for prehistoric rock art studies at the French Ministry of Culture and chairman of the International Committee for Rock Art. An archeologist by training, Clottes served for twenty-one years as director of prehistoric antiquities for the Midi-Pyrénées region, where he studied and helped to conserve the painted caves. His current research involves the application of new laboratory techniques for analyzing ancient art; he is also interested in other archeological evidence that may throw light on the artists' motivations, technology, and culture.

On Thursday, December 29, 1994, I was at my home in Foix, France, preparing for a New Year's celebration. My three children, their spouses, and my seven grandchildren (ranging in age from six months to ten years) were arriving that day and the next for a crowded family week-end. At noon the phone rang. Jean-Pierre Daugas, the regional conservator in charge of archeology for the Rhône-Alpes region, was calling to tell me that there had been a major discovery in the Ardèche Valley in southeast France. A few days before, on Christmas, three men had discovered a big cave with hundreds of paintings and engravings representing lions, rhinos, bears, horses, bison, and even a leopard and a hyena. By chance, they had felt a draft through stone rubble that blocked a small hole at the foot of a cliff in the valley. After moving the stones, they managed to wriggle through a narrow passage into a hitherto unknown painted cave and believed they were the first humans to enter it in 20,000 years.

Leopards and hyenas were unknown in Paleolithic cave art, and lions, rhinos, and bears were rare. Situated near the town of Vallon-Pont d'Arc, the cave is in a very touristy area where more than a million visitors, including many cave explorers, roam every summer. Could this be a hoax? Daugas insisted it was not. One of the discoverers, Jean-Marie Chauvet, was well known to him, as he was employed by the Ministry of Culture as a guard at the painted caves in the Ardèche region. He was trustworthy and so were his two companions, Eliette Deschamps and Christian Hillaire, who had discovered several minor painted or engraved caves in the Ardèche and Gard areas during the past ten years. I said I would go the following week. But Daugas pressed me, saying, "This looks extremely important and I really wish you could come right away." Reluctantly, I decided to disappoint my family and go check out the cave. The same afternoon I packed my cave overalls, miner's lamp, helmet, camera, and flashlight and drove to Vallon-Pont d'Arc, about 250 miles away.

The next morning, Daugas, along with one of his colleagues and the three cave explorers, met me at the hotel and we set off for the cave. I felt duty bound to tell them that I would have to question everything because my first concern was to ascertain whether such a spectacular discovery could be a fake. They just laughed and said they were not worried.

It was a bleak winter day, and heavy fog shrouded the normally beautiful countryside. We climbed briskly through thick woods to the foot of a cliff. After following along its base for a while and passing several small caves, we reached an unpromising cavity, several feet wide, which my guides said was our entry point. We scrambled down the sloping hole for about thirty feet to a heap of loose rocks that covered a much narrower opening. It was here that the discoverers had first noticed the air current rising. When they first came upon this much deeper hole, they had to spend an entire day removing rocks that had been blocking it. Before leaving the site, however, they had stacked enough rocks over the entrance to hide it again. Now they removed this small pile and crawled into the cave. Then it was my turn. The seven-foot passage was so narrow that I had to strip down to my overalls before attempting to go through. After a difficult ten minutes, getting stuck repeatedly and creeping forward only while exhaling, I emerged on the other side, where

I descended a thirty-foot hanging ladder they had left there. At the bottom I found myself inside a vast chamber.

Obviously, the Paleolithic artists had not used the access we had been through, which opened into the ceiling of the cave. Hours later, we found the cave's original entrance some hundreds of feet on the other side of the chamber. It had long been blocked by a huge pile of rocky debris, perhaps soon after the cave had been visited by humans. This blocked entrance will remain as it is, so as not to change the climatic conditions inside the cavern.

My first impression of the cave was that it was vast, pristine, and beautiful. Stalactites and stalagmites sparkled everywhere under our lights. The ground seemed untrodden, and on the other side of the chamber I could distinguish a first panel of red dots. We went over to it, and I examined it closely. The dots were large (two and a half to three inches in diameter) and numerous, resembling those in the cave of Pech-Merle in Quercy. The ancient paint had long ago penetrated into the wall, and a thin veil of calcite covered a few dots. They were undoubtedly authentic. We followed Jean-Marie Chauvet closely, stepping where he told us in order not to destroy any traces or even dirty the ground. He carefully unrolled long slips of black plastic in front of us, choosing a path where the ground was solid rock or covered with thick calcite, and skirting the soft places where prints might be preserved.

In the first chambers, most of the art consisted of red figures. Next to a few hand stencils and red dots, we saw only one black horse, half-hidden under an old layer of calcite. In a smaller gallery, the outlined head of a red deer was followed by three cave bear images and one of a horse. In creating one of the bears, the prehistoric artist had utilized the natural relief of the wall as a three-dimensional shoulder for the animal. Elsewhere, three rhinos followed one another in a long frieze. As is always the case in Paleolithic painted caves, there were many geometric signs: several panels of dots, similar to the one we had first seen; a semicircle of much smaller dots; and a few

cryptic drawings. Two of these strange geometrics resembled birds or bats, while others were reminiscent of insects with multiple legs.

The recognizable creatures painted in red included several rhinos, bears, and lions, at least one ibex, four mammoths, one bovid, and two other animals close to each other. One was indisputably a leopard, recognizable by its spots and its tail, which was devoid of the tuft all lions possess. The other one was bigger. At first, I identified it as a bear, but I was bothered by its spindly legs, its shortened hindquarters, and the spots on the front part of the body. I then let myself be persuaded that it might indeed be a hyena, as Chauvet had said in the first place. If it really was a hyena, it would be the first depiction of that animal in Paleolithic art, just as the leopard is the first known example of its kind. However, I am far from certain what it is; it still could be a bear.

After a low passage full of stalactites, we reached other chambers. In one of them, the ground had collapsed, and a deep crater about thirty feet wide had opened up. Above it, an owl, two mammoths, and a horse had been engraved on an overhang at a time when it was easy to reach. Now the engravings stood about fifteen feet above the bottom of the crater. This was further evidence that no forger could have been at work on the walls.

Farther on, we came to several extensive panels crowded with numerous black figures. These paintings were truly astonishing: on the whole they were well preserved and distinct. Most of the animals were recognizable as to species and sometimes even as to sex or behavior. Contrary to what can be seen in most painted caves, these animal depictions seem to be grouped into compositions. For example, one of the main panels appears to be organized on both sides of a small recess, inside of which a horse, a mammoth, and a rhino have been painted. On the right, there is another, young-looking mammoth, several rhinos, and some bison followed by a group of fourteen lions with their heads stretching in the direction of other animals. Behind the lions

is a solitary rhino. On the other side of the recess is a spectacular series of at least thirteen or fourteen rhinos, some superimposed on the others; most are facing left while two face right. Then there are four big lions all on the alert and looking to the right. In the middle of the group, one sees a reindeer and at least two series of red spots of various sizes—the smaller ones in a line; the bigger ones in a sort of semicircle.

Could this really be a composition rather than the placing of unrelated animals on the same walls? Already I thought of what would have to be done to try and find an answer to this question. Analyses of paint constituents might reveal whether all the animals had been done at the same time, with the same paint. All the images would have to be traced carefully and the techniques used by the artists investigated. We could not go up to that panel because the ground in front of it was untrodden and fragile, so we stayed about thirty feet back and examined it from a distance.

We could, however, get close to another one, equally complex and beautiful. There, on one wall, animals of different species had also been represented in black, and some of the images had been superimposed on others. Detailed chemical analysis would in time tell us which animals had been done first or last and enable us to establish the different phases in the composition. A first examination showed, for instance, that some small rhinos had been partly covered by four big aurochs, while another rhino was on top of one of the aurochs and four horses' heads were on top of this rhino. Two other male rhinos seemed to be fighting; such a scene is unique in Paleolithic rock art.

While I was gazing at the panel, trying to distinguish the succession of the images and, in particular, looking closely at the splendid heads of the four horses, I was suddenly overcome with emotion. I felt a deep and clear certainty that here was the work of one of the great masters, a Leonardo da Vinci of the Solutrean revealed to us for the first time. It was both humbling and exhilarating. Humbling because of the admiration one could not help but feel for the artist, forever unknown, whose works had spanned the millennia, and because the discovery underlined the immensity of our ignorance. If after more than a century of research such original and important paintings could still come to light, how many had been destroyed or were still unknown in the depths of concealed caves? On the other hand, I was thoroughly exhilarated to be there, one of the fortunate few to first behold such a masterpiece.

After a whole day spent in the cave it was possible to make a preliminary assessment. The authenticity of the paintings and engravings is beyond question. The cave is a major discovery because of the number of animals represented on its walls, their esthetic quality, and their originality. Of course, years of study lie ahead. For now, nothing can be said as to the precise dates for the works of art, the activities of prehistoric people in the cave, the meaning of the paintings, or the choice of panels. That will come later. But the indisputable authenticity makes the Chauvet Cave, as the discoverers want to call it, one of the great archeological finds of the century.

I saw more than 150 animal images that day, and I probably missed many more, as it was impossible to walk to the other side of some chambers in which the ground was littered with cave bear bones and where undisturbed prints could be seen on the surface. Across one of those chambers, we could just make out the outlines of more images, unrecognizable from a distance. Most probably, when the cave is explored in detail, there will be 200 to 300 animal figures and possibly even more. In comparison, among French caves considered among the most important in Paleolithic cave art, 145 animal paintings or engravings have been found in the Cosquer Cave near Marseille (see "Neptune's Ice Age Gallery," *Natural History,* April 1993) and 110 in Niaux, in the Ariège.

Most of the animals in the Chauvet Cave are rhinos, lions, and bears,

which is very surprising. Generally, those most often represented at the time were horses, bison, aurochs, mammoths, deer, and ibexes. Images of these animals are also present in the cave, but the emphasis on predatory animals that were probably not hunted testifies to a regional difference in the Ardèche culture during that time.

Exact dates for the paintings are still a matter of conjecture. However, some details point to a pre-Magdalenian period—the Solutrean, about 18,000 to 21,000 years ago, which is already represented in the Ardèche caves but is rare elsewhere. The panels of big dots and at least one deer are similar to the ones in Pech-Merle, a cave where stenciled red hands have also been painted and which is generally attributed to the Solutrean. Several bison are pictured with their horns facing front, while their bodies are shown in profile and their heads in three-quarters view. The style reminded me of a similar bison in the recently discovered Cosquer Cave, which is half-submerged in a seacliff on the Mediterranean and has been radiocarbondated to about 18,500 years ago. Three animals that appear to be Irish elk—an extinct deer with giant antlers—have been painted in the Chauvet Cave. Those animals appear very rarely in Paleolithic art but happen to be present in several caves dated to the Solutrean or even earlier times, such as Cougnac and Pech-Merle in the Lot region, just south of the Massif Central, and again in the Cosquer Cave. If the Chauvet Cave is indeed Solutrean, which we shall know after radiocarbon analyses and archeological studies have been done, it will be the most important sanctuary ever discovered for that culture. In any case, the Ardèche, and more generally the southeast of France, is no longer a minor area for rock art. It now ranks among the best, along with the Pèrigord, the Pyrenees, and Cantabria.

Finally, the Chauvet Cave stands out because it has been so well preserved. The discoverers were extremely care-

ful to walk where they would cause no damage. In places, the remains of fires can still be seen. Elsewhere, the ancient soil is covered with bear and human prints. Cave bear bones litter the whole cave. It will be necessary to determine whether the bears hibernated in the cave thousands of years before humans came or were present at the same time. An in-depth study of all traces should also tell us whether children went there with the adults and possibly what sorts of activities went on. In one chamber, for example, a cave bear skull has been placed on top of a big block of stone in a very dramatic way. What could this mean? Have any other bear bones been moved? And why? Did the bears go back into the cave after humans had decorated the walls? Many such questions are unanswered for the time being.

In the months and years to come, much research will be carried out in the cave. However, our first priority will have to be its preservation. A discovery such as this is exceptional from many points of view, and exceptional care is therefore in order. We have often regretted that the excavation of such caves as Lascaux and Altamira destroyed their archeological context, either through carelessness or to answer some questions of the time. In future years, our successors will have different theories and models, and they will use different techniques. Nothing should be done to destroy the primary evidence. Strict precautions must be taken against vandalism, and some restrictions placed on research. After preservation, scientific study will be our second priority. Research will take years to complete and must be nondestructive. Our third priority is to respond to the enormous public demand for films, CD-ROMs, and replicas of the images. These will become possible in time, but there is no hurry. After all, what are a few years to wait for a cave that has waited for us for fifteen or twenty millennia!

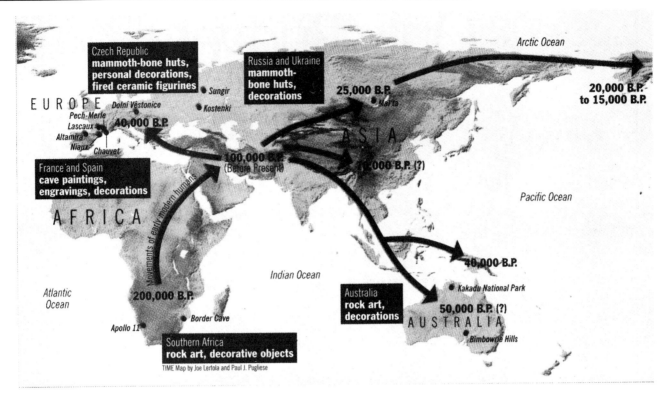

TIME Map by Joe Lertola and Paul J. Pugliese

Ancient Odysseys

As early humans migrated around the globe, image making spread rapidly

Michael D. Lemonick

The human mind can't easily comprehend huge expanses of time. Once the years run into the tens of thousands, our brain lumps them together into an undifferentiated mass. The catchall term prehistoric art works perfectly with this sort of thinking. It sounds like just another episode in art history—modern art, Renaissance art, Byzantine art, prehistoric art.

In reality, the artworks created before history began—prior, say, to about 10,000 B.P. (before the present)—cover a much longer time span than what has come afterward. Southwestern European cave painting, only the most familiar expression of ancient creativity, was done over a period of at least 10,000 years. And when Paleolithic people first crawled into the Chauvet cave to daub the walls with images of rhinos and bears, nearly half of all art history was already over with.

When art first appeared, presumably around 40,000 B.P., it spread quickly. Within a mere 5,000 years—barely the blink of an eye on paleontological time scales—the work of early artists popped up in several corners of the globe. Archaeologists have found more than 10,000 sculpted and engraved objects in hundreds of locations across Europe, southern Africa, northern Asia and Australia. The styles range from realistic to abstract, and the materials include stone, bone, antler, ivory, wood, paint, teeth, claws, shells and clay that have been carved, sculpted and painted to represent animals, plants, geometric forms, landscape features and human beings—virtually every medium and every kind of subject that artists would return to thousands of years later.

This creative explosion is best documented in Europe, largely because that is where most of the excavations have taken place. Early body decoration, for example, was found in the 1950s by

Soviet archaeologists at Sungir, near the Russian city of Vladimir. From graves dating back to 28,000 B.P., they unearthed the remains of a 10-year-old girl, a 12-year-old boy and a 60-year-old man. The three are festooned with beads, more than 14,000 all told. But each is adorned in a different way, evidence that body decoration was used to emphasize gender and age distinctions in social groups. In addition to the beads, the girl has delicate snow-flake-like carvings around her head and torso. The boy has no snowflakes but wears a belt made from 240 fox canine teeth. And the man is wearing a single pendant made of stone in the middle of his chest. Another distinction: the beads on the children's bodies are approximately two thirds the size of those the man is wearing.

At about the same time that the three were being buried—give or take a few millenniums—a new sort of artifact begins to appear in the prehistorical

Art through the Prehistoric Ages

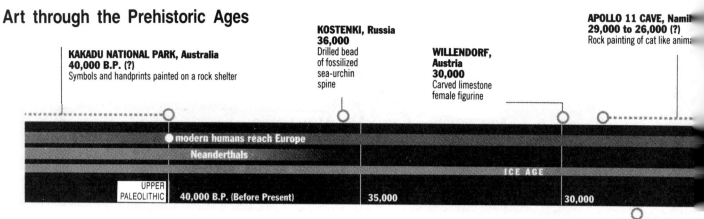

KAKADU NATIONAL PARK, Australia
40,000 B.P. (?)
Symbols and handprints painted on a rock shelter

KOSTENKI, Russia
36,000
Drilled bead of fossilized sea-urchin spine

WILLENDORF, Austria
30,000
Carved limestone female figurine

APOLLO 11 CAVE, Namib[
29,000 to 26,000 (?)
Rock painting of cat like anima[

● modern humans reach Europe

Neanderthals

ICE AGE

UPPER PALEOLITHIC | 40,000 B.P. (Before Present) | 35,000 | 30,000

SUNGIR, Russia
28,000
Ivory animal pendant with traces of paint

record. Archaeologists working at sites all across Europe and well into Russia have found dozens of so-called Venus figurines: miniature sculptures of big-breasted, broad-hipped women. The statuettes, which may have been used in fertility rites or even religious ceremonies, suggest a worshipful attitude toward fertility and reproduction.

By 22,000 B.P., archaeologists have found, the first evidence of the cave paintings that appeal so strongly to modern eyes begins to appear. The paintings, some of them realistic portraits of animals, others depicting half-human, half-animal figures or abstract symbols, soon became the dominant form of prehistoric European art. They remained important until 10,000 B.P., when, along with the glaciers of the last Ice Age, they seem to have melted away from human consciousness.

Those are the broad outlines, at least, of early art history. The details are much messier: it's not as though one phase gave way smoothly to another. Beadwork and statuette carving didn't stop just because cave painting began—and the presence of caves didn't automatically inspire people to cover them with images. Says Jean Clottes, one of France's pre-eminent authorities on prehistoric art: "There are a lot of caves in Yugoslavia, for example, but no paintings in them." Moreover, there is enormous regional variation in what sorts of art were produced at what times.

The story is even less straightforward in other parts of the world. Not only have extensive explorations been less common outside Europe, but also what's been found has proved difficult to date. Nonetheless, it is clear that

artists were at work in Australia and southern Africa, at least, at roughly the same time as their European cousins.

The Australian continent abounds in Aboriginal rock art, both paintings and engravings. Much of it lies in a 1,500-mile-long, boomerang-shaped area across the country's north coast. Archaeologist Darrell Lewis of the Australian National University estimates that there are at least 10,000 rock-art sites on the Arnhem Land plateau alone, in the Northern Territory. "Each of these sites," he says, "can have several hundred paintings." But unlike early inhabitants of Europe, who frequently decorated caves over a short period and then abandoned them, the Australian Aborigines would return over and over to the same sites—a practice that still goes on today. Unraveling the history of a single site can thus be extremely complicated.

How old is Australia's art? Some archaeologists insist that certain paintings of human hands and life-size crocodiles and kangaroos were done 50,000 years ago, but these experts may be overconfident of their dating techniques. Another controversial assertion is the claim by anthropologist Alan Thorne of the Australian National University that a small piece of red ochre (a kind of clay), dated to 50,000 B.P., was worn down on one side like a piece of chalk by humans. "Whether it was ground to paint a shelter or a person or part of a wall, I don't think anyone would disagree that it is evidence of art," says Thorne. Even if Australia's art is not as ancient as Thorne thinks, there is strong evidence that at least two rock carvings found in the Bimbowrie Hills are more than

40,000 years old, and that scores of others in the area fall between 30,000 and 20,000 B.P.

Southern Africa's artistic record is much sparser. Scientists have unearthed a pendant made from a seashell that may be more than 40,000 years old, carved bones and beads made from ostrich eggshells that probably date from around 27,000 B.P., and paintings on slabs of rock in a Namibian cave that may be nearly as old. But like Australia's Aborigines, southern Africa's indigenous people carried on their rock-art tradition into modern times, confusing anthropologists' tasks considerably.

And in the rest of the world . . . nothing. Not in the Middle East, not in Southeast Asia, not in China or Japan or Korea, and not in North Africa before 15,000 B.P. at the very earliest—although there is ample evidence of an ancient human presence in all these areas. This may mean the people there weren't interested in art, or it may simply be that they painted or carved on wood or animal skins, which have long since rotted away.

Nobody can do more than speculate about the answer. That uncertainty, along with the spottiness of the archaeological record—even in an intensively studied area like southern France—makes it hard to know whether art, once invented, was a universal practice. Probably not, argues archaeologist Olga Soffer, of the University of Illinois at Urbana-Champaign: "Art is

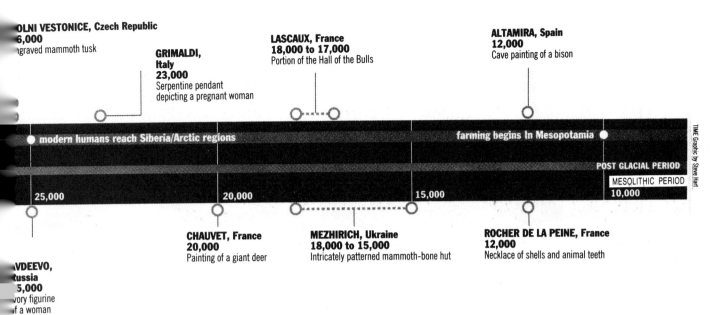

OLNI VESTONICE, Czech Republic
6,000
ngraved mammoth tusk

GRIMALDI,
Italy
23,000
Serpentine pendant
depicting a pregnant woman

LASCAUX, France
18,000 to 17,000
Portion of the Hall of the Bulls

ALTAMIRA, Spain
12,000
Cave painting of a bison

modern humans reach Siberia/Arctic regions

farming begins In Mesopotamia

POST GLACIAL PERIOD

MESOLITHIC PERIOD

25,000   20,000   15,000   10,000

TIME Graphic by Steve Hart

AVDEEVO,
Russia
5,000
vory figurine
f a woman

CHAUVET, France
20,000
Painting of a giant deer

MEZHIRICH, Ukraine
18,000 to 15,000
Intricately patterned mammoth-bone hut

ROCHER DE LA PEINE, France
12,000
Necklace of shells and animal teeth

a social phenomenon that appears and disappears and, in some places, may not arise at all." But many anthropologists counter that the term art is usually defined too narrowly. What paleolithic humans really invented, they say, is symbolic representation, and by that definition art may well appear in every culture—though it might not be easy for us to recognize.

It's also difficult to say whether art originated in a specific part of the world. By the time of humanity's great artistic awakening, Homo sapiens had probably already traveled from its African homeland through most of Europe and Asia. The urge to make art could have arisen in any of these places and spread throughout the world, or it could have happened in many areas independently.

There are problems with either scenario, however. "The pattern is puzzling," observes anthropologist Randall White. "One of the most common forms of body adornment in Western Europe during this early period is canine teeth from carnivores, drilled with holes and worn as dangling ornamentation. And damned if in Australia, some 35,000 to 40,000 years ago this isn't exactly what they're doing too." It might seem like an unremarkable coincidence—after all, carnivores must have loomed large in every culture. But an-

thropologists have learned that such coincidences are actually quite rare. If art did spread around the world, it moved with astonishing speed (on a paleontological time scale, that is), and, says White, "it's a long way from southern France to Australia."

One possible explanation: art was percolating along for tens of thousands of years before most of the known examples show up. Perhaps the original Homo sapiens populations in Africa invented art and carried it to other regions. The reasons nothing much has been found dating before 40,000 B.P., goes the argument, are that scientists haven't looked hard enough and most of the evidence has perished. As appealing as it may seem though, this art-is-older-than-we-think theory has attracted little support; the demarcation line at 40,000 B.P. is just too sharp.

New discoveries like the one at the Chauvet cave, and more intensive study of existing sites, are constantly giving archaeologists more information to work with. Also, dating techniques are becoming more refined. It used to be that scientists needed to test a large sample of paint to pinpoint its age. And, says anthropologist Margaret Conkey, "no one was willing to scrape a bison's rump off the wall." Now it takes only a tiny sample. French prehistory expert Arlette Leroi-Gourhan

estimates dates by using pollen particles preserved on cave floors.

The results of all these studies, while always enlightening, don't necessarily simplify things for scientists. A new analysis of the Cosquer cave on the French Riviera, for example, has shown that painted handprints on the walls date to 27,000 B.P., while images of horses and other animals came some 9,000 years later. Rather than being decorated in a single, prolonged burst of creativity, the cavern was painted over scores of centuries, quite possibly by artists who had no connection of any kind with one another, unlike Aborigines, whose culture has direct links to the distant past.

Prehistoric art was created over so long a period by so many different humans in so many parts of the world, and presumably for so many different reasons, that it may never fit into a tidy catalog. These ancient masterpieces are telling us that our prehistoric forebears had modes of expression more varied than we once imagined—and also that we'll never truly understand just how rich their lives must have been.

—Reported by David Bjerklie and Andrea Dorfman/New York, Tim Blair/Melbourne, Peter Hawthorne/ Cape Town and Thomas Sancton/ Paris

Toward Decolonizing Gender

Female Vision in the Upper Paleolithic

Catherine Hodge McCoid
LeRoy D. McDermott

Catherine Hodge McCoid is Professor, Department of History and Anthropology, Central Missouri State University, Warrensburg, MO 64093. LeRoy D. McDermott is Associate Professor, Department of Art, Central Missouri State University, Warrensburg, MO 64093.

THE CHINESE PROVERB "We see what is behind our eyes" captures one of the major dilemmas currently engaging both anthropological scholarship and the broader public. All of us look at the world and, at least partially, see what is inside our own heads. To the extent that we do not recognize this, we remain behind our cultural screens.

The first images of the human body from the European Upper Paleolithic, primarily three-dimensional, palm-sized female statuettes often referred to as Venus figurines, offer a case in point. Though little consensus exists about why the figures were created or what purposes they served, they have generally been interpreted as sex objects made from a male point of view.[1] This view assumes women were passive spectators of the creative mental life of prehistory, their bodies relevant only as representative of male concerns and interests. The apparently exaggerated sexual attributes of the figurines have often been seen as magical symbols of fecundity ultimately concerned with the increase of both animal and human populations.[2] Whether magical or not, the belief that these figurines reflect a symbolic interest in sex and fertility has been most influential.[3] Yet there is another plausible explanation for their creation and purpose: the figurines began as a form of self-representation by women (McDermott 1985, 1996). When examined, this proposal becomes so compelling that the only remaining question is, Why did it take so long to consider the logical possibility that a female point of view was involved?

HUMAN FIGURES IN THE EUROPEAN UPPER PALEOLITHIC

Since Édouard Piette (1895) and Salomon Reinach (1898) first described the distinctive small-scale sculptures and engravings of human figures found in the rock shelters and caves of southern France, several hundred more European Upper Paleolithic figures have been identified. The earliest of these, the so-called Stone Age Venuses or Venus figurines, constitute a distinctive class and are among the most widely known of all Paleolithic art objects. As a group they have frequently been described in the professional and popular literature.[4] Most of the figures are about 150 millimeters in height and depict nude women usually described as obese.

In spite of many difficulties in dating, there is growing belief that most of these early sculptures were created during the opening millennia of the Upper Paleolithic (circa 27,000–21,000 B.C.) and are stylistically distinct from those of the later Magdalenian.[5] These first representations of the human figure are centered in the Gravettian or Upper Perigordian assemblages in France and in related Eastern Gravettian variants, especially the Pavlovian in the former Czechoslovakia, and the Kostenkian in the former Soviet Union.

Most Pavlovian-Kostenkian-Gravettian (PKG) statuettes are carved in stone, bone, and ivory, with a few early examples modeled in a form of fired loess (Vandiver et al. 1989). Carved reliefs are also known from four French Gravettian sites: Laussel, La Mouthe, Abri Pataud, and Terme Pialet. These images show a formal concern with three-dimensional sculpted masses and have the most widespread geographical distribution of any form of prehistoric art. This contrasts sharply with the two-dimensional form and restricted scope of later Magdalenian engraved and painted figures. The unfortunate habit of collapsing both early PKG and later Magdalenian (circa 13,000–9,000 B.C.) figurines into one category has created much unnecessary confusion about stylistic variability within the Upper Paleolithic. As much as 10,000 years separates these two periods of artistic activity, so they constitute separate, though related, traditions. While considerable variation occurs among PKG figurines, claims of true diversity ignore a central tendency that defines the group as a whole.[6] The overwhelming majority of these images reflect a most unusual anatomical struc-

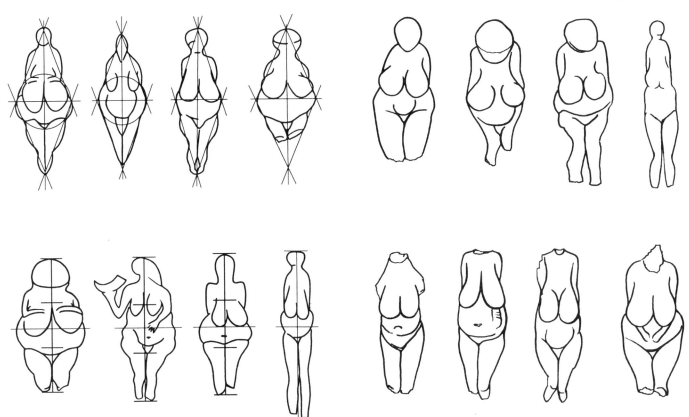

Figure 1
The PKG "lozenge composition." Above, left to right: Lespugue, Grimaldi "LeLosange," Kostenki No. 3, and Gagarino No. 1. Below, left to right: Willendorf No. 1, Laussel "La femme à la corne," Dolni Vestonice No. 1, and Gagarino No. 3. The abdominal circle used by Leroi-Gourhan (above left) is not essential to the anatomical distortions of these figurines. PKG images routinely elevate both the vertical midpoint and greatest width of the female body, and most make what should be one-half of the body closer to one-third (below). (Figures redrawn and simplified based on information in Leroi-Gourhan 1968.)

Figure 2
Additional figurines illustrating the same departures from anatomical accuracy seen in Figure 1. Above, left to right: Grimaldi "Statuette en stéatite jaune," Khotylevo No. 2, Gagarino No. 4, and Avdeevo No. 1. Below, left to right: Moravany and Kostenki nos. 1, 2, and 4.

ture, which André Leroi-Gourhan (1968) has labeled the "lozenge composition." What makes this structural formula so striking is that it consists of a recurring set of apparent departures from anatomical accuracy (see Figures 1–3). The characteristic features include a faceless, usually downturned head; thin arms that either disappear under the breasts or cross over them; an abnormally thin upper torso; voluminous, pendulous breasts; large fatty buttocks and/or thighs; a prominent, presumably pregnant abdomen, sometimes with a large elliptical navel coinciding with the greatest physical width of the figure;

and often oddly bent, unnaturally short legs that taper to a rounded point or disproportionately small feet. These deviations produce what M. D. Gvozdover (1989:79) has called "the stylistic deformation of the natural body." Yet these apparent distortions of the anatomy become apt renderings if we consider the body as seen by a woman looking down on herself. Comparison of the figurines with photographs simulating what a modern woman sees of herself from this perspective reveals striking correspondences. It is possible that since these images were discovered, we have simply

been looking at them from the wrong angle of view.

COMPARING MODERN BODIES AND PREHISTORIC ARTIFACTS

Although it is the center of visual self-awareness, a woman's face and head are not visible to her without a reflecting surface. This may explain why—although there are variations in shape, size, and position in the heads of these piece—virtually all are rendered without

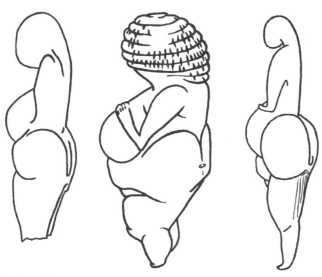

Figure 3
The PKG style in profile, illustrating common massing of three-dimensional forms. Note especially the thinness of upper torsos and the "inaccurate" relationships between buttocks and tailbones. The Willendorf (center) tailbone is an arbitrary bar without representational content, whereas the buttocks of the Grimaldi "Statuette en stéatite jaune" (left) and the Lespugue figurine (right) appear above the tailbone or upside down (see also Figures 8 and 9).

Other apparent distortions of the upper body undergo similar optical transformations from this perspective. For example, the inability to experience the true thickness of the upper body may account for the apparently abnormal thinness seen in the torsos of many figurines. Several figurines also have what seem to be unnaturally large, elliptical navels located too close to the pubic triangle. In a foreshortened view, however, the circular navel forms just such an ellipse, and when pregnant, a woman cannot easily see the space below the navel. Thus, when viewed as women survey themselves, the apparent anatomical distortions of the upper body in these figurines vanish (see Figures 4 and 5).

Similarly, as a woman looks down at the lower portion of her body, those parts farthest away from the eyes look smallest. A correct representation of the foreshortened lower body would narrow toward the feet, thus explaining the small size of the feet in these figurines. It is also true that, for a pregnant woman, inspection of the upper body terminates at the navel with the curving silhouette of the distended abdomen (see Figure 4). Without bending forward, she cannot see her lower body. Thus for a gravid female, the visual experience of her body involves two separate views whose shared boundary is the abdomen at the level of the navel, which is also the widest part of the body in the visual field. The ap-

facial features and most seem to be turned down, as is necessary to bring the body into view. A woman looking down at herself sees a strongly foreshortened view of the upper frontal surface of the thorax and abdomen, with her breasts looming large. Such a perspective helps to explain the apparently voluminous size and distinctive pendulous elonga-

tion routinely observed in the breasts of the figurines. Viewed in this way, the breasts of the figurines possess the natural proportions of the average modern woman of childbearing age (see Figures 4 and 5). Even pieces such as the one from Lespugue, in which the breasts seem unnaturally large, appear naturalistic when viewed from above.

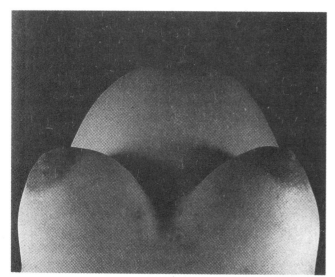

Figure 4
View of her own upper body by 26-year-old female who is five months pregnant and of average weight.

Figure 5
View of upper body of Willendorf figurine from same perspective used in Figure 4.

parent misrepresentation of height and width in the figurines results from the visual experience of this anatomical necessity. The location of the eyes means that for an expectant mother the upper half of the body visually expands toward the abdomen, whereas the lower half presents a narrow, tapering form. Efforts to represent the information contained in these two views naturally resulted in the lozenge compositional formulation, which others have seen as anatomically "incorrect" proportions (see Figures 1 and 2).

The perception of distortion is similarly resolved in a woman's view of the side and back of her own body. When one rotates at the hips and raises an arm to look down the side, one's field of vision includes an expanding strip of lower torso and then a diminishing view of the leg. The feet may or may not be visible, often being obscured by the intervening body. From above, the forward projecting mass of the thigh and the posterior location of the calf muscle are identical with a similar view of the bent-knee posture seen in numerous figurines (see Figures 6 and 7). The outline of this oblique silhouette coincides not only with the arrangement of muscles seen in these images, but with the buttocks or profile image that dominates the later Upper Paleolithic: Magdalenian III through VI, circa 13,000 to 9,000 B.C. (Leroi-Gourhan 1968:493).

Depending on the effort expended to rotate and look under the arm at one's

backside, a woman's view will either encompass a lateral segment of the lower back to the tailbone or, with greater exertion, include a strongly foreshortened, silhouetted sliver of the upper buttock. With or without maximal rotation, the view of this region will be dominated by the more proximal lateral bulge of the gluteus medius muscle, while the distal gluteus maximus of the buttocks proper is occluded entirely or reduced to a foreshortened fragment. The structure of the visual information inherent in this point of view explains not only the lateral displacement of adipose tissue or fatty thighs but also the continuum of regional variation. Many Russian pieces have what appear to be unnaturally long loins or flanks and atrophied or disproportionately short buttocks, while figures from the West (Luquet 1934) present supposedly upside-down buttocks (see Figure 3). What have been seen as buttocks in the past are really properly positioned glutei medii muscles. When correctly viewed from above, the backsides of the statuettes from Lespugue, Grimaldi, and Willendorf, which make no anatomical sense from any other point of view, are optically transformed into highly naturalistic, foreshortened images of the lower back above a correctly located tailbone (see Figures 8 and 9).

Other Upper Paleolithic peoples may have preferred the more difficult of the two routes by which the human back-

side can be directly inspected. In an over-the-shoulder view, the dual masses of the glutei maximi muscles appear to project posteriorly into the visual field exactly as in the rare rearward enlargement of the buttocks identified as steatopygia. Seen in only three pieces from Italy and southern France ("Le Polichinelle," Savignano, and Monpazier), this condition nevertheless demonstrates that the possibilities for self-inspection echo the actual range of regional and cultural variations encountered. It is possible that cultural differences in feminine self-inspection routines—with some cultures in Italy and southern France preferring to look over the shoulder while other cultures looked under the arm—account for the regional variations encountered. Again, what had been puzzling extremes of human representation become surprisingly realistic when considered from the probable point of view employed by their feminine creators.

The idea that women sought to gain and preserve knowledge about their own bodies provides a direct and parsimonious interpretation for general as well as idiosyncratic features found among female representations from the middle European Upper Paleolithic. The needs of health and hygiene, not to mention coitus and childbirth, ensure that feminine self-inspection actually occurred during the early Upper Paleolithic. Puberty, menses, copulation, conception,

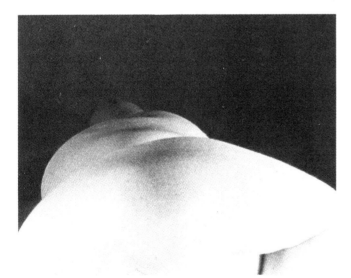

Figure 6
Woman's view of the side of her own body.

Figure 7
View of side of Willendorf figurine from same perspective.

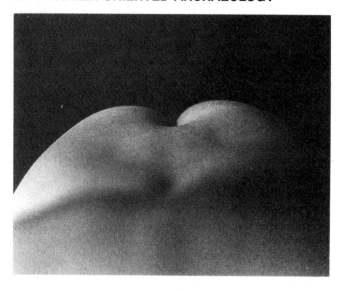

Figure 8
Woman's under-the-arm view of her own buttocks.

Figure 9
View of buttocks of Willendorf figurine from perspective similar to that used in Figure 8.

pregnancy, childbirth, and lactation are regular events in the female cycle and involve perceptible alterations in bodily function and configuration (Marshack 1972). Mastery and control of these processes continues to be of fundamental importance to women today. It is possible that the emergence and subsequent propagation of these images across Europe occurred precisely because they played a didactic function with actual adaptive consequences for women.

POPULATION, REPRODUCTION, AND NATURAL SELECTION

In interpreting female images in pre-Columbian art, Anna Roosevelt explores the hypothesis that "the figures were specifically related to a cult of human female fertility, a demographic strategy appropriate for the expanding economies of early sedentary agricultural societies" (1988:5). She suggests that the images are characteristic of chiefdoms or early states and that they disappeared shortly after state development, with its focus on war and royalty. These Upper Paleolithic figurines were probably made

at a time when there was similarly significant population increase along with cultural and economic restructuring.[7] The early to middle Upper Paleolithic was characterized by productive changes that harnessed energy and by reproductive changes that helped make possible the population expansion and technological changes that followed in the later European Upper Paleolithic.[8] Could women have made a recognizable contribution to the fluorescence of art and technology seen in the opening millennia of this era? Anything they did to improve their understanding of reproduction and thereby reduce infant and maternal mortality would clearly have contributed to this productive and reproductive change. Perhaps the figurines served as obstetrical aids, the relative sizes of the abdomens helping women to calculate the progress of their pregnancies.

Arguing for the value of using Darwinian evolution as a framework in cultural anthropology and archaeology, Steven Simms (1987:12) suggests that selection should be examined on the individual as well as the group level. These figurines might have been used to gain greater control of reproduction over time, thus offering an example of natural selection in action. As Roosevelt has pointed out, "The existing information

in the ethnographic literature is scattered and cryptic, but women in many preindustrial societies are known to make images of females, children, or genitals to aid in conception" (1988:15). Decreasing depictions of pregnancy over time, which Jean-Pierre Duhard's (1993b) work shows, would offer some support for this hypothesis. Analyzing these and other Paleolithic figures as a gynecologist, Duhard reports that 68 percent of the Gravettian figures show evidence of pregnancy as opposed to 36 percent from the Magdalenian, although Patricia Rice (1981), who includes cave art in her analysis, infers a much lower pregnancy rate.

Whether or not McDermott's hypothesis is ultimately accepted, it suggests a number of directions that might productively be explored by anthropologists. A great deal more needs to be known about patterns of production and reproduction at specific sites and over time. Marcia-Anne Dobres (1992a) points out that the rich finds of PKG figurines in the domestic context at important Russian sites—under floors and in storage pits and niches—could be particularly rewarding in locating meaningful associational patternings, including perhaps the identification of areas where figurines were made and used. Another area of possible research involves exploring stylistic variations by region to see if they support the suggestion that cultural differences in body inspection routines (under the arm versus over the shoulder) may account for the different appearances of figurines from Italy and southern France and those of other areas. Furthermore, in what ways could systematic ethnographic and ethnohistoric work help elucidate possible uses for these figurines? Assessments of the literature, as well as new field observations, could suggest new ethnographic parallels to explore.

Theoretically, if these figurines were used to improve reproductive success, keep more women alive and healthy, and produce healthier children, then natural selection would have been acting directly on the women who made and/or used them. If these Upper Paleolithic figures are naturalistic, accurate self-representations made by women, then it is reasonable to speculate that they might have had such direct, pragmatic purposes.

NOTES

Acknowledgments. Earlier drafts of this paper were presented at the 91st Annual Meeting of the American Anthropological Association, San Francisco, December 2–6, 1992, and the Annual Meeting of the Midwest Art History Society, Lawrence, Kansas, April 4–6, 1991. Particular appreciation is expressed to Anna Roosevelt and Marcia-Anne Dobres for their thoughtful criticisms regarding a previous draft of the manuscript, to Sue Ellen Jacobs for her encouragement, and to W. Christopher Hodge, Manuel Vargas, H. Clyde Wilson, Carol Mickett, Mary Jo Grinstead Schneider, and Ralph Rowlett for their helpful suggestions.

1. See Collins and Onians 1978; Conkey 1983; and Reinach 1903.

2. See Begouen 1929a, 1929b; Breuil 1952; and Reinach 1903.

3. See Abramova 1967; Burkitt 1934; Pales and de Saint Pereuse 1976; and Ucko and Rosenfeld 1967.

4. See Abramova 1967; Bahn and Vertut 1988; Burkitt 1934; Conkey 1987; Delporte 1979, 1993; Duhard 1993a; Feustel 1967; Gamble 1982; Giedion 1962; Graziosi 1960; Gvozdover 1989; Hadingham 1979; Hancar 1939–40; Jelinek 1975, 1988; Leroi-Gourhan 1968, 1982; Luquet 1930, 1934; Marshack 1972, 1991; McDermott 1985; Pales and de Saint Pereuse 1976; Passemard 1938; Pfeiffer 1982; Praslov 1985; Putnam 1988; Saccasyn-Della Santa 1947; Ucko and Rosenfeld 1967; and White 1986.

5. See Delporte 1979:226, 1993:243 and Dobres 1992a:245.

6. See Dobres 1992a, 1992b; Gvozdover 1989; Hadingham 1979:222; Nelson 1993:51; and Pales and de Saint Pereuse 1976:93.

7. See Gamble 1983; Jochim 1983, 1987; Mellars 1989; and Mellars and Stringer 1989.

8. See Conkey 1983; de Beaune and White 1993; de Sonneville-Bordes 1974; Jochim 1987; and Leroi-Gourhan 1968:498.

REFERENCES CITED

Abramova, Z. A. 1967. Paleolithic Art in the USSR. Arctic Anthropology 4:1–179.

Bahn, Paul G., and Jean Vertut 1988. Images of the Ice Age. New York: Facts on File.

Begouen, H. 1929a. A propos de l'idée de fécondité dans l'iconographie préhistorique. Bulletin de la Sociéte' Préhistorique Française 26:97–199.
1929b. The Magic Origin of Prehistoric Art. Antiquity 3:5–19.

Breuil, Abbé Henri 1952. Four Hundred Centuries of Cave Art. Montignac, France: Centre d'Études et de Documentation Préhistoriques.

Burkitt, M. C. 1934. Some Reflections on the Aurignacian Culture and Its Female Statuettes. Eurasia Septentrionalis Antiqua 9:113–122.

Collins, Desmond, and John Onians 1978. The Origins of Art. Art History 1:1–25.

Conkey, Margaret W. 1983. On the Origins of Paleolithic Art: A Review and Some Critical Thoughts. In The Mousterian Legacy: Human Biocultural Change in the Upper Pleistocene. E. Trinkaus, ed. Pp. 201–227. British Archaeological Reports, International Series 164. Oxford.
1987. New Approaches in the Search for Meaning: A Review of Research in "Paleolithic Art." Journal of Field Archaeology 14:413–430.

de Beaune, Sophie A., and Randall White 1993. Ice Age Lamps. Scientific American 266(3):108–113.

Delporte, Henri 1979. L'image de la femme dans l'art préhistorique. Paris: Picard.
1993. Gravettian Female Figurines: A Regional Survey. In Before Lascaux: The Complex Record of the Early Upper Paleolithic. H. Knecht,
A. Pike-Tay, and R. White, eds. Pp. 243–257. Boca Raton: CRC Press.

Dobres, Marcia-Anne 1992a. Re-considering Venus Figurines: A Feminist-Inspired Re-analysis. In Ancient Images, Ancient Thought: The Archaeology of Ideology. A. Sean Goldsmith, Sandra Garvie, David Selin, and Jeannette Smith, eds. Pp. 245–262. University of Calgary Archaeological Association.
1992b. Representations of Palaeolithic Visual Imagery: Simulacra and Their Alternatives. Kroeber Anthropological Society Papers 73–74:1–25.

Duhard, Jean-Pierre 1993a. Réalisme de l'image féminine Paléolithique. Paris: CNRS Éditions.
1993b. Upper Palaeolithic Figures as a Reflection of Human Morphology and Social Organization. Antiquity 67:83–91.

Feustel, Rudolf 1967. Statuettes féminines Paléolithiques de la République Démocratique Allemande. Bulletin de la Société Préhistorique Française 67:12–16.

Gamble, Clive 1982. Interaction and Alliance in Paleolithic Society. Man 17:92–107.
1983. Culture and Society in the Upper Palaeolithic of Europe. In Hunter-Gatherer Economy in Prehistory: A European Perspective. G. N. Bailey, ed. Pp.201–211. Cambridge: Cambridge University Press.

Giedion, Sigfried 1962. The Eternal Present: The Beginnings of Art. Vol. 6. Bollingen Series, 35. New York: Pantheon Books.

Graziosi, Paolo 1960. Palaeolithic Art. New York: McGraw-Hill.

Gvozdover, M. D. 1989. The Typology of Female Figurines of the Kostenki Paleolithic Culture. Olga Soffer-Bobyshev, ed. Soviet Anthropology and Archeology 27:32–94.

Hadingham, Evan 1979. Secrets of the Ice Age: The World of the Cave Artists. New York: Walker.

Hancar, Franz 1939–40. Zum Problem der Venusstatuetten in eurasiates-chen Jung-palaolithikum. Praehistorische Zeitschrift 30–31:85–156.

Jelinek, Jan 1975. The Pictorial Encyclopedia of the Evolution of Man. London: Hamlyn.
1988. Considérations sur l'art Paléolithique mobilier de l'Europe centrale. L'Anthropologie 92:203–238.

Jochim, Michael A. 1983. Palaeolithic Cave Art in Ecological Perspective. In Hunter-Gatherer Economy in Prehistory, a European Perspective. Geoff Bailey, ed. Pp. 212–219. Cambridge: Cambridge University Press.
1987. Late Pleistocene Refugia in Europe. In The Pleistocene Old World. Olga Soffer, ed. Pp. 317–348. New York: Plenum Press.

Leroi-Gourhan, André 1968. The Art of Prehistoric Man in Western Europe. London: Thames and Hudson.
1982. The Dawn of European Art: An Introduction to Palaeolithic Cave Painting. Cambridge: Cambridge University Press.

Luquet, G.-H. 1930. The Art and Religion of Fossil Man. New Haven: Yale University Press.
1934. Les Vénus Paléolithiques. Journal de Psychologie 31:429–460.

Marshack, Alexander 1972. The Roots of Civilization: The Cognitive Beginnings of Man's First Art, Symbol and Notation. New York: McGraw-Hill.
1991. The Female Image: A Time-Factored Symbol: A Study in Style and Aspects of Im-

age Use in the Upper Paleolithic. Proceedings of the Prehistoric Society 57:17–31.

McDermott, LeRoy D. 1985. Self-Generated Information and Representation of the Human Figure during the European Upper Paleolithic. Ph.D. dissertation, University of Kansas, Lawrence.

1996. Self-Representation in Upper Paleolithic Female Figurines. Current Anthropology 37:227–275.

Mellars, Paul 1989. Major Issues in the Emergence of Modern Humans. Current Anthropology 30:349–385.

Mellars, Paul, and C. B. Stringer, eds. 1989. The Human Revolution: Behavioural and Biological Perspectives on the Origins of Modern Humans. Edinburgh: Edinburgh University Press.

Nelson, S. M. 1993. Diversity of Upper Paleolithic "Venus" Figurines and Archeological Mythology. In Gender in Cross-Cultural Perspective. C. B. Brettel and C. F. Sargent, eds. Pp. 51–58. Englewood Cliffs, NJ: Prentice-Hall.

Pales, Leon, and Marie Tassin de Saint Pereuse 1976. Les gravures de la marche: Les humains. Paris: Ophrys.

Passemard, Luce 1938. Les statuettes féminines Paléolithiques dites Vénus Stéatopyges. Nîmes: Imprimerie Coopérative "La Laborieuse."

Pfeiffer, John E. 1982. The Creative Explosion: An Inquiry into the Origins of Art and Religion. New York: Harper and Row.

Piette, Édouard 1895. La station de Brassempouy et les statuettes humains de la période glyptique. L'Anthropologie 6:129–151.

Praslov, Nicolas D. 1985. L'art du Paléolithique Supérieur à l'est de l'Europe. L'Anthropologie 89:181–192.

Putnam, J. 1988. In Search of Modern Humans. National Geographic 174:439–481.

Reinach, Salomon 1898. Statuette de femme nue découverte dans une des Grottes de Menton. L'Anthropologie 9:26–31.

1903. L'art et la magie: A propos des peintures et des gravures de l'âge du renne. L'Anthropologie 14:257–266.

Rice, Patricia C. 1981. Prehistoric Venuses: Symbols of Motherhood or Womanhood? Journal of Anthropological Research 37(4):402–414.

Roosevelt, Anna C. 1988. Interpreting Certain Female Images in Prehistoric Art. In The Role of Gender in Pre-Columbian Art and Architecture. Virginia E. Miller, ed. Lanham, MD: University Press of America.

Saccasyn-Della Santa, E. 1947. Les figures humaines du Paléolithique Supérieur Eurasiatique. Antwerp: De Sikkel.

Simms, Steven R. 1987. Behavioral Ecology and Hunter-Gatherer Foraging: An Example from the Great Basin. British Archaeological Reports, International Series 381. Oxford.

Sonneville-Bordes, Denise de 1974. The Upper Palaeolithic: c. 33,000–10,000 B.C. In France before the Romans. Stuart Piggott, Glyn Daniel, and Charles McBurney, eds. Pp. 30–60. London: Thames and Hudson.

Ucko, Peter J., and Andree Rosenfeld 1967. Paleolithic Cave Art. New York: McGraw-Hill.

Vandiver, Pamel B., Olga Soffer, Bohuslav Klima, and Jiri Svoboda. 1989. The Origins of Ceramic Technology at Dolni Vestonice, Czechoslovakia. Science 246:1002–1008.

White, Randall 1986. Dark Caves, Bright Visions, Life in Ice Age Europe. Exhibition catalog. New York: American Museum of Natural History.

Lithic Technology and the Hunter-Gatherer Sexual Division of Labor

Kenneth E. Sassaman

South Carolina Institute of Archaeology and Anthropology, University of South Carolina

ABSTRACT

A technological change from formal to expedient core reduction marks the "transition" from mobile to sedentary prehistoric societies in many parts of the world. The phenomenon has often been attributed to changes in the organization of men's activities, particularly hunting. Considering, however, that the change coincides with the adoption of pottery, technology usually attributed to women, an alternative explanation must be considered. From the standpoint of archaeological systematics, the addition of pottery turns our focus away from places where hafted bifaces were discarded toward places where pottery was discarded. The latter are largely domestic contexts: locations at which women, as well as men, employed expedient core technology for a variety of tasks. Thus, the perceived change in core technology reflects the increased visibility of women's activities in the archaeological record. This recognition provides a basis for incorporating gender variables into our interpretations of prehistoric technology and labor organization.

Within American archaeology, studies of lithic technology are burgeoning in new and productive directions. Moving away from the traditional pursuits of chronology and function, lithic analysts are developing method and theory for relating stone tool technology to issues of broad anthropological relevance. These efforts have been particularly important in the study of hunter-gatherers, societies whose traces are often limited to stone tools and the by-products of their manufacture and use. Interpretations of hunter-gatherer settlement-subsistence organization (Amick, 1987; Jeffries, 1982; Raab et al., 1979), mobility (Kelly, 1988; Lurie, 1989; Parry and Kelly, 1987; Shott, 1986), time management (Torrence, 1983), and risk avoidance (Bleed, 1986; Myers, 1989; Torrence, 1989) have all been derived from studies of lithic technology (see Nelson, 1991 for recent review).

A common denominator in this work is that technology variation is referable to environmental variation—the geological occurrence of rock, the seasonality and spatial distribution of food resources, and so forth. Lithic studies that focus on social dimensions of technology are lagging behind the ecological or techno-environmental efforts. With few exceptions (e.g., Cross, 1990), studies addressing social issues—the organization of labor, inequality, control, and the like—concern relatively complex societies (e.g., Clark, 1987; Gero, 1989). The lack of similar approaches to hunter-gatherer technology might be traced to stereotypes about simple societies—that by being egalitarian, all members of the group have access to technology, including the materials and information needed to make and use tools, as well as the products of labor. We simply do not expect much social differentiation in the manufacture, distribution, and consumption of hunter-gatherer stone tools.

While this assumption is itself a subject of debate, there is one dimension of social variation that we accept in hunter-gatherers ethnographically, but do not explicitly incorporate into our models of hunter-gatherers archaeologically. That dimension is the division of labor by sex.

Nearly all recent attempts at modeling hunter-gatherer lithic technology have treated groups as if they were composed of undifferentiated members. The issue I want to address in this article is simply whether or not we can continue to develop models of lithic technology while ignoring the sexual division of labor. It seems apparent that most lithic analysts have implicitly assumed that only men made and used flaked stone tools. However, recent reviews of ethnographic literature render this position untenable (Bird, 1988; Gero, 1991). Moreover, even if women did not make and use stone tools in some prehistoric societies, it is unrealistic to assume that the economic activities of women were not factored into decisions about the production, use, and discard of men's technology.

I want to add to the growing recognition of women's roles in stone tool

From *North American Archaeologist*, Volume 13, Number 3, 1992, pp. 249-262. © 1992 by Baywood Publishing Company, Inc. Reprinted by permission.

production and use by pointing out how attention to gender variables can enhance extant interpretations of technological variation and change. My basic argument is quite simple: if we allow that women and men alike used stone tools, we should anticipate that any differences in the productive activities of men and women involving stone tools would contribute to technological variation in the material records of those activities. Such differences might include spatial patterns of work, work schedules, scale of production, access to raw materials, and discard behavior, to name but a few potential axes of variation. Needless to say, these sorts of variables are central to our perceptions and interpretations of prehistoric society.

I employ as a case study the purported change from formal to expedient core technology that is thought to mark the transition from mobile to sedentary prehistoric societies in many parts of the world. This shift has been recently attributed to changes in the organization of male hunting activities (Torrence, 1989) and to changes in patterns of residential mobility (Parry and Kelly, 1987). I will show how a consideration of gender provides alternative readings of the data.

ARCHAEOLOGICAL TIME-SPACE SYSTEMATICS

To begin, I propose that the perceived transition from formal to expedient core technology is in part shaped by the categories used to order archaeological time. As a foundation for this proposition, let us assume that there was a basic division of labor whereby men hunted game, and women collected plants and small animal resources. Let us also assume that hunting technology was distinct from other lithic technology, and that the technological requirements of hunting game contributed to regularities in tool design that are now useful in dividing archaeological time into meaningful phases or periods. It follows that time-space systematics in archaeology are largely based on continuity and change

in the design of tools used by men; in North America these consist largely of hafted bifaces, both projectiles and other bifacial tools associated with hunting activity.

While hafted bifaces comprise the primary diagnostic artifacts for early North American prehistory, pottery types replace bifaces as the chief time markers during late prehistory. Cross-cultural evidence allows us to safely assume that women made and used most of the pottery in these prehistoric societies (Arnold, 1985:108). It follows, then, that late prehistory is subdivided temporally by variation in technology usually attributed to women.

The significance of this observation becomes apparent when we consider the distinct disposal patterns of hafted bifaces versus pottery, and how these differences predetermine the distribution of associated archaeological remains (Figure 1). Specifically, hafted bifaces used in hunting are discarded at some domestic sites (where tools are replaced; represented in Figure 1 by the intersection of male and female activity loci), and at hunting-related and quarry-related locations used exclusively by men. In contrast, pottery is discarded at most, if not all domestic sites, and perhaps also at some locations where women conducted specialized activities. In short, the archaeological record of the preceramic period consists almost exclusively of locations at which hafted bifaces were discarded, while the ceramic period record consists largely of locations at which pottery was discarded. Inasmuch as the sexual division of labor ensures that these locations are not completely isomorphic, the preceramic and ceramic period archaeological records represent distinct samples of settlement variation. Our disregard for gender roles in this respect renders comparisons of the preceramic and ceramic periods untenable. As a result, observed differences in the records of these periods are interpreted as the result of anything other than gender.

I must interject at this point that the model I propose applies to the hunting of solitary game such as white-tailed deer, but not herd or migratory species

such as bison, reindeer, and caribou. In hunting the latter, entire co-resident groups relocate to kill sites after a successful hunt. Under these circumstances, we should not anticipate spatial separation of men's and women's activities at the intersite level of analysis. Unfortunately, equivalent analogs for the organization of white-tailed deer hunting are not available. I can only assume that some of the intersite assemblage variability observed in the archaeological record of temperate forest hunter-gatherers reflects a spatial (and sexual) dichotomy in the logistical organization of deer hunting. Even if this dichotomy is exaggerated, the addition of pottery to the archaeological record of temperate forest hunter-gatherers assures that we are focused on locations at which women worked. This alone creates a potential bias in the way we perceive functional differences between preceramic and ceramic period sites.

Such gender bias is illustrated in recent models for the apparent shift from formal to expedient core reduction in flaked stone industries. Because it seemingly reflects a degeneration of the art of flintknapping, the change is sometimes referred to as "devolutionary" (Torrence, 1989:58). What is interesting about the change is that it occurs in so many different places across the globe, and at similar junctures in the histories of local prehistoric populations. Two models have been developed to account for these broad patterns. One developed by Torrence (1989) points to changes in the risk avoidance strategies of hunters as societies become increasingly dependent on agricultural production. An alternative articulated by Parry and Kelly (1987) focuses on the diminishing need for portable bifacial cores as the residential mobility of hunter-gatherers decreased through time. Both arguments are logically sound and supported by evidence. However, because the technological change coincides with the adoption of pottery in many parts of the globe, our perceptions of it are partly shaped by a shift in focus from men's roles to women's roles in stone tool production and use. If we include

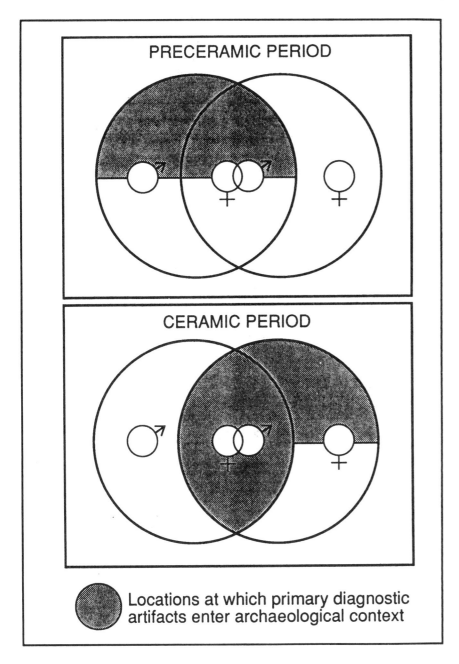

Figure 1. Model of the spatial relationships between the sexual division of labor and distributions of diagnostic artifacts in preceramic and ceramic period contexts.

gies of hunter-gatherers. Of particular relevance is the short-term risk involved in capturing food. The abundance of a food resource at a particular point in space and time is an essential component of such risk, but the greatest risk arises when there is a dependence on mobile prey for food (Torrence, 1989:59). Conversely, relatively little short-term risk is expected when there is dependence on foods that are stationary, particularly plant foods. Torrence concludes that "the percentage of plant versus animal resources in the diet can be taken as a very rough indication of the strength of a potential risk faced by a hunter-gatherer group" (Torrence, 1989:60).

To illustrate the role of risk avoidance in tool design, Torrence draws a contrast between *instruments* on the one hand, and *weapons* and *facilities* on the other. She shows that instruments dominate the tool assemblages of hunter-gatherers whose diets consisted mainly of plant foods, while weapons and facilities characterized the technologies of groups dependent on mobile games (see Torrence, 1983). She further describes how hunting technology consists of complex, formalized tools designed for long-lasting, reliable service (see Bleed, 1986). That is, hunting tools are ready when needed, unlikely to fail, and easy to repair. These properties, Torrence argues, avert much of the uncertainty of hunting by minimizing the chance of technological failure.

In contrast, the instruments of the more vegetarian hunter-gatherers need not be maintainable or reliable because the timing and severity of risk are insignificant. Instruments are thus simple in design and rarely maintained for continuous or long-term use. In this regard, instruments are equivalent to the *expedient* technology described by Lewis Binford (1979).

Torrence (1989) employs this model to explain the shift from complex to simple lithic technology that characterizes archaeological sequences throughout the world. In eastern North America, the change is characterized as a decrease in the use of formal bifaces (weapons), and an increase in

gender in the extant models of this technological change, we not only eliminate this bias, but also introduce a variable that accounts for more of the variation in the design, use, and discard of lithic stone tools cross-culturally.

STONE TOOLS AND RISK AVOIDANCE

Robin Torrence (1989) proposes that cross-cultural variation in design and use of stone tools can be understood as a function of the risk avoidance strate-

the use of informal, expedient tools (instruments). Torrence claims that the technological change coincides with the shift in subsistence from hunting and gathering to food production. As a consequence of this fundamental subsistence change, she argues, the nature of short-term risk changed. Hunting no longer occupied a risk-prone position in the economy, and thus did not require the application of elaborate and costly technology to avert failure.

My criticism of Torrence's model is that it downplays the importance of plant foods in nonagricultural economies, and thus portrays the technological change from formal to expedient core technology as abrupt. To be fair, Torrence confesses to the oversimplification of her model and points out that most assemblages will reflect a mix of technological responses to risk avoidance. The challenge, she suggests, is to determine how particular tool forms, not entire technologies, are subject to different levels and types of risk.

Her challenge offers a point of departure for addressing gender roles. If we can develop predictions about the types of subsistence activities men and women respectively perform and relate these to the timing and severity of risk, we can begin to refer the bridging arguments Torrence makes between risk and tool design to gender-specific technology. We can expect, as Torrence notes, that the risks of hunting mobile game are different than the risks of collecting plant foods, and that tools will be designed and used accordingly. That hunting and gathering were conducted simultaneously through a sexual division of labor suggests that technologies will indeed contain a mix of formal and expedient core technology. The co-occurrence of these distinct core types will depend on local factors such as the organization of land-use, duration of occupation, and site reoccupation, as well as the availability of raw materials. In more general terms, however, the relative contributions that formal and amorphous core technology make to hunter-gatherer technology can be a gauge to

the relative contribution of women to subsistence production.

In eastern North America, bifaces and other formalized core tool forms dominate assemblages dating to the late Pleistocene and early Holocene. Many of these assemblages also contain expedient cores that were used for on-site flake production, and these lend indirect support to the increasing awareness that plant foods comprised a significant portion of Paleoindian and Early Archaic diet (Meltzer and Smith, 1986). Expedient tool technology becomes increasingly important over subsequent millennia, at times eclipsing biface technology. The manufacture of formal unifacial tools likewise abates. Following Torrence, these changes probably reflect the waning need for risk-averting technology, presumable due to the increasing importance of plant foods and, presumably, women's contribution to production. However, hunting did not cease, and, indeed, it probably intensified in areas of high population density. Nor did biface technology disappear altogether. Changes are evident in the design and production of bifaces and, at certain times and places, the production of bifaces and expedient cores converged. It is important to keep in mind that these trends are nonlinear. Because they appear to fluctuate from region to region, and at different rates, we should be able to track changes in the relative contributions of men and women through changes in flaked stone technology. Importantly, the model that Torrence provides, with its emphasis on hunting technology, permits us to view changes in men's technology as a response to changes in the subsistence activities of women, and this indeed is a promising avenue for future research.

STONE TOOLS AND MOBILITY

An alternative to Torrence's model is an argument posed by William Parry and Robert Kelly (1987) on the relationship between flaked stone technology and hunter-gatherer mobility. Building upon the work of several authors (Bin-

ford, 1977, 1979; Goodyear, 1979; Kelly, 1988; Nelson 1987), they look at biface technology as an adaptive solution to the spatial and temporal incongruity between tool production and tool use. This relates not only to the constraints of tool function and tool design, but also to "behavioral variables which mediate the spatial and temporal relations among activity, manufacturing, and raw material loci" (Kelly, 1988: 717). They consider mobility to be the key behavioral factor that mediates these relations. Because there is no necessary relationship between geologic sources of rock and the locations of other resources people require, particularly food and water, stone tools have to be transported (see also Shott, 1986). And, because the functional requirements for stone tools cannot always be predicted, stone tool technology must also be flexible (see also Goodyear, 1979). Thus, mobility simultaneously dictates access to raw material, tool needs, and portability. Throughout prehistoric North America, bifacial core technology was used to meet the organizational contingencies of mobility.

Several authors have commented on the advantages of bifacial core technology to mobile hunter-gatherers (Goodyear, 1979; Kelly, 1988; Nelson, 1987; Parry and Kelly, 1987). For instance, Kelly (1988) suggests that formalized bifacial technology was selected whenever mobile settlement systems included occupations in areas lacking lithic raw material. Under these conditions, bifaces served as portable cores that could be reduced for usable flakes and shaped into formal tools that were flexible, maintainable, and recyclable. As this was a long-term, planned reduction strategy that hinged on one's ability to predictably flake stone, good-quality raw material was obviously a must (Goodyear, 1979). Parenthetically, the need to utilize good quality rock perpetuated the need for biface technology. That is, because sources of good material generally have spotty distributions, a reliance on these sources by mobile peoples created spatial incongruity between locations of procurement and locations of tools use.

Like the dichotomy set up by Torrence, Parry and Kelly (1987) juxtapose bifacial core technology with expedient core technology. They argue that the transition from bifacial to expedient core technology in several parts of North America coincided with the rise of sedentism. Residential stability, they argue, allowed tool makers to stockpile rock for immediate use. They further suggest that the tool-using activities of sedentary people were largely restricted to residential bases, so there was little spatial incongruity between raw material and tool use. It follows that there was little need to make formal bifaces for the anticipated needs of a lithic-poor environment.

In contradiction to the argument posed by Parry and Kelly are numerous examples of expedient core technology throughout eastern North America by mobile hunter-gatherers who also employed formal biface technology. These cases have been attributed by a number of authors to the luxury of local raw material abundance (Bamforth, 1986; Custer, 1987; Johnson, 1986). Here a mixed strategy of biface technology for anticipated needs and expedient technology for immediate needs seems to be the case.

The other problem with Parry and Kelly's argument is that groups that spent long periods of time at bases, and/or reoccupied bases on a seasonal basis continued to practice logistical mobility, ostensibly for hunting game. Thus, the need for bifacial core technology, both as weapons and as cores, continued.

How do the shortcomings of Parry and Kelly's thesis play themselves out in the sexual division of labor? To begin, we need to disentangle the different types of mobility embedded in the seasonal rounds of hunter-gatherers. Parry and Kelly (1987) consider residential mobility—the mobility of entire coresident groups—to be the critical consideration in technological design. Alternatively, I agree with Torrence (1989:62) that the relevant amount of mobility for the transport of tools is the distance travelled by the tool-user.

In this sense, the distances and patterns of mobility of men and women differ. Thus, the sexual division of labor is a variable that potentially accounts for combinations of formal and expedient core technology in terms of the mobility parameters spelled out by Parry and Kelly. Rather than seeing the two technologies as being mutually exclusive, we should expect the use of these to be complementary and interdependent.

In terms of production, for example, bifacial and expedient core technologies varied from being independent to being interdependent. When occupying nonsource areas, portable tools provided all of the raw material needs of stone tool-uses. Insofar as men were responsible for producing bifacial cores, women may have had little direct access to usable flakes, and instead depended on the by-products of men's work. In contrast, at residential bases near source areas, both men and women could have procured, manufactured, and used tools. Bifacial cores still comprised an important male technology for hunting forays into areas with either uncertain or unreliable raw material sources. Under these conditions, the production of bifaces remained distinct from the production of flakes from expedient cores irrespective of the availability of raw material at domestic sites.

The two strategies of tool production converged when bifaces were made from flakes removed from expedient cores at residential sites. This occurred in parts of the Southeast during the Early Woodland, and continued into late prehistory. The strategy can be partly explained by changes in biface technology itself, not the least of which was the adoption of bow and arrow technology in the Late Woodland period. In addition, though, we need to consider how women's uses of flaked stone helped to support the shift from bifacial to expedient core technology within men's technology. In this respect, the celebrated trends toward increased residential stability that mark the Woodland period had immediate and significant ramifications for women's work. As residential mobility became more difficult to maintain, a

variety of other strategies was engaged to cope with the economic stresses that constraints on fissioning imposed. Many, if not most, of the economic changes associated with this trend are implicitly attributed to women: the adoption of pottery and the expansion of the food base to include starchy seeds, shellfishing, and incipient horticulture. As Cheryl Claassen (1991) observes, if we consider all the innovations and changes that we implicitly attribute to women, we have written into prehistory a time and energy crisis for women.

If this depiction of women's labor is correct, and I believe it may be, it goes without saying that women experienced a greater need for technology, including flaked stone technology. I think it is reasonable to propose that women sought raw materials and reduced rock for their own purposes. It is unrealistic to think that women depended solely on the by-products of men's flintknapping. Instead, women had intimate knowledge of the local landscape and were able to locate and exploit sources of rock that otherwise may have been ill-suited for biface manufacture. Women also had ample opportunity and motive for scavenging the lithic refuse of abandoned sites (Sassaman and Brooks, 1990). Both sources of raw material would have been well-suited to the needs of food processing and maintenance activities at residential bases.

Eventually, the roles that formal bifaces played in men's hunting activities were filled by more expedient forms made from flakes, and finally by bow and arrow technology that required only small modified flakes for tipping arrows. This change from long-lived, curated bifaces to short-lived, throwaway bifaces marks a significant change in the technology of men's hunting weapons, but it does not necessarily reflect a major organizational change in the men's activities *per se*. Rather, the change in men's technology may in part reflect the increased contribution of women to raw material procurement and core reduction at domestic sites. The removal of flakes for immediate on-site use and for the manufacture of projectiles for hunting now fell under a single production trajectory. It is likely that women, as well as men, participated in expedient core reduction. In any event, the process was simplified so that the steps of production no longer required spatial, temporal, technological or sexual differentiation.

Whatever became of the ill-fated formal biface? Across Eastern North America well-made formal bifaces do not disappear altogether, but they do seem to be relegated to special functions within society. Ceremonial uses of bifaces, including mortuary offerings, persisted well into late prehistory. It is tempting to suggest that formal bifacial technology remained under the domain of males and became relegated to ceremonial functions as an expression of male control over certain resources and productive processes. This idea might be further substantiated if we allow that within the secular world, flaked stone had developed into an androgynous technology, bearing little to no differentiation along lines of gender. Male rituals involving formal biface technology might therefore embody a form of male resistance to the changing conditions of technology.

SUMMARY AND CONCLUSION

The sexual division of labor that we accept as a basic feature of hunter-gatherer organization obviously contributed to the patterns of technological variation we read in the archaeological record. The extant models for explaining the shift from formal biface to expedient core technology stand to gain from a consideration of gender. The changes in risk avoidance strategies that Torrence identifies, and the effects of sedentism on tool design that Parry and Kelly identify, can be recast to include the sexual division of labor. If we deny women a role in stone tool production and use, a stance that now seems wholly unfounded, then the attention on division of labor may seem extraneous. However, the decisions men make about the design, production, and use of flaked stone tools obviously have some bearing on the

overall opportunities and constraints of the entire economy; so we should expect that changes in men's technology will reflect changes in the organization and success of women's activities.

Thus, models of the organization of hunter-gatherer technology need to be expanded to account for the social units that comprise divisions of labor involving stone tools. Perhaps separate models need to be developed for men and women (cf. Jochim, 1988). But we should also focus attention on variation in the integration or interdependence of male-female tool-using activities. Given the basic dichotomy we have between hunting and gathering, many of the well-developed bridging arguments of technological organization lend themselves to this problem. If we include gender in the models, we may begin to account for variation that cannot be fully explained by tool function, raw material constraints, or group mobility.

The goal, of course, is not to define particular men and women in the record, but to look for variation in gender relations and roles that can help us to model processes of culture changes and continuity. I have no doubt that stone tools hold answers to these issues, and, the lack of ethnographic analogs notwithstanding, significant gains in these areas can be made if serious attention is brought to the subject. This is not an issue of politics; rather it is simply a natural part of the ongoing process of improving our ability to describe and explain human variation. It is unfortunate, though explicable (Wylie, 1989), that the question of gender has taken so long to enter archaeological analysis (especially lithic studies), but it is fundamental to human organization and requires our further consideration.

ACKNOWLEDGMENTS

A shorter version of this article was presented in a plenary session on the Archaeology of Gender at the 1991 Middle Archaeological Conference. My thanks to Joe Dent and Christine Jirikowic for inviting me to participate in the session. Support for this research was provided by the United States Department of Energy-Savannah River Operations Office. Revisions of an earlier draft of this article benefitted from the comments of Mark Brooks, Joan Gero, Bill Green, Alice Kehoe and Keith Stephenson. These colleagues did not agree with all of my claims, so only I, not they, can be held responsible for the final version.

REFERENCES CITED

AMICK, D. S., 1987. *Lithic Raw Material Variability in the Central Duck River Basin: Reflections of Middle and Late Archaic Organizational Strategies,* Report of Investigation 46, Department of Anthropology, University of Tennessee, Knoxville.

ARNOLD, D. E., 1985. *Ceramic Theory and Cultural Process,* Cambridge University Press, Cambridge.

BAMFORTH, DOUGLAS B., 1986. Technological Efficiency and Tool Curation, *American Antiquity, 51,* pp. 38–50.

BINFORD, LEWIS R., 1977. Forty-seven Trips: A Case Study in the Character of Archaeological Formation Processes, in *Stone Tools as Cultural Markers: Change, Evolution and Complexity,* R. V. Wright (ed.), pp. 24–36, Australian Institute of Aboriginal Studies, Canberra.

————, 1979. Organization and Formation Processes: Looking at Curated Technologies, *Journal of Anthropological Research, 35,* pp. 255–273.

BIRD, C. F. M., 1988. Women and the Toolmaker: Evidence of Women's Use and Manufacture of Flaked Stone Tools in Australia and New Guinea, paper presented at the Second New England Conference on Technological Analysis in Australian Archaeology.

BLEED, P., 1986. The Optimal Design of Hunting Weapons: Maintainability or Reliability, *American Antiquity, 51,* pp. 737–747.

CLAASSEN, CHERYL, 1991. Shellfishing and the Shellmound Archaic, in *Engendering Archaeology: Women in Prehistory,* J. M. Gero and M. W. Conkey (eds.) pp. 276–300, Blackwell, Cambridge.

CLARK, J. E., 1987. Politics, Prismatic Blades, and Mesoamerican Civilization, in *The Organization of Core Technology,* J. K. Johnson and C. A. Morrow (eds.), pp. 259–284, Westview Press, Boulder, Colorado.

CROSS, J. R., 1990. *Craft Specialization in Nonstratified Society: An Example from the Late Archaic in the Northeast,* Ph. D. dissertation, Department of Anthropology, University of Massachusetts, Amherst.

CUSTER, JAY F., 1987. Core Technology at the Hawthorne Site, New Castle County, Delaware: A Late Archaic Hunting Camp, in *The Organization of Core Technology,* J. K. Johnson and C. A. Morrow (eds.), pp. 45–62, Westview Press, Boulder, Colorado.

GERO, J. M., 1989. Assessing Social Information in Material Objects: How Well Do Lithics Measure Up?, in *Time, Energy and Stone Tools,* R. Torrence (ed.), pp. 92–105, Cambridge University Press, Cambridge.

_____, 1991. Genderlithics: Women in Stone Tool Production, in *Engendering Archaeology: Women in Prehistory*, J. M. Gero and M. W. Conkey (eds.), pp. 163–193, Blackwell, Cambridge.

GOODYEAR, ALBERT C., 1979. *A Hypothesis for the Use of Cryptocrystalline Raw Materials Among Paleo-Indian Groups in North America*, Research Manuscript Series 165, South Carolina Institute of Archaeology and Anthropology, University of South Carolina, Columbia.

JEFFRIES, R. W., 1982. Debitage as an Indicator of Intraregional Activity Diversity in Northwest Georgia, *Midcontinental Journal of Archaeology, 7*, pp. 94–132.

JOCHIM, M. A., 1988. Optimal Foraging and the Division of Labor, *American Anthropologist, 90*, pp. 130–136.

JOHNSON, JAY K., 1986. Amorphous Core Technologies in the Midsouth, *Midcontinental Journal of Archaeology, 11*, pp. 135–151.

KELLY, ROBERT L., 1988. The Three Sides of a Biface, *American Antiquity, 53*, pp. 717–731.

LURIE, R., 1989. Lithic Technology and Mobility Strategies: The Koster Site Middle Archaic, in *Time, Energy and Stone Tools*, R. Torrence (ed.), pp. 46–56, Cambridge University Press, Cambridge.

MELTZER, DAVID J. and B. D. SMITH, 1986. Paleoindian and Early Archaic Subsistence Strategies in Eastern North America, in *Foraging, Collecting and Harvesting: Archaic Period Subsistence and Settlement in the Eastern Woodlands*, S. W. Neusius (ed.), pp. 3–31, Occasional Papers 6, Center for Archaeological Investigations, Southern Illinois University, Carbondale.

MYERS, A., 1989. Reliable and Maintainable Technological Strategies in the Mesolithic of Mainland Britain, in *Time, Energy and Stone Tools*, R. Torrence (ed.), pp. 78–91, Cambridge University Press, Cambridge.

NELSON, M. C., 1987. The Role of Biface Technology in Adaptive Planning, paper presented at the 27th Annual Meeting of the Northeastern Anthropological Association, Amherst, Massachusetts.

_____, 1991. The Study of Technological Organization, in *Archaeological Method and Theory*, Vol. 3, M. B. Schiffer (ed.), pp. 57–100, University of Arizona Press, Tucson.

PARRY, WILLIAM J. and ROBERT L. KELLY, 1987. Expedient Core Technology and Sedentism, in *The Organization of Core Technology*, J. K. Johnson and C. A. Morrow (eds.), pp. 285–304, Westview Press, Boulder, Colorado.

RABB, L. MARK, R. F. CANDE and D. W. STAHLE, 1979. Debitage Graphs and Archaic Settlement Patterns, *Midcontinental Journal of Archaeology, 4*, pp. 167–182.

SASSAMAN, KENNETH E. and MARK J. BROOKS, 1990. Cultural Quarries: Scavenging and Recycling Lithic Refuse in the Southeast, paper presented at the Southeastern Archaeological Conference, Mobile, Alabama.

SHOTT, M. J., 1986. Technological Organization and Settlement Mobility: An Ethnographic Examination, *Journal of Anthropological Research, 42*, pp. 15–52.

TORRENCE, ROBIN, 1983. Time-Budgeting and Hunter-Gatherer Technology, in *Hunter-Gatherer Economy in Prehistory: A European Perspective*, G. Bailey (ed.), pp. 11–22, Cambridge University Press, Cambridge.

_____, 1989. Re-tooling: Towards a Behavioral Theory of Stone Tools, in *Time, Energy and Stone Tools*, R. Torrence (ed.), pp. 57–66, Cambridge University Press, Cambridge.

WYLIE, A., 1989. Feminist Critiques and Archaeological Challenges, paper presented at the CHACMOOL Conference, Calgary.

Denizens of the Desert

Geophysical imaging maps subterranean settlements in the hard hillsides of Israel's Negev Desert.

Thomas E. Levy, Alan J. Witten, and David Alon

Thomas E. Levy is Professor of Anthropology and Judaic Studies at the University of California, San Diego. Alan J. Witten is the Frank A. and Henrietta E. Schulz Professor of Geophysics at the University of Oklahoma, Norman. David Alon is a researcher at the Israel Antiquities Authority, Jerusalem. The

Shiqmim excavation is a joint project of the University of California, San Diego, and the Hebrew Union College–Jewish Institute of Religion (HUC-JIR), Jerusalem. The authors would like to acknowledge the assistance of the U.S. Department of Energy; the U.S. Environmental Protection Agency (EPA);

Oak Ridge National Laboratory, Tennessee; Admiral James Watkins, former U.S. Secretary of Energy; Professor Yuval Ne'eman, former Minister of Science and Technology, Jerusalem; and Professor A. Biran, director of the Nelson Glueck School of Biblical Archaeology (NGSBA) of the HUC-JIR. Financial support came from the National Endowment for the Humanities, the National Geographic Society, the C. Paul Johnson Family Charitable Foundation, and the Samuel H. Kress Foundation.

(THOMAS E. LEVY)

Underground rooms at Shiqmim, Israel, were inhabited ca. 4500–4200 B.C. and later used for grain storage.

Once one of the world's most inhospitable places, Israel's Negev Desert stretches more than 100 miles south from the modern city of Beersheva to the Gulf of Eilat. Today, thanks to modern methods of irrigation, it is dotted with farms and settlements. Some 6,500 years ago, at the beginning of the Chalcolithic period when people settled and farmed here, rainfall was more plentiful and water seems to have run year-round in some streams. Despite a milder climate, these early settlers chose to live underground, digging vast complexes of chambers and connecting tunnels into the hillsides bordering the streams. These chambers have puzzled scholars ever since they were first discovered in 1951 (by Israeli archaeologist and coauthor David Alon) and excavated by Jean Perrot, a French prehistorian. Perrot dug at Tel Abu Matar and Bir es-Safadi, two sites with underground and aboveground settle-

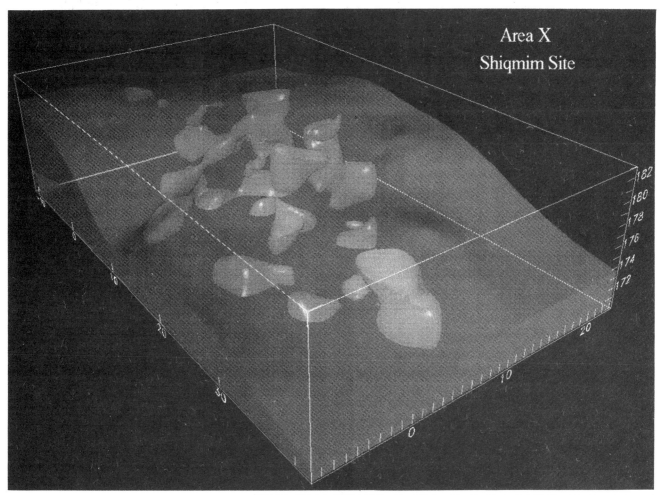

(COURTESY ALAN J. WITTEN, OAK RIDGE NATIONAL
LABORATORY)

Three-dimensional computer map of some of Shiqmim's tunnels and chambers, above, was created before the site was excavated, using Geophysical Diffraction Tomography, which generates images from sound waves bounced off underground features. At right is an artist's reconstruction of several of the site's rooms.

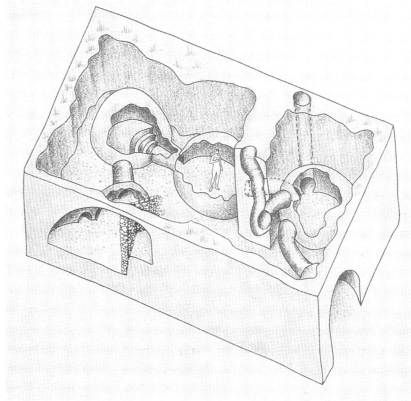

(BETTE DUKE AFTER CARL MEHLER)

2. PROBLEM-ORIENTED ARCHAEOLOGY

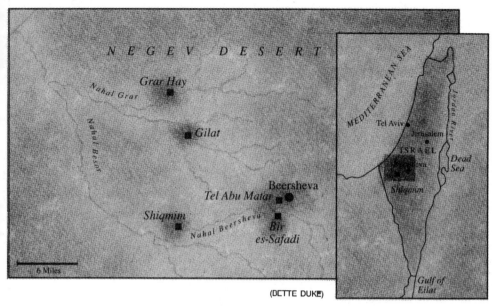

(BETTE DUKE)

(THOMAS E. LEVY)

Map indicates fifth-millennium B.C. sites, and the modern city of Beersheva, in Israel's Negev Desert. Students set up geophones to record surface vibrations caused by sound waves reflected by underground features. The vibrations were then analyzed with computers, which generated three-dimensional images of Shiqmim's underground complexes.

ments on the Nahal Beersheva *(Nahal* is a Hebrew word meaning a stream that only runs in the winter rainy season). He concluded that the underground rooms predated the aboveground villages and allowed settlers to stay cool in a hot desert environment. Isaac Gilead of Ben Gurion University, who excavated in the mid-1980s at Grar Hay in the Grar Valley, 14 miles north of the Nahal Beersheva, believed they were built by inhabitants of aboveground villages to store grains such as wheat and barley.

Since 1977 we have been investigating Shiqmim, a 24-acre site on the Na-

hal Beersheva 11 miles west of Perrot's sites. During the past three years we have supplemented traditional excavation with a new mapping technique known as Geophysical Diffraction Tomography, which allows us to map underground features such as tunnels and chambers by generating sound waves that help produce digital pictures of underground anomalies. Our new data are forcing us to rethink old ideas about how the subterranean rooms were used and their relationship to surface villages. Perrot was partly right: people did live in the earliest underground complexes before the aboveground villages were

built. But he was wrong about why they lived there. We believe these people dug into the hillsides not to keep cool, but because initially there was no floodplain on which to build settlements. There is also evidence that they may have used these subterranean chambers to defend themselves against warring rival villages. Eventually a floodplain developed, beginning around 4200 B.C., about the time that the underground chambers were abandoned as dwellings in favor of surface villages. The old tunnels and chambers were reused and new ones dug, but now primarily to store barley and wheat.

Farmers first settled the lower Jordan Valley and the fertile areas north of the Negev around 8000 B.C., but only between ca. 4500 and 4300 B.C. did they penetrate the more arid inland region. These people cultivated barley, wheat, and lentils, and raised cattle, goats, and sheep. In areas bordering the more humid coastal plain, some villages raised pigs. They also made the earliest metal tools in the Levant, beautifully carved bowls of imported basalt, and shell jewelry with incised geometrical designs. It was these farmers who first dug tunnels and chambers into the hard hillside soils of the desert. Some underground rooms were as large as 13 by 26 feet and eight feet high. Grinding stones, pottery vessels still in their earthen floor supports, and preserved barley grains indicate that at least some rooms were used for food storage and processing.

In 1977, while making a foot survey along the Nahal Beersheva and lower Nahal Besor, we found Shiqmim, a site untouched by developers, the military, and archaeologists. Two years later we began excavating there and discovered the well-preserved stone foundations of mud-brick buildings. We also found cast copper tools, including axes, adzes, chisels, and awls, and copper ceremonial items, such as mace heads and a one-foot-long scepter decorated with elaborate spiral motifs. In 1987, with support from the National Endowment for the Humanities, we began exploring the earliest occupation at the site. In the side walls of trenches more than 20 feet deep we could see dark stains, the outlines of subterranean tunnels, rooms, and silos, indicating that Shiqmim's prehistoric settlers had, like the early settlers at Tel Abu Matar and Bir es-Safadi, dug their homes into the desert hills. In 1989 we discovered a vertical tunnel with hand and foot holds leading from the site surface into a subterranean doorway blocked by a stone portal. After removing the blocking stone and large quantities of fill, we found ourselves in a ten-by-15-foot room. By the end of the season we had found a complex of ten interconnected rooms with artifacts such as a carefully carved ivory vial and the pear-shaped polished hematite heads of several maces. Some rooms had hearths and small grain-storage pits, along with cooking vessels, food debris, and stone tools, confirming Perrot's thesis that the earliest settlers had once lived there. We also verified Perrot's observation that the open-air villages were built atop older underground complexes.

New data about the Nahal Beersheva's ancient climate are casting doubt on Perrot's contention that people dug the underground complexes to keep cool. By analyzing geological deposits, Paul Goldberg of Boston University and his environmental studies colleagues found that the northern Negev was significantly more humid between ca. 4500 and 4300 B.C., having at least 12 inches of rainfall per year compared to eight now. Fragments of ancient floodplains preserved at the edge of the modern channel indicate that the stream flowed more rapidly at the beginning of the Chalcolithic, which would have discouraged the earliest inhabitants from building houses too close to the water lest they be washed away. Their alternative was to dig their homes into the earthen hills at the edges of the stream. The aboveground village at Shiqmim was built only after ca. 4300 B.C., when a rich, 20-mile-long floodplain had developed in the Beersheva Valley.

The earliest subterranean complexes may also have been used for defense during raids by neighboring villages. Historical sources document the Jews' use of underground refuges during the A.D. 132–135 revolt against Roman rule, and in the 1950s British anthropologist Henry A. Fosbrooke recorded at least four Tanzanian tribes that still used subterranean defensive complexes strikingly similar to those of Chalcolithic Palestine. Earlier scholars had described the late fifth and fourth millennia B.C. in Israel as a period during which many small villages existed peacefully but independently. Now, after more than 60 years of research in the Negev, we see increasing evidence of warfare. Ash and burnt and destroyed buildings dating ca. 4300–4200 B.C. have been unearthed at Gilat, some ten miles north of Shiqmim, suggesting violent conflict. Several underground rooms at Shiqmim were filled with ash radiocarbon-dated to ca. 4300–4000 B.C. Stone and copper mace heads have been found at many Chalcolithic archaeological sites throughout Israel and Jordan, including Shiqmim, and early Egyptian art shows these objects being used in combat. Perhaps larger settlements ruled the smaller ones, and the roots of Chalcolithic warfare lay in disputes between emerging chiefdoms.

One of the factors that made Shiqmim such a well-preserved site has also made it difficult to excavate. After the 1948 Israeli War of Independence, the area became part of a military reservation, and each season of fieldwork must be coordinated with activities of the Israel Defense Forces (IDF). With many acres occupied by the IDF, we could not be sure of permission to excavate. In 1992, to locate and map subterranean complexes without having to

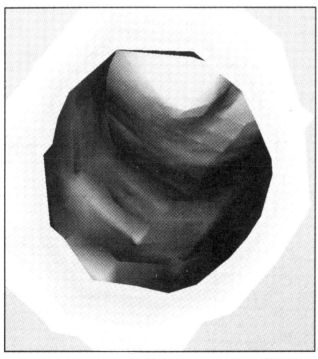

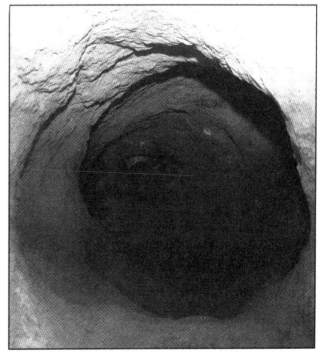

At left, archaeologists computer excavated a tunnel, located and mapped with GDT. At right is a similar tunnel after excavation.

dig, we decided to use GDT. Developed between 1984 and 1987 (by coauthor Alan J. Witten) at the Oak Ridge National Laboratory in Tennessee, GDT is based on an idea by Anthony Devaney, a professor of electrical engineering at Northeastern University in Boston. Its first successful use was the 1987–1988 imaging of the skeleton of a seismosaurus, the largest known dinosaur, in the New Mexico desert. Between 1989 and 1992 it was used to detect tunnels beneath the demilitarized zone separating North and South Korea. In 1992 and 1993 the Environmental Protection Agency used GDT to find buried drums of toxic waste in the clean-up of two dump sites in Michigan and Minnesota.

Shiqmim was the first archaeological application of GDT. There, beginning in 1992, we used a sledgehammer to strike a metal plate, generating sound waves that reflected off subsurface features. We recorded the reflections and made digital pictures of the features that we then combined to create a three-dimensional model. We used two kinds of receivers to record the reflected sound waves: hydrophones and geophones. Hydrophones record sound waves in vertical, water-filled bore holes drilled to depths of more than 30 feet. Geophones are placed on the surface and measure vibrations caused by sound waves. The data from these receivers were recorded on a laptop computer, where two-dimensional vertical slices, or transects, of subsurface features were reconstructed. These slices were transferred to a more powerful Silicon Graphics workstation. There, computer programmer Paul White, from Dynamic Graphics of Alameda, California, used a software package known as EarthVision to generate three-dimensional models from the two-dimensional slices. With EarthVision's ability to rotate, pan, zoom, and strip away horizontal or vertical layers of an image, it was possible to computer excavate portions of subterranean features located and mapped with GDT.

Traditional excavation methods had already revealed subterranean tunnels and rooms in the western portion of the ancient village, but we believed that they were more widespread. In 1993, to test our hypothesis, we used GDT to image a hilltop one-quarter mile east of the old excavations. We began by drilling a series of 23-foot-deep bore holes for hydrophones. Fragments of Chalcolithic artifacts found in the bore holes at depths of 16 to 20 feet suggested that we were above something. Unfortunately, high winds destroyed the cables connecting the hydrophones to the computer, so we switched to geophones, with which we made 14 transects, six atop the hill and eight on the slope leading down to the nahal. From these, we reconstructed images of what lay beneath the hilltop. We saw contours of a tunnel leading to a subterranean room nearby—a tunnel and room whose existence we later confirmed by excavation. As we mapped the rest of the hilltop, we discovered that it was honeycombed with other chambers. GDT imaging also revealed a number of hitherto unknown underground features, including a 40-foot-long tunnel leading from a room in one complex, which we labeled Subterranean Room 8, to a chamber in another complex that measured barely five feet wide and six and one-half deep. Later excavations in Room 8 uncovered a large grain-storage silo and an alcove with a grinding stone; charcoal found here was carbon-dated between ca. 4200 and 4000 B.C. That the entrance to the tunnel from Room 8 is too small for a human, even a child, may indicate that this was a secret tunnel, never used, but constructed as an emergency entrance to the silo in time of need.

Hundreds of underground rooms—far more than we ever suspected—still await excavation.

Our survey of Shiqmim has demonstrated the archaeological value of GDT. We have shown that hundreds of underground rooms, far more than we ever suspected, still await excavation. Many fascinating questions remain. Are the tunnels and subterranean chambers more extensive than those at Perrot's sites? How many of Shiqmim's chambers were lived in during the site's early occupation between ca. 4500 and 4300 B.C.? Which ones were dug only later to store grain for a flourishing aboveground village? Only traditional excavation can fully address such questions, but GDT has given us a head start without ever touching trowel to dirt.

FURTHER READING

Recommended are A. Ben-Tor, ed., *The Archaeology of Ancient Israel* (New Haven: Yale University Press, 1992); T. E. Levy, ed., *The Archaeology of Society in the Holy Land* (New York: Facts On File, 1995); A. Mazar, *Archaeology of the Land of the Bible, 10,000–586 BCE* (New York: Doubleday, 1990); A. J. Witten, et al., "Geophysical Diffraction Tomography: New Views on the Shiqmim Prehistoric Subterranean Village Site (Israel)" *Geoarchaeology* 10 (1995), pp. 97–118.

Find Suggests Weaving Preceded Settled Life

Discovery pushes date of earliest cloth back 7,000 years, to 27,000 years ago.

Brenda Fowler

MINNEAPOLIS

Some 27,000 years ago, an innovative group of hunters and gatherers were in the habit of setting up their summer base camps near a river along the Pavlov Hills in what is now the southeastern Czech Republic. They mixed the fine soil with water and molded it into human and animal figurines and fired them, creating the oldest known fired ceramics. They took the two-and-a-half-million-year-old technology of flaking stone tools a step further by grinding them into smoothly polished pendants and rings, the earliest known examples of ground stone technology in Europe.

And now, at a meeting here last week of the Society for American Archeology, scientists announced that this same group, contemporaries of the earliest cave painters of France and northern Spain, has left the oldest evidence of weaving in the world. The site has yielded clay fragments bearing impressions of textiles or basketry, which according to Dr. James M. Adovasio of Mercyhurst College in Erie, Pa., and Dr. Olga Soffer of the University of Illinois at Urbana, push back the known origin of these technologies at least 7,000 years, to 27,000 years ago.

It also validates a suggestion long offered by some archeologists that the origin of textile technology by far predates the Neolithic period of plant and animal domestication to which it had traditionally been assigned. Archeologists tended to believe that people did not weave until they abandoned the migratory hunting and gathering way of life and settled into permanent agricultural villages with domesticated plants and animals, a process that was getting under way in many parts of the world by around 8000 B.C. and is known as the Neolithic. Once they were sedentary, the story went, they could develop such technologies as ceramics and weaving.

"I think this will really blow the socks off the Neolithic people because they always think they've got the first of everything," Dr. Soffer said in an interview. "We have this association of fabric and ceramics and ground stone technology with the Neolithic although we've known about ceramics from these people at Pavlov for a while, but it was written in Czech or German and it didn't make an impact."

Some scholars of the Upper Paleolithic, which in that part of the world stretches from about 40,000 to 12,000 years ago, had predicted that textiles might have been around at that time. "It's not very unexpected but it's very important," said Dr. Anthony Marks, an archeologist at Southern Methodist University in Dallas.

Textile specialists, especially, were encouraged by the discovery.

"It indicates how important textile structures are," said Dr. John Peter Wild, an archeologist at the University of Manchester in England. "You're way ahead of metals. The only technologies you have to compare it with in sheer brilliance of execution are stone implements. This is the organic technology that matches it."

Previously, the earliest known basketry dated to no earlier than around 13,000 years ago and the oldest piece of woven cloth was a 9,000-year-old specimen from Cayonu in southern Turkey. The oldest known twisted fibers, which could have been woven into basketry or textiles, were found in Israel and date to about 19,300 years ago.

Because baskets and textiles are made of organic materials, they perish rapidly once deposited, Dr. Adovasio said in an interview. Not surprisingly, the absence of hard evidence for textiles in the Paleolithic molded the theories on the origins and development of weaving technology.

People invented textiles in the hunter-gatherer stage of development.

The evidence presented last week consists of four small fragments of fired clay bearing negative impressions of a textile or finely twined basket, Dr. Soffer said. Along with hundreds of thousands of other artifacts at the rich site, they were excavated in 1954 by Dr. Bohuslav Klima, a retired Moravian archeologist. In the summer of 1990, Dr. Soffer, sorting through about 3,000 clay fragments in an effort to categorize them stylistically, noticed four pieces, about the size of a quarter, with markings on their concave sides.

She photographed them, with the notation "plant fibers?" and the next year showed them to her colleague, Dr. Adovasio, who, she said, went "absolutely ballistic."

Three radiocarbon dates of ashes at the site ranged from 24,870 to 26,980 years ago, so the pieces could not have come from any other layers deposited later.

Analyzing magnified, high resolution photographs of the fragments, Dr. Adovasio determined that two fragments bore two different weaves and two bore indistinct parallel impressions that might be from warps, the vertical threads of a weave. He could see the alignment of the plant fibrils in the photographs so he knew the fibers were made of plant material, or bast, and not sinew, which can also be woven. Among the plants that could have provided bast were the yew and alder trees or the milkweed and nettle, the researchers said.

The archeologists did not know whether the impressions were made intentionally or accidentally. Many of the fragments were found in ash deposits. Analysis of all four showed that they had been fired at 600 to 800 degrees Fahrenheit, which is consistent with a simple kiln or a bonfire, or even a dwelling burning down, Dr. Soffer said. One possibility is that the woven item was unintentionally pressed into wet clay near a hearth—perhaps by walking on it—and subsequently fired.

Because the fragments are so small and no selvage, or defined edge, is apparent on them, Dr. Adovasio could not determine what they came from. He said the mesh would have been similar to that in a potato sack and might have come from a bag, mat, clothing or a basket. While it would have been possible to make the pieces without some sort of loom, it would

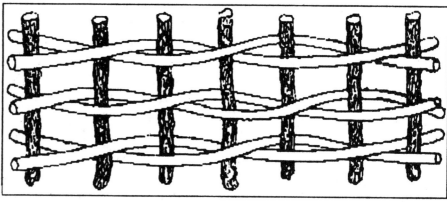

Dr. J. M. Adovasio

One clay impression of early weaving from Pavlov Hills site shows pattern above, called open diagonal twining, S-twist weft. Diagram depicts rigid vertical warp threads; specimen had flexible warps.

have been far easier using one, he said, even if that meant only tying one end of the warp around a tree and the other around one's waist.

"This demonstrates an amazing investment of energy," he said.

Dr. Elizabeth J. W. Barber, a prehistoric textile scholar at Occidental College in Los Angeles, noted that plain, or true weave, involved passing a weft, or horizontal, thread over one warp thread, under the next warp thread, over the next and so on. If a nonflexible stick is woven through the warp like this, then the process can be mechanized halfway. Raising the stick lifts up every other thread of the warp (or whichever warp threads are required for the desired weave) and the weft thread can be speedily pulled through. For the following pass, the position of the separated warp threads must be reversed and that is where a heddle, which individually holds the warp threads of the second group and attaches them to a bar, comes in.

The type of weave in the Pavlov clay fragments is "twining"; though it too can produce a cloth, it cannot be mechanized because the parallel weft threads cross each other. Dr. Barber said twining produced a more stable weave because the weft threads twisted around each other and prevented sliding.

"When you see them switching from twining over to the true weave or plain weave by around 7000 B.C., then they've figured out mechanization," she said. "They've given up stability of weave for speed of production."

Dr. Adovasio noted that twining itself was already a relatively advanced form of weaving technology. He suggested twining might even be as much as 40,000 years old.

"If they're making this, then they're making cordage," said David Hyland, an archeologist at Gannon University in Erie, Pa. Cordage, essentially plant fibers twisted together, includes string and rope.

"And if they can make this, they can make anything in the way of a net, trap or snare," said Dr. Adovasio, who believes that because of the scarcity of evidence, prehistorians had underestimated the importance of woven materials in early peoples' lives. Conversely, he said, because of their relative abundance, stone tools have been overemphasized in archeologists' interpretations of prehistoric economies.

"I don't buy a lot of the gender studies stuff," began Dr. Adovasio.

"But mostly men have done the analysis of Paleolithic sites and they have in their minds the macho hunter of extinct megafauna. Guys who hunt woolly mammoths are not supposed to be making these."

The model of the Paleolithic men going off with spears to hunt while the women stayed home and gathered plants around the camp may be too simple, he said.

"Maybe they killed one mammoth every 10 years and never stopped talking about it," Dr. Soffer said.

At the Pavlov and nearby Dolni Vestonice sites, for example, Dr.

Klima unearthed far more bones of smaller animals than of mammoths. While the former may have been hunted with spears, it is more likely that nets were used to capture small animals like rabbits, the archeologists said.

"This tool,' noted Dr. Hyland, of cloth, "represents a much greater level of success where used for hunting than lithic tools."

Dr. Adovasio, who has been working with textiles for more than 25 years, said he hoped the discovery would inspire archeologists to learn more about how textiles and basketry decayed and to pay more attention to the possibility that textiles or their impressions are preserved on sites.

One mystery is what became of the apparently advanced technologies of these Central European hunters and gatherers after 22,000 years ago, when, as the weather gradually turned colder, the archeological record of their presence in the Pavlov Hills suddenly ceased.

"You've got the huge Scandinavian ice sheet coming down from the north and glaciers coming from the Alps and you get this no-man's land and people get out of there," Dr. Soffer said.

She suspects that some went east and some southest. But except for a few random fired ceramics and bits of net or cord in eastern Europe, the technologies themselves remain silent for the next 7,000 to 10,000 years. When they resurface, the skills the Pavlov people employed so fancifully have been converted to practical purpose. The technique of stone grinding, instead of being used in decorative items alone, is now applied to making hoes and axes. Fired clay turns up not in figurines but in cooking and storage vessels.

"It had never dawned on these people that they could make a pot," Dr. Soffer noted.

Textiles and basketry, too, anchor themselves firmly into the technological landscape.

"It's like who invented the first flying machine? Leonardo da Vinci," Dr. Soffer said. "But Boeing didn't start making them until this century. There has to be a social and economic context for new technology. If you don't have the context, then it won't really go anywhere."

Thailand's Good Mound

*Twenty generations of burials provide an intimate portrait of
a Stone Age village*

Charles Higham and Rachanie Thosarat

About 650 feet wide and 40 feet high, Khok Phanom Di, "the good mound," stands out on the flat flood plain of Thailand's Bang Pakong River. Unoccupied in living memory except for a Buddhist temple, the site passed as a natural hill until a bulldozer, cutting a new path to the top, revealed a deep sequence of archeological deposits. These contained abundant remains of shellfish adapted to coastal mud flats, although nowadays the sea lies fourteen miles to the west. Damrongkiadt Noksakul, a staff member of the local teachers' college, excavated a small test square, which we visited in 1981. Peering into the inky gloom, we saw layer upon layer of hearths, ash, and discarded shellfish remains stretching down twenty-eight feet. This preliminary excavation had yielded eleven human burials, numerous pottery shards, abundant remains of rice, and shells from species of mollusks and crustaceans adapted to life in an estuary and along the seashore.

The site intrigued us because little was known of prehistoric settlements in Thailand so close to the sea. Most archeological work on early groups had been done along small tributary streams in the interior. Yet the wealth of resources on the coast or along major rivers probably played an important role in the spread of rice cultivation and in making mainland Southeast

Asia the home of some of the world's great early civilizations. The best known of these civilizations had as its court center Angkor (in present-day Cambodia), a site that represented heaven in stone and incorporated vast temple mausoleums for its deified lords.

Toward the end of 1984, we returned to Khok Phanom Di with an archeological team to excavate a square measuring one hundred square meters, or about 1,075 square feet. We had no illusions about the ease of our undertaking, which eventually involved the removal of 28,000 cubic feet of prehistoric material. We chose this single large square, however, in hopes of discovering the spatial arrangement of ancient life—perhaps house plans, the layout of a cemetery, or distinct areas for different activities. Our research was designed to find out about the way of life of the occupants and how their environment may have changed over the generations.

We erected a steel roof to shelter the square from rain and sun and arranged for electrical wiring. Water was piped in to allow us to clean the finds before sorting and packing them. Jill Thompson, a member of the team, set up a large metal tank to float plant remains out of the archeological deposits. Brian Vincent processed much of the pottery as it was recovered, and Bernard Maloney was on hand to analyze the remains of pollen, a key to understanding the changing environment in the vicinity of the site. After seven months of digging, we reached a com-

pacted, sandy layer at a depth of about twenty-one feet. At last, we were able to stand on the river flood plain that was first occupied in antiquity. The Thai workers who were helping us—and who had shown as much interest in our discoveries as we did—were equally relieved to reach bottom.

In our square—still only a fraction of the total mound—we encountered part of a cemetery. We also observed that nearer the edge of the mound, the road-cut exposed layers of debris where prehistoric pots had been fired. The remains of houses probably lay elsewhere. In the earliest layers of the excavated material, we found extensive spreads of ash and much charcoal, along with pottery shards and blunted, well-used stone adz heads. Some of the pottery shards were encrusted with marine barnacles; judging from the species of ostracods and foraminifers, the earliest inhabitants established their settlement on a sheltered estuary of a major river near its entrance to the open sea. Dating of the charcoal showed that these early deposits were about 4,000 years old.

To determine the environment prior to the site's occupation, Bernard Maloney removed a series of cores from the natural sediments that surround the site (the base of the site itself was too hard for our equipment to penetrate). Beneath the present day rice fields he found about eighteen feet of stiff, blue clay that had been laid down under a shallow sea. The clay contained microscopic fragments of charcoal and the

The inhabitants of ancient Khok Phanom Di, map below, exploited many resources, including rice, which was originally cultivated in China's Yangtze Valley.

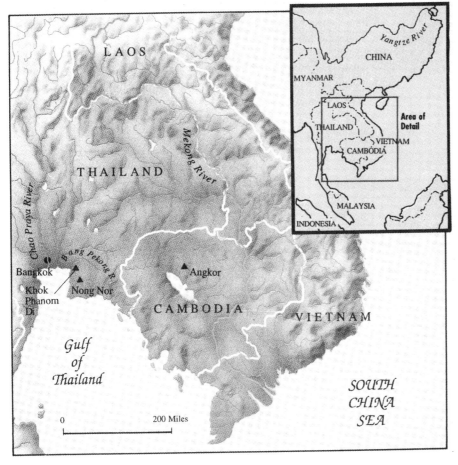

we have found tell us that they set nets in the estuary for the many species of passing fish. They also took their boats out to coastal waters to fish by line, using barbed fishhooks made of bone, and cultivated rice in the freshwater swamps behind the coastal mangrove belt. These ideal conditions favored permanent settlement, and during the ensuing years, from 4,000 until 3,500 years ago, twenty-one feet of cultural debris built up.

The inhabitants of Khok Phanom Di were in a good position to trade upriver with people inhabiting the interior and along the coast with other maritime settlements. A sedentary way of life means that trading partners know where to find one another. It permits the accumulation of weighty personal possessions and makes the construction of buildings worthwhile. And not least, it opens up the possibility of an expanding population. Where mobility is the rule, births need to be widely spaced, or there will be too many young children to carry. Permanence removes this constraint, and women can reduce the interval between pregnancies. The need to feed more mouths within such sedentary communities may help explain the rapid spread of agriculture that took place in many different parts of the world beginning 12,000 years ago.

Long-term occupation also allows for the maintenance of a cemetery as a resting place for dead ancestors. Such was the custom at Khok Phanom Di, where we found about twenty generations of burials (assuming an average interval of twenty-five years between generations). In preliterate times, the continuing presence of the ancestors may have helped signify the ownership of local land and resources.

Covered in red ocher and wrapped in shrouds fashioned from beaten bark cloth or sheets of asbestos fiber, the dead were interred face-up with their heads to the east. The oldest level of burials in the excavated part of the cemetery included only six interments, and they were very simple. Only one contained a durable grave offering—a necklace of twelve shell beads. Thereafter, burials accumulated steadily, and

remains of pollen. By dating samples of the charcoal taken at different levels in the cores, he was able to estimate that the clay was deposited between 8,000 and 4,000 years ago. And by identifying and counting the pollen grains in samples taken at intervals throughout the deposit, Maloney was also able to get a picture of the vegetation.

Mangrove pollen dominated, reinforcing other evidence that the area was near the seashore. At times, however, the quantity of charcoal rose spectacularly and the pollen of grasses and some plants that flourish in rice fields today became more prominent. Such episodes occurred sporadically beginning 7,800 years ago. Several explanations are possible: natural forest fires, burn-offs by local hunters and gatherers, and the clearing of land by rice cultivators. Possibly, people frequented the area long before they settled at Khok Phanom Di itself about 4,000 years ago. A modern fish pond dug into the marine clay near the site

revealed a deep layer of ash and pottery that may belong to this earlier time (we didn't venture to date this material, since it was not covered by our research permit).

Toward the top of the sediment cores, Maloney found evidence for a major episode of burning and the proliferation of grass pollen. This stratum was dated to the early period when Khok Phanom Di was occupied and surely reflects the activities of its inhabitants. They probably were cutting the coastal forests for fuel, including that needed to fire clay vessels, which they shaped from the rich local source of clay. They may also have been burning off dry-season plant growth in order to make way for their rice.

Because their estuary provided a wide range of renewable food resources, the inhabitants of Khok Phanom Di were probably rarely, if ever, short of food. At low tide they collected the abundant shellfish that lived on the mud flats. The clay net weights

the accompanying grave goods became more elaborate, until the cemetery was abandoned.

The cemetery was arranged in a grid of at least six separate clusters. With time, new burials were placed over preceding ones, continuing the same pattern of clusters. We noted many post holes, the residue of building foundations. Their distribution is irregular, but some alignments hint that each of the grave clusters was housed within a wooden structure, forming, in effect, a collective tomb. Doubtless the wood decayed with time, and the structures had to be refurbished or replaced.

The space between the burials contained the remains of much activity. We found middens (refuse heaps), circular pits containing the remains of unopened—and therefore uneaten—shellfish, and thin layers of ash. Very likely burial was an occasion for funerary ritual, including grave-side feasting and, perhaps, the placing of food in pits to provision the ancestors. At inland sites of comparable age, archeologists find bones from the legs of cattle or pigs, with no sign of cut marks from butchering. The animals were probably slaughtered for a mortuary feast and a limb placed with the dead. These practices seem to have disappeared with the introduction of Buddhism and cremation.

When one of our Thai colleagues, Praphid Choosiri, examined the human remains, she sometimes found rare or unusual bone structures thought to be genetically determined. Two examples of these, with the technical names *metopic suture* and *os inca,* concern the presence of extra sutures between bones in the skull. She noted that successive interments in the grave clusters sometimes exhibit the same rare characteristic, suggesting that each of the burial areas was devoted to a particular lineage. Based on this assumption, we set out to reconstruct prehistoric family trees and consider their ups and downs.

We found that two lineages were especially stable, in that they continued for the full complement of generations for the life of the cemetery. For

one reason or another, however, some lineages failed to maintain themselves. In general, we observed that infant mortality was high for the first eight or so generations, so perhaps these families died out. An alternative explanation is that, as the number of inhabitants grew, the leaders of some lineages left with their relatives to found new settlements elsewhere.

In studying the two stable lineages, we found that the quantity of grave goods varied considerably between burials: some had nothing, while others were very rich. They included lustrously burnished and decorated pots, iridescent shell beads, translucent shell disks, and stone adz heads. Small clay anvils used in making pots were found only with the remains of women, children, and infants. (Such an anvil would have been held inside the vessel as it was shaped with a wooden paddle.) On the other hand, twelve-inch-wide plaques fashioned from sea turtle carapaces, apparently worn as chest ornaments, were found only with the skeletons of men. Both men and women were interred with the stones used to burnish pottery vessels until they shone.

Neither of the two stable lineages appeared consistently wealthier than the other. Fortunes rose or fell after a generation or two, or at most three. This suggests that esteem and status—assuming these translated into mortuary wealth—had to be attained through personal achievement. They were not inherited by right, except to the extent that when infants died, wealthy parents were able to endow them with rare and beautiful grave goods. (Interestingly, infants less than a month or two old were not accorded such attention; perhaps they were still too young to be regarded as official members of society.)

Evidence of important changes at Khok Phanom Di emerged after the actual excavation, as our team of specialists completed their analyses of various kinds of data. Up to the ninth or tenth generation, the inhabitants of the village continued to exploit both the river and seacoast. Men had strong muscular development in their upper

bodies, and men and women apparently had somewhat different diets—women had more caries and tooth loss, while men kept their teeth longer and therefore showed more tooth wear. People were interred with beautifully decorated pots, and many wore shell jewelry. Infant mortality was high.

Then, about the tenth generation, something happened to the maritime connection. Marine and coastal shellfish gave way to species from freshwater or backwater mangrove stands. Mangrove wood became less common in the charcoal. From this time on, men appeared less muscular. Shell jewelry practically disappeared, and even pottery vessels became less common and lacked ornate decoration. Men and women shared a new diet pattern, probably including fewer shellfish. And infant mortality rates dropped.

We think these changes were a reaction to a swift alteration in the environment, probably a major flood followed by a shift in the river channel away from Khok Phanom Di. A gradual deposition of sediment also left the site farther from the sea. Men, whose previous strength probably reflected habitual paddling of boats, now embarked on fewer coastal voyages. The local source of high-quality shell for ornaments also suffered as the sediments killed off preferred species. And the change in habitat or diet may have reduced the danger of certain diseases, improving infant survival.

After three or four generations of relative poverty, yet another pattern emerged. We encountered a very large grave belonging to one of the two main clusters. It contained the remains of a woman in her mid-thirties. Her body was covered with a pile of clay cylinders, which may represent clay destined for conversion into pots, and the broken pieces of five ornately decorated vessels. Her personal jewelry included 120,000 shell beads, two shell disks, a headdress, and on her left wrist, a bangle made of an exotic shell. In life this woman must have been dazzling in her finery. Beside her right ankle lay a shell containing two burnishing pebbles next to a clay anvil. We think that she must have been an outstanding potter. She had well-developed wrist muscles, consistent with preparing and molding clay.

Beside her was a matching grave containing the remains of a fifteen-month-old infant. Again, we encountered a pile of clay cylinders, the body festooned with 12,000 shell beads, a bangle placed over the left wrist, beautiful pots, and a miniature clay anvil beside the right ankle.

Despite the opulence of these two burials, the succeeding generation in what we believe was the same lineage displayed very little wealth. In contrast, the other main lineage now attained greater status within the community. We found the remains of two women and a nine-year-old child buried beneath the two-foot-high raised floor of a rectangular mortuary building. Both women were buried with clay anvils, and one was buried with 11,000 shell beads. The child was accompanied by a thick shell disk and at least 18,000 beads.

Our interpretation is that the community adapted to its now more inland habitat by expanding its ceramic industry, already established owing to the settlement's rich resources and favorable location. This craft, apparently the province of women, might have provided a valuable commodity for trade. Perhaps more than ever, a potter's skill became a source of individual prestige and a route to wealth. Jewelry came to include new styles of heavy bracelets and disks made of tridacna and trochus shell. These species of mollusks are adapted to a clean, coralline habitat and so must have been obtained by exchange from some distance away.

As before, while individuals might attain the prestige evident in a rich burial, they do not seem to have been able to convert this into inherited status and rank. Rather, one family might be successful in one generation, only to be followed by less able or less fortunate descendants in the next. This might have reflected success or failure in craftsmanship and in exchange dealings with other communities, depending on individual skill or charisma. Only when a mortuary tradition in a single community can be followed over so many generations can we gain such an intimate glimpse into its operating principles. No similar site exists elsewhere in Southeast Asia, and very few in the rest of the prehistoric world.

Any community that relies on female potters for making vessels for mortuary ritual and exchange would be reluctant to lose them to other communities through marriage. We believe that the custom at Khok Phanom Di, at least for this later period, was for women to remain at their place of birth. In such a "matrilocal" community, failure to produce a female heir would have spelled the end of the lineage. This may explain the attention given to the details of child or infant burials, some of whom, presumably the young girls, were interred with clay anvils.

We also noted that proportionately fewer men were buried in the cemetery during the later phase, although at least one was well provided with grave goods. A possibility is that men were now using sailing craft to engage in long-distance trade, taking pots and returning with shells. The present-day seafaring people of southern Thailand have a tradition of such voyaging, which is usually the work of men. When they die at sea, their bodies are interred in caves remote from their home base.

Despite its renewed prosperity, Khok Phanom Di was eventually abandoned, about 3,500 years ago. Perhaps the inhabitants chose to move closer to the coast. While we cannot say what happened to them, we have subsequently excavated another cemetery about eight miles to the south, at Nong Nor. This cemetery was in use from about 500 to 800 years after Khok Phanom Di was abandoned. In some ways it shows a similar mortuary ritual, with the bodies oriented with the head to the east and clusters containing men, women, and children (but there is no buildup of successive graves that would enable us to trace individual family groups through time). At Nong Nor, the men were buried with the potter's anvils and usually had the richest grave goods.

The artifacts include ornaments cast in bronze and tin as well as jewelry of serpentine, talc, carnelian, and jade, indicating wider trade contacts.

Khok Phanom Di is one in a series of sites that mark the origins and expansion of rice-growing agriculturists in the hot, densely forested lands of Southeast Asia. The spread of agriculturists can be reconstructed by identifying similarities between many languages spoken in southern China and Southeast Asia today and by tracing them back to a common origin. According to this linguistic and associated radiocarbon evidence, there was a transition to rice farming in the Yangtze Valley of China about 8,500 years ago. The ancestors of the Vietnamese and Khmer, as well as the Munda speakers of eastern India, apparently moved down the major rivers, bringing their farming economy along with them.

Recent evidence suggests that the first farmers reached Thailand about 4,500 years ago. Occupied between 4,000 and 3,500 years ago, Khok Phanom Di has provided us with the clearest available evidence for their way of life. At the time the site was abandoned, Southeast Asia was entering the Bronze Age, as copper and tin began to be cast separately or alloyed to create ornaments, weapons, and tools. The later site of Nong Nor already includes some of these artifacts.

In terms of social organization, however, little changed in Southeast Asia until about 2,500 years ago, when the smelting of iron ores was discovered or introduced. Regional leaders began to control metal-working specialists, who cast a new range of luxury bronzes, including drinking vessels and drums. Over the next 500 years, Southeast Asia joined ever widening trade networks, and powerful regional chiefdoms arose as the rivalry and competition over luxury goods grew. The later chiefs forged the first states in Southeast Asia, a heritage that culminated 1,000 years ago in the founding of the great holy city of Angkor.

Experimental Archaeology

Some archaeologists would like to see experimental archaeology became a major subfield of the science of archaeology. Until recently, most archaeologists have viewed this approach as a supplementary technique to enhance archaeological data.

The criteria of experimental archaeology in the strictest sense are that an experiment must be set up in the present that will in some way reenact or recreate a past archaeological process. The idea underlying experimental archaeology is similar to the principle of uniformitarianism that Charles Lyell presented in the nineteenth century in order to interpret geological phenomena.

This principle is based on two ideas. One is that geological processes that occur in the present also occurred in the past. These processes include earthquakes, water erosion, mountain building, continental drift, and volcanic activity. The second idea is that the rate at which geological processes modified the crust of Earth is uniform, the same in the present as it was in the past. For example, consider the Grand Canyon in the United States. This great wonder of geology was formed by water erosion. The canyon's depth consists of about 1 mile of sedimentary rock layers that were exposed by the tremendous pressure of ages of water literally cutting into the rock. It is this same process that continues to erode rock at Niagara Falls. The processes that modify Earth's crust are universal.

In the case of Niagara Falls, for many years observers have been monitoring the rate at which the rock face recedes each year due to water erosion. In this manner they have been able to establish a uniform rate of erosion. This does not mean that the rate of erosion at Niagara Falls is exactly the same every year. It means that given X amount of water pressure, a rock density of Y will erode at the rate of Z inches per year. Usually the sum total of the different rates of erosion over a period of years is aver-

aged, producing a statement such as "the average rate of erosion per year at Niagara Falls is 4½ inches of rock."

Experimental archaeology is based on the same general principles. Usually archaeologically derived processes involve shorter time spans and can be stated with greater accuracy. However, archaeological processes also involve the eccentricities of human behavior and must be treated with considerable caution.

Questions about the state of preservation of archaeological materials may be answered by experimental archaeology. In archaeology there are many absolute dating methods that give good approximations of how old a thing is. One of the most frequently used is the radiocarbon dating method.

The state of preservation of archaeological materials is dependent upon many variables, most particularly the original material of the artifact and the conditions of the medium (site) in which it is preserved. A nineteenth-century adobe mission in the Mojave desert in California may be so weathered as to be unrecognizable. This is due to the fact that extreme temperatures, varying from very hot to very cold, typical of a low desert climate, tend to rapidly destroy any kind of matter. On the other hand, consistently wet or consistently dry conditions tend to preserve organic matter in a relatively pristine state for long periods of time. The preservation of human remains is therefore very good in bogs (such as in Denmark) that are constantly damp and in the coastal deserts of Peru, where the conditions are consistently dry over the millennia.

But archaeologists need not wait for such discoveries to be made. They may set up their own experiments to study preservation. Both material (artifacts) and medium (soil) may be infinitely varied and repeatedly tested and fine-tuned under laboratory conditions. Not only does this generate a set of relationships that may be used as a basis in archaeological situations, it also acts as a cross-check on other dating methods.

For example, radiocarbon dates can be seriously skewed by unusual chemical conditions in the artifact, the soil, or by inadvertent contamination in the process of excavation or laboratory analysis. These dates may be salvaged by using experimentally generated data to correct for such contamination.

Experimental archaeology may also elucidate cultural historical reconstruction and questions of human behavior. In this unit, William Rathje's famous Garbage Project is examined. Modern garbology presents archaeologists with an opportunity to practice a kind of sociology of garbage. What people say they do, eat, or practice is often quite different from what their garbage tells of their actual behavior.

The study of modern garbology has also reinforced what archaeologists already know, that is, the recognition that written history or the information received from living informants is sometimes heavily biased in certain directions. These biases in turn may be discerned through archaeological excavation. A healthy dose of skepticism is always part of the recipe for scientific thinking.

Looking Ahead: Challenge Questions

Why do archaeologists study modern garbage? Does any other discipline do this? Why or why not?

Have you ever looked at your own garbage after a week? What might it tell you?

How can seemingly impossible feats be accomplished by ancient peoples? Give an example.

What did the innovation of stone lamps contribute to the cultural advancement of humankind? What can we learn about the use and effectiveness of stone lamps by making replicas of them?

What can we learn from experiments in cave painting? Give examples.

Cultural anthropologists use "participant observation." Could an archaeologist do this? If so, how?

Why do people give lip service to cultural values they no longer practice? Give an example and discuss it.

Yes, Wonderful Things

William Rathje and Cullen Murphy

On a crisp October morning not long ago the sun ascended above the Atlantic Ocean and turned its gaze on a team of young researchers as they swarmed over what may be the largest archaeological site in the world. The mound they occupied covers three thousand acres and in places rises more than 155 feet above a low-lying island. Its mass, estimated at 100 million tons, and its volume, estimated at 2.9 billion cubic feet, make it one of the largest manmade structures in North America. And it is known to be a treasure trove—a Pompeii, a Tikal, a Valley of the Kings—of artifacts from the most advanced civilization the planet has ever seen. Overhead sea gulls cackled and cawed, alighting now and then to peck at an artifact or skeptically observe an archaeologist at work. The surrounding landscape still supported quail and duck, but far more noticeable were the dusty, rumbling wagons and tractors of the New York City Department of Sanitation.

The site was the Fresh Kills landfill, on Staten Island, in New York City, a repository of garbage that, when shut down, in the year 2005, will have reached a height of 505 feet above sea level, making it the highest geographic feature along a fifteen-hundred-mile stretch of the Atlantic seaboard running north from Florida all the way to Maine. One sometimes hears that Fresh Kills will have to be closed when it reaches 505 feet so as not to interfere with the approach of aircraft to Newark Airport, in New Jersey, which lies just across the waterway called Arthur Kill. In reality, though, the 505-foot elevation is the result of a series of

calculations designed to maximize the landfill's size while avoiding the creation of grades so steep that roads built upon the landfill can't safely be used.

Fresh Kills was originally a vast marshland, a tidal swamp. Robert Moses's plan for the area, in 1948, was to dump enough garbage there to fill the marshland up—a process that would take, according to one estimate, until 1968—and then to develop the site, building houses, attracting light industry, and setting aside open space for recreational use. ("The Fresh Kills landfill project," a 1951 report to Mayor Vincent R. Impelliteri observed, "cannot fail to affect constructively a wide area around it. It is at once practical and idealistic.") Something along these lines may yet happen when Fresh Kills is closed. Until then, however, it is the largest active landfill in the world. It is twenty-five times the size of the Great Pyramid of Khufu at Giza, forty times the size of the Temple of the Sun at Teotihuacan. The volume of Fresh Kills is approaching that of the Great Wall of China, and by one estimate will surpass it at some point in the next few years. It is the sheer physical stature of Fresh Kills in the hulking world of landfills that explains why archaeologists were drawn to the place.

To the archaeologists of the University of Arizona's Garbage Project, which is now entering its twentieth year, landfills represent valuable lodes of information that may, when mined and interpreted, produce valuable insights—insights not into the nature of some past society, of course, but into the nature of our own. Garbage is among humanity's most prodigious physical legacies to those who have yet to be born; if we can come to understand our discards, Garbage Project archaeologists argue, then we will better understand the

world in which we live. It is this conviction that prompts Garbage Project researchers to look upon the steaming detritus of daily existence with the same quiet excitement displayed by Howard Carter and Lord George Edward Carnarvon at the unpillaged, unopened tomb of Tutankhamun.

"Can you see anything?" Carnarvon asked as Carter thrust a lighted candle through a hole into the gloom of the first antechamber. "Yes," Carter replied. "Wonderful things."

Garbage archaeology can be conducted in several ways. At Fresh Kills the method of excavation involved a mobile derrick and a thirteen-hundred-pound bucket auger, the latter of which would be sunk into various parts of the landfill to retrieve samples of garbage from selected strata. At 6:15 a.m. Buddy Kellett of the company Kellett's Well Boring, Inc., which had assisted with several previous Garbage Project landfill digs, drove one of the company's trucks, with derrick and auger collapsed for travel, straight up the steep slope of one of the landfill mounds. Two-thirds of the way up, the Garbage Project crew directed Kellett to a small patch of level ground. Four hydraulic posts were deployed from the stationary vehicle, extending outward to keep it safely moored. Now the derrick was raised. It supported a long metal rod that in turn housed two other metal rods; the apparatus, when pulled to its full length, like a telescope, was capable of penetrating the landfill to a depth of ninety-seven feet—enough at this particular spot to go clear through its bottom and into the original marsh that Fresh Kills had been (or into what was left of it). At the end of the rods was the auger, a large bucket made of high-tension steel: four feet high, three feet in diameter, and open at the bottom like a cookie cutter, with six graphite-and-steel teeth around the bottom's circumference. The bucket would spin at about thirty revolutions per minute and with such force that virtually nothing could impede its descent. At a Garbage Project excavation in Sunnyvale, California, in 1988, one of the first things the bucket hit in the cover dirt a few feet below the surface of the Sunnyvale Landfill was the skeleton of a car. The bucket's teeth snapped the axle, and drilled on.

The digging at Fresh Kills began. Down the whirring bucket plunged. Moments later it returned with a gasp, laden with garbage that, when released, spewed a thin vapor into the chill autumnal air. The smell was pungent, somewhere between sweet and disagreeable. Kellett's rig operator, David Spillers, did his job with the relaxation that comes of familiarity, seemingly oblivious to the harsh grindings and sharp clanks. The rest of the archaeological crew, wearing cloth aprons and heavy rubber gloves, went about their duties with practiced efficiency and considerable speed. They were veteran members of the Garbage Project's A-Team—its landfill-excavating arm—and had been through it all before.

Again a bucketful of garbage rose out of the ground. As soon as it was dumped Masakazu Tani, at the time a Japanese graduate student in anthropology at the University of Arizona (his Ph.D. thesis, recently completed, involves identifying activity areas in ancient sites on the basis of distributions of litter), plunged a thermometer into the warm mass. "Forty-three degrees centigrade," Tani called out. The temperature (equivalent to 109.4 degrees Fahrenheit) was duly logged. The garbage was then given a brusque preliminary examination to determine its generic source and, if possible, its date of origin. In this case the presence of telltale domestic items, and of legible newspapers, made both tasks easy. Gavin Archer, another anthropologist and a research associate of the Garbage Project, made a notation in the running log that he would keep all day long: "Household, circa 1977." Before the next sample was pulled up Douglas

Wilson, an anthropologist who specializes in household hazardous waste, stepped up to the auger hole and played out a weighted tape measure, eventually calling out, "Thirty-five feet." As a safety precaution, Wilson, like any other crew member working close to the sunken shaft on depth-measure duty, wore a leather harness tethered to a nearby vehicle. The esophagus created by the bucket auger was just large enough to accept a human being, and anyone slipping untethered a story or two into this narrow, oxygen-starved cavity would die of asphyxiation before any rescue could be attempted.

Most of the bucketfuls of garbage received no more attention than did the load labeled "Household, circa 1977." Some basic data were recorded for tracking purposes, and the garbage was left on a quickly accumulating backdirt pile. But as each of what would finally be fourteen wells grew deeper and deeper, at regular intervals (either every five or every ten feet) samples were taken and preserved for full-dress analysis. On those occasions Wilson Hughes, the methodical and serenely ursine co-director and field supervisor of the Garbage Project, and the man responsible for day-to-day logistics at the Fresh Kills dig, would call out to the bucket operator over the noise of the engine: "We'll take the next bucket." Then Hughes and Wilson would race toward the rig in a running crouch, like medics toward a helicopter, a plywood sampling board between them. Running in behind came a team of microbiologists and civil engineers assembled from the University of Oklahoma, the University of Wisconsin, and Procter & Gamble's environmental laboratory. They brought with them a variety of containers and sealing devices to preserve samples in an oxygen-free environment—an environment that would allow colonies of the anaerobic bacteria that cause most of the biodegradation in landfills (to the extent that biodegradation occurs) to survive for later analysis. Behind the biologists and engineers came other Garbage Project personnel with an assortment of wire mesh screens and saw horses.

Within seconds of the bucket's removal from the ground, the operator maneuvered it directly over the sampling board, and released the contents. The pile was attacked first by Phillip Zack, a civil engineering student from the University of Wisconsin, who, as the temperature was being recorded, directed portions of the material into a variety of airtight conveyances. Then other members of the team moved in—the people who would shovel the steaming refuse atop the wire mesh; the people who would sort and bag whatever didn't go through the mesh; the people who would pour into bags or cannisters or jars whatever did go through the mesh; the people who would label everything for the trip either back to Tucson and the Garbage Project's holding bins or to the laboratories of the various microbiologists. (The shortest trip was to the trailer-laboratory that Procter & Gamble scientists had driven from Cincinnati and parked at the edge of the landfill.) The whole sample-collection process, from dumping to sorting to storing, took no more than twelve minutes. During the Fresh Kills dig it was repeated forty-four times at various places and various depths.

As morning edged toward afternoon the bucket auger began to near the limits of its reach in one of the wells. Down through the first thirty-five feet, a depth that in this well would date back to around 1984, the landfill had been relatively dry. Food waste and yard waste—hot dogs, bread, and grass clippings, for, example—were fairly well preserved. Newspapers remained intact and easy to read, their lurid headlines ("Woman Butchered-Ex-Hubby Held") calling to mind a handful of yesterday's tragedies. Beyond thirty-five feet, however, the landfill became increasingly wet, the garbage increasingly unidentifiable. At sixty feet, a stratum in this well containing garbage from the 1940s and 1950s, the bucket grabbed a sample and pulled it toward the surface. The Garbage Project team ran forward with their equipment, positioning themselves underneath. The bucket rose majestically as the operator sat at the controls, shouting something over the noise. As near as anyone can reconstruct it now, he was saying, "You boys might want to back off some, 'cause if this wind hits that bucket. . . ." The operator broke off because the wind did hit that bucket, and the material inside—a gray slime, redolent of putrefaction—thoroughly showered the crew. It would be an exaggeration to suggest that the victims were elated by this development, but their curiosity was certainly piqued, because on only one previous excavation had slime like this turned up in a landfill. What was the stuff made of? How had it come to be? What did its existence mean? The crew members doggedly collected all the usual samples, plus a few extra bottles of slime for special study. Then they cleaned themselves off.

It would be a blessing if it were possible to study garbage in the abstract, to study garbage without having to handle it physically.* But that is not possible. Garbage is not mathematics. To understand garbage you have to touch it, to feel it, to sort it, to smell it. You have to pick through hundreds of tons of it, counting and weighing all the daily newspapers, the telephone books; the soiled diapers, the foam clamshells that once briefly held hamburgers, the lipstick cylinders

*A note on terminology. Several words for the things we throw away—"garbage," "trash," "refuse," "rubbish"—are used synonymously in casual speech but in fact have different meanings. *Trash* refers specifically to discards that are at least theoretically "dry"—newspapers, boxes, cans, and so on. *Garbage* refers technically to "wet" discards—food remains, yard waste, and offal. *Refuse* is an inclusive term for both the wet discards and the dry. *Rubbish* is even more inclusive: It refers to all refuse plus construction and demolition debris. The distinction between wet and dry garbage was important in the days when cities slopped garbage to pigs, and needed to have the wet material separated from the dry; it eventually became irrelevant, but may see a revival if the idea of composting food and yard waste catches on. We will frequently use "garbage" in this book to refer to the totality of human discards because it is the word used most naturally in ordinary speech. The word is etymologically obscure, though it probably derives from Anglo-French, and its earliest associations have to do with working in the kitchen.

coated with grease, the medicine vials still encasing brightly colored pills, the empty bottles of scotch, the half-full cans of paint and muddy turpentine, the forsaken toys, the cigarette butts. You have to sort and weigh and measure the volume of all the organic matter, the discards from thousands of plates: the noodles and the Cheerios and the tortillas; the pieces of pet food that have made their own gravy; the hardened jelly doughnuts, bleeding from their side wounds; the half-eaten bananas, mostly still within their peels, black and incomparably sweet in the embrace of final decay. You have to confront sticky green mountains of yard waste, and slippery brown hills of potato peels, and brittle ossuaries of chicken bones and T-bones. And then, finally, there are the "fines," the vast connecting mixture of tiny bits of paper, metal, glass, plastic, dirt, grit, and former nutrients that suffuses every landfill like a kind of grainy lymph. To understand garbage you need thick gloves and a mask and some booster shots. But the yield in knowledge—about people and their behavior as well as about garbage itself—offsets the grim working conditions.

To an archaeologist, ancient garbage pits or garbage mounds, which can usually be located within a short distance from any ruin, are always among the happiest of finds, for they contain in concentrated form the artifacts and comestibles and remnants of behavior of the people who used them. While every archaeologist dreams of discovering spectacular objects, the bread-and-butter work of archaeology involves the most common and routine kinds of discards. It is not entirely fanciful to define archaeology as the discipline that tries to understand old garbage, and to learn from that garbage something about ancient societies and ancient behaviors. The eminent archaeologist Emil Haury once wrote of the aboriginal garbage heaps of the American Southwest: "Whichever way one views the mounds—as garbage piles to avoid, or as symbols of a way of life—they nevertheless are features more productive of information than any others." When the British archae-

ologist Sir Leonard Woolley, in 1916, first climbed to the top of the ancient city of Carchemish, on the Euphrates River near the modern-day Turkish-Syrian border, he moistened his index finger and held it in the air. Satisfied, he scanned the region due south of the city—that is, downwind—pausing to draw on his map the location of any mounds he saw. A trench dug through the largest of these mounds revealed it to be the garbage dump Woolley was certain it was, and the exposed strata helped establish the chronological sequence for the Carchemish site as a whole. Archaeologists have been picking through ancient garbage ever since archaeology became a profession, more than a century ago, and they will no doubt go on doing so as long as garbage is produced.

Several basic points about garbage need to be emphasized at the outset. First, the creation of garbage is an unequivocal sign of a human presence. From Styrofoam cups along a roadway and urine bags on the moon there is an uninterrupted chain of garbage that reaches back more than two million years to the first "waste flake" knocked off in the knapping of the first stone tool. That the distant past often seems misty and dim is precisely because our earliest ancestors left so little garbage behind. An appreciation of the accomplishments of the first hominids became possible only after they began making stone tools, the debris from the production of which, along with the discarded tools themselves, are now probed for their secrets with electron microscopes and displayed in museums not as garbage but as "artifacts." These artifacts serve as markers—increasingly frequent and informative markers—of how our forebears coped with the evolving physical and social world. Human beings are mere placeholders in time, like zeros in a long number; their garbage seems to have more staying power, and a power to inform across the millennia that complements (and often substitutes for) that of the written word. The profligate habits of our own country and our own time—the sheer volume of the garbage that we create and must dispose of—

will make our society an open book. The question is: Would we ourselves recognize our story when it is told, or will our garbage tell tales about us that we as yet do not suspect?

That brings up a second matter: If our garbage, in the eyes of the future, is destined to hold a key to the past, then surely it already holds a key to the present. This may be an obvious point, but it is one whose implications were not pursued by scholars until relatively recently. Each of us throws away dozens of items every day. All of these items are relics of specific human activities—relics no different in their inherent nature from many of those that traditional archaeologists work with (though they are, to be sure, a bit fresher). Taken as a whole the garbage of the United States, from its 93 million households and 1.5 million retail outlets and from all of its schools, hospitals, government offices, and other public facilities, is a mirror of American society. Of course, the problem with the mirror garbage offers is that, when encountered in a garbage can, dump, or landfill, it is a broken one: our civilization is reflected in billions of fragments that may reveal little in and of themselves. Fitting some of the pieces back together requires painstaking effort—effort that a small number of archaeologists and natural scientists have only just begun to apply.

A third point about garbage is that it is not an assertion but a physical fact—and thus may sometimes serve as a useful corrective. Human beings have over the centuries left many accounts describing their lives and civilizations. Many of these are little more than self-aggrandizing advertisements. The remains of the tombs, temples, and palaces of the elite are filled with personal histories as recorded by admiring relatives and fawning retainers. More such information is carved into obelisks and stelae, gouged into clay tablets, painted or printed on papyrus and paper. Historians are understandably drawn to written evidence of this kind, but garbage has often served as a kind of tattle-tale, setting the record straight.

It had long been known, for example, that French as well as Spanish forts had been erected along the coast of South Carolina during the sixteenth century, and various mounds and depressions have survived into our own time to testify to their whereabouts. Ever since the mid-nineteenth century a site on the tip of Parris Island, South Carolina, has been familiarly known as the site of a French outpost, built in 1562, that is spelled variously in old documents as Charlesfort, Charlesforte, and Charles Forte. In 1925, the Huguenot Society of South Carolina successfully lobbied Congress to erect a monument commemorating the building of Charlesfort. Subsequently, people in nearby Beaufort took up the Charlesfort theme, giving French names to streets, restaurants, and housing developments. Gift shops sold kitschy touristiana with a distinctly Gallic flavor. Those restaurants and gift shops found themselves in an awkward position when, in 1957, as a result of an analysis of discarded matter discovered at Charlesfort, a National Park Service historian, Albert Manucy, suggested that the site was of Spanish origin. Excavations begun in 1979 by the archaeologist Stanley South, which turned up such items as discarded Spanish olive jars and broken majolica pottery from Seville, confirmed Manucy's view: "Charlesfort," South established, was actually Fort San Marcos, a Spanish installation built in 1577 to protect a Spanish town named Santa Elena. (Both the fort and the town had been abandoned after only a few years.)

Garbage, then, represents physical fact, not mythology. It underscores a point that can not be too greatly emphasized: Our private worlds consist essentially of two realities—mental reality, which encompasses beliefs, attitudes, and ideas, and material reality, which is the picture embodied in the physical record. The study of garbage reminds us that it is a rare person in whom mental and material realities completely coincide. Indeed, for the most part, the pair exist in a state of tension, if not open conflict.

Americans have always wondered, sometimes with buoyant playfulness, what their countrymen in the far future will make of Americans "now." In 1952, in a monograph he first circulated privately among colleagues and eventually published in *The Journal of Irreproducible Results,* the eminent anthropologist and linguist Joseph H. Greenberg—the man who would one day sort the roughly one thousand known Native American languages into three broad language families—imagined the unearthing of the so-called "violence texts" during an excavation of the Brooklyn Dodgers' Ebbets Field in the year A.D. 2026; what interpretation, he wondered, would be given to such newspaper reports as Yanks Slaughter Indians" and "Reese made a sacrifice in the infield"? In 1979 the artist and writer David Macaulay published *Motel of the Mysteries,* an archaeological site-report setting forth the conclusions reached by a team of excavators in the year A.D. 4022 who have unearthed a motel dating back to 1985 (the year, Macaulay wrote, in which "an accidental reduction in postal rates on a substance called third- and fourth-class mail literally buried the North Americans under tons of brochures, fliers, and small containers called FREE"). Included in the report are illustrations of an archaeologist modeling a toilet seat, toothbrushes, and a drain stopper (or, as Macaulay describes them, "the Sacred Collar . . . the magnificent 'plasticus' ear ornaments, and the exquisite silver chain and pendant"), all assumed to be items of ritual or personal regalia. In 1982 an exhibit was mounted in New York City called "Splendors of the Sohites"—a vast display of artifacts, including "funerary vessels" (faded, dusky soda bottles) and "hermaphrodite amulets" (discarded pop-top rings), found in the SoHo section of Manhattan and dating from the Archaic Period (A.D. 1950-1961), the Classical Period (1962-1975), and the Decadent Period (1976- c.1980).

Greenberg, Macaulay, and the organizers of the Sohites exhibition all meant to have some fun, but there is an uneasy undercurrent to their work, and it is embodied in the question: What are we to make of ourselves? The Garbage Project, conceived in 1971, and officially established at the University of Arizona in 1973, was an attempt to come up with a new way of providing serious answers. It aimed to apply *real* archaeology to this very question; to see if it would be possible to investigate human behavior "from the back end," as it were. This scholarly endeavor has come to be known as garbology, and practitioners of garbology are known as garbologists. The printed citation (dated 1975) in the *Oxford English Dictionary* for the meaning of "garbology" as used here associates the term with the Garbage Project.

In the years since its founding the Garbage Project's staff members have processed more than 250,000 pounds of garbage, some of it from landfills but most of it fresh out of garbage cans in selected neighborhoods. All of this garbage has been sorted, coded, and catalogued—every piece, from bottles of furniture polish and egg-shaped pantyhose packaging to worn and shredded clothing, crumpled bubble-gum wrappers, and the full range of kitchen waste. A unique database has been built up from these cast-offs, covering virtually every aspect of American life: drinking habits, attitudes toward red meat, trends in the use of convenience foods, the strange ways in which consumers respond to shortages, the use of contraceptives, and hundreds of other matters.*

*A question that always comes up is: What about garbage disposers? Garbage disposers are obviously capable of skewing the data in certain garbage categories, and Garbage Project researchers can employ a variety of techniques to compensate for the bias that garbage disposers introduce. Studies were conducted at the very outset of the Garbage Project to determine the discard differential between households with and without disposers, and one eventual result was a set of correction factors for various kinds of garbage (primarily food), broken down by subtype. As a general rule of thumb, households with disposers end up discarding in their trash about half the amount of food waste and food debris as households without disposers. It should be noted, however, that the fact that disposers have ground up some portion of a household's garbage often has little relevance to the larger issues the Garbage Project is trying to address. It means, for example, not that the Garbage Project's findings about the extent of food waste are invalid, but merely that its estimates are conservative.

The antecedents of the Garbage Project in the world of scholarship and elsewhere are few but various. Some are undeniably dubious. The examination of fresh refuse is, of course, as old as the human species—just watch anyone who happens upon an old campsite, or a neighbor scavenging at a dump for spare parts or furniture. The first systematic study of the components of America's garbage dates to the early 1900s and the work of the civil engineers Rudolph Hering (in New York) and Samuel A. Greeley (in Chicago), who by 1921 had gathered enough information from enough cities to compile *Collection and Disposal of Municipal Refuse,* the first textbook on urban trash management. In academe, not much happened after that for quite some time. Out in the field, however, civil engineers and solid-waste managers did now and again sort and weigh fresh garbage as it stood in transit between its source and destination, but their categories were usually simple: paper, glass, metal. No one sorted garbage into detailed categories relating to particular consumer discard patterns. No one, for example, kept track of phenomena as specific as the number of beer cans thrown away versus the number of beer bottles, or the number of orange-juice cans thrown away versus the number of pounds of freshly squeezed oranges, or the amount of candy thrown away in the week after Halloween versus the amount thrown away in the week after Valentine's Day. And no one ever dug into the final resting places of most of America's garbage: dumps (where garbage is left in the open) and sanitary landfills (where fresh garbage is covered every night with six to eight inches of soil).

Even as America's city managers over the years oversaw—and sometimes desperately attempted to cope with—the disposal of ever-increasing amounts of garbage, the study of garbage itself took several odd detours—one into the world of the military, another into the world of celebrity-watching, and a third into the world of law enforcement.

The military's foray into garbology occurred in 1941, when two enlisted

men, Horace Schwerin and Phalen Golden, were forced to discontinue a survey they were conducting among new recruits about which aspects of Army life the recruits most disliked. (Conducting polls of military personnel was, they had learned, against regulations.) Schwerin and Golden had already discovered, however, that the low quality of the food was the most frequently heard complaint, and they resolved to look into this one matter with an investigation that could not be considered a poll. What Schwerin and Golden did was to station observers in mess halls to record the types of food that were most commonly wasted and the volume of waste by type of food. The result, after 2.4 million man-meals had been observed, was a textbook example of how garbage studies can produce not only behavioral insights but also practical benefits. Schwerin and Golden discovered that 20 percent of the food prepared for Army mess halls was eventually thrown away, and that one reason for this was simply excess preparation. Here are some more of their findings, as summarized in a wartime article that appeared in the *The Saturday Evening Post:*

Soldiers ate more if they were allowed to smoke in the mess hall. They ate more if they went promptly to table instead of waiting on line outside—perhaps because the food became cold. They ate more if they fell to on their own initiative instead of by command. They cared little for soups, and 65 percent of the kale and nearly as much of the spinach went into the garbage can. Favorite desserts were cakes and cookies, canned fruit, fruit salad, and gelatin. They ate ice cream in almost any amount that was served to them.

"That, sergeant, is an excellent piece of work," General George C. Marshall, the Army chief of staff, told Horace Schwerin after hearing a report by Schwerin on the research findings. The Army adopted many of Schwerin and Golden's recommendations, and began saving some 2.5 million pounds of food a day. It is perhaps not surprising to learn that until joining the Army Horace Schwerin had been in market research, and, among other things, had helped CBS to perfect a device for measuring audience reaction to radio shows.

The origins of an ephemeral branch of garbage studies focused on celebrities—"peeping-Tom" garbology, one might call it—seem to lie in the work of A. J. Weberman. Weberman was a gonzo journalist and yippie whose interest in the songs of Bob Dylan, and obsession with their interpretation, in 1970 prompted him to begin stealing the garbage from the cans left out in front of Dylan's Greenwich Village brownstone on MacDougal Street. Weberman didn't find much—some soiled Pampers, some old newspapers, some fast-food packaging from a nearby Blimpie Base, a shopping list with the word vanilla spelled "vannilla." He did, however, stumble into a brief but highly publicized career. This self-proclaimed "garbage guerrilla" quickly moved on to Neil Simon's garbage (it included a half-eaten bagel, scraps of lox, the Sunday *Times*), Muhammad Ali's (an empty can of Luck's collard greens, an empty roach bomb), and Abbie Hoffman's (a summons for hitchhiking, an unused can of deodorant, an estimate of the cost for the printing of *Steal This Book,* and the telephone numbers of Jack Anderson and Kate Millet). Weberman revealed many of his findings in an article in *Esquire* in 1971. It was antics such as his that inspired a prior meaning of the term "garbology," one very different from the definition established today.

Weberman's work inspired other garbage guerrillas. In January of 1975, the *Detroit Free Press* Sunday magazine reported on the findings from its raids on the garbage of several city notables, including the mayor, the head of the city council, the leader of a right-wing group, a food columnist, a disk jockey, and a prominent psychiatrist. Nothing much was discovered that might be deemed out of the ordinary, save for some of the contents of the garbage taken from a local Hare Krishna temple: a price tag from an Oleg Cassini garment, for example, and four ticket stubs from the Bel-Aire Drive-In Theater, which at the time was showing *Horrible House on the*

Hill and *The Night God Screamed.* Six months after the *Free Press* exposé, a reporter for the *National Enquirer,* Jay Gourley, drove up to 3018 Dumbarton Avenue, N.W., in Washington, D.C., and threw the five garbage bags in front of Secretary of State Henry A. Kissinger's house into the trunk of his car. Secret Service agents swiftly blocked Gourley's departure, but after a day of questioning allowed him to proceed, the garbage still in the trunk. Among Gourley's finds: a crumpled piece of paper with a dog's teeth marks on it, upon which was written the work schedules of the Secret Service agents assigned to guard the Secretary; empty bottles of Seconal and Maalox; and a shopping list, calling for a case of Jack Daniel's, a case of Ezra Brooks bourbon, and a case of Cabin Still bourbon. Gourley later returned most of the garbage to the Kissingers—minus, he told reporters, "several dozen interesting things."

After the Kissinger episode curiosity about the garbage of celebrities seems to have abated. In 1977 the *National Enquirer* sent a reporter to poke through the garbage of President Jimmy Carter's press secretary, Jody Powell. The reporter found so little of interest that the tabloid decided not to publish a story. In 1980 Secret Service agents apprehended A. J. Weberman as he attempted to abduct former President Richard Nixon's garbage from behind an apartment building in Manhattan. Weberman was released, without the garbage.

The third detour taken by garbage studies involves police work. Over the years, law enforcement agents looking for evidence in criminal cases have also been more-than-occasional students of garbage; the Federal Bureau of Investigation in particular has spent considerable time poring over the household trash of people in whom it maintains a professional interest. ("We take it on a case-by-case basis," an FBI spokesman says.) One of the biggest criminal cases involving garbage began in 1975 and involved Joseph "Joe Bananas" Bonanno, Sr., a resident of Tucson at the time and a man with alleged ties to organized crime that

were believed to date back to the days of Al Capone. For a period of three years officers of the Arizona Drug Control District collected Bonanno's trash just before the regular pickup, replacing it with "fake" Bonanno garbage. (Local garbagemen were not employed in the operation because some of them had received anonymous threats after assisting law enforcement agencies in an earlier venture.) The haul in evidence was beyond anyone's expectations: Bonanno had apparently kept detailed records of his various transactions, mostly in Sicilian. Although Bonanno had torn up each sheet of paper into tiny pieces, forensic specialists with the Drug Control District, like archaeologists reconstructing ceramic bowls from potsherds, managed to reassemble many of the documents and with the help of the FBI got them translated. In 1980 Bonanno was found guilty of having interfered with a federal grand jury investigation into the business operations of his two sons and a nephew. He was eventually sent to jail.

Unlike law-enforcement officers or garbage guerrillas, the archaeologists of the Garbage Project are not interested in the contents of any particular individual's garbage can. Indeed, it is almost always the case that a given person's garbage is at once largely anonymous and unimaginably humdrum. Garbage most usefully comes alive when it can be viewed in the context of broad patterns, for it is mainly in patterns that the links between artifacts and behaviors can be discerned.

The seed from which the Garbage Project grew was an anthropology class conducted at the University of Arizona in 1971 that was designed to teach principles of archaeological methodology. The University of Arizona has long occupied a venerable place in the annals of American archaeology and, not surprisingly, the pursuit of archaeology there to this day is carried on in serious and innovative ways. The class in question was one in which students undertook independent projects aimed precisely at showing links between various kinds of artifacts and various kinds of behavior. For example, one student, Sharon Thomas, decided to look into the relationship between a familiar motor function ("the diffusion pattern of ketchup over hamburgers") and a person's appearance, as manifested in clothing. Thomas took up a position at "seven different hamburger dispensaries" and, as people came in to eat, labeled them "neat" or "sloppy" according to a set of criteria relating to the way they dressed. Then she recorded how each of the fifty-seven patrons she studied—the ones who ordered hamburgers—poured ketchup over their food. She discovered that sloppy people were far more likely than neat people to put ketchup on in blobs, sometimes even stirring it with their fingers. Neat people, in contrast, tended to apply the ketchup in patterns: circles, spirals, and crisscrosses. One person (a young male neatly dressed in a body shirt, flared pants, and patent-leather Oxfords) wrote with ketchup what appeared to be initials.

Two of the student investigations, conducted independently by Frank Ariza and Kelly Allen, led directly to the Garbage Project. Ariza and Allen, wanting to explore the divergence between (or correlation of) mental stereotypes and physical realities, collected garbage from two households in an affluent part of Tucson and compared it to garbage from two households in a poor and, as it happens, Mexican-American part of town. The rich and poor families, each student found, ate about the same amount of steak and hamburger, and drank about the same amount of milk. But the poor families, they learned, bought more expensive child-education items. They also bought more household cleansers. What did such findings mean? Obviously the sample—involving only four households in all—was too small for the results even to be acknowledged as representative, let alone to provide hints as to what lay behind them. However, the general nature of the research effort itself—comparing garbage samples in order to gauge behavior (and, what is more, gauging behavior unobtrusively, thereby avoiding one of the great biases inher-

ent in much social science)—seemed to hold great promise.

A year later, in 1972, university students, under professorial direction, began borrowing samples of household garbage from different areas of Tucson, and sorting it in a lot behind a dormitory. The Garbage Project was under way. In 1973, the Garbage Project entered into an arrangement with the City of Tucson, whereby the Sanitation Division, four days a week, delivered five to eight randomly selected household pickups from designated census tracts to an analysis site that the Division set aside for the Project's sorters at a maintenance yard. (Wilson Hughes, who as mentioned earlier is the Garbage Project's co-director, was one of the first undergraduate garbage sorters.) In 1984 operations were moved to an enclosure where many of the university's dumpsters are parked, across the street from Arizona Stadium.

The excavation of landfills would come much later in the Garbage Project's history, when to its focus on issues of garbage and human behavior it added a focus on issues of garbage management. The advantage in the initial years of sorting fresh garbage over excavating landfills was a basic but important one: In landfills it is often quite difficult and in many cases impossible to get some idea, demographically speaking, of the kind of neighborhood from which any particular piece of garbage has come. The value of landfill studies is therefore limited to advancing our understanding of garbage in the aggregate. With fresh garbage, on the other hand, one can have demographic precision down to the level of a few city blocks, by directing pickups to specific census districts and cross-tabulating the findings with census data.

Needless to say, deciding just which characteristics of the collected garbage to pay attention to posed a conceptual challenge, one that was met by Wilson Hughes, who devised the "protocol" that is used by the Garbage Project to this day. Items found in garbage are sorted into one of 150 specific coded categories that can in turn be clustered into larger categories representing food

(fresh food versus prepared, health food versus junk food), drugs, personal and household sanitation products, amusement-related or educational materials, communications-related materials, pet-related materials, yard-related materials, and hazardous materials. For each item the following information is recorded on a standardized form: the date on which it was collected; the census tract from which it came; the item code (for example, 001, which would be the code for "Beef"); the item's type (for example, "chuck"); its original weight or volume (in this case, derived from the packaging); its cost (also from the packaging); material composition of container; brand (if applicable); and the weight of any discarded food (if applicable). The information garnered over the years from many thousands of such forms, filled out in pursuit of a wide variety of research objectives, constitutes the Garbage Project's database. It has all been computerized and amounts to some two million lines of data drawn from some fifteen thousand household-refuse samples. The aim here has been not only to approach garbage with specific questions to answer or hypotheses to prove but also to amass sufficient quantities of information, in a systematic and open-minded way, so that with the data on hand Garbage Project researchers would be able to answer any future questions or evaluate any future hypotheses that might arise. In 1972 garbage was, after all, still terra incognita, and the first job to be done was akin to that undertaken by the explorers Lewis and Clark.

From the outset the Garbage Project has had to confront the legal and ethical issues its research involves: Was collecting and sorting someone's household garbage an unjustifiable invasion of privacy? This very question has over the years been argued repeatedly in the courts. The Fourth Amendment unequivocally guarantees Americans protection from unreasonable search and seizure. Joseph Bonanno, Sr., tried to invoke the Fourth Amendment to prevent his garbage from being used as evidence. But garbage placed in a garbage can in a public thoroughfare, where it awaits removal by impersonal refuse collectors, and where it may be picked over by scavengers looking for aluminum cans, by curious children or neighbors, and by the refuse collectors themselves (some of whom do a thriving trade in old appliances, large and small), is usually considered by the courts to have been abandoned. Therefore, the examination of the garbage by outside parties cannot be a violation of a constitutional right. In the Bonanno case, U.S. District Court Judge William Ingram ruled that investigating garbage for evidence of a crime may carry a "stench," but was not illegal. In 1988, in *California v. Greenwood,* the U.S. Supreme Court ruled by a margin of six to two that the police were entitled to conduct a warrantless search of a suspected drug dealer's garbage—a search that led to drug paraphenalia, which led in turn to warrants, arrests, and convictions. As Justice Byron White has written, "The police cannot reasonably be expected to avert their eyes from evidence of criminal activity that could have been observed by any member of the public."

Legal issues aside, the Garbage Project has taken pains to ensure that those whose garbage comes under scrutiny remain anonymous. Before obtaining garbage for study, the Project provides guarantees to communities and their garbage collectors that nothing of a personal nature will be examined and that no names or addresses or other personal information will be recorded. The Project also stipulates that all of the garbage collected (except aluminum cans, which are recycled) will be returned to the community for normal disposal.

As noted, the Garbage Project has now been sorting and evaluating garbage, with scientific rigor, for two decades. The Project has proved durable because its findings have supplied a fresh perspective on what we know—and what we think we know—about certain aspects of our lives. Medical researchers, for example, have long made it their business to question people about their eating habits in order to uncover relationships between patterns of diet and patterns of disease. These researchers have also long suspected that people—honest, well-meaning people—may often be providing information about quantities and types and even brands of food and drink consumed that is not entirely accurate. People can't readily say whether they trimmed 3.3 ounces or 5.4 ounces of fat off the last steak they ate, and they probably don't remember whether they had four, five, or seven beers in the previous week, or two eggs or three. The average person just isn't paying attention. Are there certain patterns in the way in which people wrongly "self-report" their dietary habits? Yes, there are, and Garbage Project studies have identified many of them.

Garbage archaeologists also know how much edible food is thrown away; what percentage of newspapers, cans, bottles, and other items aren't recycled; how loyal we are to brand-name products and which have earned the greatest loyalty; and how much household hazardous waste is carted off to landfills and incinerators. From several truckloads of garbage and a few pieces of ancillary data—most importantly, the length of time over which the garbage was collected—the Garbage Project staff can reconstruct the community from which it came with a degree of accuracy that the Census Bureau might in some neighborhoods be unable to match.

Garbage also exposes the routine perversity of human ways. Garbage archaeologists have learned, for example, that the volume of garbage that Americans produce expands to fill the number of receptacles that are available to put it in. They have learned that we waste more of what is in short supply than of what is plentiful; that attempts by individuals to restrict consumption of certain foodstuffs are often counterbalanced by extra and inadvertent consumption of those same foodstuffs in hidden form; and that while a person's memory of what he has eaten and drunk in a given week is inevitably wide of the mark, his guess as to what a family member or even neighbor has eaten and drunk usually turns out to be more perceptive.

Some of the Garbage Project's research has prompted unusual forays into arcane aspects of popular culture. Consider the matter of those "amulets" worn by the Sohites—that is, the once-familiar detachable pop-top pull tab. Pull tabs first became important to the Garbage Project during a study of household recycling practices, conducted on behalf of the federal Environmental Protection Agency during the mid-1970s. The question arose: If a bag of household garbage contained no aluminum cans, did that mean that the household didn't dispose of any cans or that it had recycled its cans? Finding a way to answer that question was essential if a neighborhood's recycling rate was to be accurately determined. Pull tabs turned out to hold the key. A quick study revealed that most people did not drop pull tabs into the cans from which they had been wrenched; rather, the vast majority of people threw the tabs into the trash. If empty cans were stored separately for recycling, the pull tabs still went out to the curb with the rest of the garbage. A garbage sample that contained several pull tabs but no aluminum cans was a good bet to have come from a household that recycled.

All this counting of pull tabs prompted a surprising discovery one day by a student: Pull tabs were not all alike. Their configuration and even color depended on what kind of beverage they were associated with and where the beverage had been canned. Armed with this knowledge, Garbage Project researchers constructed an elaborate typology of pull tabs, enabling investigators to tease out data about beverage consumption—say, beer versus soda, Michelob versus Schlitz—even from samples of garbage that contained not a single can. Detachable pull tabs are no longer widely used in beverage cans, but the pull-tab typology remains useful even now. Among other things, in the absence of such evidence of chronology as a newspaper's dateline, pull tabs can reliably help to fix the dates of strata in a landfill. In archaeological parlance objects like these that have been widely diffused over a short period of time, and then abruptly disappear, are known as horizon markers.

The unique "punch-top" on Coors beer cans, for example, was used only between March of 1974 and June of 1977. (It was abandoned because some customers complained that they cut their thumbs pushing the holes open.) In landfills around the country, wherever Coors beer cans were discarded, punch-top cans not only identify strata associated with a narrow band of dates but also separate two epochs one from another. One might think of punch-tops playfully as the garbage equivalent of the famous iridium layer found in sediment toward the end of the Cretaceous Era, marking the moment (proponents of the theory believe) when a giant meteor crashed into the planet Earth, exterminating the dinosaurs.

All told, the Garbage Project has conducted nine full-scale excavations of municipal landfills in the United States and two smaller excavations associated with special projects. In the fall of 1991 it also excavated four sites in Canada, the data from which remains largely unanalyzed (and is not reflected in this book). The logistics of the landfill excavations are complex, and they have been overseen in all cases by Wilson Hughes. What is involved? Permission must be obtained from a raft of local officials and union leaders; indemnification notices must be provided to assure local authorities that the Garbage Project carries suffi-

cient insurance against injury; local universities must be scoured for a supply of students to supplement the Garbage Project team; in many cases construction permits, of all things, must be obtained in advance of digging. There is also the whole matter of transportation, not only of personnel but also of large amounts of equipment. And there is the matter of personal accommodation and equipment storage. The time available for excavation is always limited, sometimes extremely so; the research program must be compressed to fit it, and the staff must be "tasked" accordingly. When the excavation has been completed the samples need to be packed and shipped—frequently on ice—back to headquarters or to specialized laboratories. All archaeologists will tell you that field work is mostly laborious, not glamorous; a landfill excavation is archaeology of the laborious kind.

For all the difficulties they present, the Garbage Project's landfill digs have acquired an increasing timeliness and relevance as concerns about solid-waste disposal have grown. Even as the Garbage Project has trained considerable attention on garbage as an analytical tool it has also taken up the problem of garbage itself—garbage as a problem, garbage as symbolized by *Mobro 4000*, the so-called "garbage barge," which sailed from Islip, Long Island, on March 22, 1987, and spent the next fifty-five days plying the seas in search of a place to deposit its 3,168

tons of cargo. Strange though it may seem, although more than 70 percent of America's household and commercial garbage ends up in landfills, very little reliable data existed until recently as to a landfill's contents and biological dynamics. Much of the conventional wisdom about garbage disposal consists of assertions that turn out, upon investigation, to be simplistic or misleading: among them, the assertion that, as trash, plastic, foam, and fast-food packaging are causes for great concern, that biodegradable items are always more desirable than nonbiodegradable ones, that on a per capita basis the nation's households are generating a lot more garbage than they used to, and that we're physically running out of places to put landfills.

This is not to say that garbage isn't a problem in need of serious attention. It is. But if they are to succeed, plans of action must be based on garbage realities. The most critical part of the garbage problem in America is that our notions about the creation and disposal of garbage are often riddled with myth. There are few other subjects of public significance on which popular and official opinion is so consistently misinformed. . . .

Gaps—large gaps—remain in our knowledge of garbage, and of how human behavior relates to it, and of how best to deal with it. But a lighted candle has at least been seized and thrust inside the antechamber.

Moving the Moai

Transporting the megaliths of Easter Island: How did they do it?

Jo Anne Van Tilburg

Jo Anne Van Tilburg is a research associate of the Institute of Archaeology, UCLA, and has directed the Moai Documentation Project on Easter Island since 1982.

Easter Island's stone statues—sacred objects, emblems of status, and the dominant symbol of a complex ideology—have astounded and perplexed nearly all who have seen or read about them. Pioneering British ethnographer Katherine Scoresby Routledge was the first to investigate the meaning and function of the sculptures, known as *moai*. She and her husband William mounted the 1914–15 Mana Expedition to Easter Island, or Rapa Nui, and mapped Rano Raraku quarry, the volcanic crater where 95 percent of the statues were carved. They discovered and traced the unpaved roads that led from Rano Raraku to ceremonial platforms called *ahu*. Scattered along these roads were 45 statues, presumably abandoned "in transport."

In 1982 I joined the Instituto de Estudios, Universidad de Chile, in its archaeological survey of the island. During the past 12 years my Chilean colleagues and I have located, measured, photographed, drawn, and mapped 883 moai. This number includes visible quarry statues, those on ahu sites, many hidden in caves or partially buried, statues taken from the island to foreign museums, and 47 recorded as "in transport." In mapping Rano Raraku, the Chilean team located 397 of the total number of statues. With 80 percent of the island surveyed, it is possible that another 35–50 moai will be found.

Our goal was to produce a comprehensive description of moai form, style, context, and distribution. In the process we collected a massive amount of data about the political and ideological contexts of the statues. This information holds answers to many questions, not the least of which is how the moai were moved.

To answer this question, I first researched contemporary observations of large stone transport in many parts of the world. In Indonesia, huge gravestones weighing many tons are still hauled on sledges by as many as 150 men, women, and children pulling on attached ropes. In northeastern India, stones of two tons or more were moved over narrow trails as late as the 1940s. Other sources of information are the ethnographically documented cases of stone transport in Madagascar, Tonga, Micronesia, and the Marquesas Islands, and experimental archaeology projects at La Venta in Mexico, at the Giza Plateau in Egypt, and at Stonehenge and elsewhere in Great Britain. In virtually all cases, the stones were moved in a horizontal or occasionally, lateral position on a sledge over rollers.

Next, I studied how eight Rapa Nui statues were collected by foreign museums. In 1886 U.S. Navy Paymaster William J. Thomson and the crew of the USS *Mohican* removed one that is now in the Smithsonian Institution. Islanders and draft animals hauled it two and one-half miles from an inland ahu to Anakena Bay, from which the *Mohican* sailed. The British Museum's

Reprinted with permission from *Archaeology* magazine, January/February 1995, pp. 34-43. © 1995 by the Archaeological Institute of America.

statue, called Hoa Hakananai'a ("stolen or hidden friend"), was removed in 1868 from a stone house then dragged by Rapa Nui people and crew members of HMS *Topaze,* without benefit of a sled. A missionary on the island noted the "precautions" taken to avoid damaging the statue as it was dragged face down, "tracing with its nose, a long furrow on the ground." In 1935 a statue was taken to the Musée d'Art et d'Histoire in Brussels from a site near the village of Hanga Roa. It was wrapped in a cargo net, then placed in a prone position on a wooden sledge, hauled to a nearby bay, and loaded on the Belgian training ship *Mercator.* Alfred Métraux, an ethnographer who witnessed the event, took the opportunity to ask questions about prehistoric transport methods. He found that the Rapa Nui were "unable to explain the methods used by their ancestors for transporting the stone images." In 1955 scientists of Thor Heyerdahl's Norwegian Archaeological Expedition attached a 13-foot-tall statue in a horizontal position to a Y-shaped sledge made from a forked tree trunk with cross pieces over the runners. Ropes were attached to the sledge, and between 75 and 180 people hauled it a few yards over flat ground.

Three additional methods of transportation have been suggested. American archaeologist William Mulloy, who directed the re-erection of statues on several restored sites, speculated that a 32-foot-tall, 89-ton statue called Paro could have been moved using a bipod of tree trunks about 30 feet tall. He believed the statue, suspended by ropes from the bipod, could have been inched forward by rocking it on its protruding belly. One or two of the larger statues lying along a transport road may have inspired Mulloy's fulcrum idea, but neither Paro nor the majority of the other larger-than-average statues have sufficient depth through the midsection to make the method feasible.

More recently, a crew directed by Thor Heyerdahl demonstrated that a 13-foot-tall moai could be inched forward in an upright position on completely flat terrain by tilting and rocking the statue back and forth while manipulating ropes attached to the statue's head and base, much as one would move a heavy piece of furniture. The statue they used, which now stands near Ahu Tongariki, was broken at the base during this operation.

Concrete replicas of moai, not particularly well designed or accurately proportioned, have been used in experiments similar to Heyerdahl's. American geologist Charles Love devised a variation on the upright, tilting method by attaching a pod—a small platform of short logs—to the base of his replica. Once upright on the pod, rollers were placed underneath and the replica was pulled forward over flat ground by attached ropes. This was an improvement over the tilting method, but spacing the rollers unevenly caused the replica to come crashing down.

These experiments were largely shots in the dark. I wanted to find a way to experiment with transport methods that didn't endanger a real statue and didn't depend on awkward and inexact replicas. It was also important to conduct experiments that were controlled and replicable, and which could be generalized from one statue to many. The moai measurements we so painstakingly gathered over the years would be used to build a computer-simulated moai.

Of the statues inventoried thus far, 134 have ten crucial measurements that define body and head shapes and allow us to determine volume, weight, and center of gravity. All 134 are found on ahu or lying "in transport" between Rano Raraku and various ahu. Analyses of size, shape, weight, and proportionate relationships of head to body have allowed us to clarify statue forms.

The statistically average statue for the whole island is 14 feet, six inches tall and weighs 14 tons. Of the dozen or more that we could have used as our reference moai, we chose Statue 01 at Ahu Akivi, a restored and dated ahu lying about 460 feet above sea level on the southwestern slope of Maunga Terevaka. Statue 01 is 13 feet tall and weighs 14 tons. It is five feet wide at its base, almost five feet wide at its head, and has a total depth of three feet through the midpoint of the body. It has a total volume of 210 cubic feet, and its center of gravity is at four and one-half feet. Metric and photogrammetric data collected in 1991 allowed artist Gary Lloyd to sculpt a 1:10 scale model of Statue 01. A computer image of the model produced by laser scan was used to experiment with a variety of hypothetical transport methods.

When Europeans entered the Pacific, the great double-hulled canoes for which Polynesia is now famous were few in number, seen mostly in Samoa, Tonga, and Fiji. Estimates of length vary, but 65 to 70 feet was typical. Canoe hulls from Fiji, Hawaii, and the Society Islands were hewn from massive hardwood tree trunks, weighed from 6 to 12 tons, and were between 108 and 118 feet long. Construction of such vessels was in the hands of master craftsmen with hereditary status and specialized knowledge. The work progressed in accordance with the availability of food. According to Fijian craftsmen, *"a tata tu i kete"* ("the chopping is in the belly"). Sometimes the canoes were built inland, where the best timber was available, and then hauled overland to a beach. In Fiji, the great war canoes are said to have been launched over the bodies of men, sacrificed to serve as rollers allowing the vessel to slide into the water. It is not unreasonable to speculate that moai were commissioned and paid for by Rapa Nui chiefs in much the same way that canoes were built and paid for elsewhere.

We can presume that the Rapa Nui called upon generations of experience in marine exploration and canoe construction and that principles of the fulcrum lever, forked lever, balance beam, pivot, and moving pivot would have been easily adapted to statue transportation. Ancient skills in the production of stone adzes and chisels, strong cordage, and boring and lashing techniques would have been utilized, as would methods for raising and securing masts using side, back, and fore stays. Fibers from the bark of the hau tree would have been twisted into long, strong ropes. Skilled master carvers would have employed a highly stylized design template, probably using

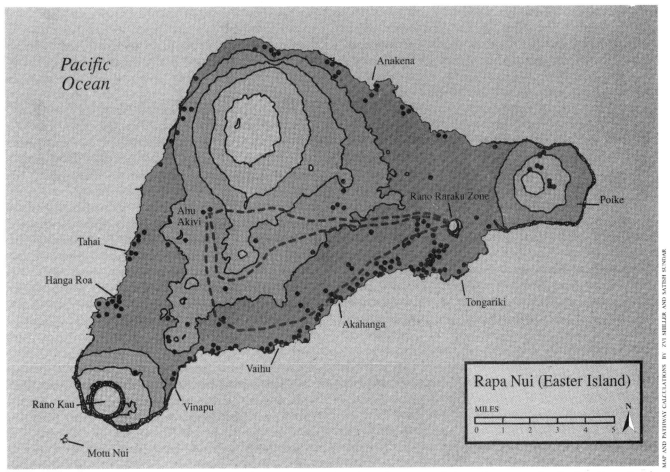

Rapa Nui surface map based on a computer-generated image shows locations of statues and alternative transport paths from Rano Raraku quarry to Ahu Akivi. Path 1 (the optimal path of about six miles) is at top.

knotted cords and charcoal to mark dimensions on the stone before a statue was roughed out.

We decided—based on Polynesian ethnographies, previous experimental archaeology projects in other megalithic societies, Rapa Nui terrain, and statue attributes—that a horizontal transport method was the most logical. The flat backs of the statues and lines of the shoulders were ideally shaped for such transport. Experiments with our scale model helped us to design a light and economical sledge. When transferred to our computer model, it consisted simply of two simulated nonparallel wood beams 18 feet long and almost ten inches in diameter. These were placed under our computer reference statue so that they extended and met about three feet beyond the statue's head. The V-shaped alignment of the transport beams would help in pulling the sledge. The weight of the statue alone would hold the beams

snugly in place. Fifteen to 20 "rollers" about ten inches in diameter were placed under the simulated beams. The statue was then "pulled" forward with ropes.

Of the 383 statues we have measured to date outside of Rano Raraku, 163 are lying face down, 122 are on their backs, and 31 are on their sides. Does the face down position of "in transport" statues mean they were being moved that way? Perhaps, although the experience of Hoa Hakananai'a being dragged with its nose "tracing a furrow in the ground" suggested to us that adjustments to our model would have to be made. To accommodate the face-down position, two crossbeams six and one-half feet long were required. One was placed at the neck to keep the nose and face clear of the ground, and the other, smaller one was placed at the base. Face-down or face-up, the stone experiences stress at the neck. In the face-up mode, a simple

padding of vegetable material under the back of the neck solves the problem, but in the face-down position, the stress is not completely relieved by padding. Some of the statues found "in transport" are broken at the neck, possibly from being transported face-down.

The most difficult aspect of moai transport was positioning and then erecting the statue on an ahu. The statues, whether they were in a face-up or face-down position on the sledge, were probably transported head-first. In the case of Ahu Akivi, statues could have approached the platform in either a face-up or face-down position and from either the front or the rear. Remaining on its transport sledge, the statue was aligned on the site with its base perpendicular to the platform. It was then pulled up a gently sloping earth ramp about three or four times the length of the statue. The base was raised about four feet and positioned

109

on a flat pedestal on top of the platform. Using rocks, earth, rope stays, wedges, and levers, the statue would have been raised to an angle, where it was then guided slowly into place. At this point, the upright, tilting method would have been helpful in adjusting the statue's position on the flat pedestal. Any scars on the smoothly polished surface would have been abraded out with lumps of coral or pumice.

Some coastal ahu were built with high rear walls facing steep seaside cliffs. Moai were moved onto these platforms from the front. Houses and other structures were kept at a distance from the ahu, and the cleared, flat ground in front of the platforms provided ease of access. Earth ramps used in erecting statues were modified and beach cobble paving added to create platform extensions.

Katherine Scoresby Routledge, noting the patterns of breakage on some "in transport" statues, first considered and then rejected the idea that they were being transported upright. Instead, she believed that most had stood erect in place to form a ceremonial road to Rano Raraku. Testing this hypothesis, archaeologist Arne Skjølsvold of the Kon-Tiki Museum conducted excavations of two "in transport" statues in 1986. One had a patterned arrangement of stone at the base, suggesting that it had supported the weight of the upright statue, and lending some credibility to Routledge's hypothesis. Her excavations in Rano Raraku quarry, and Skjølsvold's own in 1955, revealed human bone, stone bowls, and tools associated with some moai standing on the volcano's slopes. In 1774 Captain Cook's party sought the lunchtime shade of a standing statue that may be one lying "in transport" near Ahu Oroi. This huge moai is almost 30 feet tall, more than double the height of the statistical average. It has a notched base, which suggests that levers were used to help move it while in a horizontal position, but it is shattered in such a way that it appears to have fallen from an upright position. All of this evidence suggests that at least some upright statues in the quarry, and others that *appear* to be "in transport," may actually have been deliberately placed

upright at their current non-ahu locations for use in ceremonial activity.

To test Routledge's idea of a ceremonial road further, we plotted the positions and orientations of moai lying along the main road from Rano Raraku to Rano Kau and the populous southeastern coast. The majority of statues either on their sides or face-down are lying with their heads oriented away from the quarry, while the heads of the face-up statues are toward the quarry. This means that nearly all of the statues, if standing upright, were looking southwest toward the massive bulk of the crater Rano Kau. There, from about A.D. 1450–1500 until well after contact with Europeans in 1722, the pan-island ceremonial center of Orongo flourished as the site of "birdman" rites. Predicated on the seasonal arrival of flocks of sooty terns and other birds following migratory schools of fish such as tuna, the birdman cult was a vital focus of Rapa Nui spiritual life. This cult emerged and evolved, in part, as a response to food resource scarcity and a changing sociopolitical environment. If Routledge's ceremonial road was, in fact, adorned with standing moai, the two spiritual centers of Rano Raraku and Rano Kau would have been visually linked in an extremely dramatic way.

The ahu to which the "in transport" statues were theoretically being moved were not prepared to receive them. None had been cleared of broken sculpture, and their walls had not been strengthened to support the new statues, all of which are larger than average. The cumulative evidence suggests that, at about the time Orongo became important, the ahu were adapted to uses that did not require moai. Instead, the statues remained in Rano Raraku, where many were used in new ways. Taking everything as a whole, it appears to me that Routledge's ceremonial road is a very real possibility.

In our computer modeling we sought the optimal path the Rapa Nui would have taken to haul Statue 01 from Rano Raraku to Ahu Akivi. We invited Zvi Shiller and his engineering graduate students at the University of California at Los Angeles Robotics Lab to participate in this stage of our research. First, they

digitized a topographic map of Rapa Nui to produce a three-dimensional map of the terrain. Using their computer programs and our statue data, they proposed three alternate routes.

Path 1 was the shortest, most direct route, requiring the least expenditure of energy. It ran westward and directly inland. Between 55 and 70 people would have been able to haul Statue 01 from Rano Raraku to Ahu Akivi along this route. A concerted pull on the hauling ropes would have moved the statue 14 feet. Taking into account pauses to adjust the statue, move the rollers, and tighten any lashings, the work could have been accomplished in five to seven days, calculated on the basis of a five-hour workday. Paths 2 and 3 were also viable, and neither required substantially more people to move the statue. However, Path 2 was longer and Path 3 the longest. Each demanded that laborers expend substantially more energy, thus requiring more food and water to get the job done.

The maximum force required to pull the statue in a horizontal position is two and one-half tons. In an upright position a 14-ton statue with a flat rectangular base requires two and one-third tons of force to tilt. Thus little energy is saved by tilting, although this transport method does not require wood. Pulling an upright statue on a "pod" over rollers requires nearly the same amount of wood as the horizontal method we designed. Manpower needs, however, are about half. The most obvious argument against upright transport is the Rapa Nui terrain. Our calculations show that an upright statue will fall often on a ten-degree slope and nearly all of the time on a 20-degree slope. Tilting an upright statue or pulling one on a "pod" of logs up or down even the gentlest slopes can be tricky and dangerous. Why would the Rapa Nui have resorted to such methods if, in fact, they even did? The only logical explanation would be a lack of wood and/or lack of sufficient manpower. The statues at Ahu Akivi were erected sometime after A.D. 1400 and before the mid-1600s, when the simple, rectangular stone platform was renovated to hold seven statues. Was wood available on Rapa Nui then?

Swamps and lakes in the craters of Rano Raraku and Rano Kau, and on Maunga Terevaka, hold thousands of years of pollen, evidence of the island's history of vegetation and ecological change. Pollen was collected by several investigators, including the Norwegian Archaeological Expedition in 1955. In the early 1930s John Flenley of Massey University in New Zealand and his colleagues analyzed core samples collected on Rapa Nui. They found that the island was once lushly if not lavishly forested, and that a species of palm similar to the gigantic *Jubaea chilensis* was once present, along with other trees.

More recently, Chilean agronomist Gerardo Velasco discovered dozens of large, round holes in ancient, hardened lava flows along the island's coast. The holes are the "prints" left by the trunks of trees once entombed in lava. Close examination reveals patterned ridges in the stone, clearly made by the distinctive trunks of palms. Velasco has measured dozens of these holes, which average 18 inches in diameter. This size is a great deal smaller than that of *Jubaea chilensis,* suggesting that more than one type of palm may have existed on the island. Eighteen inches, however, is a perfect size for transport frames and rollers.

Deforestation took place on the island in various locales at different times, with Rano Raraku probably stripped of its trees by A.D. 1000. American archaeologist Chris Stevenson has found evidence of palms and other as yet unidentified trees at inland sites dating to the 1400s and 1500s. It is safe to assume, therefore, that trees of appropriate dimensions were available for horizontal statue transport at about the time the Ahu Akivi statues were moved.

What about manpower? We used osteological data to calculate the stature of the prehistoric Rapa Nui man who would have transported and erected statues. Our Rapa Nui "reference man" was between the age of 18 and 30, in generally good health. He was five and one-half feet tall and weighed approximately 150 pounds. His daily nutritional requirement would have been 2,880 calories, of which he would have expended roughly 50 percent in energy. According

to the ethnographer Alfred Métraux, the typical Rapa Nui family consisted of nine members. Data from western Polynesia clearly show an extended family could be expected to have 45 to 50 members. Virtually every member contributed some form of labor to the economic life of the whole. Conservatively, each extended family would have had eight males of appropriate age and vigor available to haul statues, meaning that between eight and nine extended families would have had to cooperate to move the average moai.

We calculated an optimal daily diet for our Rapa Nui reference man. About 25–35 percent of the 2,880 calories would have been provided by fat. In order to replace the energy and body tissue he was expending in the work task, he would have needed 65–75 grams of protein and 15 grams of iron, in addition to calcium, phosphorous, carbohydrates, and various vitamins. To accomplish this each man would have had to consume either 200 grams of chicken or an equal amount of non-oily fish (preferably tuna or something similar) to gain 500–600 calories of protein. The remaining calories would have been supplied by sweet potatoes, sugar cane, and bananas, all important Rapa Nui crops with a high water content—a key factor in avoiding work fatigue. Water was also available in the crater lake of Rano Raraku and in the vicinity of Ahu Akivi.

To meet the food requirements of the laborers, a Rapa Nui chief (*ariki*) who commissioned an average statue and had it moved along Path 1 would have needed three to six acres per crop above and beyond the normal one-half acre required to feed each person. He would also have required a surplus of crops at least equal to what he was dispensing to pay for the fish or other protein. It is a conservative estimate that agricultural resources provided by 50 acres, or about double the extended family norm, were required to complete the Ahu Akivi transport task.

In the same way that Polynesian chiefs throughout the Pacific commissioned and paid for canoes, Rapa Nui chiefs called upon their communities to make and move statues. Work parties

were formed of combined, co-resident family groups or cooperating extended family units at the behest of chiefs who exploited ties of kinship, shared religious beliefs, and personal status to marshall the resources of lineage lands and fishing grounds. Master craftspeople with extensive, formal, and institutionalized knowledge, training, talent, and skill directed work crews. Food, water, and timber were produced on lineage lands or traded for by chiefs, and appropriate ceremonies were conducted at all stages of the work. Polynesians distinguish between food needed for sustenance and feast food, and prodigious amounts of both were required for statue transport.

Transporting and raising seven statues at Ahu Akivi is typical of what a Rapa Nui chief could do, and is no small accomplishment. Transport methods used by Rapa Nui experts would logically have been those that were most efficient and of proven utility, and the horizontal method seems most appropriate. Adaptation to time, manpower, or resource shortages would have required flexibility and could have produced individual innovations.

The evidence throughout the Pacific is that limited island ecosystems with short food chains were dramatically transformed by humans. On Rapa Nui from about A.D. 1000, deforestation and agricultural land-use policies apparently caused serious soil erosion. Birds and eggs, once easily attainable foods, were significantly depleted and consequently more valuable. Natural disasters may have occurred that have not, as yet, been investigated. Rapa Nui cultural practices interacted with the island's marginal and isolated environment to precipitate a series of environmental problems, resource shortages, and probable social crises as yet not fully understood.

Not all Rapa Nui people experienced the same kind of problems at the same time, however. Polynesian people held their island homes in high regard, and chiefs were responsible for maintaining individual lineage land-use rights and managing resources. Some were more successful than others. There is direct archaeological evidence that many people tried to mitigate some of their environmental crises as they recognized and understood them. Practical innovations such as *manavai* (stone garden enclosures), which protected fragile plants from the wind, worked fairly well. The Rapa Nui also conceived the birdman cult and other dramatically new religious practices out of old ideas.

The moai were not abandoned, however. Instead of being transported to ahu, they were used in new ways. It appears that increasingly larger moai were erected on the slopes of Rano Raraku. This may reflect a general movement away from narrowly defined, ahu-based lineage concerns and toward more integrated, supralineage ideological practices concentrated on the two main sites of pan-island significance, Rano Raraku and Rano Kau. In the same time frame, however, and possibly less than 200 years before the 1722 arrival of Europeans, our simulated transport studies suggest that a typical Rapa Nui chief was still able to make and move an average-size statue.

The Rapa Nui courageously faced the open and empty sea when they founded and settled their tiny island. As they cleared and used the land and fished the surrounding ocean, they called upon their gods, their leaders, their families, and their own strengths. They interacted with their island environment in traditional ways. Their repertoire of coping skills was shaped by their heritage as Polynesians. European "discoverers" of Rapa Nui perceived the culture, with its fallen statues, as in a state of collapse. This is an ethnocentric Western interpretation rather than an archaeological one. As cultural outsiders, we can now see where the Rapa Nui went wrong. But because the course of Rapa Nui history was interrupted and redirected by the impact of Europeans, we will never know for certain just how successful they might have been in dealing with the environmental crises they faced.

Ice Age Lamps

*The invention of fat-burning lamps toward the end of the Ice Age
helped to transform European culture. It coincided with
several other major technological advances.*

Sophie A. de Beaune and Randall White

Sophie A. de Beaune and Randall White share a fascination with the culture and technology of Ice Age humans. De Beaune is a member of the Laboratory of Prehistoric Ethnology at the National Center for Scientific Research (CNRS) in Paris. She also teaches biological and cultural anthropology to high school students in France. Her current research focuses on nonflint artifacts from the Paleolithic era; she has participated in and directed several excavations in southwest France. White is an associate professor of anthropology at New York University. He specializes in Upper Paleolithic art and technology and is currently preparing a monograph on the earliest forms of personal adornment among European cultures. White co-edited French Upper Paleolithic Collections in the Logan Museum of Anthropology, *which brought to light important late Ice Age art and artifacts in an important U.S. repository. De Beaune contributed most of the new research for this article, which White has helped place in a broader scientific context.*

The controlled use of fire, first achieved at least half a million years ago, is one of the great innovations in human culture. Although archaeologists and anthropologists generally emphasize the importance of

fire for cooking, warmth and protection from predators, the light accompanying fire was also a precious resource, one that made it possible to extend human activity to times and places that are naturally dark. The invention of stone, fat-burning lamps, which happened in Ice Age Europe nearly 40,000 years ago, offered the first effective, portable means of exploiting this aspect of fire. The appearance of lamps broadly coincides with a number of other extraordinary cultural changes, including the emergence of art, personal adornment and complex weapons systems.

Many scholars have hypothesized about how Ice Age lamps functioned and were used, but nobody had ever undertaken a systematic study of them. One of us (de Beaune) therefore set out to examine these lamps in detail and to classify them by type. In conjunction with that project, we built working replicas of stone lamps in order to analyze their effectiveness as light sources and to learn about their design, fabrication and use. The results of this investigation provide a provocative insight into the technology and behavior of some of the earliest modern humans in Europe.

The first object explicitly identified as an Ice Age lamp was discovered in 1902, the year researchers authenticated the wall art in the cave at La Mouthe, France. Archaeologists had presumed that the creation of paintings and engravings hundreds of meters underground must have required an arti-

ficial light source. In the course of exploring La Mouthe, they uncovered compelling support of that notion: a carefully fabricated and heavily burned sandstone lamp bearing the engraved image of an ibex on its underside.

Since then, hundreds of more or less hollowed-out objects have been excavated and rather indiscriminately lumped into the category of lamps. The initial research goals were to sift through the potpourri, establish criteria for identifying lamps and examine variation within this category of objects. A search of the literature and of museum collections turned up 547 artifacts that had been listed as possible lamps. The first hurdle was to distinguish lamps from other similarly shaped implements, such as grinding stones. It quickly became obvious that the size and shape of an object are insufficient as defining criteria. For example, lamps need not have a bowl-shaped depression; many perfectly flat slabs show clear traces of localized burning, which in these and other instances provide only incontrovertible evidence that an object served as a lamp.

We judged that 245 of the 547 putative lamps clearly served other purposes (mortars, ocher receptacles and so on). The remaining 302 objects were of uncertain status as lamps. We then divided that sample (285 of which have a well-known site of origin) into two categories. We considered 169 of the items to be certain, probable or

Aquitaine basin has yielded 60 percent of the lamps, the Pyrenean region 15 percent. Considerably fewer lamps have been recovered from other parts of France, and lamps found outside France—in Spain, Germany and Czechoslovakia—are exceedingly rare. Although this pattern may be explained in part by the historically greater intensity of research and the greater number of sites in southwest France, it seems that lamp-producing cultures were in fact restricted to a particular European region.

The vast majority of the known stone lamps consist of limestone or sandstone, both of which are fairly abundant. Limestone has the advantage of often occurring naturally in slab-like shapes that require little alteration. Moreover, limestone conducts heat poorly, so lamps of this material do not get hot enough to burn the user's fingers. Sandstone is a much better heat conductor, so simple sandstone lamps quickly become too hot to hold after they are lit. Paleolithic people solved this problem by carving handles into most sandstone lamps. Perhaps part of the appeal of sandstone lay in its attractive red color and smooth texture.

Our experiments suggest that the size and shape of the bowl are the primary factors that control how well a stone lamp functions. Setting bowl shape as our primary criterion, we divided the 302 Upper Paleolithic lamps into three main types: open-circuit lamps, closed-circuit bowl lamps and closed-circuit lamps with carved handles.

Open-circuit lamps are the simplest kind. They consist of either small, flat or slightly concave slabs or of larger slabs having natural cavities open to one side to allow excess fuel to drain away as the fat melts; the largest ones are roughly 20 centimeters across. Because open-circuit lamps show no noticeable signs of carving or shaping, large numbers of them may have gone unrecognized in premodern excavations. As a result, open-circuit lamps probably are underrepresented in the current sample.

Any slab of rock will work as an open-circuit lamp, so fashioning one

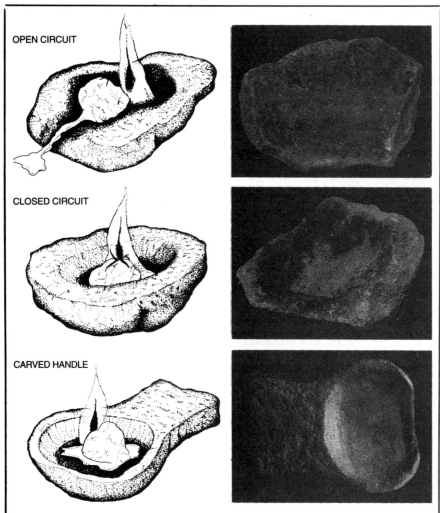

LAMP DESIGNS fall into three main categories. Open-circuit lamps (*top*) consist of largely unaltered slabs of rock. When the lamp is lit, melted fat runs off through natural crevices in the rock. Closed-circuit lamps (*middle*) have carved depressions to contain the runoff. Carved-handle, closed-circuit lamps (*bottom*) also have bowl-shaped fuel chambers but are more finely finished and have formed extensions for easier handling. Burn marks indicate that the wick was placed away from the handle.

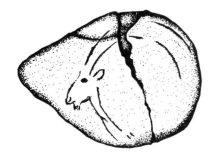

ENGRAVED DECORATIONS often appear on the sides or bottoms of closed-circuit lamps. This carved-handle lamp, which features the incised image of an ibex, was found at La Mouthe in 1902. It was the first object explicitly identified as a lamp.

possible lamps. The other 133 we classified as doubtful or unavailable for study. Markings left by the burning of fuel and wick tend to disappear over time, so the oldest lamps were the most likely to fall into the dubious category.

The lamps that we consider here all date from the Upper Paleolithic era, between 40,000 and 11,000 years ago.

The 285 lamps of known origin come from 105 different archaeological sites, mainly in southwest France. The

requires extremely little effort. The trade-off is that these kinds of lamps inevitably waste a lot of fuel. Open-circuit lamps may be best interpreted as makeshift or expedient devices, easily made and freely discarded. Studies of the modern Inuit show that human groups, even those capable of building large, elaborate lamps, occasionally burn a piece of fat on a stone slab when no alternative lies readily at hand.

Closed-circuit bowl lamps are the most common variety. They are in all regions, in all periods and in all types of sites where lamps have been recovered. Closed-circuit bowl lamps have shallow, circular or oval depressions designed to retain the melted fuel. The recovered lamps of this kind range from crude to elaborate. Some bowl lamps are entirely natural, some have a slightly retouched bowl and others are completely fabricated. The exterior part of the lamp also may be natural, partly retouched or entirely sculpted. These lamps consist of oval or circular pieces of limestone that are usually the size of a fist

or slightly larger. The bowl has sloping sides capable of retaining liquid when the lamp is placed on a horizontal surface. A typical bowl measures a few centimeters across but only 15 to 20 millimeters deep. The largest bowls can hold about 10 cubic centimeters of liquid.

Ice Age closed-circuit lamps resemble those employed by certain Inuit peoples—such as the Caribou, Netsilik and Aleut—who had access to wood for fuel and were therefore not dependent on lamps for heat. Inuit living north of the treeline, where wood was scarce, designed large lamps from slabs of soapstone that were up to a meter across. Those giant lamps (perhaps more correctly thought of as stoves) served many of the same functions as hearths elsewhere, including drying clothes, cooking and heating. There may be direct relations between the quality and abundance of locally available wood for fuel, the presence of fireplaces and the form of lamps at a site.

The most intricate lamps are those we classified as closed-circuit lamps

with carved handles. The 30 such lamps in our sample are shaped, smoothed and finely finished entirely by abrasion. Each has a carved handle; 11 of them are decorated with engravings. These lamps appear in the archaeological record somewhat later than the others. The first carved-handle lamps show up in either the Solutrean (22,000 to 18,000 years ago) or Lower Magdalenian (18,000 to 15,000 years ago) cultures. They are particularly abundant in the Middle and Upper Magdalenian (15,000 to 11,000 years ago). Most carved-handle lamps are found in the Dordogne region of France. They are most abundant in rock-shelter sites but are also found in caves and open-air camps.

The elegant design, rarity and limited distribution in time and space of carved-handle lamps may imply that they served primarily ceremonial purposes. A well-known example from Lascaux, which has been dated to 17,500 years ago, was found on the cave floor at the bottom of a vertical shaft, below a drawing of a hunter confronting a wounded bison. This

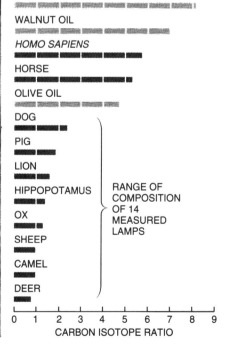

EXPERIMENTAL CLOSED-CIRCUIT LAMP (*left*) clarifies how these objects were used in Paleolithic times. A lump of fat serves as the fuel; the wick consists of bits of bark, lichen or moss. Melted fat collects in a depression in the rock and must occasionally be poured off. Chemical analysis of Ice Age lamps reveals the presence of residues whose composition resembles that of fat from animals that were common in Paleolithic France (*right*); vegetable fats clearly were not used.

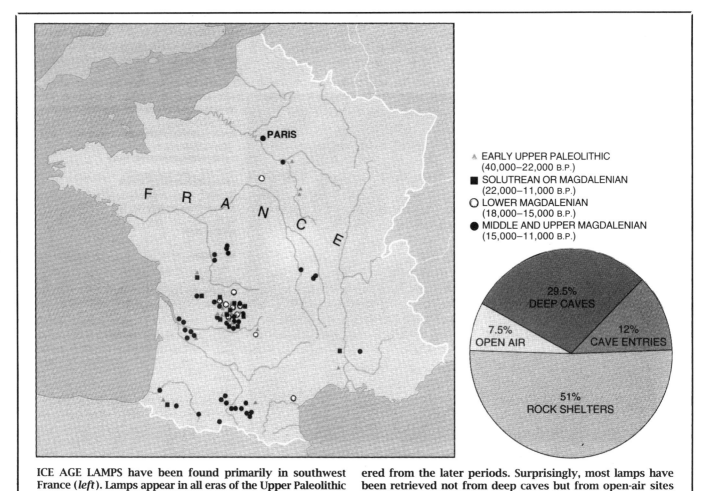

ICE AGE LAMPS have been found primarily in southwest France (*left*). Lamps appear in all eras of the Upper Paleolithic (40,000 to 11,000 years ago); more of them have been recov- ered from the later periods. Surprisingly, most lamps have been retrieved not from deep caves but from open-air sites and from under rock shelters (*right*).

Legend:
- △ EARLY UPPER PALEOLITHIC (40,000–22,000 B.P.)
- ■ SOLUTREAN OR MAGDALENIAN (22,000–11,000 B.P.)
- ○ LOWER MAGDALENIAN (18,000–15,000 B.P.)
- ● MIDDLE AND UPPER MAGDALENIAN (15,000–11,000 B.P.)

Pie chart:
- 29.5% DEEP CAVES
- 12% CAVE ENTRIES
- 7.5% OPEN AIR
- 51% ROCK SHELTERS

lamp was discovered by the Abbé Glory, a Catholic lay priest who suggested that such lamps were used to burn aromatic twigs and hence were analogous to incense burners. Too few chemical analyses have been performed, however, to test this hypothesis adequately. The other kinds of stone lamps probably served exclusively as sources of light.

To be effective, a fat-burning lamp must be reliable, easy to handle and bright enough to throw usable light a distance of a few meters in, for example, a darkened cave. The form of lamp that predominates in our sample of Paleolithic lamps is precisely that which our experiments revealed to be optimally efficient. It is a closed-circuit lamp having an oval or circular depression and gently sloping rather than vertical sides. Sloping the side of the bowl facilitates emptying the lamp (so that the wick does not become swamped

in melted fat) without dislodging the wick. Carving a gap or notch in the rim of the lamp offers an alternative way to empty the bowl while keeping the wick in place. Eighty percent of the Paleolithic lamps we studied use the sloped-side approach.

Anthropologists have long assumed that animal fat was the fuel burned in Ice Age lamps. From our experiments, we learned that the best fats are those that melt quickly and at a low temperature. Also, they must not contain too much adipose tissue, the connective tissue in fat. Fat from seals, horses and bovids proved most effective in experimental lamps. But were these in fact the fuels favored by Paleolithic humans?

Guy L. Bourgeois of the University of Bordeaux and de Beaune analyzed residues from several Paleolithic lamps to identify the substances they con-

tained. Using two sensitive chemical analysis techniques (vapor-phase chromatography and mass spectrometry), they measured the carbon isotope ratios in fatty acids in the residues. The abundance ratios resemble those in animal fats from modern herbivores, such as cattle, pigs and horses. Unfortunately, scientists have no samples of fat from the actual animals that lived during the late Pleistocene. Nevertheless, the observed ratios of carbon isotopes are quite unlike those in vegetable fats, proving that animals were indeed the source of fuel for Ice Age lamps.

Our investigations also provided new information about the materials from which wicks were made. A good wick must be able to attract melted fat by capillary action and convey it to the free, burning end without being too quickly consumed. Of the wicks we tested, lichen (known to be used by modern Inuit), moss and then juniper worked best. Fritz H. Schweingrüber of the Swiss Federal Research Institute for Forest, Snow and Landscape analyzed several lamp residues. He detected remnants of conifers, juniper and grass, as well as nonwoody residues, possibly lichen or moss. In our experience, juniper wicks are never completely consumed by the flame and so may be better preserved than wicks composed of other plants.

The traces of use on our experimental lamps make it possible to interpret with confidence the markings observed on Paleolithic lamps. Those signs of usage come in three broad forms: light accumulations of soot, deposits of charcoal and reddening of the rock itself, a process known as rubefaction. In 80 percent of all the lamps observed, soot and charcoal deposits are situated within or on the rim of the fuel chamber, where one would expect the wick to lie. Occasional blackening of the side or underside of the lamp can be produced by trickles of melted fat that carried with them small particles of soot. Charcoal deposits result from carbonization of the wick or from the heat alteration, or calcination, of adipose tissue in the burning fat.

Thermal reddening often appears on the sides and undersides of lamps, but it, too, most frequently appears in or on the rim of the fuel chamber (in 67.5 percent of the cases). Experience with modern replicas indicates that such reddening took place when hot, melted fat ran onto the side or bottom of the lamp, either as the lamp was being emptied or when it overflowed on its own. Thermal reddening evidently can occur after only a few uses and so provides a helpful indicator of which artifacts served as lamps.

Repeated reuse of a lamp leaves distinct patterns. If a standard open- or closed-circuit lamp is lit on several occasions, the placement of the fat and wick tends to change from one time to the next. Because there is no preferred orientation for those simple lamps, they eventually become blackened and reddened over the entire bowl or surface. The carefully worked closed-circuit lamps that have handles display strikingly different signs of usage.

They are oriented the same way each time they are lit, so soot deposits build up on one part of the bowl only, generally the area opposite the handle.

Open-circuit and simple closed-circuit lamps probably were lit only a few times before being discarded. They are so easy to manufacture that there would have existed little incentive to carry them from site to site; we found that we could make a decent lamp in about half an hour. Decorated, carved-handle lamps, which represent a greater investment of labor, were more likely to have been used repeatedly.

To evaluate the effectiveness of Paleolithic fat-burning lamps, one needs to know how much light those lamps could provide. De Beaune investigated this matter by measuring the light output of modern replicas in the metrology laboratories of Kodak-Pathé, France. In quantity, intensity and luminescence, the experimental lamps provided distinctly less light than a standard candle but nonetheless would have been sufficient to guide a person through a cave or to illuminate fine work when placed nearby—assuming, of course, that the visual acuity of Paleolithic people was the same as ours.

The limitations of Ice Age lamps suggest that the creators of cave drawings never saw them as they appear in modern photographs. Human color perception is constrained and distorted at levels less than 150 lux (for comparison, 1,000 lux is typical in a well-lit office). It seems doubtful that the creators of the cave art worked under such bright conditions. Achieving full and accurate color perception of the cave images along a five-meter-long panel would require 150 lamps, each of them placed 50 centimeters from the cave wall. Torches could have provided supplementary light, but few traces of torches have been found in deep caves. On the other hand, the absence or scarcity of lamps in vast cave galleries such as those at Rouffignac, Niaux and Les Trois Frères implies that the creator of the paintings had access to some alternative light sources.

Today when one views the famous cave art in France and Spain, the artificial illumination creates an effect fundamentally unlike that experienced by Paleolithic visitors. Electric lights in the cave of Font de Gaume yield a steady light level of about 20 to 40 lux across a full panel of drawings. Ten to 15 thoughtfully placed stone lamps would be needed to attain 20 lux. A person carrying a single lamp would get a very different impression of the cave art and could view only small portions of the wall at a time. The dim illumination produced by flickering lamps may well have been part of the desired effect of viewing art deep within a cave. The illusion of animals suddenly materializing out of the darkness is a powerful one, and some cave images are all the more convincing if one cannot see them too well.

Of course, fat-burning lamps were employed for many tasks other than creating and viewing cave art. Lamps are found in such abundance at sites throughout southwest France that they must have been a fairly ordinary item of day-to-day existence. Only about 30 percent of the known lamps were recovered in deep caves. Open-air sites, rock shelters exposed to plentiful daylight and cave entries have provided the rest. The number of lamps at each site (two to three, on average) does not differ significantly from caves to rock shelters to open-air sites.

The location of lamps within sites provides clues to how people exploited them. In deep caves, lamps are often recovered from places where people had to pass, such as cave entrances, the intersections of different galleries and along walls. It would seem that lamps were placed at strategic or predictable points where they could easily be found and reused. The discovery of many lamps lying together—most notably at Lascaux, where 70 lamps have been recovered—implies that lamps were stored in particular locations between uses. Unfortunately, one cannot deduce how many of the lamps were lit at any one time.

Lamps are frequently discovered near fireplaces. Perhaps they were preheated in the fire in order to warm the fat and make it easier to ignite or were abandoned and reused as hearthstones. More likely, fireplaces served as central points of heat and light from which people departed into and returned from the darkness. Many lamps are found inverted in the soil, implying that on returning, people extinguished them simply by turning them over.

In at least one location, a lamp seems to have provided a permanent, fixed source of light within a campsite. Archaeologists found two lamps in a small, natural cavity in the wall of the rock shelter of La Garenne. One lamp had been turned over as if to extinguish the flame. The other was placed upright in a natural hollow in the rock that held it level. The cavity itself would have served as a natural reflector that maximized the lamp's light output.

Sorting through the sample of fat-burning lamps, we sought to learn how their abundance and design changed over time. That analysis is somewhat restricted by the paucity of data. Accurate radioactive dates are available for only the most recently discovered lamps. In most cases, ages are inferred from the archaeological levels in which the lamps were found, and in many early excavations even that information was not recorded. Nevertheless, enough information exists for us to make some general observations.

Many more lamps appear in the last cultural period of the Upper Paleolithic, the Magdalenian, than in preceding periods. This may reflect the fact that there are simply more Magdalenian sites known than is the case for earlier periods, as well as the fact that most deep-cave painting took place in the Magdalenian. Older lamps are also harder to identify with certainty.

The form of lamps seems to have evolved surprisingly little through the ages. Some variation in form, material and design occurred, but there is no clear progression from crude to elaborate. Although carved-handle lamps are more common in the later eras, all three primary types of lamp are found throughout the Magdalenian, and even the most elaborate lamp designs date back to the earliest Upper Paleolithic periods, which roughly corresponds to the time when Cro-Magnon, anatomically modern humans, appeared in Europe. The various forms of lamp most likely represent functional responses to particular contexts of use; the need for both simple, easy-to-make lamps and carved, aesthetically pleasing ones apparently was common to all Paleolithic cultures in France.

It is difficult to overstate the importance of artificial light in freeing humans from their evolutionary adaptation to the daylight world. Cave art specialist Denis Vialou of the Museum of Natural History in Paris lauds the Magdalenian cave artists as the people who conquered the world of the underground. But perhaps it is more accurate to see them as the most daring of a long line of our Cro-Magnon ancestors, who, through intelligence and technological innovation, changed the human experience forever by domesticating the realm of darkness.

FURTHER READING

DARK CAVES, BRIGHT VISIONS: LIFE IN ICE AGE EUROPE. Randall White. American Museum of Natural History and W. W. Norton & Company, 1986.
PALEOLITHIC LAMPS AND THEIR SPECIALIZATION: A HYPOTHESIS. S. de Beaune in *Current Anthropology,* Vol. 28, No. 4, pages 569–577; August/October 1987.
TECHNOLOGICAL CHANGES ACROSS THE MIDDLE-UPPER PALEOLITHIC TRANSITION: ECONOMIC, SOCIAL AND COGNITIVE PERSPECTIVES. P. Mellars in *The Human Revolution: Behavioural and Biological Perspectives on the Origins of Modern Humans.* Edited by P. Mellars and C. Stringer. Princeton University Press, 1989.
NONFLINT STONE TOOLS OF THE EARLY UPPER PALEOLITHIC. Sophie de Beaune in *Before Lascaux: The Complex Record of the Early Upper Paleolithic.* Edited by H. Knecht, A. Pike-Tay and R. White. CRC Press, 1993.

Paleolithic Paint Job

Two French archeologists are trying to get closer—much closer—to an ancient act of creation.

Roger Lewin

Roger Lewin is a writer in Washington, D.C., who specializes in human prehistory. His most recent book on the subject, Origins Reconsidered, *written with anthropologist Richard Leakey, was published in 1992. In 1989 Lewin was the recipient of the inaugural Lewis Thomas Award for Excellence in the Communication of Life Sciences. "Ancient human fossils stir the imagination," Lewin says, "but nothing matches the immediacy of prehistoric cave paintings in their ability to connect us with our past."*

"You have to be dressed right for this job," says Michel Lorblanchet, whose beret-capped head and white goatee make him a virtual caricature of a Frenchman. Lorblanchet, an archeologist with France's National Center for Scientific Research, slips out of mud-caked overalls and, with a colleague's help, struggles free of a pair of snug rubber boots. "It's pretty tight in there," he says, referring to a cave he has been working in, not to his boots. "You have to crawl a long way," he adds. "That's how we get so filthy." Lorblanchet is describing his efforts to study the ancient paintings deep inside the caves of the Lot Valley in southwest France. These depictions of a lost world—of Ice Age bison, horses, mammoths, and deer—were painted between 30,000 and 10,000 years ago.

They remain among the most haunting of all archeological finds.

The region here, known as Quercy, is dominated by rugged gray limestone plateaus intermittently sliced by fertile valleys and farmland. The cuisine of the area—a matter of constant and weighty discussion among the locals—is rich and robust: truffles, foie gras, duck confit, deeply flavorful lamb, and strong, dark wines. There is an earthy sensuosity about the place. When Lorblanchet, a native son of the area, describes it simply as "my country," you know he is speaking not only for himself but for generations of people whose roots are planted in this land. The Quercy sensuosity also apparently imbues Lorblanchet's unorthodox approach to studying cave art.

Traditionally cave art archeologists, perhaps to beef up their scientific credentials, have striven to understand the meaning of these paintings through objective inquiry. They have relied heavily on statistical analysis (which animals were represented where in the caves, for example) to test their hypotheses about the art. Lorblanchet's approach, by contrast, is freewheeling, subjective, experimental. He wants to get inside the minds of the early artists by reproducing some of their most famous works—not merely by tracing their outlines onto paper, as others have done in the past, but by replicating whole paintings on rock. Although he hopes to gain new insights, he has

no theory to prove or disprove. "Some of my colleagues think that experimentation without a preliminary theory is a waste of time," says Lorblanchet, the usual soft timbre of his voice gaining a slight edge of defiance. "But I totally disagree with them. I don't know what I will learn by temporarily becoming a Paleolithic painter, but I know I'll learn something."

Actually, for all its apparent unorthodoxy, Lorblanchet's work fits right into a new trend in cave art archeology. The Quercy archeologist is interested in how the early artists went about painting. Jean Clottes, another French archeologist, working in the Pyrenees, studies what their pigments were composed of. Although the two men's styles could hardly be more dissimilar—one personal and intuitive, the other extremely high-tech—they converge on the same novel question: What can we learn from the *paint* in these paintings? This investigative avenue doesn't ignore all that has gone before, of course, but builds on it.

The scholarly study of Ice Age art began in the 1920s with the great French prehistorian Abbé Henri Breuil, who saw it as an expression of hunting magic. Breuil based his conclusions on contemporary anthropological observations of the Arunta aborigines in central Australia. To ensure a plentiful supply of prey, the Arunta performed rituals during which they painted images of the prey—principally kangaroos—on rock faces. (Rituals of this kind are now well known among many of the world's remaining foraging peoples.)

Gradually though, archeologists began to doubt that hunting magic alone could explain all prehistoric cave art. The overthrow of this hypothesis in the 1960s was led by another French prehistorian, André Leroi-Gourhan. After surveying more than 60 painted caves, Leroi-Gourhan came to see order in the images' distribution. Stags often appeared in entrance-ways, ibex at the caves' peripheries, and horses, bison, oxen, and mammoths in the main chambers. As Leroi-Gourhan saw it, this structure represented the division of the world into males and females—or, more mystically, maleness and femaleness. The horse, the stag, and the ibex embodied maleness; the bison, the mammoth, and the ox embodied femaleness. According to this "structuralist" interpretation, all caves were decorated systematically to reflect this male-female duality, which suffused the mythology of Upper Paleolithic people.

This mode of structuralism was eventually done in by its all-embracing scope. It could be true, but there was no way of knowing: How could you test a rule with no exceptions? These days archeologists are taking more diverse approaches. Structure could still play a role, for example, but a more limited one—individual caves may well have been decorated with an overall pattern in mind. More attention is now being paid to the art's context. For example, Margaret Conkey, an archeologist at the University of California at Berkeley, argues that to understand what made the art meaningful you have to understand its social context. Which members of society produced the images? Was it the sacred right of a few important males? Were females involved, or even responsible for the art?

Still, even with a diversity of approaches, you can only hope for shadowy glimpses of Paleolithic life. "You know we should admit that it may never be possible to bridge the gap between the Paleolithic mind and the modern mind," cautions Lorblanchet. "There are many barriers that stop us." The most immediate barrier, he says, is that our perspective on the world is so utterly different from that of the Ice Age artists. The country here was once a frigid steppe, roamed by herds of exotic species that have long since gone extinct; and the lives of the hunters, so intimately attuned to the rhythms of nature, were vastly different from our own. "We are city dwellers, surrounded by angular build-ings, following artificial rhythms of life," says Lorblanchet. "How can we expect to be able to view the art as Upper Paleolithic people did?" Lorblanchet hopes his new approach will help answer that.

Lorblanchet's recent bid to re-create one of the most important Ice Age images in Europe was an affair of the heart as much as the head. "I tried to abandon my skin of a modern citizen, tried to experience the feeling of the artist, to enter the dialogue between the rock and the man," he explains. Every day for a week in the fall of 1990 he drove the 20 miles from his home in the medieval village of Cajarc into the hills above the river Lot. There, in a small, practically inaccessible cave, he transformed himself into an Upper Paleolithic painter. And not just any Upper Paleolithic painter, but the one who 18,400 years ago crafted the dotted horses inside the famous cave of Pech Merle.

You can still see the original horses in Pech Merle's vast underground geo-

Spit-painting in action: Michel Lorblanchet blows paint under his left hand to achieve an outline with a soft lower edge for the horse's back; spits pigment between parallel hands to paint the legs; makes a handprint; and spits dots through a hole in an animal skin.

logic splendor. You enter through a narrow passageway and soon find yourself gazing across a grand cavern to where the painting seems to hang in the gloom. "Outside, the landscape is very different from the one the Upper Paleolithic people saw," says Lorblanchet. "But in here, the landscape is the same as it was more than 18,000 years ago. You see what the Upper Paleolithic people experienced." No matter where you look in this cavern, the eye is drawn back to the panel of horses.

The two horses face away from each other, rumps slightly overlapping, their outlines sketched in black. The animal on the right seems to come alive as it merges with a crook in the edge of the panel, the perfect natural shape for a horse's head. But the impression of naturalism quickly fades as the eye falls on the painting's dark dots. There are more than 200 of them, deliberately distributed within and below the bodies and arcing around the right-hand horse's head and mane. More cryptic still are a smattering of red dots and half-circles and the floating outline of a fish. The surrealism is completed by six disembodied human hands stenciled above and below the animals.

Lorblanchet began thinking about re-creating the horses after a research trip to Australia over a decade ago. Not only is Australia a treasure trove of rock art, but its aboriginal people are still creating it. "In Queensland I learned how people painted by spitting pigment onto the rock," he recalls. "They spat paint and used their hand, a piece of cloth, or a feather as a screen to create different lines and other effects. Elsewhere in Australia people used chewed twigs as paintbrushes, but in Queensland the spitting technique worked best." The rock surfaces there were too uneven for extensive brushwork, he adds—just as they are in Quercy.

When Lorblanchet returned home he looked at the Quercy paintings with a new eye. Sure enough, he began seeing the telltale signs of spit-painting—lines with edges that were sharply demarcated on one side and fuzzy on the other, as if they had been airbrushed—instead of the brushstrokes he and others had assumed were there. Could you produce lines that were crisp on both edges with the same technique, he wondered, and perhaps dots too? Archeologists had long recognized that hand stencils, which are common in prehistoric art, were produced by spitting paint around a hand held to the wall. But no one had thought that entire animal images could be created this way. Before he could test his ideas, however, Lorblanchet had to find a suitable rock face—the original horses were painted on a roughly vertical panel 13 feet across and 6 feet high. With the help of a speleologist, he eventually found a rock face in a remote cave high in the hills and set to work.

Following the aboriginal practices he had witnessed, Lorblanchet first made a light outline sketch of the horses with a charred stick. Then he prepared black pigment for the painting. "My intention had been to use manganese dioxide, as the Pech Merle painter did," says Lorblanchet, referring to one of the minerals ground up for paint by the early artists. "But I was advised that manganese is somewhat toxic, so I used wood charcoal instead." (Charcoal was used as pigment by Paleolithic painters in other caves, so Lorblanchet felt he could justify his concession to safety.) To turn the charcoal into paint, Lorblanchet ground it with a limestone block, put the powder in his mouth, and diluted it to the right consistency with saliva and water. For red pigment he used ocher from the local iron-rich clay.

He started with the dark mane of the right-hand horse. "I spat a series of dots and fused them together to represent tufts of hair," he says, unselfconsciously reproducing the spitting action as he talks. "Then I painted the horse's back by blowing the pigment

below my hand held so"—he holds his hand flat against the rock with his thumb tucked in to form a straight line—"and used it like a stencil to produce a sharp upper edge and a diffused lower edge. You get an illusion of the animal's rounded flank this way."

He experimented as he went. "You see the angular rump?" he says, pointing to the original painting. "I reproduced that by holding my hand perpendicular to the rock, with my palm slightly bent, and I spat along the edge formed by my hand and the rock." He found he could produce sharp lines, such as those in the tail and in the upper hind leg, by spitting into the gap between parallel hands. The belly demanded more ingenuity; he spat paint into a V-shape formed by his two splayed hands, rubbed it into a curved swath to shape the belly's outline, then finger-painted short protruding lines to suggest the animals' shaggy hair. Neatly outlined dots, he found, could not be made by blowing a thin jet of charcoal onto the wall. He had to spit pigment through a hole made in an animal skin.

"I spent seven hours a day for a week," he says. "Puff . . . puff . . . puff. . . . It was exhausting, particularly because there was carbon monoxide in the cave. But you experience

something special, painting like that. You feel you are breathing the image onto the rock—projecting your spirit from the deepest part of your body onto the rock surface."

Was that what the Paleolithic painter felt when creating this image? "Yes, I know it doesn't sound very scientific," Lorblanchet says of his highly personal style of investigation, "but the intellectual games of the structuralists haven't got us very far, have they? Studying rock art shouldn't be an intellectual game. It is about understanding humanity. That's why I believe the experimental approach is valid in this case."

In contrast to Lorblanchet's free-wheeling style, Jean Clottes's research looks much more like science as usual—technical and analytical. Clottes, a scientific adviser on rock art to the French Ministry of Culture, works in the Midi-Pyrénées, a wild and mountainous region that abuts France's border with Spain. Many of the caves in these mountains contain fine examples of Ice Age art. The most celebrated of the decorated caves is Niaux, which is approached by a gaping entrance on the steep northern slope of the Vicdessos Valley. About half a mile into this long, meandering cave is the Salon Noir, a towering

cavern containing black images of horses, bison, ibex, and deer. Among the questions that preoccupied Clottes during his many visits to the Salon Noir was the age of these images. Were they all created at about the same time? And who created them?

One of the toughest problems in the study of rock art is accurately dating it. Radiocarbon dating, the surest method can be done only if charcoal is present in the paint. (The first such dates were obtained in 1989, when a technological advance—carbon dating by accelerator mass spectrometry—made it possible to use much smaller paint samples.) For the most part, however, archeologists have had to rely on what they term stylistic chronology. This basically depends on a subjective assessment of painting styles and on the assumption that particular conventions—such as the use of perspective—belong to particular periods. According to Leroi-Gourhan's chronology, nearly universally accepted, the paintings in the Salon Noir were painted in a uniform style typical of the period known as the Middle Magdalenian, which occurred some 13,000 to 14,000 years ago. But the pigment analysis that Clottes undertook with physicists Michel Menu and Philippe Walter revealed a different story.

Clottes's study was inspired by some work that Menu and Walter had done previously at the cave of La Vache, some 450 feet from Niaux, as the crow flies, on the southern side of the Vicdessos Valley. Although La Vache had no paintings, it did contain engraved bone objects, along with charcoal remains, that carbon dating established as being between 12,000 and 13,000 years old, an age corresponding to the period known as the Late Magdalenian. Trapped within the grooves of the engraved artifacts were residues of red and black paint Menu and Walter decided to find out what these paints were made from.

Back in Paris, at the Research Laboratory of the Museums of France, the

Lorblanchet's re-creation of the ancient dotted horses; it took him a week to complete his Paleolithic masterpiece.

Flightless Bird in Waterlogged Cave

The cave has been hailed as a sort of underwater Lascaux, the most exciting find since Lascaux's painted galleries were discovered five decades ago in southwest France. The hyperbole is understandable. The Cosquer cave, whose discovery was formally documented last year, can't really match Lascaux for artistry, but its images are unique and its place in prehistory is pivotal. The cave was found in 1991 by Henri Cosquer, a professional diver, while he was exploring the underwater grottoes at Cap Morgiu, near Marseilles. Its narrow entrance lies 121 feet below the surface of the Mediterranean, making it inaccessible to all but the most expert scuba divers—and enormously frustrating for landlubbing archeologists like Jean Clottes.

"I'd love to visit the Cosquer cave," says Clottes, who heads the committee formed by the French Ministry of Culture to plan future work at the promising site. "But I'm no diver, and the passage to it is very dangerous." Already the cave has claimed three lives. Shortly after its discovery, three diving enthusiasts died in the water darkness while worming their way along the 500-foot-long tunnel that leads from the entrance to the partially flooded inner caverns. The French government

has since blocked the entrance to prevent further tragedy. Clottes himself has seen only video images of the paintings, transmitted by the cameras of the diving research team to a TV monitor on dry land.

The cave is important for several reasons, explains Clottes. While painted caves are common in southwest France and in the Pyrenees, nothing like Cosquer had ever been found in the country's southeast. Although Cosquer is half underwater, the walls above sea level are covered in decorations. There are hand stencils, finger tracings, cryptic symbols, and cross-hatchings and more than 100 engraved and painted animal images. Many of these show horses, bison, and ibex, which are typical of Ice Age art from Europe. But the images of marine animals—what look like jellyfish, and a kind of seabird—are unlike anything seen before. Early English-language reports referred to the large, portly birds with stunted wings as penguins. In fact, says Clottes, they are auks, flightless seabirds that became extinct in the Mediterranean about a century and a half ago.

The cave is all the more important because it is possible to carbon-date some of the images from charcoal

flakes in the paint and from charcoal in hearths found on the cave floor. Carbon dating has shown that the hand stencils were done between 27,800 and 26,500 years ago, which makes them contenders for the oldest known paintings in the world. The animal images, some of which appear on top of the negative handprints, were crafted more than 8,000 years later. "In the short time since its discovery, Cosquer has become the most thoroughly dated painted cave known," observes Clottes.

Although getting to the cave is hard nowadays—a sort of athletic event in itself, as Clottes puts it—the prehistoric people who used the cave for their ancient rituals would have had no trouble reaching it. Sea levels at the time were at least 300 feet lower than they are today, so the cave was dry. Archeologists hope to make access easier by sinking a shaft through the limestone to a passage near the caverns. But first they will have to determine what effect such an opening would have on very fragile paintings that have been sealed in an air pocket for thousands of years. "Our first priority," says Clottes, "is the preservation of the paintings."

—*Roger Lewin*

two physicists used scanning electron microscopy, X-ray diffraction, and proton-induced X-ray emission to examine the physical and chemical properties of these paints. The pigment minerals held no surprises: the red was hematite and the black was basically manganese dioxide. The interest lay in the extender, a general term for materials that artists use to stretch pigment and, along with water, enhance its ease of application. Menu and Walter's analysis revealed that the extender in the La Vache paint was a mixture of biotite and feldspar, minerals easily obtained in the valley. But what intrigued the researchers was that biotite and feldspar don't occur together. "The

Paleolithic painters had to mix them together, then grind them with the pigment to form paint," says Clottes. Quartz grinding stones bearing traces of paint production were discovered in the caves. "This tells us that the Paleolithic painters didn't just use whatever was available," Clottes points out "They had a specific recipe."

Was the La Vache recipe—call it recipe B, for biotite and feldspar—also used at Niaux? "Because of their proximity, there seemed a good chance that the hunters of La Vache belonged to the same social group that frequented Niaux," explains Clottes. "If so, they probably used the same pigments."

Traditionally archeologists would have hesitated to take paint from prehistoric images to test the idea, but Menu and Walter's methods required only a tiny quantity—less than half a milligram. In 1989 they received permission to lift 59 pinhead-size pieces of pigment from images in the Salon Noir and other locations in the cave. When these paint samples were analyzed, Clottes's intuition was proved correct: most were indeed recipe B, suggesting that they, too, might be 12,000 to 13,000 years old, just like those in the cave across the valley. His deductions were recently confirmed in a follow-up study capitalizing on one of the surprises of the Niaux pigment analysis. Tests revealed that the recipe B paint was layered: there were traces of charcoal under the black manganese pigment. Carbon dating on the charcoal flakes under one of the images corroborated that the paint was 12,800 years old, consistent with the paint at La Vache.

The confirmation of Clottes's hunch, however, opened a can of worms. Based on Leroi-Gourhan's stylistic chronology, the Niaux paintings were up to 14,000 years old. Yet at least some of the Niaux paintings employed a paint recipe—recipe B—that carbon dating established as 12,000 to 13,000 years old. Did this mean that the recipe had been in use for at least 1,000 years? Or could there be something wrong with the chronology based on stylistic similarity?

"We didn't know what to make of it," says Clottes. "And the situation became more complicated, because in *some* paint samples from Niaux, we found a different recipe." In this paint mixture, call it recipe F the extender was only feldspar. It contained no biotite, and there was no charcoal beneath it. "We toyed with the idea of different paint recipes being used by groups of different social status, or even one recipe for men, the other for women. But it seemed just as likely that the different recipes were used during different periods."

To settle this puzzle, Clottes, Menu, and Walter analyzed the paint recipes from a wide range of decorated caves in the region that have been firmly carbon-dated. Would the two recipes at Niaux turn out to correspond to two different prehistoric periods? So far— and Clottes points out that the sample is small, about ten sites—recipe B has been found consistently with Late Magdalenian work (about 12,000 to 13,000 years old), while recipe F is exclusively Middle Magdalenian (about 13,000 to 14,000 years old). "We don't know why Paleolithic painters changed the recipe for the extender around 13,000 years ago," asserts Clottes. Perhaps, he speculates, it made the paint easier to apply or gave it a slightly different color. "But whatever

the reason, it gives us a way of attaching a date to paintings when radiocarbon methods are not possible."

Thus the Niaux paint studies answered Clottes's question in a completely unexpected way: despite their similarity, the paintings in the cave were not all created within a short period of time. Many generations could have separated recipe B and recipe F paintings. The more general implication—one that archeologists will have to struggle with in the years to come—is that style is no certain guide to chronology. The methodology that supported years of archeological work has suddenly crumbled. But that isn't the only ripple the studies have left in their wake.

Archeologists have long believed that the Salon Noir at Niaux was a sanctuary—a sort of Ice Age cathedral where important ceremonies were held. Clottes himself subscribes to this gut feeling. "There is something special about the Salon Noir," he says, as he leads the way along the uneven corridor that takes you to the cave's inner chamber. "When you enter with a small lamp, you naturally follow the right-hand wall, retreating from that great black void to the left. Eventually, inevitably, you reach the Salon Noir, with its soaring ceiling beyond the reach of torchlight. It's as if the place draws you here." Clottes shifts the beam of light to the walls, dramatically revealing the panels of black bison, horses, ibex, and deer. He swings the beam from panel to panel, creating an eerie sense of movement in the ancient images as he points out how stylistically homogeneous they are. "This homogeneity," he explains, "has been very important to our perception of the cave as a sanctuary."

When archeologists speak of a sanctuary, they typically imagine a richly decorated cave in which the paintings seem to form a planned, cohesive body of work. The two most famous examples are Altamira in Spain, with its huge polychrome extravaganzas, and Lascaux in France, with its fabulous friezes. But by that logic, wouldn't the discovery of different paint recipes in the Salon Noir, spanning as much as

two millennia, cast doubt on Niaux's status as a sanctuary? "That *seems* logical, but it turns out to be wrong," asserts Clottes. For evidence, he returns to the pigment studies that uncovered charcoal fragments under the most commonly used paint in the Salon Noir. "That indicated to us that the Upper Paleolithic artists first made a sketch using a charcoal stick, then painted over the outline," says Clottes.

This technique—a preliminary sketch followed by careful painting—is not common in Paleolithic art. The combination of sketch and painting not only takes more time, says Clottes, but also implies premeditation. It suggests that the artist had some sort of composition in mind, sketching first and only filling in the outlines with paint after he or she was satisfied with the overall effect. That kind of care, argues Clottes, is much more consistent with paintings found in heavily decorated sanctuaries than in the more run-of-the-mill caves with their scattered images that look as if they've been hastily dashed off on brief visits.

"I believe people repeatedly came to the spot we're standing on now," says Clottes. It was, he is sure, a gathering place of lasting social and mythological significance. "You know," he finally confides, "I've been in this cave many times. I've stood in the place where the Upper Paleolithic painter stood. I've traced the images. You put your hand where his or her hand once was; you move it, producing the same lines. Sometimes it feels uncanny. It brings you closer to them. Closer, but still frustratingly distant."

At moments like this the differences in style between Clottes and Lorblanchet seem to evaporate. "The first time I did my own hand stencil, I was shocked," recalls Lorblanchet. "There it was, my hand, separate and distant from me, but very definitely me, a more powerful signature than any writing. I had put myself into the rock, become part of another world." For Paleolithic people, that "other world," a potent mythological world mediated by simple images, was probably as real as life on the frigid steppe. Today we see only images on the rock.

BUSHMEN

John Yellen

John Yellen, director of the anthropology program at the National Science Foundation, has returned to the Kalahari four times since 1968.

I followed Dau, kept his slim brown back directly in front of me, as we broke suddenly free from the dense Kalahari bush and crossed through the low wire fence that separated Botswana from Namibia to the West. For that moment while Dau held the smooth wires apart for me, we were out in the open, in the full hot light of the sun and then we entered the shadows, the tangled thickets of arrow grass and thorn bush and mongongo trees once again. As soon as the bush began to close in around us again, I quickly became disoriented, Dau's back my only reference point.

Even then, in that first month of 1968, while my desert boots retained their luster, I knew enough to walk behind, not next to Dau. I had expected the Kalahari Desert to be bare open sand. I had imagined myself looking out over vast stretches that swept across to the horizon. But to my surprise, I found that the dunes were covered with trees and that during the rains the grasses grew high over my head. The bare sand, where I could see it, was littered with leaves, and over these the living trees and brush threw a dappled pattern of sunlight and shade. To look in the far distance and maintain a sense of direction, to narrow my focus and pick a way between the acacia bushes and their thorns, and then to look down, just in front of my feet to search out menacing shapes, was too much for me. Already, in that first month, the Bushmen had shown me a puff adder coiled motionless by the base of an acacia tree, but not until Cumsa the Hunter came up close to it, ready to strike it with his spear, could I finally see what all those hands were pointing at.

As Dau walked, I tried to follow his lead. To my discomfort I knew that many of these bushes had thorns—the Kalahari cloaks itself in thorns—some hidden close to the ground just high enough to rake across my ankles and draw blood when I pushed through, others long and straight and white so they reflected the sun. That morning, just before the border fence, my concentration had lagged and I found myself entangled in wait-a-bit thorns that curved backwards up the branch. So I stopped and this short, brown-skinned Bushman pushed me gently backwards to release the tension, then worked the branch, thorn by thorn from my shirt and my skin.

In the mid-1960s, the South African government had decided to accurately survey the Botswana border, mark it with five-strand fence, and cut a thin firebreak on either side. At intervals they constructed survey towers, strange skeletal affairs, like oil drilling rigs, their tops poking well above the highest mongongo trees. It was to one of these that Dau led me across the border, through the midday sun. Although he would not climb it himself, since it was a white man's tower, he assumed I would. I followed his finger, his chain of logic as I started rather hesitantly up the rusted rungs. I cleared the arrow grass, the acacia bushes, finally the broad leafy crowns of the mongongo nut trees. Just short of the top I stopped and sat, hooked my feet beneath the rung below, and wrapped my arms around the metal edges of the sides.

From *Science 85,* May 1985, pp. 41-48. © 1985 by John Yellen, National Science Foundation, Arlington, VA. Reprinted by permission.

3. EXPERIMENTAL ARCHAEOLOGY

For a month now I had copied the maps—the lines and the circles the !Kung tribesmen had drawn with their fingers in the sand. I had listened and tried to transcribe names of those places, so unintelligible with their clicks, their rising and falling tones. I had walked with Dau and the others to some of those places, to small camps near ephemeral water holes, but on the ground it was too confusing, the changes in altitude and vegetation too subtle, the sun too nearly overhead to provide any sense of where I was or from where I had come.

For the first time from the tower, I could see an order to the landscape. From up there on the tower, I could see that long thin border scar, could trace it off to the horizon to both the north and south. But beyond that, no evidence, not the slightest sign of a human hand. The Bushmen camps were too few in number, too small and well-hidden in the grass and bush to be visible from here. Likewise, the camp where we anthropologists lived, off to the east at the Dobe waterhole, that also was too small to see.

As Dau had intended, from my perch on that tower I learned a lot. At least now I could use the dunes, the shallow valleys, to know whether I was walking east and west or north and south.

In those first years with the Dobe Bushmen, I did gain at least a partial understanding of that land. And I learned to recognize many of those places, the ones that rate no name at all but are marked only by events—brief, ephemeral happenings that leave no mark on the land. I learned to walk with the Bushmen back from a hunt or a trip for honey or spear-shaft wood and listen. They talked, chattered almost constantly, decorating the bus, these no-name places as they went, putting ornaments of experience on them: "See that tree there, John? That's where we stopped, my brother and I, long before he was married, when he killed a kudu, a big female. We stopped under that tree, hung the meat up there and rested in the shade. But the flies were so bad, the biting flies, that we couldn't stay for long."

It took me a long time to realize that this chatter was not chatter at all, to understand that those remarks were gifts, a private map shared only among a few, an overlay crammed with fine, spidery writing on top of the base map with its named waterholes and large valleys, a map for friends to read. Dau would see a porcupine burrow, tiny, hidden in the vastness of the bush. And at night he could sit by the fire and move the others from point to point across the landscape to that small opening in the ground.

But as an archeologist, I had a task to do—to name those places and to discover what life had been like there in the past. "This place has a name now," I told Dau when I went back in 1976. Not the chicken camp, because when I was there I kept 15 chickens, or the cobra camp, for the cobra we killed one morning among the nesting hens, but Dobe Base Camp 18. Eighteen because it's the eighteenth of these old abandoned camps I've followed you to in the last three days. See? That's what goes into this ledger, this fat bound book in waterproof ballpoint ink. We could get a reflector in here—a big piece of tin like some metal off a roof and get some satellite or a plane to photograph it. We could tell just where it is then, could mark it on one of those large aerial maps down to the nearest meter if we wanted.

We came back to these camps, these abandoned places on the ground, not once but month after month for the better part of a year. Not just Dau and myself but a whole crew of us, eight Bushmen and I, to dig, to look down into the ground. We started before the sun was too high up in the sky, and later Dau and I sat in the shade sipping thick, rich tea. I asked questions and he talked.

"One day when I was living here, I shot a kudu: an adult female. Hit it with one arrow in the flank. But it went too far and we never found it. Then another day my brother hit a wildebeest, another adult female and that one we got. We carried it back to camp here and ate it."

"What other meat did you eat here, Dau?"

"One, no two, steenbok, it was."

1948: 28 years ago by my counting was when Dau, his brothers, his family were here. How could he remember the detail? This man sat in the shade and recalled trivial events that have repeated themselves in more or less the same way at so many places over the last three decades.

We dug day after day in the old camps—and found what Dau said we should. Bones, decomposing, but still identifiable: bones of wildebeest and steenbok among the charcoal and mongongo nut shells.

We dug our squares, sifting through the sand for bones. And when I dumped the bones, the odd ostrich eggshell bead, the other bits and pieces out onto the bridge table to sort, so much of what my eyes and ears told me was confirmed in this most tangible form. If excavation in one square revealed the bones of a wildebeest or kudi or other large antelope, then the others would contain them as well. In an environment as unpredictable as the Kalahari, where the game was hard to find and the probability of failure high, survival depended on sharing, on spreading the risk. And the bones, distributed almost evenly around the individual family hearths confirmed that. What also impressed me was how little else other than the bones there was. Most archeological sites contain a broad range of debris. But in those years the Bushmen owned so little. Two spears or wooden digging sticks or strings of ostrich eggshell beads were of no more use than one. Better to share, to give away meat or extra belongings and through such gifts create a web of debts, of obligations that some day would be repaid. In 1948, even in 1965, to accumulate material goods made no sense.

When it was hot, which was most of the year, I arranged the bridge table and two chairs in a patch of nearby shade. We sat there with the bound black and red ledger and dumped the bones in a heap in the center of the table, then sorted them out. I did the easy stuff, separated out the turtle shells, the bird bones, set each in a small pile around the table's edge. Dau did the harder part, separated the steenbok from the duiker, the wildebeest from kudu, held small splintered bone fragments and turned them over and over in his hands. We went through the piles then, one by one, moved each in its turn to the center of the table, sorted them into finer categories, body part by body part, bone by bone. Cryptic notes, bits of data that accumulated page by page. The bones with their sand and grit were transformed into numbers in rows and columns, classes and subclasses which would, I hoped, emerge from some computer to reveal a grander order, a design, an underlying truth.

Taphonomy: That's the proper term for it. The study of burial and preservation. Archeologists dig lots of bones out of the ground, not just from recent places such as these but from sites that span the millions of years of mankind's existence. On the basis of the bones, we try to learn about those ancient people. We try to reconstruct their diet, figure out how the animals were hunted, how they were killed, butchered, and shared.

What appealed to me about the Dobe situation, why I followed Dau, walked out his youth and his early manhood back and forth around the waterhole was the neat, almost laboratory situation Dobe offered. A natural experiment. I could go to a modern camp, collect those discarded food bones even before the jackals and hyenas had gotten to them, examine and count them, watch the pattern emerge. What happened then to the bones after they'd been trampled, picked over, rained on, lain in the ground for five years? Five years ago? Dobe Base Camp 21, 1971. I could go there, dig up a sample and find out.

What went on farther and farther back in time? Is there a pattern? Try eight years ago. 1968, DBC 18. We could go there to the cobra camp and see. Thirty-four years ago? The camp where Tsaa with the beautiful wife was born. One can watch, can see how things fall apart, can make graphs, curves, shoot them back, watch them arc backwards beyond Dau, beyond Dau's father, back into the true archeological past.

We dug our way through the DBCs, back into the early 1940s, listening day after day to the South African soap operas on the short-wave radio, and our consumption of plastic bags went down and down. Slim pickings in the

bone department. And the bones we did find tended to be rotten: They fragmented, fell apart in the sieve.

So we left the 1940s, collapsed the bridge table and the folding chairs and went to that site that played such a crucial role for anthropologists: DBC 12, the 1963 camp where those old myths about hunters and gatherers came up against the hard rock of truth.

They built this camp just after Richard Lee, the pioneer, arrived. They lived there through the winter and hunted warthog with spears and a pack of dogs so good they remember each by name to this day. Richard lived there with them. He watched them—what they did, what they ate, weighed food on his small scale slung with a rope from an acacia tree. He weighed people, sat in camp day after day with his notebook and his wristwatch and scale. He recorded times: when each person left camp in the morning, when each returned for the day.

In this small remnant group, one of the last in the world still living by hunting and gathering, it should be possible, he believed, to see a reflection, a faint glimmer of the distant universal past of all humanity, a common condition that had continued for millions and millions of years. He went there because of that and for that reason, later on, the rest of us followed him.

What he found in that desert camp, that dry, hard land, set the anthropological world back on its collective ear. What his scale and his wristwatch and his systematic scribbles showed was that we were fooled, that we had it all wrong. To be a hunter and gatherer wasn't that bad after all. They didn't work that hard, even in this land of thorns: For an adult, it came to less time than a nine-to-five office worker puts in on the job. They lived a long time, too, didn't wear out and die young but old-looking, as we had always thought. Even in this camp, the camp with the good hunting dogs, it was plants, not meat, which provided the staff of life. Women walked through the nut groves and collected nuts with their toes, dug in the molapos and sang to each other through the bush. Unlike the game, which spooked so easily and

followed the unpredictable rains, the nuts, roots, and berries were dependable, there in plenty, there for the picking. Another distinguished anthropologist, Marshall Sahlins, termed those DBC 12 people "the original affluent society"— something quite different from the traditional conception of hunting and gathering as a mean, hard existence half a step ahead of starvation and doom.

Over the years that name has held— but life in the Kalahari has changed. That kind of camp, with all the bones and mongongo nuts and dogs, is no more.

By the mid-1970s, things were different at Dobe. Diane Gelburd, another of the anthropologists out there then, only needed to look around her to see how the Bushman lifestyle had changed from the way Richard recorded it, from how Sahlins described it. But what had changed the people at DBC 12 who believed that property should be commonly held and shared? What had altered their system of values? That same winter Diane decided to find out.

She devised a simple measure of acculturation that used pictures cut from magazines: an airplane, a sewing machine, a gold mine in South Africa. (Almost no one got the gold mine right.) That was the most enjoyable part of the study. They all liked to look at pictures, to guess.

Then she turned from what people knew to what they believed. She wanted to rank them along a scale, from traditional to acculturated. So again she asked questions:

"Will your children be tattooed?"

To women: "If you were having a difficult childbirth and a white doctor were there, would you ask for assistance?"

To men: "If someone asked you for permission to marry your daughter would you demand (the traditional) bride service?"

Another question so stereotyped that in our own society one would be too embarassed to ask it: "Would you let your child marry someone from another tribe—a Tswana or a Herero—a white person?"

First knowledge, then belief, and finally material culture. She did the less sensitive questions first. "Do you

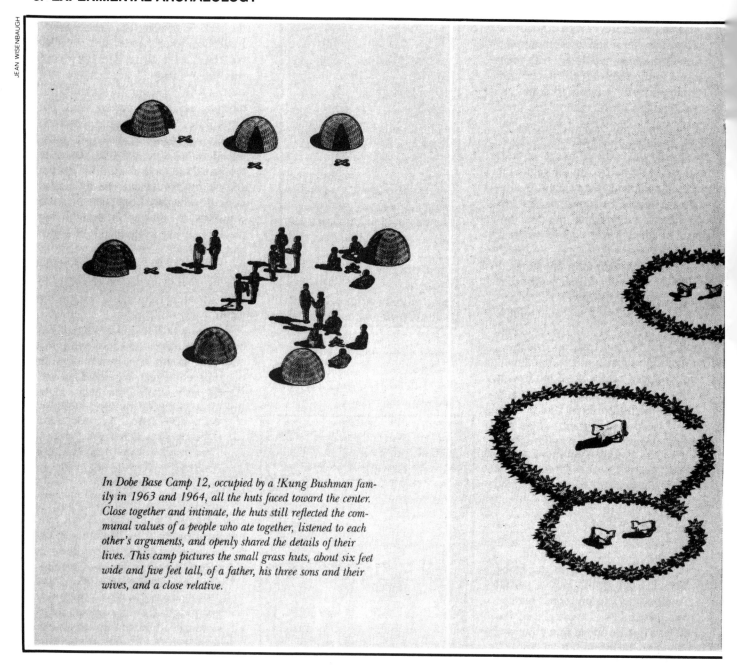

In Dobe Base Camp 12, occupied by a !Kung Bushman family in 1963 and 1964, all the huts faced toward the center. Close together and intimate, the huts still reflected the communal values of a people who ate together, listened to each other's arguments, and openly shared the details of their lives. This camp pictures the small grass huts, about six feet wide and five feet tall, of a father, his three sons and their wives, and a close relative.

have a field? What do you grow? What kind of animals do you have? How many of what?" Then came the hard part: She needed to see what people actually owned. I tagged along with her one day and remember the whispers inside one dark mud hut. Trunks were unlocked and hurriedly unpacked away from the entrance to shield them from sight. A blanket spread out on a trunk revealed the secret wealth that belied their statements: "Me? I have nothing." In the semidarkness she made her inventory. Then the trunks were hastily repacked and relocked with relief.

She went through the data, looked at those lists of belongings, itemized them in computer printouts. Here's a man who still hunts. The printout shows it. He has a bow and quiver and arrows on which the poison is kept fresh. He has a spear and snares for birds. He has a small steenbok skin bag, a traditional carryall that rests neatly under his arm.

He also has 19 goats and two donkeys, bought from the Herero or Tswana, who now get Dobe Bushmen to help plant their fields and herd their cows. They pay in livestock, hand-me-down clothing, blankets, and sometimes cash. He has three large metal trunks crammed full: One is packed to the top

with shoes, shirts, and pants, most well-worn. He has two large linen mosquito nets, 10 tin cups, and a metal file. He has ropes of beads: strand upon strand—over 200 in all, pounds of small colored glass beads made in Czechoslovakia that I had bought in Johannesburg years earlier. He has four large iron pots and a five-gallon plastic jerry can. He has a plow, a gift from the anthropologists. He has a bridle and bit, light blankets, a large tin basin. He has six pieces of silverware, a mirror and hairbrush, two billycans. His wife and his children together couldn't carry all that. The trunks are

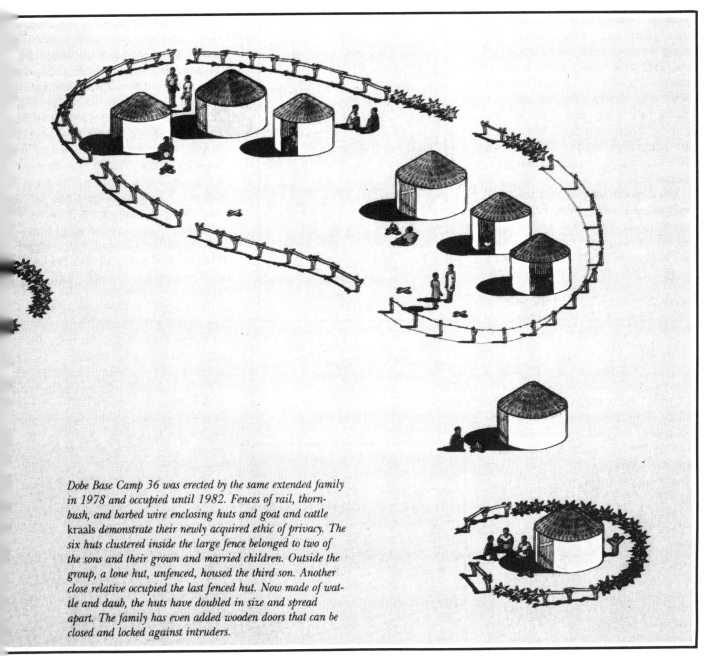

Dobe Base Camp 36 was erected by the same extended family in 1978 and occupied until 1982. Fences of rail, thornbush, and barbed wire enclosing huts and goat and cattle kraals demonstrate their newly acquired ethic of privacy. The six huts clustered inside the large fence belonged to two of the sons and their grown and married children. Outside the group, a lone hut, unfenced, housed the third son. Another close relative occupied the last fenced hut. Now made of wattle and daub, the huts have doubled in size and spread apart. The family has even added wooden doors that can be closed and locked against intruders.

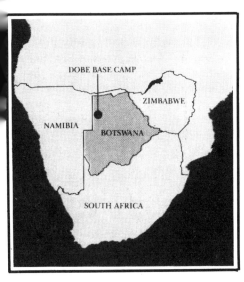

too heavy and too large for one person to carry so you would have to have two people for each. What about the plow, those heavy iron pots? Quite a job to carry those through bush, through the thick thorns.

But here is the surprising part. Talk to that man. Read the printout. See what he knows, what he believes. It isn't surprising that he speaks the Herero language and Setswana fluently or that he has worked for the Herero, the anthropologists. Nothing startling there. A budding Dobe capitalist. But then comes the shock: He espouses the traditional values.

"Bushmen share things, John. We share things and depend on each other, help each other out. That's what makes us different from the black people."

But the same person, his back to the door, opens his trunks, unlocks them one by one, lays out the blankets, the beads, then quickly closes each before he opens the next.

Multiply that. Make a whole village of people like that, and you can see the cumulative effect: You can actually measure it. As time goes on, as people come to own more possessions; the huts move farther and farther apart.

In the old days a camp was cosy, initimate and close. You could sit there by one fire and look into the other grass huts, see what the other people were doing, what they were making or eating. You heard the conversations, the arguments and banter.

We ask them why the new pattern?

Says Dau: "It's because of the livestock that we put our huts this way. They can eat the grass from the roofs and the sides of our houses. So we have to build fences to keep them away and to do that, you must have room between the huts."

I look up from the fire, glance around the camp, say nothing. No fences there. Not a single one around any of the huts, although I concede that one day they probably will build them. But why construct a lot of separate small fences, one around each hut? Why not clump the huts together the way they did in the old days and make a single large fence around the lot? Certainly a more efficient approach. Why worry about fences now in any case? The only exposed grass is on the roofs, protected by straight mud walls and nothing short of an elephant or giraffe could eat it.

Xashe's answer is different. Another brief reply. An attempt to dispose of the subject politely but quickly. "It's fire, John. That's what we're worried about. If we put our houses too close together, if one catches fire, the others will burn as well. We don't want one fire to burn all our houses down. That's why we build them so far apart."

But why worry about fire now? What about in the old days when the huts were so close, cheek by jowl? Why is it that when the huts were really vulnerable, when they were built entirely of dried grass, you didn't worry about fires then?

You read Diane's interviews and look at those lists of how much people own. You see those shielded mud huts with doors spaced, so far apart. You also listen to the people you like and trust. People who always have been honest with you. You hear their explanations and realize the evasions are not for you but for themselves. You see things they can't. But nothing can be done. It would be ludicrous to tell these brothers: "Don't you see, my friends, the lack of concordance be-

tween your values and the changing reality of your world?"

Now, years after the DBC study, I sit with data spread out before me and it is so clear. Richard's camp in 1963: just grass huts, a hearth in front of each. Huts and hearths in a circle, nothing more. 1968: more of the same. The following year though the first *kraal* appears, just a small thorn enclosure, some acacia bushes cut and dragged haphazardly together for their first few goats. It's set apart way out behind the circle of huts. On one goes, from plot to plot, following the pattern from year to year. The huts change from grass to mud. They become larger, more solidly built. Goats, a few at first, then more of them. So you build a fence around your house to keep them away from the grass roofs. The *kraals* grow larger, move in closer to be incorporated finally into the circle of huts itself. The huts become spaced farther and farther apart, seemingly repelled over time, one from the next. People, families move farther apart.

The bones tell the same story. 1947: All the bones from wild animals, game caught in snares or shot with poisoned arrows—game taken from the bush. By 1964 a few goat bones, a cow bone or two, but not many. Less than 20 percent of the total. Look then at the early 1970s and watch the line on the graph climb slowly upwards—by 1976 over 80 percent from domesticated stock.

But what explains the shattering of this society? Why is this hunting and gathering way of life, so resilient in the face of uncertainty, falling apart? It hasn't been a direct force—a war, the ravages of disease. It is the internal conflicts, the tensions, the inconsistencies, the impossibility of reconciling such different views of the world.

At Dobe it is happening to them all together. All of the huts have moved farther apart in lockstep, which makes it harder for them to see how incompatible the old system is with the new. But Rakudu, a Bushman who lived at the Mahopa waterhole eight miles down the valley from Dobe, was a step ahead of the rest. He experienced, before the rest of them, their collective fate.

When I was at the Cobra Camp in

1969, Rakudu lived down near Mahopa, off on his own, a mile or so away from the pastoral Herero villages. He had two hats and a very deep bass voice, both so strange, so out of place in a Bushman. He was a comical sort of man with the hats and that voice and a large Adam's apple that bobbed up and down.

The one hat must have been a leftover from the German-Herero wars because no one in Botswana wore a hat like that—a real pith helmet with a solid top and a rounded brim. It had been cared for over the years because, although soiled and faded, it still retained the original strap that tucks beneath the chin. The second hat was also unique—a World War I aviator's hat, one of those leather sacks that fits tightly over the head and buckles under the chin. Only the goggles were missing.

I should have seen then how out of place the ownership of two hats was in that hunter-gatherer world. Give two hats like that to any of the others and one would have been given away on the spot. A month or two later, the other would become a gift as well. Moving goods as gifts and favors along that chain of human ties. That was the way to maintain those links, to keep them strong.

When I went to Rakudu's village and realized what he was up to, I could see that he was one of a kind. The mud-walled huts in his village made it look like a Herero village—not a grass hut in sight. And when I came, Rakudu pulled out a hand-carved wood and leather chair and set it in the shade. This village was different from any of the Bushman camps I had seen. Mud huts set out in a circle, real clay storage bins to hold the corn—not platforms in a tree—and *kraals* for lots of goats and donkeys. He had a large field, too, several years before the first one appeared at Dobe.

Why shouldn't Bushmen do it—build their own villages, model their subsistence after the Herero? To plant a field, to tend goats, to build mud-walled houses like that was not hard to do. Work for the Herero a while and get an axe, accumulate the nucleus of a herd, buy or borrow the seeds. That year the rains were long and heavy. The sand held the water and the crickets and the birds didn't come. So the harvest was good, and I could sit there in the carved chair and look at Rakudu's herd of goats and their young ones and admire him for his industry, for what he had done.

Only a year later I saw him and his eldest son just outside the Cobra Camp. I went over and sat in the sand and listened to the negotiations for the marriage Rakudu was trying to arrange. His son's most recent wife had run away, and Rakudu was discussing a union between his son and Dau the Elder's oldest daughter who was just approaching marriageable age. They talked about names and Dau the Elder explained why the marriage couldn't take place. It was clear that the objection was trivial, that he was making an excuse. Even I could see that his explanation was a face-saving gesture to make the refusal easier for all of them.

Later I asked Dau the Elder why he did it. It seemed like a good deal to me. "Rakudu has all that wealth, those goats and field. I'd think that you would be anxious to be linked with a family like that. Look at all you have to gain. Is the son difficult? Did he beat his last wife?"

"She left because she was embarrassed. The wife before her ran away for the same reason and so did the younger brother's wife," he said. "Both brothers treated their wives well. The problem wasn't that. It was when the wives' relatives came. That's when it became so hard for the women because

Rakudu and his sons are such stingy men. They wouldn't give anything away, wouldn't share anything with them. Rakudu has a big herd just like the Herero, and he wouldn't kill goats for them to eat."

Not the way Bushmen should act toward relatives, not by the traditional value system at least. Sharing, the most deeply held Bushman belief, and that man with the two hats wouldn't go along. Herero are different. You can't expect them to act properly, to show what is only common decency; you must take them as they are. But someone like Rakudu, a Bushman, should know better than that. So the wives walked out and left for good.

But Rakudu understood what was happening, how he was trapped—and he tried to respond. If you can't kill too many goats from the herd that has become essential to you, perhaps you can find something else of value to give away. Rakudu thought he had an answer.

He raised tobacco in one section of his field. Tobacco, a plant not really adapted to a place like the northern Kalahari, has to be weeded, watered by hand, and paid special care. Rakudu did that and for one year at least harvested a tobacco crop.

Bushmen crave tobacco and Rakudu hoped he had found a solution—that they would accept tobacco in place of goats, in place of mealie meal. A good try. Perhaps the only one open to him. But, as it turned out, not good enough. Rakudu's son could not find a wife.

Ironic that a culture can die yet not a

single person perish. A sense of identity, of a shared set of rules, of participation in a single destiny binds individuals together into a tribe or cultural group. Let that survive long enough, let the participants pass this sense through enough generations, one to the next, create enough debris, and they will find their way into the archeological record, into the study of cultures remembered only by their traces left on the land.

Rakudu bought out. He, his wife, and his two sons sold their goats for cash, took the money and walked west, across the border scar that the South Africans had cut, through the smooth fence wire and down the hard calcrete road beyond. They became wards of the Afrikaaners, were lost to their own culture, let their fate pass into hands other than their own. At Chum kwe, the mission station across the border 34 miles to the west, they were given numbers and the right to stand in line with the others and have mealie meal and other of life's physical essentials handed out to them. As wards of the state, that became their right. When the problems, the contradictions of your life are insoluble, a paternalistic hand provides one easy out.

Dau stayed at Dobe. Drive there today and you can find his mud-walled hut just by the waterhole. But he understands: He has married off his daughter, his first-born girl to a wealthy Chum kwe man who drives a tractor—an old man, more than twice her age, and by traditional Bushmen standards not an appropriate match. Given the chance, one by one, the others will do the same.

History and Ethnoarchaeology

How many times have you misplaced your car keys? Locked yourself out of the house? Lost your wallet? Your address book? Sometimes these artifacts are recovered and brought back into the historical present. Sometimes they are lost forever, becoming part of the rubbish of an extinct culture. Have you ever noticed that lost things, when found, are always in the place you look? Is this a law of science?

Here is an opportunity to practice historical archaeology. You may wish to try this puzzler in order to practice thinking like an archaeologist. (Do not forget to apply the basics discussed in Unit 1.) The incident recounted here is true. Only the names and places were changed to protect the privacy of the famous personages involved in this highly charged mystery.

Problem: Dr. Wheeler, an archaeologist at a large university, left his office on December 20, 1989, around 9 P.M. on a cold Wednesday evening, preceding the long holiday. Immediately before he left his office, he stated that he placed a thin, reddish, three-ring notebook in an unlocked cupboard in his office.

Dr. Wheeler then proceeded to go directly to his designated campus parking place, got into his motorcar and drove directly to his flat in Marshalltown Goldens. When he arrived at home, he went straightaway to his study.

Dr. Wheeler had a jolly holiday with his family and thought nothing more of his notebook until the university resumed its session on Wednesday, January 3, 1990. Upon returning to his office, Dr. Wheeler could not find his notebook in the cupboard, and he became very agitated.

He chased his assistant, Miss Mortimer, around the office, wielding a wicked looking Acheulean hand-ax. Poor Miss Mortimer claimed she had no knowledge of the whereabouts of the notebook. But Dr. Wheeler had always suspected that Miss Mortimer pinched pens and pencils from his desk, so, naturally. . . . But Miss Mortimer protested so earnestly that Dr. Wheeler eventually settled in, had a cup of tea, and decided that perhaps he had absentmindedly taken the notebook home after all.

However, a thorough search of his flat indicated that the notebook was clearly not there. It was lost! Dr. Wheeler was almost bloody well lost himself when his wife, Sophia, caught him excavating her rose garden in the vain hope that Tut, the family dog, had buried the lost article there. It was a professor's nightmare, since the notebook contained the only copy of all his class records for the entire term. What could he do? He knew he was in danger of being fired from his chair for moral ineptitude.

Thus, Dr. Wheeler approached the problem in the manner of a proper, eccentric archaeologist. He had another cup of tea and generated several hypotheses about where his notebook might be. He tested these hypotheses, but none of them yielded his notebook. So, being a good archaeologist, he kept on generating hypotheses.

Now, as is sometimes the case, luck intervened, and his faithful assistant Miss Mortimer received a phone call on January 9 from a woman who had found the missing notebook on the evening of December 31, in a gutter! To be precise, she found it in a family neighborhood located on the corner of Olduvai Drive and East Turkana Avenue in Hadar Heights, about 1 mile from the university. Please note that this area is in the opposite direction from Dr. Wheeler's flat in Marshalltown Goldens. The notebook was jolly well wet and muddy, and furthermore, it was wedged down onto a gutter grill.

Greatly relieved, the next day Dr. Wheeler had Miss Mortimer run over to the kind woman's flat, and thus he recouped his class records. Dr. Wheeler was so delighted that when Miss Mortimer returned with the notebook, he invited her to sit and join him for a spot of tea. Yet, Dr. Wheeler was not satisfied with merely recovering his notebook. He was curious to know what had happened to it and why. He continued to generate more sophisticated hypotheses, until . . . ?

The Challenge: Now it is your turn to be Dr. Wheeler. Trace the general whereabouts of the lost three-ring notebook from the night of Wednesday, December 20, 1989, to the time of its return to Dr. Wheeler on January 10, 1990.

How do you do this? Review everything you believe to be true, carefully and skeptically. Using this as your initial database, set up a hypothesis to account for the lost notebook. This means a plausible series of events to account for the mysterious traveling notebook. Continue to refine your hypothesis and/or make alternative hypotheses until you arrive at the *simplest* possible explanation that is largely supported by direct or deduced data.

Consider that you are doing historical archaeology. Ask your living informant(s) for information first. What could you ask Dr. Wheeler? You could ask, Did you go to the lavatory before you left the building on December 20? Where was your motorcar parked? Was it raining? Did you stop and talk to anybody on the way to your motorcar? Where were you on December 31? Let your imagination run free. Creativity is the essence of all science.

Hints: Dr. Wheeler's university office was never broken into. Poor Miss Mortimer and the kind woman who found the notebook had nothing to do with the whereabouts of the notebook. Dr. Wheeler's family and his dog Tut were not involved in the missing notebook. Don't look now, but you are thinking like an archaeologist. It is a lot of fun, and it will reward you well.

Looking Ahead: Challenge Questions

How have recent excavations revised the stereotypes of the lives of slaves on American plantations? Give examples.

What was the influence of the Spanish on certain runaway slaves in eighteenth-century Florida?

What is *battlefield archaeology*? Give an example.

What happens when the archaeological record rewrites history? Give an example.

In the Donner Party incident, how is predictability about human behavior revealed? How can this be used for the purposes of cultural historical reconstruction?

What do ancient Peruvian textiles have to do with modern drug cartels?

What kinds of evidence do forensic anthropologists use to solve past murders? Give examples. How could this be used as a tool for archaeology?

The Earth Is Their Witness

Archaeology is shedding new light on the secret lives of American slaves

Larry McKee

Larry McKee is staff archaeologist at the Hermitage in Hermitage, Tennessee, and adjunct assistant professor of anthropology at Vanderbilt University. He is working on a book about the Hermitage slave community, with support from the Ladies' Hermitage Association, the National Endowment for the Humanities and Earthwatch.

In the spring of 1835, as Andrew Jackson approached his last year in the White House, his mind was already back at the Hermitage, the cotton plantation near Nashville where he would die ten years later. In a letter to Andrew Jackson Jr., his adopted son and temporary master of the Hermitage, the president tried to pass on some of what he had learned about plantation management. "One willing hand is really worth two who only does what labour he is forcibly compelled to perform," he wrote, after praising the plantation overseer, who had "reduced the hands to good subordination, and in doing this [had] obtained their confidence and attachment."

Jackson's "hands" were, of course, slaves. In the first half of the nineteenth century the Hermitage was home to more than 130 slaves and one of the largest plantations in the fertile central basin of Tennessee. In contrast to Thomas Jefferson, who compared his own slave ownership to holding a "wolf by the ears," Jackson never questioned his right to own other human beings. Fervently populist yet racist to his

bones, pragmatic yet prone to furious rages that often ended in fisticuffs and in one case a formal duel, Jackson was a great champion of the southern status quo. Slave ownership was a purely practical matter to him, an organizational problem no more anguishing than the weather or the price of cotton.

In an earlier letter to his son, Jackson had declared without irony that slaves "will complain often, without cause." To a modern reader, taught to think of slavery as a nightmare of backbreaking labor and unrelenting brutality, that statement seems shockingly insensitive. If Jackson seems to have been blind to the psychological horror of slavery, however, the modern understanding of plantation life too often translates that horror into physical terms. Slaves were the most valuable assets on any plantation: common sense required planters to provide them with adequate food, clothing and shelter, and to keep workloads moderate, and brutal, corporal punishments to a minimum. Plantation life, however demeaning, must have also fostered at least a fragile consensus between blacks and whites. Why else would the great majority of slaves never have run away or directly revolted against their oppressors? How else could a handful of white owners and overseers have controlled hundreds of slaves twenty-four hours a day?

Making sense of Jackson's offhand comments requires a calm, nuanced assessment of slavery, one that moves beyond the inflammatory rhetoric that has always surrounded the subject.

From the start, studies of slavery have been hampered by a dearth of hard data or reasonably objective accounts by contemporary observers. In delivering speeches, writing letters or even filling out the pages of diaries, participants in the slavery debate seem to have been always conscious of the eyes of history upon them, of the need to record for posterity their most extreme—and often, therefore, their least objective—arguments.

Those in the pro-slavery camp stressed the humane paternalism of plantation owners and their role in "civilizing" a "savage" people. As one planter wrote in 1846:

Our slaves will bear a favorable contrast with that of any other laboring population in the world, so far as comfort and happiness is concerned, and will not fall below them in any other point of view than that of mere abstract notions of human rights, about which, it is true, there has been much nonsensical prating in this as well as in other countries.

Abolitionists, for their part, usually matched their opponents' rhetorical excesses. Frances Anne Kemble, author of *Journal of a Residence on a Georgian Plantation in 1838–1839* put it this way:

Though the Negroes are fed, clothed, and housed, and though the Irish peasant is starved, naked, and roofless, the bare name of freemen . . . are blessings beyond food, raiment, or shelter; possessing which, the want of every comfort of life is yet more tolerable than their fullest enjoyment without them.

To withstand the buffeting winds of such rhetoric, an understanding of slavery needs to be anchored in simple facts about day-to-day plantation life. Because the historical documents are nearly devoid of such facts, one has to examine the actual remains of slave life—the bones, potsherds, bottle glass and broken trinkets buried on plantation grounds throughout the South. Paltry, as they seem, such remains, together with information gathered from documents, folklore, anthropological theory and whatever else may be of use, can help build (to use a term coined by the anthropologist Clifford Geertz of the Institute for Advanced Study in Princeton, New Jersey) "thick descriptions" of the world that slave and master made and occupied together.

The archaeological study of slavery began in the late 1960s, with the pioneering work of the late Charles H. Fairbanks along the southeastern coastal lowlands. In the quarter-century since that time, the study has spread through all former slave-holding regions of the United States and the Caribbean, as well as parts of Central and South America. Archaeologists have excavated the remains of dozens of slave quarters and have pieced together an understanding of power structures, trade networks and social relations within slave communities.

The permanent, family-based slave quarters built later in the nineteenth century were a result of complicated, mostly indirect negotiations.

In the 1980s, excavations of slave dwellings at Monticello, by William M. Kelso of the Association for the Preservation of Virginia Antiquities, added a new dimension to the understanding of Thomas Jefferson. More recently, excavations at the colonial-period African Burial Ground site in lower Manhattan provided a sobering reminder that slavery was not confined to the South. Poor interdisciplinary communication and the usual scholarly turf wars have kept mainstream historians from appreciating the significance of such discoveries, much less incorporating them into their work. It now seems, however, that in the next decade archaeology will be firmly accepted as an indispensable tool in the study of slavery.

My own work, as staff archaeologist at the Hermitage since 1988, has uncovered dramatic evidence of initiative and autonomy among Hermitage slaves. In hunting for wild meat after work, surreptitiously bartering for goods or observing their ancestors' beliefs, Hermitage slaves refused to accept their dispossession, and they strove to improve their lives rather than submit passively to their owner's orders. If Jackson's overseer did indeed reduce Hermitage slaves to "good subordination," the slaves' remains show that he often did so by subordinating his own wishes to their needs.

A visitor taking the current public tour at the Hermitage gets little sense that 130 slaves once lived on the property. Most of the tour is devoted to the Jackson family's Greek Revival mansion, set within a bucolic landscape. Gone are the rutted roads, squealing hogs and crowds of slaves toiling in the fields to make the planters' high life possible. A log cabin behind the mansion provides the only hint of slavery on the tour. Signs describe it as the home of Alfred Jackson, a Hermitage slave who stayed on after emancipation until his death in 1901. His gravestone, in the garden near the family tomb, commemorates him as "Uncle Alfred, faithful servant of Andrew Jackson."

No other African-Americans are buried in the garden, and the slave burial ground has never been found. Lacking any antebellum maps of the Hermitage slave quarters, or any diaries or letters written by the slaves themselves, historians have been largely at a loss to recover the slaves' side of the plantation's history. But archaeologists, by locating the remains of the slave quarters, have begun to clarify Jackson's intentions toward his slaves.

Like many planters, Jackson divided his slaves into two groups: those assigned to household duties lived in cabins set up near the mansion; those assigned to farming lived in cabins in the fields, clustered in two subgroups, one 250 yards and the other 600 yards from the mansion. In designing the cabins, Jackson almost certainly consulted southern farm journals in the Hermitage library. Constructed of brick and, in plan, nearly always a square twenty feet on a side, the cabins bespeak an effort at "social engineering" of the kind advocated by essays in those journals.

"The ends aimed at in building negro cabins should be: First, the health and comfort of the occupants," one planter wrote in 1856. "Secondly, the convenience of nursing, surveillance, discipline, and the supply of wood and water; and Thirdly, economy of construction." Like plain, sturdy stables built to shelter valuable livestock, such housing kept slaves literally and figuratively in their place, implying that the contrast between shabby slave quarters and the grand mansion was part of an immutable natural order.

In Jackson's time each slave family at the Hermitage occupied a single 400-square-foot room with a wooden floor, an attic loft, one door and one window. Larger Hermitage families, which had as many as ten children, according to the 1850 farm census, must have found life in such cramped quarters chaotic. Yet the cabin design Jackson chose was a product of more than a century of give-and-take between owner and slave. As late as 1820, our excavations show slaves on the Hermitage (as elsewhere in the South) were crammed together in hut-like log buildings that offered families little or no privacy.

The permanent, family-based slave quarters built later in the nineteenth century, like many other improvements in slave life, were a result of complicated, mostly indirect negotiations. Surly behavior, work slowdowns, theft, sabotage or flight were the slaves' only weapons in this cold war. The owners might have retaliated with whippings or worse, but more often they tried gentler methods. Coaxing was preferable to coercing, three planters wrote in 1846, in "promoting [the slaves'] happiness, and consequently their usefulness to us." Compliant slaves might be allowed to travel off the property when not at work, or to take extra time off following the harvest or during holidays. They might get cash bonuses for chopping extra firewood or for producing crafts. Such noblesse oblige was meant to win the slaves' "confidence and attachment" while demonstrating the owner's self-confident authority and managerial savvy.

Like military barracks, the rows of identical slave cabins at the Hermitage seem to suggest lives shaped and dictated by a local authority. But beneath their façades, the cabins hid evidence of less regimented lives, conducted in near secret. The most direct gateways to those secret lives were found under each cabin floor: small squared-off pits dug into the stiff clay soil and sometimes lined with brick. Such pits served primarily as cool, dry root cellars, but they were often also used as places for items (and, on occasion, people) that had to be kept hidden from master and overseer.

Jackson and many other plantation owners allowed slaves to dig the pits for food storage, although they probably knew that the "hidey holes" could also be used for clandestine activities and stolen goods. One planter, writing in 1851, cautioned that houses should have "no place to stow away anything." Another, writing the year before, recommended that slave dwellings be placed on piers: "When thus elevated, if there should be any filth under them, the master or overseer, in passing, can see it and have it removed."

Small game and baskets of root crops were among the most common items stored in the pits, and their remains are among the most revealing to the archaeologist. Food was always a major point of contention on any plan-

tation. Planters disagreed with slaves as well as with one another about what constituted adequate rations and how those rations ought to be distributed. Some thought it best to distribute a week's worth of raw rations at a time, whereas others favored a central kitchen where slaves could go for their meals. Although it appears that many planters believed, in the words of one essayist, that "A negro slave is so constituted that he is dependent in a great measure for happiness on his food," the rations provided hardly seem to bear out that dictum. Research into plantation records from all over the South shows that between thirty-two and forty-eight cups of cornmeal and three and a half pounds of meat a week was all a slave could expect to receive from his owner.

Contrary to popular belief, however, few slaves were content to eat only their rations. Of the more than 100,000 animal bones we have excavated so far, most came from pigs. Moreover, in some years, according to Hermitage records, more than nine tons of pork was processed on the property; Those numbers imply that every household at the site, including the Jackson family itself, chose pork for 70 to 80 percent of its meals. Mutton and beef were about equally favored as alternatives. Each slave family rounded out those provisions with foods as varied as family members were resourceful. Depending on which cabin site we excavated, we found bones from chickens; geese, ducks and other wild birds; opossums, raccoons, groundhogs and other small mammals; and turtles, fish, shellfish and other aquatic animals.

Secret trade networks, run by the slaves, moved goods all over the South from ports as distant as Europe and the Caribbean.

By allowing slaves to hunt and collect wild foods and to raise garden crops and livestock, the planters saved

the cost of providing truly sufficient rations and, perhaps, promoted a sense of self-satisfaction within the plantation community. Keeping rations to a minimum also enabled planters to reward good behavior and added effort with extra rations. "If occasionally a little molasses be added to the allowance," an essayist wrote in 1850, "the cost will be but a trifle, while the negro will esteem it a great luxury."

Such rewards may have helped fulfill Jackson's goal of creating "willing hands," but at a cost of some loss of authority and control. Slaves often chose to sell their personal produce rather than consume it themselves. As one planter from Alabama put it:

A privilege to work in their patches until 9 or 10 o'clock at night is often construed into a privilege to visit a neighbor's hen house or pig yard; or perhaps to get a mule and take a turn of corn to some market and barter it for a jug of whiskey, or something of little more value.

If slaves stashed important items beneath cabin floors, one might assume the cabins themselves held little of value. But excavations at the Hermitage have revealed an astonishing wealth of artifacts among cabin remains, and in one slave cabin at Monticello archaeologists unearthed fragments of fifteen matching porcelain dinner plates from China. Jackson and Jefferson were particularly wealthy planters, able to offer their slaves gifts of chipped or outmoded objects along with a few basic furnishings. But mansion castoffs alone cannot account for all the Hermitage artifacts, including coins, bone-handled cutlery and combs, a brass thermometer backing plate, glass beads in a variety of styles and colors, and 1,190 ceramic shards, mostly from refined white earthenware vessels made in England.

Some of those items might have made their way to Tennessee with new slaves from Florida or New Orleans. Given their diverse origins, however, many items probably arrived through surreptitious trade networks run by the slaves themselves. Passing from hand to hand, coat lining to coat lining, in a continual yet ephemeral system of barter and trade, goods reached slaves all over the South from ports as distant as Europe and the Caribbean. Cities such as Nashville, Memphis and New Orleans, linked by land and river, were key nodes in the trade network.

Among the Hermitage slaves, as among their white owners, success at trade would have been regarded as one sign of social rank. Given the conventional wisdom that house slaves were better treated and generally more comfortable than field slaves, one would expect their material remains to be richer. At the Hermitage, however, cabins belonging to house slaves and cabins belonging to field slaves yielded equally impressive artifacts. Such evidence seems to suggest that class structure at the Hermitage had less to do with the social order Jackson tried to impose than with the slaves' own reckoning of their talents and achievements. Field slaves might have received fewer castoffs from the mansion, but living further from the overseers eyes gave them more freedom to hunt and trade.

Such discoveries serve as reminders that plantation slaves, against all odds, formed true communities, complete with social mobility, scandal, gossip and ceremony. Bones and trade goods document the daily struggle for food and minor liberties, but the most intriguing artifacts offer a window on those parts of slave life that made bondage bearable. In the course of three excavating seasons, for instance, our teams have uncovered three beautifully wrought brass amulets shaped like human fists. Only one similar charm has been recovered by archaeologists—on the grounds of a house in Annapolis, Maryland, occupied by white families and their slave attendants during the eighteenth and nineteenth centuries. Elsewhere in the world, however, hand images are common and are often believed to confer spiritual power. In Islamic folklore, the "Hand of Fatima" is used to ward off the evil eye. In Brazil and elsewhere in Latin America, hand-shaped charms and votive items, known as *figas* and *mil-*

agros, respectively, are still widely used to confer good luck and fertility, as defenses against witchcraft and as religious offerings. The meaning that Hermitage slaves probably bestowed on their charms is clearly linked to the use of the word *hand* in African-American folklore as a generic term for any item intended to bring good luck or to ward off evil.

Hundreds of other items uncovered at the Hermitage and at other southern plantations were probably thought to have similar spiritual powers: quartz crystals, medicine vials, lumps of sulfur, cut silver coins and a pierced coin-like medallion, glass beads used to protect slaves from witchcraft, gaming pieces made from shards of European pottery, prehistoric projectile points, and a smoothed and polished raccoon penis bone. More than any other artifacts, such spiritual items show how slaves created an independent world within the bounds of their bondage—a culture within a culture, defined by its own beliefs concerning supernatural powers.

When the issue of race so deeply divides society, common sense about slave life has a hard time escaping the distorting gravity of myth.

Slave owners usually dismissed slave superstitions as primitive and childlike, forbidding them to be openly observed for fear they might disrupt plantation discipline. That slaves almost uniformly ignored such orders demonstrates how spirituality helped build solidarity in the slave community and thus provided a moral compass in a world that must have seemed largely senseless and evil.

To nurture a culture in the heart of oppression, slaves had to become masters of disguise, shielding their inner lives from prying eyes, hiding or even burying their most precious belongings, assuming the trappings

of obedience while secretly subverting their role. Archaeologists can sometimes get to the truth behind those disguises, but not without getting fooled themselves from time to time. Am I right in thinking the odd smooth stones sometimes found at the Hermitage are spiritual items—akin to similar stones found in medicine bundles used by African curers—or are they just leftovers from a child's collection of curios? If Hermitage slaves managed to conduct trade networks and forbidden rituals beneath their owners' noses, might they not easily deceive me a century later? I often imagine the slaves themselves watching me at work, listening to the tales I spin based on their garbage and ruins. Do they feel exposed—violated, even—watching me piece together the remains of their secrets? Or do they just laugh, shaking their heads at the persistence of delusion?

After spending more than a decade digging up slave quarters in Virginia and Tennessee, I realize that the "truth" of slavery will always remain elusive. As long as race, oppression and inequality remain burning, contemporary issues, the scholars of every generation will reinterpret slavery for their own time. In Tennessee today the world of plantation slavery seems simultaneously familiar and unthinkable. Blacks and whites live in relative harmony, yet they are only three or four generations removed from slaves and slave owners. Slavery may not be a constant topic of discussion, but a confederate flag, a hymn to old Dixie, or a hiring based on affirmative action can still stir up a fight.

When the issue of race so deeply divides society, common sense about slave life has a hard time escaping the distorting gravity of myth. On the one hand, a minister for Louis Farrakhan's Nation of Islam describes slavery as the worst crime "in the history of humanity. . . . The Holocaust did not equal it." On the other hand, some southern whites call slavery a necessary step in our national development. In comparison, the conclusions my colleagues and I have reached about life at the Hermitage may seem self-evident: anyone who has read a line of Faulkner knows that slaves and masters endlessly negotiated the details of daily life. For all its apparent mundanity, however, archaeology can help prepare new ground for such sensible old ideas, extinguishing the fires of ideology with a rain of specific detail.

To their credit, some plantation museums in the U.S. are evolving from shrines for southern myths into places where visitors can confront facts about the past. At the Hermitage, on a busy day in the summer, more than a thousand people stop by to watch the excavations behind the mansion. Some move on quickly; others stop just long enough to crack jokes about finding

gold; a few pace along the edge of the excavation pit, asking questions that they have never had answered. Most of the truths they take away are only partial, but one is complete: that the Hermitage was a home to slaves as well as slave owners—elegance as well as injustice—although the mansion stands unblemished and the cabins are survived by holes in the ground.

Legacy of Fort Mose

*A Florida marsh yields the remnants of colonial America's
first free black settlement.*

Darcie MacMahon and Kathleen Deagan

Darcie MacMahon is Exhibit Coordinator at the Florida Museum of Natural History. Kathleen Deagan is the museum's Distinguished Research Curator. Work at Fort Mose was funded by the state of Florida.

For more than 175 years the remains of the first free black town in the North American colonies lay forgotten in a salt marsh north of St. Augustine, Florida. Known as Fort Mose, after an Indian name for the area, it was in 1738 the northernmost outpost protecting the capital of Spanish Florida, a vast territory stretching west to the Gulf of Mexico and north into what are today Georgia and South Carolina. The fort's origins derived from a Spanish effort to destabilize the slave-based economy of English settlers in the Carolinas, particularly those in Charleston, established in 1670. The Spanish encouraged enslaved Africans to flee south promising them sanctuary if they converted to Catholicism. King Charles II of Spain sanctioned the policy of granting runaways religious sanctuary in 1693 with a royal proclamation "giving liberty to all . . . the men as well as the women . . . so that by their example and by my liberality others will do the same." The effort reflected Spain's customary inclusion of Africans at many levels of society, an outgrowth of 700 years of Moorish occupation of the Iberian peninsula.

The first group of runaways—eight men, two women, and a nursing child—arrived in St. Augustine in 1687. By the early 1730s more than 100 fugitives had arrived. In 1738 governor Manuel de Montiano formed them into a military company and stationed them with their families at a frontier post two miles

Silver medal found at the second Fort Mose depicts St. Christopher and a compass rose. It may have been worn by an African sailor. Photo by James Quine, courtesy the F. E. Williams Collection

north of St. Augustine. Established on St. Teresa's feast day, the post was named Gracia Real de Santa Teresa de Mose.

Fort Mose was abandoned in 1763 when Spain ceded its colony to Britain, and St. Augustine's colonists and the residents of the fort moved to Cuba. Forty-nine years later the abandoned fort was used by a group of American adventurers, known as the Florida Patriots, in a battle with Spanish forces that had returned to Florida in 1784 as part of a settlement ending the American Revolution. The Patriots were defeated and the fort was destroyed.

St. Augustine resident Jack Williams, convinced by his study of the Florida Patriots that the fort was on his property, contacted University of Florida archaeologist Charles H. Fairbanks in 1971. Fairbanks' subsequent test excavations confirmed the presence of pottery, musket balls, and other items from the Spanish period. Although the artifacts dated to the time of the fort, the 1971 expedition found no evidence of the fort itself. In 1985, we resumed the search, inspired by Florida's Black Legislative Caucus led by State Representative Bill Clark.

There were actually two forts named Mose. The site of the first lies under a foot of water in a tidal marsh created by rising sea levels and the blocking of drainage creeks by road construction. No excavations have been conducted, but thermal images of the area have re-

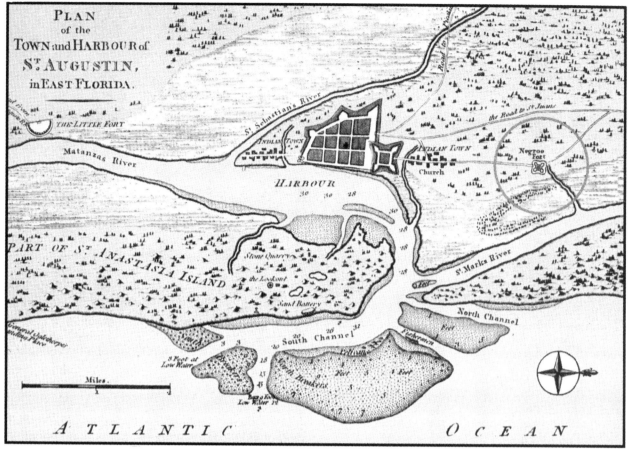

This 1762 map by Thomas Jefferys shows coastline of the time and the first Fort Mose, labeled "Negroe Fort."

vealed the outline of a ground disturbance that conforms to the shape and dimensions of the fort as described in maps and documents. The images were created using an aircraft-mounted scanner that measures the amount of heat held in the ground; areas occupied or altered by settlers have more organic matter and thus retain more heat.

British General James Oglethorpe, who founded Georgia in 1739 and raided the first Fort Mose in 1740, left this description:

Fort Moosa ... being about twenty Miles from Fort Diego within two Miles 'Distance and in full Sight of St. Augustine (lying near the Creek which runs up between that and Point Cartell up to Fort Diego) was made in the Middle of a Plantation for Safety of the Negroes against Indians. It was four Square with a flanker at each Corner, banked round with Earth, having a Ditch without on all Sides lined round with prickly Palmeto Royal and had

a Well and House within, and a Look Out.

The first fort was badly damaged and abandoned after a battle between British and Spanish forces in 1740. The soldiers and their families lived in St. Augustine for 12 years before establishing a second Fort Mose, built on high ground along a tidal creek one-quarter mile from the original compound.

The second fort had three 195-foot-long walls, probably about ten feet tall, made of packed earth faced with clay and sod and planted with prickly pear cactus to discourage intruders. The fourth side faced a creek. Franciscan priest Father Juan Joseph de Solana described it in 1759 during an inspection tour of Spanish Florida:

The Fort at Mose is situated on the banks of the River which runs to the north, and at a distance of 3/4 of a league from the presidio, the part that faces the river has no protection of defense whatsoever and is

formed by two small bastions which look landward on which are mounted two four-pound cannons and six swivel guns divided among them. ... The earthwork embankment is covered with thorns ... the housing which it includes are some huts of thatch. ...

We located the site by first placing scaled aerial photographs over historic maps to pinpoint the location. A topographic map indicated changes in elevation, suggesting where the earthen walls of the fort once stood. The outlying agricultural fields have eroded, leaving the site isolated in a salt marsh. Two years of excavation have revealed features of the fort itself as well as a richer picture of the daily life there.

As we were excavating, historian Jane Landers of Vanderbilt University dug into Spanish and Floridian archives for maps, census records, treasury accounts, militia lists, baptism and marriage records, death registers, official correspondence, and judicial records.

(COURTESY FLORIDA MUSEUM OF NATURAL HISTORY)

Thermal imagery revealed the location of the first Fort Mose, circled. The fort was destroyed in 1740 during a battle between English and Spanish forces.

Her research yielded evidence of a diverse community made up of people from widely varied backgrounds: Mandingos, Congos, Carabalis, Minas, Gambas, Lecumis, Sambas, Gangas, Araras, and Guineans. Most residents probably spoke some English, Spanish, and Indian languages in addition to their own. The common experiences of life in the Americas must have helped them bridge cultural and linguistic differences. The captain of the Fort Mose garrison was Francisco Menéndez, a West African Mandingo by birth. He had escaped from the Carolinas with the aid of the Yamassee Indians, and in 1726, prior to the establishment of Fort Mose, was captain of the black company at the St. Augustine garrison. Menéndez was acknowledged by the Spaniards as the *cassique,* or chief, of the community.

Fort Mose residents generally married within the community, but because there were fewer women the men also looked elsewhere for wives. In 1759 the community had 22 dwellings housing 37 men, 15 women, seven boys, and eight girls. Marriages eventually extended out of the original group of fu-

(PHOTO BY JAMES QUINE, COURTESY FLORIDA MUSEUM OF NATURAL HISTORY)

Bill Clark, Fred White, Kathleen Deagan, John Massena, and Jean-Claude Selime screen soil at the site of the second Fort Mose.

(COURTESY FLORIDA MUSEUM OF NATURAL HISTORY)

Artist's rendering of the second Fort Mose is based on archaeological and historical research by consulting project historians Albert Manucy and Luis Arana.

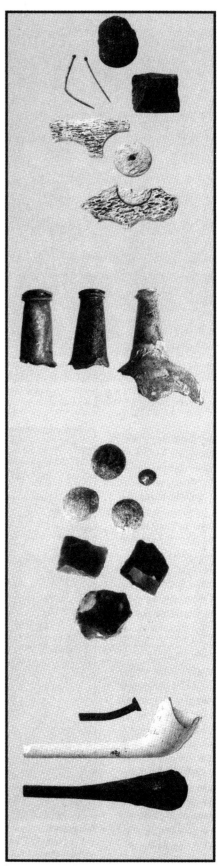

(COURTESY FLORIDA MUSEUM OF NATURAL HISTORY)

gitives and into the broader St. Augustine population, ten percent of which was composed of first generation Africans, Africans who had relocated from Spain or from Spanish colonies in the Caribbean and Latin America, or Africans who had been in Florida for generations as slaves, soldiers, or artisans. Some residents of Fort Mose married Indians from nearby villages, and some of the women residents married Spanish men, patterns of intermarriage that were common in the Spanish-American colonies.

The Spanish intended Fort Mose to produce surplus food to send to St. Augustine, but documentary evidence shows that the militia and their families occasionally received government supplies of corn, beef, pork, rice, and biscuits, suggesting that the farming activities at the fort were secondary to defense. Some of the ways in which this culturally diverse community adapted to the Florida frontier are reflected in the archaeological record. Zooarchaeologist Elizabeth Reitz of the University of Georgia studied faunal remains indicating that people ate some beef and pork, but primarily relied on a great deal of locally available wild foods, particularly deer, turtles, rabbits, opossums, squirrels, fish, and oysters. Food was prepared with Indian cooking pots and eaten from Spanish and English tableware; methods of cooking the meals or making the pots may have been African. No identifiably African artifacts have

Artifacts recovered from the second Fort Mose include from top: pins, thimbles, and a button stamped from animal bone; bottle fragments; musket balls and gunflints; and a nail, a clay tobacco pipe, and tableware.

been found at Fort Mose. The many fragments of green glass bottles suggest that the people of Fort Mose also drank wine or rum, and clay pipe fragments attest tobacco smoking, a practice with roots in American Indian traditions. Buttons, buckles, pins, and thimbles indicate that clothes were probably European in style, although by no means elegant. Buttons, for example, were stamped at the fort from animal bone. We also found musket balls and gunflints.

We know from documentary evidence that a wood and thatch Catholic chapel was located in the fort, and was administered by a Franciscan missionary. Father Solana described it as

> ... ten varas long and six wide [approx. 25 by 15 feet], the walls which are under construction are made of wood and the sacristy, which is finished, and in which the priest lives, is a very small room and serves as the chapel for the fort.

Residents of Fort Mose, as part of the parish of St. Augustine, were baptized,

married, and buried at the St. Augustine cathedral, where parish registers were maintained. Fragments of what were probably rosaries were found within the fort, and a small handmade silver medallion was discovered in the adjacent creek. One side of the medallion depicts St. Christopher as the patron saint of Havana and of travelers, who was also associated with many black religious brotherhoods that acted as mutual aid societies throughout Spanish America. The other side of the medallion bears a mariner's compass rose, showing the cardinal directions. Landers' research revealed that many men from Fort Mose served as sailors and crewmen on Spanish ships during their 12-year stay in St. Augustine. Perhaps the medallion was fashioned and worn by one of them.

Our work culminated in a traveling exhibit that places the story of Fort Mose within the context of the African experience in the Americas. Designated a National Historic Landmark in 1994, Fort Mose is now the premier site on the Florida Black Heritage Trail, a tangible reminder of the people who risked and often lost their lives in their struggle to attain freedom.

FURTHER READING

Freedom (Gainesville: University Press of Florida, 1995) presents African Americans in the Spanish colonies with more than 200 illustrations. Also recommended are J. Landers, "Gracia Real de Santa Teresa de Mose: A Free Black Town in Spanish Colonial Florida," *The American Historical Review* 95:1 (1990), pp. 9–30; D. H. Thomas, ed., "African Presence in Early Spanish Colonization of the Caribbean and the Southeastern Borderlands," pp. 315–327 in *Colombian Consequences, Volume II Archaeological and Historical Perspectives on the Spanish Borderlands East* (Washington, DC: Smithsonian Institution Press, 1990); and D. R. Colburn and J. Landers, eds., "Traditions of African American Freedom and Community in Spanish Colonial Florida," in *The African American Heritage of Florida* (Gainesville: University Press of Florida, 1995). B. D. Camp, *Fort Mose Educational Packet* (Gainesville: Florida Museum of Natural History, 1990) offers teacher information and exercises for K–12; and *Fort Mose* (Gainesville: Florida Museum of Natural History, 1991) is a 25-minute video.

The Guns of Palo Alto

Battlefield surveys indicate that Mexican maps distorted the opening engagement of the Mexican-American War. Why?

Charles M. Haecker

Charles M. Haecker is an archaeologist with the National Park Service, Intermountain Cultural Resources Center, Santa Fe, New Mexico, and the NPS Battlefield Protection Program.

When he wrote his memoirs, an aged and terminally ill Ulysses S. Grant could still vividly recall his introduction to battle almost 35 years earlier. A baby-faced second lieutenant, he, along with some 2,200 other American soldiers, had marched in column formation through shoulder-high grass "almost as sharp as darning needles" in the opening battle of the Mexican-American War. The future general of the army and president remembered cannonballs "whizzing thick and fast." This was the battle of Palo Alto, fought on a warm south Texas afternoon, May 8, 1846.

Young Grant and many of his comrades would experience battles of far greater complexity and bloodshed during the Civil War, which in time would overshadow the Mexican-American War of 1846–1848. Many Americans would quickly forget the far-reaching results of the earlier war, which wrested more than one million square miles of land from Mexico. Palo Alto was a testing ground for a new generation of professional officers, West Pointers like Grant, whose familiarity with tactical advances such as the fast moving, accurate, "flying" artillery—so called because each man in a battery had his own mount—would lead to a new and bloodier form of warfare.

Mexico had severed diplomatic relations with the United States following the annexation of Texas in February 1845. Fearful that the U.S. intended to claim their entire country, many Mexicans agitated for war to recapture Texas. Meanwhile President James K. Polk was convinced he could force Mexico into recognizing the state, and in May 1845 he ordered General Zachary Taylor to move 1,500 regular troops from Fort Jessup, Louisiana, to Corpus Christi, Texas, 140 miles north of the newly established Rio Grande border. By the end of July, Taylor's troops had been supplemented by 2,800 men, including infantry from the Indian frontier in Kansas and artillerymen from defenses on the Gulf Coast of Florida.

Learning through diplomatic channels of Mexico's eagerness "to settle the present dispute in a peaceful, reasonable, and honorable manner," Polk tried to persuade Mexico to accept the Rio Grande boundary by promising to pay several million dollars worth of property damage and unsatisfied debt claims filed against Mexico by Americans living or doing business there. He also hoped that the nearly bankrupt Mexico would settle for a sliding scale of payments for additional Mexican lands beyond Texas: $5 million for New Mexico and up to $25 million for California. When Polk was snubbed by Mexico's secretary of foreign relations, he increased the pressure with a show of force, ordering Taylor to move his troops to the Rio Grande.

In March 1846 Taylor took 2,800 troops to the northern bank of the river, where they built a star-shaped earthen garrison, called Fort Texas, opposite the Mexican town of Matamoros. In late April Mexican forces crossed the Rio Grande, intent upon severing the fort's supply line to Port Isabel 20 miles to the north. General Anastasio Torrejón crossed ten miles west of Matamoros with about 1,600 troops; shortly thereafter his commander, General Mariano Arista, forded the river 13 miles east of the town with some 3,500 troops. Learning of Torrejón's crossing, Taylor sent out patrols to determine his position. One was attacked, and 11 men were killed, six wounded, and 46 captured. The engagement led to an official declaration of war by the House of Representatives, which Polk signed on May 13. But by then the first major battle of the war had already been fought.

Taylor was convinced that the Mexican army, which now numbered more than 5,000 troops, would march toward Port Isabel, cutting off his supply route. To block such a move, he left 500 men in Fort Texas and on May 1 took 2,300 to protect Port Isabel and bring back supplies. The Mexican army followed, confident it could prevent Taylor from returning to relieve Fort Texas, under bombardment from Matamoros since May 3.

Taylor delayed his return to Fort Texas until sufficient reinforcements could be gathered to ensure the safety of Port Isabel, where he left more than 50 men in need of medical attention. Heading back on May 8 with 300 loaded supply wagons, he found the road to Fort Texas blocked by Mexican troops spread out before him on a broad prairie known as Palo Alto, or "Tall Timber," named for the mesquite forest that surrounded it. The field was covered with shoulder-high grass, and recent heavy

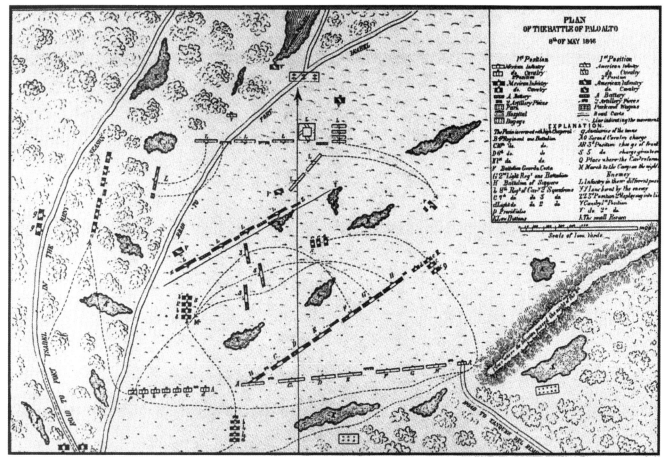

This 1850 English-language version of Berlandier's sketches depicts Mexican forces pivoting toward the American line during the final phase of the encounter. Surveys of the battlefield indicate that no such pivot maneuver ever took place.

rains had turned shallow depressions and old river beds into stagnant marshes.

Arista had arrayed his men and cannon in a mile-long line on the southern end of the battlefield, east of the Port Isabel-Matamoros road. Mounted troops armed with lances blocked the road and protected the army's flanks. When Taylor's regiments advanced, Mexican artillery opened fire. The Americans formed a battle line, with light artillery in front of the infantry and out of the range of Mexican musket fire.

The American guns rained six-, 12-, and 18-pound exploding shells on the Mexicans, whose antiquated four- and eight-pounders were no match for the American cannon in accuracy and destructive power. It soon became obvious to Taylor that his superior artillery made an infantry charge unnecessary. Mexican cavalry and light infantry tried flanking maneuvers, but were turned back by the devastating artillery fire. The broad

marsh between the battle lines discouraged a frontal attack. The battle ended at dusk, with Arista's mauled and retreating army now encamped beyond the range of American artillery. Search parties from both sides brought in wounded under a flag of truce. Some 250 to 400 Mexicans had been killed or wounded; only seven Americans had been killed and 43 wounded.

The following morning, Arista's army retreated to a more defensible position at Resaca de la Palma, a marshy area seven miles south of Palo Alto, where he was reinforced with fresh troops. Taylor's army, in hot pursuit, struck again, driving the Mexicans back across the Rio Grande. Taylor's smaller force had won the day.

The Palo Alto prairie was littered with battle refuse: fragments of exploded shells, cannonballs, ox- and horseshoes, and the bodies and belongings of dead soldiers. The victors took

lances, swords, and regimental badges as souvenirs. Seven months later a soldier from a volunteer unit stationed near Palo Alto visited the battlefield and identified the Mexican line as a roughly linear scattering of bones in tattered rags, the remains of soldiers lying where they had fallen. The Mexicans had only managed to bury a handful of their dead. Grasses eventually hid the ground laid bare by the fighting, and flooding deposited new soil on the battlefield. In time the wagon road from Matamoros to Port Isabel was abandoned, its traces obliterated and forgotten.

In June 1992 Congress passed the Palo Alto Battlefield National Historic Site Act, which recognized the significance of the engagement in American history. In so doing, it authorized the National Park Service to study Palo Alto and provide a plan for managing and interpreting the battlefield park for the public. My investigation began that year

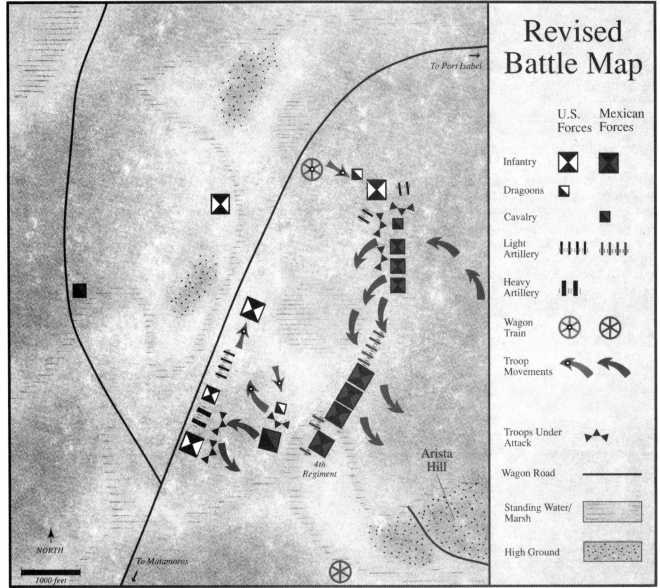

Revised Battle Map

	U.S. Forces	Mexican Forces
Infantry	◪	◼
Dragoons	◪	
Cavalry		◼
Light Artillery	⍿	⍿
Heavy Artillery	⏸	⌸
Wagon Train	⊛	⊛
Troop Movements		
Troops Under Attack	◥◤	
Wagon Road	———	
Standing Water/ Marsh		
High Ground		

(BETTE DUKE)

This revised map is based on battlefield surveys and American sketches of the final phase of the encounter. Rather than pivoting toward the American line in a last ditch attack, as indicated on Mexican maps, these studies show a retreat to the southeast and a failed flanking movement intended to destroy the U.S. wagon train.

with archival research. I was intrigued by two maps of the battle sketched by Captain Jean Louis Berlandier, one of Arista's staff officers. Berlandier's drawings formed the basis of an official government document on the battle published in Mexico in 1846, a few months after the event. During the next 100 years, maps based on these sketches were published in several major American and Mexican histories of the war. Berlandier had labeled the regiments of both armies, showing their movements during the battle. The final phase of the encounter on one sketch showed an ag-

gressive pivoting advance by the entire Mexican line. According to Berlandier, the Fourth Regiment had been stationed on the left flank, or western end, of the line, close to the Matamoros-Port Isabel road, and had acted as the "hinge" for the advancing battle line. It had thus remained largely stationary, while the other three Mexican regiments extending to the east had swung toward the American line.

An official Mexican account of the battle stated that the Fourth Regiment had suffered heavy casualties from the American 18-pounders. As pivot for a

final attack, it would have been a non-moving target. I correlated topographic features found at Palo Alto today with those labeled on Berlandier's sketches, including the broad marsh that had separated the two armies and the hillock that had anchored the Mexican army's right flank, now known as Arista Hill. I then delineated sample survey areas where Fourth Regiment artifact concentrations should exist. A team of local volunteers and I walked through the survey areas with metal detectors, later recording the locations of pieces of weapons, uniform fittings, and fragments of explosive

(LYNDA D'AMICO)

NATIONAL PARK SERVICE

Artifacts from Palo Alto battlefield include from top: Mexican Fourth Infantry cartridge-box belt plate; U.S. canister shot; American six-pound cannonball; and Mexican religious medal.

shells and cannonballs. We hoped to find concentrations of Mexican buttons, badges, and personal belongings mixed with American ordinance where this regiment had supposedly stood. We found none. More than 1,000 feet to the east we did find a concentration of Mexican-related artifacts, including badges of the Fourth and other regiments. Were Berlandier's sketches inaccurate?

Prior to our 1993 field season, I searched the Library of Congress and found several battle maps produced by American officers who had fought at Palo Alto. The American and Mexican maps are similar, except for the final phase of battle. Lieutenant Jeremiah M. Scarritt, a topographical engineer, had drawn four maps in a letter to his superior, Colonel J. G. Totten, each depicting a particular phase of the engagement. Scarritt's final sketch shows that both armies had moved from their original east-west orientation to a north-south orientation. American units were now aligned along the road, with cannon directed at the Mexican army to the east. Another American officer had produced a map for a pro-war propaganda pamphlet published a few months after the battle. This map also showed the final Mexican line as parallel to that of the Americans along the road. A third American battle map in *Campaign Sketches of the War with Mexico,* a popu-

lar book written by Captain W. S. Henry and published in 1847, shows the final phase of battle as a retreat of four Mexican regiments, including the Fourth, toward the southeast and well away from the road that they had guarded. It appeared that the Mexican Fourth had not functioned as a hinge for the other regiments advancing toward the Americans.

It was still possible, however, that traces of the Mexican Fourth lay somewhere between the road and the area 1,000 feet to the east where we had found the concentration of Mexican artifacts. If regimental badges from the Fourth were found in the immediate vicinity of the road, it would lend some support to Berlandier's interpretation. No more artifacts were found, however, until I extended the survey some 2,000 feet east of the road. We focused on this area of the battlefield, hoping that the patterns of artifacts found here might provide a clue to the orientation of the Mexican line. They did. One area contained a 20- to 30-foot-wide band of Mexican-related artifacts extending 500 feet north-south, to the edges of the test area. Here was conclusive evidence that the American maps were truer than the official Mexican one to what had actually happened.

We now know that toward the end of the battle American artillery had forced the Mexican left flank to the east or southeast and away from the road. This retreat would have compressed the Mexican units, offering an even better target for American artillery. A crowded army under constant artillery attack could not have performed the type of aggressive pivoting advance reported by Berlandier. Additional sampling of the Mexican line yielded numbered badges from four Mexican regiments within a three-acre area, testifying to the compression of regiments during the confusion of the final phase of battle.

To the north and east of the concentration of numbered badges, we found widely dispersed Mexican-related artifacts, perhaps reflecting a rapid movement of troops over a broad area and within a short time span. In fact both Mexican and American battle accounts describe such a charge by the Mexican army's right flank. This tactic was a final, desperate attempt to get around the American left flank and destroy the lightly defended wagon train parked in the rear. The charge was a brave but costly failure. Survivors of this attack retreated in disorder onto the already compressed Mexican left flank, causing even greater confusion and leading to a general retreat.

Why should there be discrepancies between Mexican and American battle maps? Granted, the fog of battle will result in some misinterpretations, but there may be an additional explanation. I believe Berlandier's map was an attempt to put the best face on an otherwise ignominious defeat. It was better to explain the heavy casualties as the result of a bold, final attack rather than the result of poorly used troops slaughtered by the superior cannon of an outnumbered enemy. I suspect that Berlandier created these battle sketches for Arista's use in his defense at a board of inquiry, where he was cleared of charges of incompetency. The sketches became part of the Mexican explanation of what had happened at Palo Alto. Mexican and American historians working from them when writing of the battle unknowingly republished the false information.

Battlefield archaeology has only recently gained respectability as a valuable way to analyze combat experience. A decade ago most scholars felt such investigations were pointless, since any recovered artifacts would have been deposited randomly in the confusion of battle and then picked over by generations of relic hunters. But studies beginning in 1984 at the site of the Battle of the Little Bighorn (see ARCHAEOLOGY, March/April 1990), convinced many scholars that battlefield surveys were not only useful but could lead to dramatic reassessments of military engagements. In the Battle of the Little Bighorn study, the findings from archaeological surveys were used to create a unique computer simulation of the final, fatal moments of the battle. Formerly undetected Indian positions indicated a skillful, coordinated encirclement of the cavalry by the Sioux and Cheyenne forces. This archaeologically based reconstruction significantly altered our traditional notions about how this battle was fought. Similarly, in the case of the battle of Palo Alto, fought 150 years ago this May, archaeology helped determine the veracity of conflicting accounts of the engagement's final phase found in historical documents. One can only imagine how such investigations might bear on the study of other battles, ancient or modern.

FURTHER READING

Charles M. Haecker, *A Thunder of Cannon: Archaeology of the Mexican-American War Battlefield of Palo Alto, Professional Papers* 52 (Santa Fe: National Park Service, Southwest Cultural Resources Center, 1994) covers the author's historical and archaeological research. K. Jack Bauer, *The Mexican War, 1846–1848* (New York: Macmillan Publishing Co., 1974) emphasizes strategy and tactics of both armies. John S. D. Eisenhower, *So Far From God: The U.S. War with Mexico 1846–1848* (New York: Anchor Books-Doubleday, 1989) is a readable account of the war. Robert Ryal Miller, *Shamrock and Sword: The Saint Patrick's Battalion in the U.S.–Mexican War* (Norman: University of Oklahoma Press, 1989) is the story of Irish immigrants who deserted the U.S. army and fought for Mexico. Also recommended are David Nevin, *The Mexican War* (Alexandria, VA: Time-Life Books, 1978); and Ulysses S. Grant, *Memoirs and Selected Letters 1839–1865* (New York: Library of America, 1990).

Living Through the Donner Party

The nineteenth-century survivors of the infamous Donner Party told cautionary tales of starvation and cannibalism, greed and self-sacrifice. But not until now are we learning why the survivors survived.

Jared Diamond

Jared Diamond is a contributing editor of DISCOVER, *a professor of physiology at* UCLA *School of Medicine, a recipient of a MacArthur genius award, and the author of* The Third Chimpanzee.

"Mrs. Fosdick and Mrs. Foster, after eating, returned to the body of [Mr.] Fosdick. There, in spite of the widow's entreaties, Mrs. Foster took out the liver and heart from the body and removed the arms and legs. . . . [Mrs. Fosdick] was forced to see her husband's heart broiled over the fire." "He eat her body and found her flesh the best he had ever tasted! He further stated that he obtained from her body at least four pounds of fat!" "Eat baby raw, stewed some of Jake and roasted his head, not good meat, taste like sheep with the rot."

—GEORGE STEWART,
Ordeal by Hunger: The Story of the Donner Party

Nearly a century and a half after it happened, the story of the Donner Party remains one of the most riveting tragedies in U.S. history. Partly that's because of its lurid elements: almost half the party died, and many of their bodies were defiled in an orgy of cannibalism. Partly, too, it's because of the human drama of noble self-sacrifice and base murder juxtaposed. The Donner Party began as just another nameless pioneer trek to California, but it came to symbolize the Great American Dream gone awry.

By now the tale of that disastrous journey has been told so often that seemingly nothing else remains to be said—or so I thought, until my friend Donald Grayson at the University of Washington sent me an analysis that he had published in the *Journal of Anthropological Research*. By comparing the fates of all Donner Party members, Grayson identified striking differences between those who came through the ordeal alive and those who were not so lucky. In doing so he has made the lessons of the Donner Party universal.

Under more mundane life-threatening situations, who among us too will be "lucky"?

Grayson's insights did not depend on new discoveries about the ill-fated pioneers nor on new analytical techniques, but on that most elusive ingredient of great science: a new idea about an old problem. Given the same information, any of you could extract the same conclusions. In fact, on page 151 you'll find the roster of the Donner Party members along with a few personal details about each of them and their fate. If you like, you can try to figure out for yourself some general rules about who is most likely to die when the going gets tough.

The Lewis and Clark Expedition of 1804 to 1806 was the first to cross the continent, but they didn't take along ox-drawn wagons, which were a requirement for pioneer settlement. Clearing a wagon route through the West's unmapped deserts and mountains proved far more difficult than finding a footpath. Not until 1841 was the first attempt made to haul wagons and settlers overland to California, and only in 1844 did the effort succeed. Until the Gold Rush of 1848 unleashed a flood of emigrants, wagon traffic to California remained a trickle.

As of 1846, when the Donner Party set out, the usual wagon route headed west from St. Louis to Fort Bridger in Wyoming, then northwest into Idaho before turning southwest through Nevada and on to California. However, at that time a popular guidebook author named Lansford Hastings was touting a shortcut that purported to cut many miles from the long trek. Hastings's route continued west from Fort Bridger through the Wasatch mountain range, then south of Utah's Great Salt Lake across the Salt Lake Desert, and finally rejoined the usual California Trail in Nevada.

In the summer of 1846 a number of wagon parties set out for California from Fort Bridger. One, which left shortly before the Donner Party, was guided by Hastings himself. Using his shortcut, the party would eventually make it to California, albeit with great difficulty.

The pioneers who would become the members of the Donner Party were in fact all headed for Fort Bridger to join the Hastings expedition, but they arrived too late. With Hastings thus unavailable to serve as a guide, some of these California-bound emigrants opted for the usual route instead. Others, however, decided to try the Hastings Cutoff anyway. In all, 87 people in 23 wagons chose the cutoff. They consisted of 10 unrelated families and 16 lone individuals, most of them well-to-do midwestern farmers and townspeople who had met by chance and joined forces for protection. None had had any real experience of the western mountains or Indians. They became known as the Donner Party because they elected an elderly Illinois farmer named George Donner as their captain. They left Fort Bridger on July 31, one of the last parties of

that summer to begin the long haul to California.

Within a fortnight the Donner Party suffered their first crushing setback, when they reached Utah's steep, brush-covered Wasatch Mountains. The terrain was so wild that, in order to cross, the men had first to build a wagon road. It took 16 backbreaking days to cover just 36 miles, and afterward the people and draft animals were worn out. A second blow followed almost immediately thereafter, west of the Great Salt Lake, when the party ran into an 80-mile stretch of desert. To save themselves from death by thirst, some of the pioneers were forced to unhitch their wagons, rush ahead with their precious animals to the next spring, and return to retrieve the wagons. The rush became a disorganized panic, and many of the animals died, wandered off, or were killed by Indians. Four wagons and large quantities of supplies had to be abandoned. Not until September 30—two full months after leaving Fort Bridger—did the Donner Party emerge from their fatal shortcut to rejoin the California Trail.

By November 1 they had struggled up to Truckee Lake—later renamed Donner Lake—at an elevation of 6,000 feet on the eastern flank of the Sierra Nevada, west of the present-day California-Nevada border. Snow had already begun to fall during the last days of October, and now a fierce snowstorm defeated the exhausted party as they attempted to cross a 7,200-foot pass just west of the lake. With that storm, a trap snapped shut around them: they had set out just a little too late and proceeded just a little too slowly. They now faced a long winter at the lake, with very little food.

Death had come to the Donner Party even before it reached the lake. There were five casualties: on August 29 Luke Halloran died of "consumption" (presumably tuberculosis); on October 5 James Reed knifed John Snyder in self-defense, during a fight that broke out when two teams of oxen became entangled; three days later Lewis Keseberg abandoned an old man named Hardkoop who had been riding

in Keseberg's wagon, and most of the party refused to stop and search for him; sometime after October 13 two German emigrants, Joseph Reinhardt and Augustus Spitzer, murdered a rich German named Wolfinger while ostensibly helping him to cache his property; and on October 20 William Pike was shot as he and his brother-in-law were cleaning a pistol.

They cut off and roasted flesh from the corpses, restrained only by the rule that no one partook of his or her own relative's body.

In addition, four party members had decided earlier to walk out ahead to Sutter's Fort (now Sacramento) to bring back supplies and help. One of those four, Charles Stanton, rejoined the party on October 19, bringing food and two Indians sent by Sutter. Thus, of the 87 original members of the Donner Party, 79—plus the two Indians—were pinned down in the winter camp at Donner Lake.

The trapped pioneers lay freezing inside crude tents and cabins. They quickly exhausted their little remaining food, then killed and ate their pack animals. Then they ate their dogs. Finally they boiled hides and blankets to make a gluelike soup. Gross selfishness became rampant, as families with food refused to share it with destitute families or demanded exorbitant payment. On December 16 the first death came to the winter camp when 24-year-old Baylis Williams succumbed to starvation. On that same day 15 of the strongest people—5 women and 10 men, including Charles Stanton and the two Indians—set out across the pass on homemade snowshoes, virtually without food and in appallingly cold and stormy weather, in the hope of reaching outside help. Four of the men left behind their families; three of the women left behind their children.

On the sixth morning an exhausted Stanton let the others go on ahead of him; he remained behind to die. On the ninth day the remaining 14 for the first time openly broached the subject of cannibalism which had already been on their minds. They debated drawing lots as to who should be eaten, or letting two people shoot it out until one was killed and could be eaten. Both proposals were rejected in favor of waiting for someone to die naturally.

Such opportunities soon arose. On Christmas Eve, as a 23-year-old man named Antoine, a bachelor, slept in a heavy stupor, he stretched out his arm such that his hand fell into the fire. A companion pulled it out at once. When it fell in a second time, however, no one intervened—they simply let it burn. Antoine died, then Franklin Graves, then Patrick Dolan, then Lemuel Murphy. The others cut off and roasted flesh from the corpses, restrained only by the rule that no one would partake of his or her own relative's body. When

Manifest of a Tragic Journey

DONNER FAMILY

Name	Sex	Age	Fate
Jacob Donner	M	65	died in Nov. in winter camp
George Donner	M	62	died in Apr. in winter camp
Elizabeth Donner	F	45	died in Mar. in winter camp
Tamsen Donner	F	45	died in Apr. in winter camp
Elitha Donner	F	14	
Solomon Hook	M	14	
William Hook	M	12	died Feb. 28 with first rescue team
Leanna Donner	F	12	
George Donner	M	9	
Mary Donner	F	7	
Frances Donner	F	6	
Isaac Donner	M	5	died Mar. 7 with second rescue team
Georgia Donner	F	4	
Samuel Donner	M	4	died in Apr. in winter camp
Lewis Donner	M	3	died Mar. 7 or 8 in winter camp
Eliza Donner	F	3	

MURPHY-FOSTER-PIKE FAMILY

Name	Sex	Age	Fate
Lavina Murphy	F	50	died around Mar. 19 in winter camp
William Foster	M	28	
William Pike	M	25	died Oct. 20 by gunshot
Sara Foster	F	23	
Harriet Pike	F	21	
John Landrum Murphy	M	15	died Jan. 31 in winter camp
Mary Murphy	F	13	
Lemuel Murphy	M	12	died Dec. 27 with snowshoers
William Murphy	M	11	
Simon Murphy	M	10	
George Foster	M	4	died in early Mar. in winter camp
Naomi Pike	F	3	
Catherine Pike	F	1	died Feb. 20 in winter camp

GRAVES-FOSDICK FAMILY

Name	Sex	Age	Fate
Franklin Graves	M	57	died Dec. 24 with snowshoers
Elizabeth Graves	F	47	died Mar. 8 with second rescue team
Jay Fosdick	M	23	died Jan. 5 with snowshoers
Sarah Fosdick	F	22	
Mary Graves	F	20	
William Graves	M	18	
Eleanor Graves	F	15	
Lavina Graves	F	13	
Nancy Graves	F	9	
Jonathan Graves	M	7	
Franklin Graves Jr.	M	5	died Mar. 8 with second rescue team
Elizabeth Graves	F	1	died soon after rescue by second team

BREEN FAMILY

Name	Sex	Age	Fate
Patrick Breen	M	40	
Mary Breen	F	40	
John Breen	M	14	
Edward Breen	M	13	
Patrick Breen Jr.	M	11	
Simon Breen	M	9	
Peter Breen	M	7	
James Breen	M	4	
Isabella Breen	F	1	

REED FAMILY

Name	Sex	Age	Fate
James Reed	M	46	
Margaret Reed	F	32	
Virginia Reed	F	12	
Patty Reed	F	8	
James Reed Jr.	M	5	
Thomas Reed	M	3	

EDDY FAMILY

Name	Sex	Age	Fate
William Eddy	M	28	
Eleanor Eddy	F	25	died Feb. 7 in winter camp
James Eddy	M	3	died in early Mar. in winter camp
Margaret Eddy	F	1	died Feb. 4 in winter camp

KESEBERG FAMILY

Name	Sex	Age	Fate
Lewis Keseberg	M	32	
Phillipine Keseberg	F	32	
Ada Keseberg	F	3	died Feb. 24 with first rescue team
Lewis Keseberg Jr.	M	1	died Jan. 24 in winter camp

MCCUTCHEN FAMILY

Name	Sex	Age	Fate
William McCutchen	M	30	
Amanda McCutchen	F	24	
Harriet McCutchen	F	1	died Feb. 2 in winter camp

WILLIAMS FAMILY

Name	Sex	Age	Fate
Eliza Williams	F	25	
Baylis Williams	M	24	died Dec. 16 in winter camp

WOLFINGER FAMILY

Name	Sex	Age	Fate
Mr. Wolfinger	M	?	killed around Oct. 13 by Reinhardt and Spitzer
Mrs. Wolfinger	F	?	

UNRELATED INDIVIDUALS

Name	Sex	Age	Fate
Mr. Hardkoop	M	60	died around Oct. 8, abandoned by Lewis Keseberg
Patrick Dolan	M	40	died Dec. 25 with snowshoers
Charles Stanton	M	35	died around Dec. 21 with snowshoers
Charles Burger	M	30	died Dec. 29 in winter camp
Joseph Reinhardt	M	30	died in Nov. or early Dec. in winter camp
Augustus Spitzer	M	30	died Feb. 7 in winter camp
John Denton	M	28	died Feb. 24 with first rescue team
Milton Elliot	M	28	died Feb. 9 in winter camp
Luke Halloran	M	25	died Aug. 29 of consumption
William Herron	M	25	
Samuel Shoemaker	M	25	died in Nov. or early Dec. in winter camp
James Smith	M	25	died in Nov. or early Dec. in winter camp
John Snyder	M	25	killed Oct. 5 by James Reed
Jean Baptiste Trubode	M	23	
Antoine	M	23	died Dec. 24 with snowshoers
Noah James	M	20	

the corpses were consumed, the survivors began eating old shoes.

On January 5, 23-year-old Jay Fosdick died, only to be cut up and boiled by Mrs. Foster over the protests of Mrs. Fosdick. Soon after, the frenzied Mr. Foster chased down, shot, and killed the two Indians to eat them. That left 7 of the original 15 snowshoers to stagger into the first white settlement in California, after a midwinter trek of 33 days through the snow.

On January 31 the first rescue team set out from the settlement for Donner Lake. It would take three more teams and two and a half months before the ordeal was all over. During that time many more people died, either in the winter camp or while fighting their way out with the rescue teams. There was never enough food, and by the end of February, cannibalism had established itself at the lake.

When William Eddy and William Foster, who had gotten out with the snowshoers, reached the lake with the third rescue team on March 13, they found that Keseberg had eaten their sons. The Foster child's grandmother accused the starving Keseberg of having taken the child to bed with him one night, strangling him, and hanging the corpse on the wall before eating it. Keseberg, in his defense, claimed the children had died naturally. When the rescuers left the lake the next day to return to California, they left Keseberg behind with just four others: the elderly Lavina Murphy, the badly injured George Donner, his 4-year-old nephew Samuel and his healthy wife Tamsen, who could have traveled but insisted on staying with her dying husband.

The fourth and last rescue team reached the lake on April 17 to find Keseberg alone, surrounded by indescribable filth and mutilated corpses. George Donner's body lay with his skull split open to permit the extraction of his brains. Three frozen ox legs lay in plain view almost uneaten beside a kettle of cut-up human flesh. Near Keseberg sat two kettles of blood and a large pan full of fresh human liver and lungs. He alleged that his four companions had died natural deaths, but he

was frank about having eaten them. As to why he had not eaten ox leg instead, he explained that it was too dry: human liver and lungs tasted better, and human brains made a good soup. As for Tamsen Donner, Keseberg noted that she tasted the best, being well endowed with fat. In a bundle held by Keseberg the rescuers found silk, jewelry, pistols, and money that had belonged to George Donner.

After returning to Sutter's Fort, one of the rescuers accused Keseberg of having murdered his companions, prompting Keseberg to sue for defamation of character. In the absence of legal proof of murder the court verdict was equivocal, and the issue of Keseberg's guilt remains disputed to this day. However, Tamsen Donner's death is especially suspicious since she had been in strong physical condition when last seen by the third rescue team.

Thus, out of 87 Donner Party members, 40 died: 5 before reaching Donner Lake, 22 in their winter camp at the lake, and 13 (plus the two Indians) during or just after efforts to leave the lake. Why those particular 40? From the facts given in the roster, can you draw conclusions, as Grayson did, as to who was in fact the most likely to die?

As a simple first test, compare the fates of Donner Party males and females irrespective of age. Most of the males (30 out of 53) died; most of the females (24 out of 34) survived. The 57 percent death rate among males was nearly double the 29 percent death rate among females.

Next, consider the effect of age irrespective of sex. The worst toll was among the young and the old. Without exception, everyone over the age of 50 died, as did most of the children below the age of 5. Surprisingly, children and teenagers between the ages of 5 and 19 fared better than did adults in their prime (age 20 to 39): half the latter, but less than one-fifth of the former, died.

By looking at the effects of age and sex simultaneously, the advantage the women had over the men becomes even more striking.

Most of the female deaths were among the youngest and oldest, who were already doomed by their age. Among those party members aged 5 to 39—the ones whose ages left them some reasonable chance of survival—half the men but only 5 percent of the women died.

Experience has taught us that the youngest and oldest people are the most vulnerable even under normal conditions, and their vulnerability increases under stress.

The dates of death provide deeper insight. Of the 35 unfortunates who died after reaching the lake, 14 men but not a single woman had died by the end of January. Only in February did women begin to buckle under. From February onward the death toll was essentially equal by sex—11 men, 10 women. The differences in dates of death simply underscore the lesson of the death rates themselves: the Donner Party women were far hardier than the men.

Thus, sex and age considered together account for much of the luck of the survivors. Most of those who died (39 of the 40 victims) had the misfortune to be of the wrong sex, or the wrong age, or both.

Experience has taught us that the youngest and oldest people are the most vulnerable even under normal conditions, and their vulnerability increases under stress. In many natural disasters, those under 10 or over 50 suffered the highest mortality. For instance, children under 10 accounted for over half the 240,000 deaths in the 1970 Bangladesh cyclone, though they constituted only one-third of the exposed population.

uch of the vulnerability of the old and young under stress is simply a matter of insufficient physical strength: these people are less able to walk out through deep snow (in the case of the Donner Party) or to cling to trees above the height of flood waters (in the case of the Bangladesh cyclone). Babies have special problems. Per pound of body weight a baby has twice an adult's surface area, which means double the area across which body heat can escape. To maintain body temperature, babies have to increase their metabolic rate when air temperature drops only a few degrees below body temperature, whereas adults don't have to do so until a drop of 20 to 35 degrees. At cold temperatures the factor by which babies must increase their metabolism to stay warm is several times that for adults. These considerations place even well-fed babies at risk under cold conditions. And the Donner Party babies were at a crippling further disadvantage because they had so little food to fuel their metabolism. They literally froze to death.

But what gave the women such an edge over the men? Were the pioneers practicing the noble motto "women and children first" when it came to dividing food? Unfortunately, "women and children last" is a more accurate description of how most men behave under stress. As the *Titanic* sank, male crew members took many places in lifeboats while leaving women and children of steerage class below decks to drown. Much grosser male behavior emerged when the steamship *Atlantic* sank in 1879: the death toll included 294 of the 295 women and children on board, but only 187 of the 636 men. In the Biafran famine of the late 1960s, when relief agencies tried to distribute food to youngsters under 10 and to pregnant and nursing women, Biafran men gave a brutally frank response: "Stop all this rubbish, it is we men who shall have the food, let the children die, we will make new children after the war." Similarly, accounts by Donner Party members yield no evidence of hungry men deferring to

women, and babies fared especially poorly.

Instead, we must seek some cause other than male self-sacrifice to account for the survival of Donner Party women. One contributing factor is that the men were busy killing each other. Four of the five deaths before the pioneers reached the lake, plus the deaths of the two Indians, involved male victims of male violence, a pattern that fits widespread human experience.

However, invoking male violence still leaves 26 of 30 Donner Party male deaths unexplained. It also fails to explain why men began starving and freezing to death nearly two months before women did. Evidently the women had a big physiological advantage. This could be an extreme expression of the fact that, at every age and for all leading causes of death—from cancer and car accidents to heart disease and suicide—the death rate is far higher for men than for women. While the reasons for this ubiquitous male vulnerability remain debated, there are several compelling reasons why men are more likely than women to die under the extreme conditions the Donner Party faced.

First, men are bigger than women. Typical body weights for the world as a whole are about 140 pounds for men and only 120 pounds for women. Hence, even while lying down and doing nothing, men need more food to support their basal metabolism. They also need more energy than women do for equivalent physical activity. Even for sedentary people, the typical metabolic rate for an average-size woman is 25 percent lower than an average-size man's. Under conditions of cold temperatures and heavy physical activity, such as were faced by the Donner Party men when doing the backbreaking work of cutting the wagon road or hunting for food, men's metabolic rates can be double those of women.

To top it all off, women have more fat reserves than men: fat makes up 22 percent of the body weight of an average nonobese, well-nourished woman, but only 16 percent of a similar man. More of the man's weight is instead

made up of muscle, which gets burned up much more quickly than does fat. Thus, when there simply was no more food left, the Donner Party men burned up their body reserves much faster than did the women. Furthermore, much of women's fat is distributed under the skin and acts as heat insulation, so that they can withstand cold temperatures better than men can. Women don't have to raise their metabolic rate to stay warm as soon as men do.

These physiological factors easily surpass male murderousness in accounting for all those extra male deaths in the Donner Party. Indeed, a microcosm of the whole disaster was the escape attempt by 15 people on snowshoes, lasting 33 days in midwinter. Of the ten men who set out, two were murdered by another man, six starved or froze to death, and only two survived. Not a single one of the five women with them died.

The Donner Party records make it vividly clear that family members stuck together and helped one another at the expense of the others.

Even with all these explanations, there is still one puzzling finding to consider: the unexpectedly high death toll of people in their prime, age 20 to 39. That toll proves to be almost entirely of the men: 67 percent of the men in that age range (14 out of 21) died, a much higher proportion than among the teenage boys (only 20 percent). Closer scrutiny shows why most of those men were so unlucky.

Most of the Donner Party consisted of large families, but there were also 16 individuals traveling without any relatives. All those 16 happened to be men, and all but two were between 20 and 39. Those 16 unfortunates bore the brunt of the prime-age mortality. Thirteen of them died, and most of them died long before any of the women. Of the survivors, one—William Herron—reached California in October, so in reality only 2 survived the winter at the lake.

Of the 7 men in their prime who survived, 4 were family men. Only 3 of the 14 dead were. The prime-age women fared similarly: the 8 survivors belonged to families with an average size of 12 people, while Eleanor Eddy, the only woman to die in this age group, had no adult support. Her husband had escaped with the snowshoers, leaving her alone with their two small children.

The Donner Party records make it vividly clear that family members stuck together and helped one another at the expense of the others. A notorious example was the Breen family of nine, every one of whom (even two small children) survived through the luck of retaining their wagons and some pack animals much longer than the others, and through their considerable selfishness toward others. Compare this with the old bachelor Hardkoop, who was ordered out of the Keseberg family wagon and abandoned to die, or the fate of the young bachelor Antoine, whom none of the hungry snowshoers bothered to awaken when his hand fell into the fire.

Family ties can be a matter of life and death even under normal conditions. Married people, it turns out, have lower death rates than single, widowed, or divorced people. And marriage's life-promoting benefits have been found to be shared by all sorts of social ties, such as friendships and membership in social groups. Regardless of age or sex or initial health status, socially isolated individuals have well over twice the death rate of socially connected people.

For reasons about which we can only speculate, the lethal effects of social isolation are more marked for men than for women. It's clear, though, why social contacts are important for both sexes. They provide concrete help in case of need. They're our source of advice and shared information. They provide a sense of belonging and self-worth, and the courage to face tomorrow. They make stress more bearable.

All those benefits of social contact applied as well to the Donner Party members, who differed only in that their risk of death was much greater and their likely circumstances of death more grotesque than yours and mine. In that sense too, the harrowing story of the Donner Party grips us because it was ordinary life writ large.

Colorful Cotton!

An ethnoarchaeologist tries to revive a 5,000-year-old
Peruvian textile tradition.

Angela M. H. Schuster

A shaft of sunlight through the window of an adobe house illuminates the chalk-covered hands of an elderly weaver. Pulling and plying chocolate-colored fiber from a cone of raw cotton held in place by a large stone, she gathers it onto a weighted spindle, the chalk allowing the fiber to pass smoothly through her fingers. In a month she will have spun enough yarn to make a poncho of the type worn by the men of her community for more than three millennia. like her mother and her grandmother before her, Margarita Farfán, a Mochica, has spent the better part of a lifetime providing her family with clothes, blankets, saddlebags, and fishing nets, all woven of naturally pigmented cotton in shades of rust, beige, mauve, and chocolate.

The cultivation of multicolored cotton, *algodón nativo (Gossypium barbadense),* has been an integral part of Andean culture for millennia. Three-thousand-year-old mummies preserved in Peru's coastal sand dunes were wrapped in layer upon layer of colored cotton fabric; royalty buried in 1,500-year-old tombs at the Moche site of Sipán in the Reque Valley were draped in cotton shrouds and wore tunics of the native fiber bearing intricate anthropomorphic figures woven in dark chocolate; and, at the 4,500-year-old site of Huaca Prieta in northern Peru's Lower Chicama Valley, archaeologist Junius B. Bird recovered more than 9,000 textile fragments, presumably from mummy wrappings and funerary offerings, most of which were woven of cotton. At all of these sites, the cotton textiles had retained their natural pigmentation.

Known for its long staple and colorful fibers, algodón nativo is naturally resistant to insects, and thrives on the eastern slopes of the Andes 3,000 feet above sea level, an elevation at which other varieties of cotton fail. The plant's deep root system allows it to survive on Peru's arid north coast, which receives less than one inch of rainfall per year. To grow the cotton

Margarita Farán pulls and plies fiber from a cone of algodón nativo. *Chalk on her hands facilitates the handling the fiber.*

An Ancient Tradition

Several days before it is ginned, freshly picked cotton is laid out to cure in the sunlight. While paler shades of mauve and beige give up their seeds easily, the fragile rust and chocolate fibers, whose seeds are firmly embedded, are difficult to gin by hand. Cleaned locks of cotton are stretched out, flattened, and gathered into bundles weighing as much as a pound. These are beaten flat with sticks, folded and beaten again until the fibers are smooth and homogeneous. The flattened bundles are rolled into cones.

The spinning process is simple. A spindle is held in a horizontal and slightly inclined position while fibers are drawn from a cone of cotton tied to a stationary post, or distaff, or held in place under a heavy object such as a large stone. Cotton spinners on the north coast use smaller and lighter spindles (the sticks around which yarn is wound) and whorls (spindle weights) than those in the highlands, who work longer and heavier camelid fibers. Both cotton and camelid textiles are woven on a traditional backstrap loom anchored to a wall or tree.—A.M.H.S.

and produce a textile from it is time-consuming and arduous, especially if ginning (removing the seeds), carding (cleaning and straightening the fiber), and spinning are done by hand, as they are to this day in remote villages of Peru.

In antiquity an estimated ten percent of the land under cultivation was devoted to algodón nativo. Today, it grows only in small family gardens along with native food crops, and sometimes wild along country roads. Margarita Farfán and her seven daughters are among the last to spin and weave it. Peru's once dominant fiber has been displaced by the more familiar white tanguis and pima cottons—cultivated for their high yield, strong fiber, and ease of spinning—and commercially produced synthetics. In recent decades much of the farmland in the nearby Andean foothills, once used to grow the native cotton, has been turned over to coca leaf. A far more lucrative crop, it is Peru's leading agricultural export, supplying some 60 percent of the world market for cocaine.

Though extensive research has been carried out on Peru's highland textiles, most of which are woven of fibers from camelids—alpaca, llama, and vicuña—until recently little was known about the textiles of the north coast, especially those woven of multicolored cotton. To document Preconquest use of the colored cotton fibers, anthropologist James Vreeland of the University of Texas, Austin, began working with traditional weavers in several coastal communities in the departments of Piura and Lambayeque. In two villages, Mórrope and Ferreñafe, he found that women still cultivated, spun, and wove the colored cotton and that more than three-quarters of them had worked the fiber in their youth. In documenting their methods of cultivation and the equipment used to spin and weave—distaffs, spindles, whorls, and looms—Vreeland noticed that in nearly every respect the tools and techniques were Precolumbian in origin, attesting an unbroken textile tradition in the region.

Vreeland's ethnographic research provided clues to an enigmatic archaeological find. During the 1970s archaeologists working in the Jequetepeque Valley had collected soil samples from a pre-Inka field system abandoned ca. A.D. 1250. Along with seeds of cotton and various squashes, crops traditionally grown in close proximity, they recovered remnants of the woody shrub *Lippia* sp., a relative of lemon verbena that seemed to serve no useful purpose. In a recent conversation with an elderly farmer in the Piura Valley, Vreeland learned that peasants in the

area grow the shrub near their cotton plants as a pesticide; smoke from burning these shrubs kills and repels a number of insects harmful to the plants.

In addition to its value as a textile fiber, algodón nativo has played an important role in traditional Mochica medicine, where it is still used to cure a host of illnesses. Recent research has revealed that cotton seed is rich in antibiotics, which may explain its widespread use in folk remedies. Women also use the ash of burned cotton to cure spider bites and tuck small wads of the chocolate fiber in their clothing for protection against *mal de ojo,* the evil eye. In some communities a small pad of the dark brown cotton is placed on a newborn's head to protect it from the nocturnal hoot of the two-horned owl, a sound thought to be capable of splitting open an infant's fragile skull. Vreeland also found that coastal fishermen still made nets of chocolate-colored cotton similar to those recovered by Junius Bird at Huaca Prieta. When he inquired about this use of the fiber, one octogenarian fisherman told him that nets made of the dark cotton are invisible to fish, especially those swimming near the surface.

What for Vreeland began as research into ancient textile production soon became a personal campaign to revitalize Peru's native cotton tradition. "The gene stock is here," he says, "as well as the knowledge of Prehispanic farming techniques that are less destructive than modern practices, which rely on fertilizers, harmful pesticides, and overtilling of the soil." In 1984 he co-founded La Sociedad de Investigacion de la Ciencia, Cultura, y Arte Norteño (SICAN), a nonprofit research institution, to promote a return to Precolumbian land-management techniques and provide a profitable alternative to growing coca leaf. With support from several nongovernmental organizations, Vreeland collected seed from family gardens and abandoned fields, and, with the help of peasant families, local graduate students, and Peruvian scientists, he planted 11 farmyard plots. Fiber generated from these plots was given to artisans to weave into traditional garments and blankets that were sold to handicraft stores in Lima and museum shops in the United States. Vreeland and his colleagues also began testing the fiber on modern spinning machines. The dark cotton tended to break when spun on machines. By blending the fiber with organically grown white cotton, they were able to strengthen it.

Last year some 500 families, both on the coast and in the Andean foothills, were involved in growing and weaving the native cotton, and the number is expected to double this year. Because the fibers and textiles are produced without chemical fertilizers, pesticides, or commercial dyes and fabric softeners, they have been favorably received by the environmentally minded in the United States, Europe, and Japan. Retailers such as L.L. Bean and Lands' End now carry socks and underwear made from the colored cotton. Vreeland, however, faces strong

opposition from drug cartels and commercial cotton producers. "It has been difficult to compete with coca as a cash crop," he says, "since it can yield $3,000–$4,000 per hectare [2.5 acres] annually, four times what a farmer can make from cotton, even if it is grown commercially." The United States Drug Enforcement Administration estimates that Peru now has more than 130,000 hectares under coca cultivation compared to 100,000 hectares for commercial cotton. Until recently farmers were heavily fined for cultivating algodón nativo in areas where tanguis and pima were grown for export. Commercial cotton producers feared cross pollination, resulting in undesirable intermediate varieties, weaker fibers, and muddled colors unacceptable in the highly competitive industrial market.

Meanwhile, farmers are under extreme pressure from the drug cartels to grow the coca leaf and to produce coca paste and refine cocaine from it. One

ginning company processing algodón nativo found rifle cartridges in its machines, presumably intended to damage the equipment. "But there is a quality-of-life issue here that many of the farmers are just now beginning to see," says Vreeland. "Though they earn more money growing coca leaf, it costs significantly more to provide for their families, since they have to purchase the food they once grew themselves. Moreover, being in business with the cartels places a great amount of strain on family life."

Cultivation regulations, the drug trade, and recent torrential rain and flash floods brought by El Niño—a climatic phenomenon caused by a periodic change in the Peru Current that runs along the Pacific coast—have significantly depleted the native cotton gene stock. In antiquity, Peruvians stored cotton seed so that crops could be replenished in the event of a disaster. During the past century, there has been virtually no preservation of seed

Seed Sleuths

When Spanish soldiers landed on Peru's north coast in 1531, they marveled at the fields of brown and mauve cotton, unknown in the Old World. The Spanish missionary Bernabé Cobo wrote in his seventeenth-century *History of the New World* that "the Indians dye the fibers of cotton on the plant." Early in the eighteenth century Spanish botanists Hipólito Ruiz and José Pavón reported the plant being grown in the valleys of Lima and Chancay, and sent specimens to the Spanish taxonomist Cavanilles for study. And at the end of the eighteenth century Bishop Martínez de Compañón included colored cotton in a book on north coast plants.

In 1983 James Vreeland of the Sociedad de Investigación de la Ciencia, Cultura, y Arte Norteño, Magda Chanco of the Museum of Natural History of Lima, Miguel Holle of the International Board for Plant Genetic

Resources/FAO, Felix Chicoma of Lambayeque University, and I began a systematic study of algodón nativo and its current distribution within Peru. We began collecting cotton from gardens in the Indian desert communities of Schura and Olmos. Seeds from plants with the most vivid fiber pigments were sown in an observation plot on the lemon plantation of Gustavo del Solar, where they survived the 1983 El Niño and the severe drought that followed. Additional seeds from Olmos were collected and planted at the Museum of Natural History of Lima.

During our decade-long project, we found that water supply and soil conditions dramatically affect the plant—it grows to a height of 18 feet on the desert coast but rarely more than six feet in jungle areas. We were surprised to find remnants of the species *Gossypium raimondii*, named for a nine-

teenth-century Italian botanist Antonio Raimondi, in the Saña Valley. Researchers had declared it extinct decades ago. On the Morañon River, a tributary of the Amazon, we found kidney cotton, a native variety whose seeds form a kidney-shaped mass.

To slow the erosion of the gene base of algodón nativo, we succeeded in having the plant declared a national plant patrimony in 1992. Today the plants that we collected can be examined in the Herbarium of the Museum of Natural History of the University of San Marcos, Lima. More than 700 samples of the cotton seed have been placed in an air-conditioned vault at the Peruvian Ministry of Agriculture for future generations to use and study.

Ramón Ferreyra is director of the Museum of Natural History, University of San Marcos, Lima, Peru.

stock. To remedy this, Vreeland and his colleagues collected seeds from throughout Peru hoping to recoup colors lost in antiquity. In 1992 SICAN succeeded in having native cotton declared a national plant patrimony under Peru's 1990 Environmental Code, and it can now be grown anywhere without penalty.

While peasant farmers are producing native cotton for export, personal use of the fiber among the indigenous population has declined. The villages of Mórrope and Ferreñafe, once isolated from mainstream Peruvian culture, are now connected by new roads to the Panamerican Highway. Villagers who once wore garments made of native cotton now prefer blue jeans and Michael Jackson T-shirts.

Esperanza Pisfil Capuñay is a weaver in Monsefú, a small town south of Chiclayo. She makes her living weaving dowries—tablecloths, napkins, bed linens, and doilies. "A generation ago women provided their own dowries," she says, "but today many of the young girls are going to work in Lima, Piura, or Trujillo and do not have the time or the inclination to spin and weave." Though the tradition of presenting a groom's family with a dowry remains strong, it is women like

Esperanza who produce it. Weaving on a traditional backstrap loom, she works primarily with imported cotton fiber in brilliant shades of pink and green. She prefers the aniline-dyed cotton yarn, which she has to purchase, to the native cotton that grows wild near her house because the indigenous fiber is time-consuming and difficult to work. Commercially spun yarns, she says, are inexpensive and readily available at the local market. The most important factor, however, is color. "Only the elderly still wear the brown and mauve," she says. "It's old-fashioned."

While use of native cotton in the villages of the north coast may end with the demise of the older generation, the technology is being kept alive by a group of weavers in Chiclayo, who have found a growing market in replicating and restoring ancient textiles for museums. Clemencia Cabrera de Bautista is the director of the Puchka Cooperative, a weavers' group formed in 1983 to manufacture blankets and ponchos for the tourist trade. "They are producing beautiful goods," says Vreeland, "but they are in no way 'traditional.' Most of the Puchka weavers came from the highlands and originally worked in alpaca and llama

wool. They were taught how to spin and weave algodón nativo by Margarita Farfán and her daughters. As a result, they are now producing cotton items whose designs are of highland origin." Cabrera agrees that the co-op has re-created many of the ancient highland patterns and that their work does not represent a continuity with the past. However, she says her weavers understand the methods used millennia ago and are comfortable deciphering lowland textiles and fragments found in excavations and replicating them. Their work can be seen in the *Royal Tombs of Sipán* exhibition now touring the United States.

While traditional spinning and weaving by hand are on the decline, Vreeland hopes that algodón nativo will prove a workable alternative to coca leaf. This past year sales of the fiber grown by the Indians exceeded $1 million and he expects to have some 10,000 hectars under cultivation next year. If he and others can continue to interest foreign markets in buying Peru's unique strain of cotton, it is conceivable that one of South America's oldest cultivars will one day help sustain a country now in urgent need of an alternative export.

Murders From the Past

Sleuthing crimes of the past, forensic anthropologists open up files on Lizzie Borden, the Colorado Cannibal, Zachary Taylor, and Huey "Kingfish" Long, among others.

James Dickerson

An electric saw buzzed through a lead container that had been sealed for 150 years. Slowly, the liner lid was removed, exposing the remains of Zachary Taylor, the twelfth president of the United States. Face to face with the former president, a blue-ribbon panel of investigators was surprised to see a thick mass of dark hair and a large cloth bow under the chin. Since the president's visit was meant to be brief, his hosts went to work immediately. University of Florida forensic anthropologist Bill Maples methodically cut away the president's clothing, finding abundant body hair beneath the one-piece, pleated shroud. Then he took hair, nail, and tissue samples, hoping they would prove whether the president had succumbed to arsenic poisoning or died of natural causes.

Ghoulish? Perhaps to most. But to forensic sleuths like Maples, who focus on murders and other mysteries a century or more old, exhuming and examining the remains of celebrities from presidents to political assassins is business as usual.

In another case, for instance, Maples seeks to identify the remains of Francisco Pizarro, the Spanish conqueror of Peru. And his colleague James Starrs, a lawyer and forensic scientist at George Washington University in Washington, DC, has exhumed the remains of Dr. Carl Austin Weiss, the alleged assassin of the controversial U.S. senator from Louisiana, Huey

Long. When held up to the scrutiny of modern science, Weiss's remains and other buried evidence may show whether the doctor was truly Long's assassin or was innocent, as his descendants have claimed.

It's possible to resolve such issues today, thanks to the extraordinary range and power of modern forensic techniques. Today's high-resolution microscopes, for instance, can analyze knife marks on bone, distinguishing between different knives or the marks left by animals. X-rays can probe beneath the surface of grave sites. Sophisticated chemical and nuclear technologies can detect trace amounts of incriminating poisons. And using computers, experts can superimpose old photos of a victim or suspect on top of x-ray images of facial bones, determining whether or not the identities are a match.

In fact, whether it's determining the identity of an eighteenth-century cannibal or investigating the fate of the princess Anastasia Romanov, forensic anthropologists have begun to rewrite the history of murder, mayhem, and sensational crime. For a look at some of the most fascinating investigations to date, open *Omni*'s murder dossier, and read on.

WHO KILLED THE KINGFISH?

VICTIM: Huey Long, U.S. senator and former governor from Louisiana.
DEATH NOTES: The politically powerful Long was shot and killed while

visiting the Louisiana State Capitol on September 8, 1935. The presumed assassin, a 29-year-old physician named Carl Weiss, was killed by Long's bodyguards in a hail of gunfire at the scene.
MURDER MYSTERY: Although the case against Weiss was considered open and shut at the time, questions began to emerge. First of all, officials were never able to establish a genuine motive. In addition, though police said Weiss's gun was found at the scene, no one could prove he had carried the gun into the Capitol. Did Carl Weiss really kill Huey Long, or was he just a patsy, a fall guy set up by one of the many bitter political enemies Long had cultivated over the years?
FORENSIC SLEUTHS: James Starrs, forensic scientist, George Washington University, Washington, DC; Douglas Ubelaker, curator of anthropology, National Museum of Natural History, Smithsonian Institution, Washington, DC; Lucien Haag, freelance "criminalist" and weapons expert, Phoenix; Irvin Sother, state medical examiner, West Virginia; and Alphonse Poklis, toxicologist, Medical College of Virginia at Richmond.
CLUES UNEARTHED: Weiss's remains were exhumed on October 20, 1991, at the Roselawn Cemetery in Baton Rouge and transported first to the Lafayette, Louisiana, pathology lab for cleaning, then to Ubelaker's lab at the National Museum of Natural History. To identify the remains as those of Weiss, Ubelaker used the technique of photographic imposition to

match the skull with old photos of the suspect. To rule out the likelihood that Weiss committed the act as a result of a brain tumor or while under the influence of drugs, toxicologist Poklis examined the anatomy of the skull and analyzed the chemical content of tissue and bones. Examining the remains, he also discovered that Weiss had been shot a minimum of 23 times, with half the wounds inflicted on his back. Several bullet wounds were found in his arms, suggesting a defensive posture. Ubelaker also found that Weiss had been shot from a "variety of angles, implying that his assailants came from many directions."

Then Haag, an expert in firearms and tool marks, stepped in to examine the contents of files squirreled away by the police superintendent. Perhaps most telling was a .32-caliber bullet thought to have come from the scene of the crime. After testing the bullet at the laboratory in Phoenix, Haag concluded it did not come from Weiss's gun. Since Long's bodyguards carried only larger .38- and .45-caliber pistols, Haag notes, the mysterious bullet raises the question of a second, never-reported .32-caliber pistol somewhere on the scene. It's possible, he proposes, that Weiss's gun was simply a plant to protect the identity of the true killer, the one that got away. Anyone who knew that Weiss carried a piece could have found one like it and committed the crime themselves, setting Weiss up for the fall, Haag says.

CONCLUSION: As a result of all the new evidence, the seemingly solid case against Weiss has been riddled with doubt.

WILL THE REAL PIZARRO PLEASE STAND?

VICTIM: Francisco Pizarro, Spanish conqueror of Peru.

DEATH NOTES: Francisco Pizarro, despised by native Peruvians because of his brutal reign, was stabbed to death by a crowd of angry subjects in 1541 at the age of 71 in full view of numerous witnesses. Pizarro subsequently faded into history where he remained a topic for academicians and scholars for more than 350 years.

QUESTION OF IDENTITY: The cir-

Back in time: To resolve some of the most gruesome and enigmatic murder mysteries of the past, physical anthropolo-

gists like Bill Maples, top center, are digging up remains of both killers and victims as well as old murder weapons and more. Maples' colleagues, for instance, have exhumed the body of Dr. Carl Austin Weiss, top left, convicted, perhaps wrongfully, of assassinating the controversial U.S. senator Huey Long. Weiss's x-rayed skull is depicted, bottom right. Experts also want to study the hatchet supposedly used by Lizzie Borden, next page, top right, to kill her father, whose skull is shown, top right, and her stepmother, whose skull

is depicted on the next page, bottom left. Bottom center on this page is another focus for forensic sleuthing: One Alferd Packer, convicted of the gruesome, cannibalistic murder of five prospectors seeking gold and silver in Colorado's San Juan Mountains. Though Packer was convicted by a jury of his peers, he always maintained his innocence and was eventually paroled. Packer died in 1907, leaving unanswered the question of whether he truly was the

vicious killer who ate his unwitting victims' remains. Shown above is a photo of the remains of the five victims shortly after

exhumation in 1989. Another historical figure currently the subject of investigation is Meriwether Lewis, of Lewis and Clark fame, at right, who died of two gunshot wounds. The

death was declared a suicide at the time but is now considered a murder. Also the topic of study was

former U.S president Zachary Taylor, bottom right, who died suddenly, allegedly of gastroenteritis; despite this official cause of death, some experts have suggested arsenic poisoning instead. To unearth the truth, a team of forensic sleuths exhumed Taylor's remains in 1991, almost a century and a half after his

untimely death. It's interesting to note that detailed chemical and nuclear tests at the Louisville medical examiner's office and at the Oak Ridge National Laboratory in Tennessee yielded

no evidence of arsenic poisoning. But despite these results, say some experts, it's remotely possible that Taylor was poisoned with arsenic after all and that the evidence has simply leached from his body over the years.

cumstances of Pizarro's death are not in question, having been well documented at the time by the Spanish, who tortured witnesses to elicit the details. However, in the 1890s, Peruvian officials decided to put Pizarro's remains on exhibit as part of an upcoming celebration of Columbus's voyage. They asked officials at the Cathedral of the Plaza de Aramis in Lima for Pizarro's body and were directed to a mummy, which they put on view. Then, in 1978, workers in the cathedral uncovered a secret niche that had been walled over. On a shelf inside the niche was a lead box with a skull and an inscription identifying the contents as the head of Pizarro. Alongside this first box was another, this one containing the bones of several unidentified individuals. Who was the real Pizarro? The mummy that had been on display

for nearly a century or the skull and bones found in the cathedral crypt?
FORENSIC SLEUTHS: Bill Maples, anthropologist, University of Florida, Gainesville, and Bob Benfer, anthropologist, University of Missouri, Columbia.
CLUES UNEARTHED: A preliminary investigation by one of Benfer's students showed that postcranial bones in the second box matched the skull in the first. The matching bones were then assembled with the skull. The challenge for Maples and Benfer: determining whether the newly discovered bones contained marks consistent with knife or sword wounds and then determining whether similar wounds appeared on the mummy. Using straightforward visual observation, the researchers determined that the skeleton had been stabbed multiple times, consistent with

the reported demise of Pizarro. From the location of the wounds, Maples and Benfer concluded that Pizarro had been stabbed about the head and body and apparently had tried to shield himself with his arm, a reaction that is common in stabbing deaths. The mummy, on the other hand, exhibited no injuries whatsoever and could not have been Pizarro at all.

CONCLUSION: The remains of Pizarro had been hidden in the Cathedral crypt all along. The mystery solved, Peruvian officials exchanged the mummy with the bones, which are now on display instead. As for the mummy, it's on a piece of plywood down in the crypt. "Fame is fleeting," Maples observes, "even after death."

SEARCH FOR ANASTASIA

VICTIMS: Czar of Russia, Nicholas II; his wife, Alexandra; their five children, Olga, Tatiana, Marie, Anastasia, and Alexis; the royal physician; and several royal servants.

DEATH NOTES: On July 17, 1918, during the Bolshevik Revolution, the Russian czar and his family along with the royal physician and some servants were awakened and taken to the basement of the house in which they stayed. There, they were greeted by a hail of bullets and then stabbed with bayonets. According to one account, their bodies were hacked to pieces and soaked in acid. Two were burned.

MURDER MYSTERY: In what may have been the ultimate game of Russian roulette, the assassins assigned to wipe out the royal family may have let two members slip through the cracks. According to rumors that have persisted ever since the fateful day, the princess Anastasia Romanov and her brother Alexis may have survived their grievous injuries and lived to tell the tale. One observer, for instance, recalled the czar's youngest daughter sitting up and screaming after the initial volley of bullets. And in the years that followed, a number of people have claimed to be Anastasia herself. Anna Anderson Manahan, who died in Charlottesville, Virginia, in 1984 at the age of 82, was probably the most publicized claimant. For 60 years she tried to convince people she was Princess Anastasia and even filed a lawsuit in Germany for an $85 million dowry supposedly held in trust. German bankers were vague about the existence of a trust fund, however, and she lost the case. Although a movie was made of her struggle, her claims were discounted, primarily because she could not speak Russian. Was Manahan or another claimant the true Anastasia Romanov? Did the youngest czarist princess survive?

FORENSIC SLEUTHS: Bill Maples; Lowell Levine, codirector of the New York State Police Forensic Sciences Unit in Albany; Michael Baden, New York City pathologist; and Catherine

One of the biggest mysteries of the past involved the lost remains of

Francisco Pizarro, top left, Spanish conqueror of Peru, stabbed to death by native Peruvians who despised his brutal reign. While the circumstances of Pizarro's death are not in question, experts have debated the legitimacy of the explorer's mummified remains, put on exhibit at the Cathedral of the Plaza de

Aramis in Lima. The mummy in question showed no evidence of a brutal attack, and when workers found

another batch of remains hidden behind a secret cathedral wall,

the identity of the true Pizarro was up for grabs. A bit of forensic sleuthing proved the mummy an imposter and the bones behind the hidden wall real.

Maples, "even after death." This page, center, is George Washington University lawyer and forensic scientist James Starrs, who investigated the

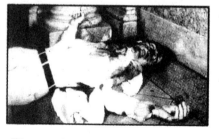

The mystery solved, Peruvian officials put the true remains on display. "Fame is fleeting," observed investigator Bill

murder of Huey Long, bottom left, and the true guilt of his

murderer, Carl Weiss, whose dead body is shown on the previous page on a Baton Rouge Capitol corridor floor. Forensic sleuths investigating the Colorado Canni-

bal have studied this sketch, above, created by artist John Randolph, the man said to have discovered the remains of the five unlucky victims brutally killed and then apparently filleted and eaten by Packer.

Photograph of the skull of victim George Noon, below, shows numerous hatchet marks. Finally,

experts trying to solve a royal murder mystery have compared photos of Anna Anderson Manahan, right, with depictions of her royal highness Anastasia Romanov, bottom right, said to have been killed with the rest of the Russian royal family during the Bolshevik revolution. To her dying day, Manahan claimed she was the real Anastasia, whose remains have never been identified.

Did Anastasia survive? To get to the truth, scientists are hoping to find and study more royal bones at the bottom of a firepit.

Oakes, microtomist, New York State police.

CLUES UNEARTHED: In 1991, Russian authorities exhumed the remains of nine bodies thought to be the czar and those who perished with him. Also retrieved from the grave site were bullets and a broken acid jar. Soon after exhumation, American experts, including Maples and Levine, arrived at a lab in Yekaterinburg, a city some 800 miles east of Moscow. Their goal: to identify the bodies and determine the cause of death. The Americans quickly declared that historical accounts of the assassination were born out by the condition of the remains. "Three of the skulls showed clear evidence of gunshot wounds," Maples says, "and teeth

and skulls showed evidence of etching and erosion by acid." There was even enough tissue on the remains of what was certainly the royal physician to hold the lower torso together. In fact, there was only one part of the story that could not be verified: the death of Anastasia. The skeleton of a 17-year-old female could not be found. Maples sees one last way to prove that Anastasia died: Locate a firepit containing the two bodies that were supposedly burned. According to historical accounts, the burned bodies belonged to Alexis, the czar's son, and a maid. But Maples says one of the burned bodies could turn out to be Anastasia. "If we found the bodies of two teenagers in a fire pit," he says, "I would feel confident that Anastasia did not survive."

CONCLUSION: DNA analysis conducted by British scientists confirmed the findings of forensic sleuths who went to Russia. After comparing blood samples taken from Prince Philip, a blood relative of the czar's wife, with tissue samples taken from the remains at Yekaterinburg, scientists were able to get a match. At the moment, the fate of Anastasia has been thrown into question. Russian investigators say Anastasia's remains were among those found. American experts are unsure. Recently, a lock of hair said to belong to Anna Anderson Manahan has been produced and will soon be subjected to DNA analysis. Hopefully, say the experts, they will be able to tell whether her genes and those of Prince Philip match.

4. HISTORY AND ETHNOARCHAEOLOGY

PRESIDENTIAL POISON

VICTIM: Zachary Taylor, twelfth president of the United States.

DEATH NOTES: On July 4, 1850, President Taylor dedicated the cornerstone for the Washington Monument. After walking home from the ceremony, he ate a bowl of cherries and drank a glass of cold milk. A short while later, he became violently ill with diarrhea, severe vomiting, and dehydration. Five days later he died.

MURDER MYSTERY: At the time, Taylor's death was attributed to deadly gastroenteritis. But according to pundits, the same symptoms are characteristic of arsenic poisoning, and, they say, Taylor may have been murdered by enemies wishing to do him in. Historical novelist Clara Rising even has two prime suspects: then–Vice President Millard Fillmore and Kentucky senator Henry Clay. Taylor was opposed to the extension of slavery, Rising explains, and supported the admission of California as a free state, something that would have made free states more numerous than slave ones. After Taylor's death, however, Fillmore supported a compromise proposal by Clay in which California, a free state, was paired with New Mexico, a slave state; the balance of power was kept intact. Motive enough to assassinate a president? Rising and others say maybe so.

FORENSIC SLEUTHS: Clara Rising, Louisville; Bill Maples; Dr. Richard Greathouse, Jefferson County coroner, Louisville; Dr. George Nichols, medical examiner, Commonwealth of Kentucky, Louisville; and Dr. William Hamilton, medical examiner, Gainesville, Florida.

CLUES UNEARTHED: Before exhuming Taylor on June 17, 1991, researchers checked with White House historical records to determine if the president had been embalmed. In the 1800s, embalming almost always involved the use of arsenic, and if he had been embalmed, it would have been impossible to tell whether Taylor had in fact been poisoned. According to Rising, records show that Taylor's wife would not allow him to be embalmed.

Oxidation of the coffin's lead liner caused by large quantities of seeping body fluids offers additional evidence that embalming did not occur. The researchers also sent tissue samples to the Louisville medical examiner's toxicology lab and to the Oak Ridge National Laboratory in Tennessee, where it was placed in a powerful research reactor and bombarded with neutrons. When bombarded with neutrons, different metals give off different levels of radiation; arsenic, of course, has its own telltale signature. When the results were in, both the chemical and nuclear tests revealed only "normal levels of arsenic" consistent with neither embalming nor poisoning. The labs also checked for the presence of other heavy metals, including mercury and antimony, and found none.

CONCLUSION: The detailed tests found no evidence of arsenic poisoning. But despite the results, says Maples, it's remotely possible that Taylor was poisoned with arsenic after all and that the evidence has simply leached from his body over the years.

COLORADO CANNIBAL

VICTIMS: Shannon Bell, Israel Swan, James Humphrey, George Noon, and Frank Miller, five prospectors seeking gold and silver in Colorado's San Juan Mountains.

DEATH NOTES: In the winter of 1874, the five victims hired one Alferd Packer to guide them through the mountains. But when Packer returned to town after six weeks, he said he had lost the others in a snow storm. There had, indeed, been a raging storm, but authorities were suspicious because of Packer's appearance: Despite his claims of hardship and a shortage of food, he was noticeably fat and more interested in drinking than eating. In addition, he seemed to have far more money than he'd had *before* the trip. When a traveling artist located the remains of the missing men, he discovered evidence of foul play and even sketched the scene for *Harper's Weekly*. Finally authorities reported "marks of extreme violence" on the

bodies of the victims and concluded that they had been murdered by ax or hatchet.

FORENSIC SLEUTHS: James Starrs; Douglas Ubelyker; Walter Birkby, forensic anthropologist, University of Arizona, Tucson; tool-mark expert Lucien Haag; and archeologist James Ayres, Tucson, Arizona.

MURDER MYSTERY: Before he could be charged with the murders, Packer escaped from authorities and remained at large for nine years. He was finally captured in 1883 and at his trial declared that four of the men had been murdered by Shannon Bell. He himself shot and then hacked Bell to death in self-defense, he claimed, after Bell attacked him. Packer was convicted and sentenced to death but won a new trial on a technicality. He was convicted a second time and sentenced to 40 years hard labor. At the turn of the century, however, a Denver newspaper columnist raised doubts about his guilt and succeeded in getting him paroled in 1901. He died in 1907. Was Packer innocent, or was he a vicious killer who ate the remains of his victims?

CLUES UNEARTHED: After the remains of the five prospectors were exhumed in July 1989, they were taken to the University of Arizona, where Walter Birkby is curator of physical anthropology. According to Birkby, the remains were in good condition, the result of soil with especially low levels of acid at the grave site. None of the bodies had been dismembered, he noted, but all had hatchet-like marks on the skull and had been defleshed. After the skeletons were assembled, Lucien Haag was called in to identify the marks found on the bones. Haag used a microscope to study the tool patterns and then made silicone rubber casts to preserve the marks for additional study.

According to investigators, the number, type, and location of implement marks leave no mystery as to how the prospectors died and what happened to them after death. "These individuals were all murdered," said Birkby. "All of them exhibited evidence of sharp implement marks on their bones, which is consistent with defleshing.

One individual had 14 hatchet marks on his skull." Some of the marks are clearly defensive, indicating some of the victims had held up their arms to ward off the blows of an ax or hatchet. Others received blows on the head, indicating they may have been sleeping when attacked. Many of the bones also showed very fine knife marks, Haag adds, an indication that these victims had, like steak, been filleted.

What about Packer's claim that Bell shot the others, causing him to shoot Bell in self-defense? Not likely, say the investigators. One individual probably committed all the murders, they explained, because the injuries were consistent from one cranium to the next. What's more, the researchers found only one bullet wound amongst all the victims—and that individual had been shot years before his death.
CONCLUSION: Packer's story did not hold up to scientific scrutiny. The jury that convicted him was right and his defenders were wrong. Alferd Packer was, indeed, "the Colorado Cannibal."

ON THE DOCKET:

Thanks to modern technology, the skeletal remains of historical figures have the potential to rewrite history by answering questions unanswerable at the time of death. Several cases still under study could rattle the cages of historians and law-enforcement officials:

Lizzie Borden. After an inept police investigation and a sensational murder trial in 1893, Lizzie Borden was found not guilty of hacking her father and 200-pound stepmother to death with an ax at their home in Fall River, Massachusetts. Despite her acquittal, Lizzie remained guilty in the eyes of the popular press and some historians. Enter forensic investigator James Starrs, who is convinced Lizzie Borden may have been innocent. Starrs wants permission from Borden family members to exhume the skulls of Lizzie's parents. If Lizzie is innocent, it can be proven scientifically, he says, "by comparing available physical evidence, such as the famous 'hoodoo hatchet,' with scientific analysis of the remains."

Meriwether Lewis. Also on Starrs' list of unsolved mysteries is the death of Meriwether Lewis (of Lewis and Clark fame). Lewis died in 1809 at an inn on the Natchez Trace southwest of Nashville, Tennessee. Governor of the Louisiana Territory at the time, he was on his way to Washington, DC, to meet with officials when he died of two gunshot wounds, one to the side and the other to the head. The death has long been labeled a suicide, but Starrs states that "the scientific evidence that he committed suicide is entirely deficient." Lewis may have been murdered,

---

'James Starrs hopes to exhume the skulls of Lizzie Borden's parents to compare with physical evidence such as the famous hoodoo hatchet.'

---

says Starrs. With the permission of Lewis's descendants, he hopes to exhume the remains and find out.

John Wilkes Booth. Abraham Lincoln was assassinated in April 1865 by John Wilkes Booth, who 12 days later was gunned down by soldiers in a barn—right? Wrong, according to Hugh Berryman, director of the Regional Forensic Center in Memphis; Nathaniel Orlowek, a religious educator at Beth Shalom Congregation in Potomac, Maryland; and Arthur Chitty, historian at the University of the South. They believe Booth may have escaped capture and lived another 38 years using the name John St. Helen before confessing his identity and committing suicide in Enid, Oklahoma. After his death, St. Helen's body was embalmed. But when the government showed no interest in investigating the claims, the lawyer to whom St. Helen confessed stored the mummy in his basement for 29 years. Eventually, the mummified body was sold to a carnival and then slipped out of sight. If the mummy can be recovered, says Berryman, it would be possible, using mod-

ern forensic technology, to make comparisons with known photographs of Booth. Meanwhile, Orlowek is attempting to exhume the body thought to belong to Booth and determine whether it is truly his.

Wild Bill Longley. On October 11, 1878, a notorious Texas outlaw named Wild Bill Longley was convicted of murder and hanged under the watchful eye of the local sheriff. His body was then buried in a cemetery near Giddings. Or was it? Family legend has it that he escaped the hangman's noose and relocated in Iberville Parish, Louisiana, where he adopted the sheriff's last name of Brown and lived a long life as a respected member of the community. According to family legend, in fact, Longley made a deal with the sheriff to fake the hanging using a harness to break his fall. Before burial, he escaped while the coffin was weighted with stones. The sheriff was subsequently killed in a gunfight with police in Chicago, and a man calling himself John Calhoun Brown began a new life in Louisiana. He fathered ten children, ran a successful timber business, and died around 1923.

These claims by the families of both the "original" Longley and the Brown descendants in Louisiana prompted Dr. Douglas Owsley, a forensic anthropologist at the Smithsonian Institution, to organize an investigative team. The first step was using a computer to compare photographs of the two men. "I was taken aback by the correspondence of the fit," he says. "They were very, very similar. "Betting on the "probability" that Longley and Brown were one and the same, Owsley worked with geologist Brooks Elwood at the University of Texas and Pat Mercado-Allinger of the Texas Historical Commission to excavate 25 graves at the cemetery where the outlaw's coffin, filled with stones, was said to lie. The outlaw's marker had been moved at least twice in more than a century, so it's no surprise that none of the 25 coffins turned out to be his. But the team will do some more historical research and then return to the cemetery, hoping to find a coffin full of stones.

The New Politics of Archaeology: A Trowel for Your Thoughts

Good morning, ladies and gentlemen. Welcome to the first annual convention of WARP, the World Archaeological Research Project. I am Dr. Derk Digger. As we all know, from the very beginning archaeology was an underground science fraught with a lot of just plain dirt flying around. By the end of the nineteenth century, disagreement within the rank and file had elevated to mud slinging.

"During the 1960s in the historical period known as the 'New Archaeology,' infighting among archaeologists reached new intellectual lows. A whole decade was spent arguing about the true meaning of Mousterian points. Heavies like 'Louie the Blade' and 'François the Flake' perpetuated pointed discussions, ignoring core materials.

"When push came to shove in the 1970s, some archaeologists viciously attacked vending machines at professional meetings. Whole dynasties of stellar archaeological families fought others for sites and National Geographic funding, sometimes misplacing whole sites or taking over small nations. Rulers of sites rose and fell, as espionage and counterespionage tossed reputations around like so much falling backdirt.

"There was much splitting and lumping during these fluctuating dates, and not much was salvaged. This pugnacious pattern of archaeological antics continued to worsen during the decades of the 1980s and 1990s until archaeology was in ruins! The garbage finally hit the pits, and archaeologists surrendered on July 4, 1999, at Point Clovis, New Mexico. The Marshalltowns hitting the ground made a sound the likes of which had not been heard since Howard Carter opened King Tut's tomb.

"Ah, but this is all history, or maybe proto-history. We remaining archaeologists hope to form a hypothetical agreement on the issues that concern all of us here today. That is, of course, the future of archaeological sites. Remember, as you sit here today, we are about to create TRASH (The Ruling Archaeological Sites Hierarchy). During this morning's session, we can consider about six demands from our various special interest groups. Please put your shards on the table before you speak.

"I would like to introduce our first speaker, Mr. Peter Potlooter of Profit, Inc. We all know of the negative impact archaeology has had on this worldwide organization representing thieves, pothunters, and looters. We now welcome our fellow enthusiasts from Profit, Inc., and hope to convert a great many of their views into TRASH. As reformed archaeologists, we are eager to make up for the past 200 years of tyranny in which we have tried to keep archaeological sites for ourselves.

"What was that? I can't hear you! Oh yes, certainly, Mr. Sharp Arrow, this afternoon we will get to your proposal to bury the Smithsonian, artifacts and all!"*

And so, the tale above goes on . . . somewhere in someone's midden-clotted brain.

In this unit, the real state of the health of the science of archaeology is examined. In any science, a good deal of infighting goes on. But it seems that something about archaeologists makes them carry on with an exquisite pugnaciousness that impresses even the most hardened veterans of other disciplines. Much speculation has been spent on the eccentric stereotype of archaeologists. If there is an answer, it probably is to be found in the nature of the subject matter and its closeness to ultimate concerns such as the nature of human beings and our very origins.

The readings presented in this section address the concerns archaeologists face in terms of a whole new set of politics. There are other serious contenders for the rights to archaeological sites, and archaeologists need to focus outward.

As long as there has been property, there have been thieves. As long as there have been archaeological sites, there have been looters. What of the native or descendant generations who feel a continuity with their past either in a specific area or in a generalized sense. For example, North American archaeology has been revolutionized by recent laws designating ownership of many archaeological sites to those who claim to be native descendants. But criteria to establish who is a descendant have not been well defined. This leads to complicated questions of repatriation of what are now archaeological materials. In fact, the rightful ownership of antiquities by museums, universities, or whole nations is continuously being challenged.

Today archaeologists must walk an ethical and political tightrope on all of these issues. It is a very hard thing to do, when our shared human past and all the wisdom it can offer us is at stake. Our species has always had an insatiable need to know who we are.

---

* Any resemblance to real persons or events in this fictional story are purely coincidental, with the exception of Howard Carter and King Tut's tomb.

UNIT 5

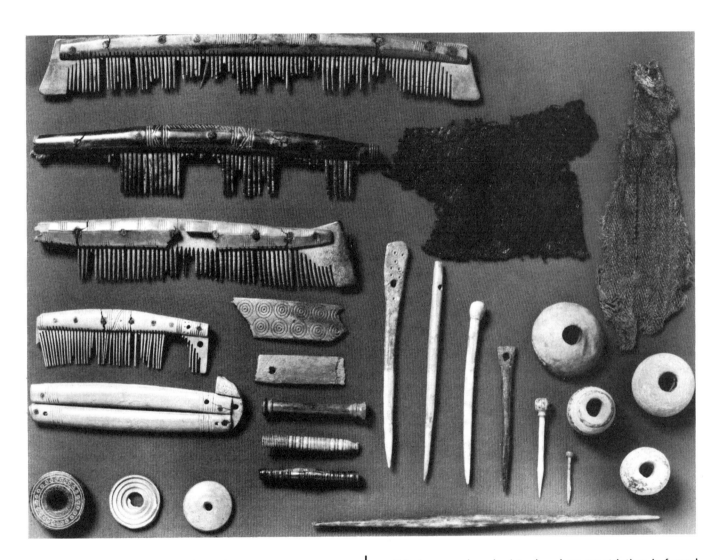

Looking Ahead: Challenge Questions

What is meant by the term native descendant generation?

What is meant by repatriation of archaeological finds?

What methods are used to settle disputes over archaeological materials gained during international wars?

How would you characterize Heinrich Schliemann as an archaeologist by today's standards of professionalism? Why?

What are the special problems of underwater archaeology in determining ownership of spoils of the deep?

What can archaeologists do when repatriation is forced, as in the Tasmanian affair? Discuss the possibilities.

What happens when urban archaeologists face modern developers? Discuss and cite examples from this book and any other information you may have.

How was archaeology used as propaganda to fuel the Nazi movement in World War II? In your judgment, did the Nazi archaeologists really believe their own lies? Explain your answer. In what other instances has archaeology been used as propaganda?

An Anthropological Culture Shift

A federal law that puts Native American rights and religion ahead of scientific curiosity is reshaping North American anthropology and archeology.

Museums, universities, and federal agencies are beginning to clean skeletons out of their closets all across the United States. They're clearing out other objects important to Native Americans as well, such as sacred shields and medicine bundles. This flurry of housecleaning is prompted not by a shortage of storage space, but by a law that recognizes Native Americans' claims to their past.

The Native American Graves Protection and Repatriation Act (NAGPRA) requires some 5000 federally funded institutions and government agencies to return Native American skeletons, funerary and sacred objects, and items of profound cultural importance to American Indian tribes and Native Hawaiians. Although NAGPRA was passed 4 years ago, it didn't really start to bite until last November, when facilities had to notify the tribes about the sacred and cultural items in their collections. That was just the first step in

a process that will see tens of thousands of scientifically valuable items handed over, many of them for reburial, over the next few years. Hundreds of scientists who depend upon this material will be cut off from their research data, and North American anthropology and archeology will be changed forever.

"The reality is there's been a shift in the equation," says Dan Monroe, executive director of the Peabody Essex Museum in Salem, Massachusetts. "It's a matter of basic human rights versus scientific rights, and in this new equation in many instances those scientific rights have been constrained, no doubt about it." But NAGPRA isn't just placing skeletons and artifacts out of reach of scientific study. It's also giving Native Americans influence over what research is conducted and published. Scientists who were once accustomed to "doing as they damned well-pleased," as one anthropologist put it,

must now involve Native Americans in almost every phase of their research—from requesting research permits to study collections to, in some cases, passing completed studies to tribal councils for prepublication review. "The shocking thing is that we really haven't spent time talking to the Indians," admits Thomas J. Green, director of the Arkansas Archeological Survey. "NAGPRA is forcing us to do that, and maybe once we get through these issues, we'll see that there's actually a natural alliance between the archeological and Indian communities."

But this bridge-building doesn't mean that the bitter debate that preceded passage of NAGPRA 4 years ago has died down. Many scientists still decry the repatriation as an improper melding of church and state, and they are particularly upset that the law provides Native Americans very broad ancestral claims—even on items that scientists say predate the origins of the tribes themselves.

State Laws Provide a Glimpse of the Future

As researchers and museum officials begin to implement a new law requiring repatriation of Native American skeletons and artifacts, some clues to what lies ahead may be found in the operation of similar state laws already on the books. One of those laws in Idaho sent "Buhla," a 10,675-year-old female skeleton, back into the ground in 1992. Idaho state archeologists had recovered the bones from a gravel pit operation near the town of Buhl just 3 years earlier. During this time the remains had only been studied for 3 days, by a single physical anthropologist—research that was delayed because of technical problems in obtaining a radiocarbon date.

The remains and the artifacts found with the skeleton were reburied on the Shoshone-Bannock reservation, 100 miles from where it was found—although archeologists doubt any Shoshone-Bannock inhabited the region 10,000 years ago. In the tradition of the Shoshone-Bannock, the woman is perceived as "our Mother; the Mother of us all," explains Diana K. Yupe, a Shoshone-Bannock anthropologist. "To us, she is our ancestor, and hers is not just a decomposed body; she is alive."

"There are about 25 skeletons in North America older than 8500 [before present]," says Thomas J. Green, the former Idaho state archeologist and now director of the Arkansas Archeological Survey. "And of these, she was one of the oldest and certainly one of the best preserved. Now, probably the most signifi-

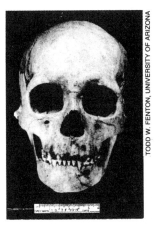

Reinterred. Skull of 10,675-year-old skeleton reburied under Idaho state law.

cant thing about Buhla is that she's reburied."

Archeologists expect to see a similar fate befall many of the funerary goods now stored in museums. A 1991 Arizona case, in which archeologists were complying with state law, suggests what might be in store on a broad scale. When a new highway in Phoenix was going to destroy a portion of a known, large Hohokam settlement called Pueblo Grande that dated from 900 to 1450 years ago, the state called in an archeological consulting firm to salvage and record what was found. Eventually, 2000 funerary vessels and 800 skeletons were recovered—the largest such collection of Hohokam pottery and individuals ever found. "It was the best collection of its kind," says Cory Breternitz, president of Soil Systems

Inc., the archeological firm that handled the dig. "And we'd worked out an agreement about the study of this material with the tribes ahead of time." But in the spring of 1991, the tribal council objected to the study of the human remains, and a few months later every item was reburied on the Ak-Chin Reservation.

Also destined for reburial is the Grasshopper Collection, skeletal and funerary material dating from 1300 to 1400 years ago that was recovered from a large Mogollan complex on the White Mountain Apache Reservation over the past 30 years. Consisting of more than 700 skeletons and thousands of artifacts, including arrow points, stone and bone tools, beads, shells, pottery, and hair ornaments, it is now housed in the Arizona State Museum. According to University of Arizona archeologist William A. Longacre, who oversaw much of the excavation, it is "the best documented and largest collection from a single Native American community that's been occupied consistently for 100 years."

But the collection is going back into the ground. Although the excavations took place on White Mountain Apache land, the material is culturally linked to the Zuni and Hopi—and the three tribes have decided they want all the skeletons and grave goods repatriated and reburied. "It's an incredible resource that we are going to lose," Longacre says. "From our perspective, it is a terrible loss. But from theirs [the Indians], it's a terrible thing that we've done." —V.M.

From the Indians' perspective, however, the return of sacred items is long overdue. "The reality is, it's our stuff," says John Pretty On Top, cultural director for the Crow. "We made it and we know best how to use it and care for it. . . . And now because of the law, we're going to get it back." Leigh Jenkins, the director of the Hopi Cultural Preservation Office, notes that graves and religious icons of all other peoples in America were never

treated the way Indian material was treated. "Every tribe has sad stories about graves being pillaged, the offerings and skeletons taken, and ritual objects removed," he says. "Scientists always had one standard for themselves and another for Indians."

A shift of power

Now that museums have notified tribes that they possess sacred and culturally important Indian material, the next step

will be to determine exactly what will be returned. By 1995, the museums must provide detailed inventories of all skeletal remains and funerary goods, and the tribes can then request that the material be shipped back to them. NAGPRA provides a set of guidelines to help Native Americans and museums sort out what can and cannot be returned, but both sides anticipate disagreements—particularly over prehistoric remains and burial goods.

"Those are emerging as the flash point," says Jonathan Haas, McArthur Curator of North American anthropology and archeology at Chicago's Field Museum of Natural History.

No anthropologist interviewed by Science objected to reburial when the remains were those of a known individual—in fact, scientists expressed dismay that such items should have found their way to a museum in the first place. But the return and reburial of skeletal material several hundreds or thousands of years old, where ancestral relationships are not always clear, has researchers groaning—especially since these materials are often scientifically the most interesting. To American Indians, however, a skeleton's age is immaterial. "We don't accept any artificial cutoff date set by scientists to separate us from our ancestors," says Walter R. Echo-Hawk, the attorney for the Native American Rights Fund, one of the groups that fought for NAGPRA. "What Europeans want do with their dead is their business," he says. "We have different values."

NAGPRA, in fact, places those values on an equal footing with scientific evidence. "The law explicitly says that their oral traditions have standing in this process," explains C. Timothy McKeown, an ethnographer and program leader for the implementation of NAGPRA at the National Park Service, the federal agency charged with overseeing the law. Thus, a tribe can claim prehistoric remains if tribal tradition says that its people were created in the same region where the remains were found—a claim that has already led to reburial of some collections under existing state laws (see box). (If a museum objects to these claims, then a special NAGPRA review committee will make the final determination, weighing both the scientific and tribal evidence.)

Many museums, in order to maintain good relations with the tribes and salvage some material for study, have already handed over, or are in the process of doing so, large collections of skeletons. The Field Museum, where more than 300 scholars a year come to use the extensive Native American materials, has given back 62 of its 2000 remains, and expects to return the rest. At the Smithsonian Institution's physical anthropological collections, 2000 skeletons have been returned for reburial, with the remaining 14,000 skeletons set to follow.

Many scientists are troubled by the prospect of massive reburials of prehistoric materials because they shut the door on studies using new techniques. "Once the material is gone, it is no longer available for restudy or for future studies using new techniques, nor can anyone check the original data for observer error—something that is fundamental to science," says Jane Buikstra, a physical anthropologist at the University of Chicago. Douglas Owsley, a physical and forensic anthropologist at the Smithsonian, points out that "we can do studies now—on health and disease, demographic rates, settlement patterns—that we simply had no inkling of when I was in graduate school [in the 1970s]. To say that we have learned all we can from these skeletons is a serious mistake."

Take the case of Ethne Barnes, a physical anthropologist at Witchita State University, who recently developed a new method for identifying developmental defects in adult skeletons. "The data collected in the past on these skeletons has very little value to my work," says Barnes, "because I'm looking at them from a completely new perspective and scaling the growth patterns differently than others have done." Barnes began her study shortly before NAGPRA, using skeletal material housed in the Smithsonian and other museums. Initially, she needed only the museums' permission to study the collections, but now she must also seek each tribe's permission, which is not always forthcoming. "The Cochiti Pueblo flat-out said no, while the Hopi were very interested," she says. However, the Hopi want to see her research results before she publishes. "It is a kind of censorship," she agrees, "but I also think we should be collaborating with the Indians."

So far, most of the attention has been focused on NAGPRA's impact on archeology and physical anthropology,

> "... For those of us doing excavations, we're going to have to be a lot more responsible collecting information and sharing it with the people we're studying."

but some scientists think it will eventually have a major effect on cultural anthropology as well. Lynne Goldstein, a mortuary archeologist at the University of Wisconsin, Milwaukee, says Native Americans aren't going to be satisfied with the return of bones and artifacts: "They'll ask next for field notes, tapes, photographs; and they'll insist that you have their permission before you publish." Goldstein's concern is more than hypothetical: The Hopi Tribe, in its response to the museums' inventory letters, asked museums to declare a moratorium on the study of any archival material pertaining to the Hopi people—a request that has stunned the museum community, although to the Hopi it seems a logical extension of NAGPRA. "We feel very strongly that there is a connection between the intellectual knowledge and the sacred objects that were collected from our religious altars: The knowledge and the object are one," says Leigh Jenkins. "The Hopi people want that esoteric knowledge protected right now."

An alliance out of adversity?
Despite all the turmoil NAGPRA has caused, scientists and Indians alike agree that the law has started to bring them together. Scientists, says Goldstein, "have to look at this situation pragmatically because the reality is, we lost. . . . [F]or those of us doing excavations, we're going to have to be a lot more responsible collecting information and sharing it with the people we're studying."

Not sharing information appears to be at the root of much of the distrust now afflicting academic researchers. Archeologists, for example, excavated homes and burials of the Pawnee people for more than a half-century before they ever contacted the tribe, says Roger Echo-Hawk, a Pawnee graduate student studying the relationship between oral history and archeology at the University of Colorado, Boulder. Indeed, scientists admit they made little effort in the past to involve Native Americans. "We've had to move from the ethics of conquest to the ethics of collaboration," says Martin Sullivan, director of Phoenix, Arizona's Heard Museum.

Still, scientists should "not look at collaboration through rose-colored glasses," says Goldstein, who points to her excavation last summer of a cemetery in California's Fort Ross State Park as an example. It took her 18 months to acquire all the necessary permissions—from state agencies, California and Alaskan tribes, the Russian Orthodox Church, and the local coroner's office—and then she went out of her way to keep all parties informed as the dig progressed. "Was it the easiest way to do archeology?" she asks. "Hell, no. But it was effective. Everybody felt they were a part of it."

Similar alliances, if they take shape, will probably coalesce around a new series of tribal museums. Not every tribe is planning to rebury all returned material; many have opened or are planning to open museums of their own, as the Confederated Tribes of the Warm Springs Reservation did last summer in Oregon. Some 120 such institutions now exist, and although some are little more than cultural centers, others maintain small research centers, which are staffed with Indian scientists.

The museums will have the material, and much of it (aside from sacred objects) will be made available to academic researchers, who are willing to work with tribal councils. "We do have common ground," says Roger Echo-Hawk. "If we build on that, we may create a new science of North American archeology."

-**Virginia Morell**

The Antiquities Market

DAVID P. STALEY

David P. Staley (M.A. 1990, Washington State University) is a research associate at the University of Alaska Anchorage's Environment and Natural Resources Institute. He has 10 years' cultural-resource management experience in Alaska. Mailing address: University of Alaska Anchorage, Environment and Natural Resources Institute, 707A Street, Anchorage, Alaska 99501.

INTRODUCTION

The market in ancient human artifacts has always had a supply problem. Apart from the resale of objects in the possession of collectors—objects, that is, already in slow circulation—maintaining a profitable market tempo has left dealers with two major options. One possibility is to attempt to create new categories of objects deemed worthy of sale, purchase, and collection; this obviously involves the manipulation of tastes and perceptions so as to imbue previously disdained or ignored objects with new value. The other possibility is far more notorious: the encouragement of continued mining of known sources for objects of established saleability. The connection, overt or covert, between dealers and those non-archaeologists who dig for artifacts is well known.

Far less understood are the diggers themselves. These people, usually called looters, are strangely anonymous in the literature on the illicit market in antiquities. Their names are not known,

or, if known, not published. Usually only the empty trenches and gaping holes they leave behind are all that is left to mark their progress. For the most part, discussions of why the past is put up for sale conclude (without more than cursory investigation) that the economic straits in which these suppliers find themselves are so dire that looting is an attractive solution.

The following article by David P. Staley seeks to develop a better understanding of the market's supply side through a look at the lives of a group of Bering Sea natives who engage in what Staley calls "subsistence digging." Certain inhabitants of St. Lawrence Island spend some time every year excavating and selling ancient ivory and other artifacts, an activity which brings them some profit. These objects command high prices when they reach the centers of the art market. Recently, a New York dealer was asking $17,500 for an ivory anthropomorphic drum handle, with inlaid metal eyes, said to date to A.C. 600 and to have been excavated on St. Lawrence Island. The dealer, Jeffrey R. Myers, apparently makes a point of spending a part of his summers on St. Lawrence, which is when subsistence digging is done.

Staley's article will also be of interest to those who enjoy the ethical dilemma of who owns the past. Since St. Lawrence is owned by its natives, their excavations are not illegal. Since they are unearthing the possessions of their own ancestors, can any outsider object?

Timothy Kaiser
Editor

ST. LAWRENCE ISLAND'S SUBSISTENCE DIGGERS: A NEW PERSPECTIVE ON HUMAN EFFECTS ON ARCHAEOLOGICAL SITES

The problem of archaeological site destruction is receiving much deserved attention from the archaeological profession and from the public. Native subsistence diggers are significant agents of destruction in Alaska and their situation is representative of third world conditions. A case study, featuring the St. Lawrence Island community of Gambell, Alaska, describes the subsistence diggers' attitudes and motivations. This study provides insight into behavioral aspects of archaeological looting, causal factors underlying site destruction, and the internal workings of the artifact market. The Gambell case illustrates an ethical dilemma that needs to be addressed, since newly adopted policies to curtail site destruction may cause significant harm to a Native population that is compelled by economic forces to cannibalize its own heritage. The introduction of alternate sources of cash income through sensible economic development offers a possible solution.

Introduction

Archaeologists are shaping public policy through lobbying efforts in the area of cultural resource legislation and through their involvement in the U.S. public education campaign. The international archaeological community has been very much concerned with site looting, artifact trafficking, and the ethics of collecting (Messenger 1989; Neumann 1989; Smith and Ehrenhard

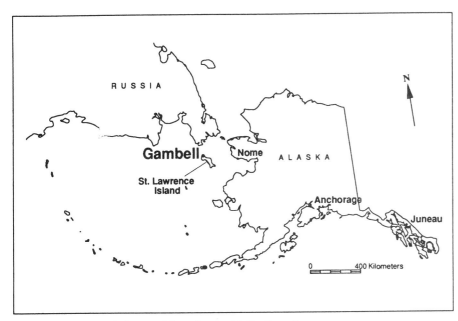

Figure 1. Map showing the location of the study areas. (By Ray Norman)

fresh ivory, trade in old or fossil ivory is not restricted by the Marine Mammal Protection Act. St. Lawrence is one of the few sources for bulk ancient or fossil ivory sold to artisans and manufacturers. Unrestricted, fee simple title to the island is held by the Gambell and Savoonga village corporations established under the Alaska Native Claims Settlement Act (ANCSA) of 1971. Thus, since the entire island is privately owned, its lands are not covered under existing laws such as the Archaeological Resources Protection Act. Site access is relatively easy, as three sites are located in Gambell or within a short walking distance. Destruction of sites around Gambell has been so severe that the sites have lost their National Historic Landmark status (Morton 1989: 2).

During July and August of 1991, I monitored a municipal construction project in Gambell. In my "off" hours, I wandered about the sites, observed work in progress, and visited with local diggers and traders. Much of the information presented in this case study was personally observed or learned through these conversations.

The Setting

Gambell is a Yupik community located at the NW end of St. Lawrence Island (FIG. 1). Only one other community, Savoonga, is located on the 160 km-long island, which is situated less than 65 km from Siberia and 200 km from the Alaskan mainland. In 1990, Gambell had a total population of 525 people. At that time, 317 adults lived in the community and the median age was 24.2 years. There were 120 houses in Gambell with 4.38 persons per household (U.S. Department of Commerce, Bureau of the Census 1991: 33).

The people of Gambell are engaged in a mixed cash and subsistence economy, with the latter being more important (Little and Robbins 1984: 64; John Muir Institute, Inc. 1984: 112). A considerable amount of cash income is required for subsistence pursuits (Nowak 1977; VanStone 1960; Wenzel 1991: 106–133). A decade ago, a family would spend an average of $6700 each

1991; Vitelli 1984). Major educational campaigns, supported by government agencies and professional organizations, have been launched to enlighten the public regarding the importance of heritage preservation (Hoffman and Lerner 1988; McManamon 1990; Rogge 1988). This is now the archaeologist's primary weapon against the destruction and degradation of historical and archaeological sites. While archaeologists are actively attempting to influence public attitudes and policies, we know very little about the people involved in site destruction. With few exceptions (Gramann and Vander Stoep 1986; Nickens, Larralde, and Tucker 1981; McAllister 1991), the behavioral aspects of looting and trafficking and the factors underlying the destruction of sites have not been evaluated.

Native subsistence diggers are significant agents in site looting in Alaska (Crowell 1985; King 1991; Morton 1989: 2; Staley 1990: 22–23). I opt for the term "digger" since both "looter" and "pothunter" have negative connotations and do not apply well in this situation. In this article, the subsistence digger is defined as a person who uses the proceeds from artifact sales to support his or her traditional subsistence lifestyle. My usage of "traditional subsistence" follows that of

Wenzel, who described the notion as having " . . . little to do with the technology used but much to do with internal relations . . ." of a culture (1991: 180). The term subsistence includes "cultural values that socially integrate the economic relations of a hunting peoples into their daily lives" (Wenzel 1991: 57). For the most part, subsistence diggers have been either overlooked by investigators of the problem or considered a limited regional phenomenon (Christensen et al. 1988; Nickens 1991; McAllister 1991). In contrast with other destructive agents, very little is known of the subsistence digger's situation, attitudes, or motivations.

On St. Lawrence Island, Eskimos are mining their ancestral archaeological sites (Scott 1984; Wardell 1986). The case study presented here, focusing on the community of Gambell, Alaska, contributes to an understanding of human impact on archaeological sites and highlights the Native subsistence digger. A brief summary of conditions and factors illustrates the extreme nature of the situation in Gambell. Economic conditions in the community are bleak (Little and Robbins 1984), yet St. Lawrence Island ivory artifacts are world renowned, and delicately carved pieces command high prices (Wardell 1986). Unlike raw or

year on transportation, weapons, ammunition, and fishing equipment used in subsistence pursuits and an additional $1700 per year on gasoline. In 1984, the average family paid out $3800 for goods and food. This included primarily cereals, tea, coffee, sugar, pilot bread, soda, and cigarettes (John Muir Institute, Inc. 1984: 121). Of course, prices have increased over the last decade. For example, in 1991, a household of seven persons spent between $200 and $300 a month on food alone. A delayed barge delivery during the summer temporarily drove gasoline prices to $5.00 per gallon, although eventually prices returned to $2.50. Other monthly expenses included $74 for water and sewer services, $72 for cable television, $70 for electric service, and a heating fuel bill around $345 a month during winter.

Jobs are relatively scarce and extremely dependent upon State and Federal appropriations. Based on a community survey of Gambell conducted by the Norton Sound Health Corporation during 1990, 51% of 95 household respondents were unemployed. Only 22% of these households included a member with full time employment (Don Smith, Bering Strait Economic Development Corporation, personal communication, 1991). Monthly wage income in Gambell averaged $85 per person (Alaska Department of Labor, personal communication, 1991). This income was supplemented by food stamps, Aid to Families with Dependent Children, Energy Assistance, Longevity Bonus, and Permanent Fund Dividend programs. The production and sale of crafts, particularly ivory carvings, is a large source of locally generated income on the island. During the 1980s, ivory-carving sales volumes were estimated at approximately $100,000 per year (Little and Robbins 1984: 68). Between September, 1983, and October, 1984, sales of bulk ivory mined from sites netted more than $100,000. Sales of artifacts totalled around $40,000 in 1983 (Crowell 1985: 20). An analysis of average household income and expenses during 1991 demonstrated the critical importance of both the subsistence oriented economy,

48% of the expenses, and cash influx from ivory and artifacts, 13% of the income. Sales of ivory and artifacts are especially important because household budgets appear to be operating in a break-even or deficit mode.

Since 1983, Sivuqaq, Inc., Gambell's village corporation established under ANCSA, has been actively involved in the sale of bulk ivory (Crowell 1985: 21–22). The corporation acts as a middleman in the trade, providing a consistent, accessible market for the ivory diggers and attempting to maximize economic returns to the resident shareholders. The village corporation's perception of archaeological sites as economic resources is contrary to the perspective of most Native groups in the United States. Native groups generally advocate protection and conservation of historical and prehistoric sites (Nichols, Klesert, and Anyon 1989; Anyon 1991). Sivuqaq, Inc. sees archaeological sites as the source of extractable commodities, whereas other Native groups perceive cultural resources as a means to economic development but through a combined strategy of preservation and tourism (Parker 1990: 67).

Gambell's Subsistence Diggers
The entire demographic spectrum of the community participates in the excavation of Gambell's archaeological sites. Young and old, male and female, single individuals and entire families mine sites for old ivory and artifacts. Children brought to the site may help, but often bring toys to entertain themselves while the adults work. Both employed and unemployed residents work at the sites, although the latter have more time to devote to this activity.

Digging is limited to the summer season while permafrost sediments are thawing. Ardent diggers tend to work between four and 10 hours a day, while casual diggers are more likely to spend a few hours at a site one evening a week. Although digging may take place at any time, it seems to be predominantly an evening affair. The work is typically cold, wet, and arduous.

A variety of tools and apparatus is used at the sites including simple hand tools such as shovels, mattocks, picks, and buckets. Ice axes, manufactured for mountaineers, are preferred by both serious and casual diggers. This may be related to their easy access through mail-order catalogs. Wheelbarrows are in short supply; a village entrepreneur was recently renting one for $20 per day. At times, gasoline-powered portable pumps are used to drain pooled water from excavations. Hydraulic excavation occurs at some sites but not at those adjacent to Gambell. Many people leave their tools and equipment at the site between digging sessions.

The focus of excavation shifts around on the sites based on other diggers' findings or rumored findings. Rumored success of diggers under one of the few road beds in town caused substantial sections of the road to be torn up in a matter of days. Word of the recovery of potentially valuable pieces travels fast through the community and often stimulates others to get out and dig.

Excavation intensity and technique vary considerably. Men tend to excavate larger and deeper holes. When working by themselves, women and children dig numerous small shallow holes and never invest much time in any one location; but they tend to do more prospecting than the men, who concentrate on mining. Patterns of permafrost thawing also tend to influence excavation strategies and techniques. At present, diggers go to great lengths to find rare, undisturbed sections of the sites. The digging undercuts paths and roads and exposes various pipes, and phone and power lines. At times, diggers are forced to move tremendous piles of backdirt and disturbed sediments extending to depths of 4 m. Plastic covers surprisingly deep limits of previous mining efforts. Once undisturbed deposits are located, excavations proceed horizontally into the face, sometimes undercutting large blocks of sediments. These blocks frequently give way and negate the time and effort used to clear the area as well as burying equipment and diggers alike. Curious passersby are sharply warned not to walk above these excavations. Diggers often follow house wall logs, as whole walrus tusks are known to have been used to support vertical posts. Other structural elements are often chopped out of the way before they are completely exposed, and rock slab flooring is often torn up as the excavation proceeds.

Some of the techniques used by diggers in Gambell were learned directly from archaeologists who have worked in the area. In the late 1920s, Otto Geist experimented with boilers and steam thawing as well as using pumps, hoses, pressure nozzles, and screens to hydraulically excavate sites and water screen artifacts (Geist and Rainey 1976: 35, 42). The use of steel rod probes to differentiate subsurface bone and ivory was adopted from Hans-Georg Bandi, who used the technique to locate human burials. One digger stated she had been shown by archaeologists how small artifacts on the surface are more easily observed after a rain storm. Gambell diggers often toss faunal remains into a separate pile as they dig. This behavior may have been adopted from Otto Geist, who also segregated bone into large piles (Geist and Raney 1976: 246).

Artifacts
The relative importance of various artifact classes to the people of Gambell is expressed in the way they sort, accumulate, and conserve artifacts. Artifacts with certain monetary values are piled separately while digging and bagged at the end of the session. These include complete or fragmentary ivory artifacts with or without incised decoration, ivory scrap, walrus tusk and teeth, large sea mammal teeth, and walrus penis bones. Artifacts of marginal value or interest, such as seal teeth, groundstone ulus and endblades, palettes, chipped stone scrapers, points or blades, baleen bucket parts, scapula shovel blades, and various whole or broken wood and bone tools, are consistently sorted from the dirt and piled near the pit. Some of these artifacts are composite tool parts that are kept sep-

arately until the digger is certain that other components are lost. Artifacts are often shown to children, visitors, and other diggers and are the main topic of discussion. Artifacts of marginal value are often displayed on a whale or walrus scapula in or on the margins of the pit. Structural elements, faunal remains, flaking debitage, and small fragments of stone artifacts are either tossed into the backdirt or segregated into piles.

Valuable artifacts are typically amassed until sold to village visitors, professional artifact dealers or, if unmarketable as art or curio, eventually sold as scrap ivory. Diggers are anxious to show their artifacts even without any potential for sale. People will invite you into their houses to see their collections. In one home, I saw composite fish hooks, harpoon heads, buttons, and a wrist-guard fragment made of ivory and decorated with Punuk design elements. Most collections, however, included large varieties of mundane, undecorated artifacts. Although most household collections are awaiting sale, there are several families that keep groups of interesting artifacts in their homes with no intention of selling them.

Old ivory begins to crack, split, and peel after it is removed from the ground. Diggers attempt to conserve ivory artifacts using a variety of techniques and substances. Most understand that the problems are caused by too-rapid drying. Therefore, many try to control temperatures and humidity by drying specimens in a cool place inside sealed plastic bags. Others attempt to replace the water in the artifacts by soaking them in baby or gun oils.

Staking Claims and Territoriality
The passage of ANCSA legally made the natural resources on St. Lawrence Island common property and essentially gave all residents access to these resources. Control over the island's natural resources is shared by the village corporations of Gambell and Savoonga. This is the latest step in the liberalization of natural-resource use

rights. Prior to ANCSA, each community claimed control over a portion of the island's resources (Burgess 1974: 78). Preceding the consolidation of the population into these communities, territories were controlled by clans (Little and Robbins 1984: 82–83). Even at present, however, clans do maintain use rights over specific camping, hunting, and fishing locations.

The archaeological sites on St. Lawrence Island are also considered a common natural resource. There appear to be some differences in use rights, however, depending on the distance between the site and the main village. At sites close to Gambell, diggers who begin an excavation or adopt an abandoned, existing pit have use rights contingent on their consistent and continuous work in the location. Claimed areas are often shared between brothers who may work together or in staggered shifts. These rights may be traded or passed to other individuals, and permission is requested to dig in areas that are not clearly abandoned.

During the summer, many families leave Gambell to stay at subsistence camps, which are positioned within larger clan territories at prime subsistence-resource locations (Little and Robbins 1984: 184–205; Crowell 1985: 18). These same resources have drawn people to these locations for millennia. As clan members have use rights for the location, they also have exclusive control over any nearby archaeological resources. Unlike the Gambell sites, there is no requirement for consistent and continuous digging at these sites to maintain use rights.

Claims on digging areas at subsistence camps follow the historical, kinship-based pattern of use rights. Closer to Gambell, no clan can claim exclusive rights to an area, therefore, a different system has developed to define digging territories within sites. This system is a reflection of the liberalization of natural-resource use rights but only at the community scale. Future research on this subject may find even further communal ownership, with Savoonga residents freely digging at Gambell and vice versa.

Use rights to digging territories are generally respected although there are interlopers. It seems likely that incidents of encroachment are more common near Gambell than at subsistence camps. Diggers complain about trespassers more for their sloppy technique than for the potential loss of ivory and artifacts. Some diggers have threatened to place booby traps in their pits to discourage poaching by their fellow villagers.

Attitudes

The people of Gambell are very friendly, generous, and kind. Their attitudes toward the profession of archaeology are generally negative, however. Early archaeological investigations on the island were sophisticated for their time, although by today's standards the methods were coarse, and the large scale trenches through mounds would appear to the uninitiated as uncontrolled massive disturbances. Other than the excavation techniques described above, one can safely assume that little effort was expended toward explaining archaeological method and theory to the residents of Gambell.

Before the early archaeological investigations on the island by Otto Geist and Henry Collins, various superstitions and fears of the dead made most residents very reluctant to dig at the sites (Keim 1969: 114, 218). Archaeologists had a hand in changing this attitude by purchasing artifacts and hiring local assistants (Collins 1975: 25, 31, 35; Geist and Rainey 1976: 25, 31–32; Keim 1969: 150; Scott 1984: 48). Due to a lack of funds, Geist could not pay his assistants an hourly or daily wage. He paid the "volunteers" according to the amount of ivory they uncovered (Geist and Rainey 1976: 32). Geist soon realized the mistake of paying for unprovenienced artifacts, as residents became uncontrollable diggers. In his biography of Geist, Keim (1969: 115) describes the result: "The car Otto had oiled, greased, and carefully cranked was running away with him and there was not much he could do until it ran out of gas."

People frequently complain about archaeologists digging up their sites and, justifiably, about the removal of the artifacts from the island. Historically, collecting artifacts for museums was a primary reason for doing archaeology. At present, the lack of an appropriate facility prevents curation on the island. The excavation of artifacts by archaeologists is variously presented as a cultural or a financial loss. Crowell (1985: 26–27) has found that buyers and collectors tend to support or encourage the notion of the archaeologist as resource competitor. Portions of the population wish the artifacts returned, and some would like to profit from the sale of these returned items. Others have proposed placing the artifacts in a local museum to be used for educational purposes and also for generating tourist revenues.

Many Gambell residents disagree with the position that only archaeologists can extract worthwhile information through controlled excavation of the sites. Local diggers contend that they have learned much about their heritage through their excavations. Traditional craftsmanship, innovations, architecture, and natural history are all learned from digging. Although not written in reports, heritage learned from digging at the site has been expressed orally to other villagers. In contrast, few, if any, archaeologists have presented their findings to the people of Gambell.

Some diggers see their work at archaeological sites as a form of recycling, realizing that previous residents gleaned materials from the sites to be reused or remade into needed tools. Similar attitudes have been expressed to other researchers (Little and Robbins 1984: 194; Crowell 1985: 25).

The Gambell diggers do not want to intensify their extraction of artifacts. Intensification would merely cause the resource to be consumed too quickly and, thus, a slower pace is preferred. A slow pace maintains prices at current levels and also extends the financial gain into the future. The diggers fear that a sudden, large influx of money would be squandered. In this instance, people do not favor strict conservation to preserve their heritage for posterity, but rather a conservative management style to provide a steady source of cash.

Motivations

Digging on St. Lawrence Island is fueled by a combination of motives including economic requirements, education, tradition, and recreation. Economic conditions provide the primary motive for digging at the sites, and the earlier overview of the Gambell economy and the cash requirements of modern subsistence practices provides a partial context for this discussion. A description of the Gambell ivory market, including rates, prices, and structure is critical for understanding residents' motivations.

The return for scrap ivory and artifacts is an important source of the community's cash income. Most of the return comes from the slow, steady recovery and sale of scrap ivory. The purchase price for this commodity varies depending upon the size and condition of the pieces, as well as seasonal supply and demand factors. During August, 1991, the prevailing rate for small ivory scrap was $20 per pound.

Prices for artifacts destined for the curio or native art markets vary considerably. Mundane utilitarian objects are sometimes sold for a few dollars to a tourist or visitor. More often, these same items are of more value if sold as scrap ivory. Those bound for the art market bring the greatest prices. These pieces include decorated ivory figurines, winged objects, tridents, and utilitarian objects of the Old Bering Sea and Punuk periods (Wardwell 1986). It is difficult to get an accurate estimate of sale prices in Gambell as these have become clouded by myth and legend. Gambell residents spoke of an ivory ulu handle in the form of a polar bear that was recently sold by a digger for $10,000. Other legendary prices paid to finders range from $45,000 up to as high as $60,000. These prices are most often mentioned in relation to the winged objects or "butterflies." Such large monetary returns, whether real and rare or purely imaginary, are a major driving force in the system.

Diggers have several avenues for converting scrap ivory and artifacts into cash. Scrap ivory is purchased by the Native store, the Native corporation, and various visiting private buyers. Visiting buyers may also buy ivory carvings and artifacts. These individuals advertise their upcoming visits through posters and flyers. It was said that in 1991 there was only one buyer, down from the annual average of three buyers, who tended to bid against each other.

Several recent developments may now be acting to preclude the necessity of actual buying trips on the part of brokers and/or collectors. A Gambell entrepreneur, particularly adept at negotiating and facilitating business deals, has established himself as a middleman between diggers and a New York City buyer. The middleman describes the find to his contact by telephone. If the buyer is interested in a piece, he asks for it to be sent along for viewing. A price is agreed upon and the middleman gets 10% of the sale price. This same middleman has sold a number of pieces for a group of diggers directly through Sotheby's auction house in New York City. He said Sotheby's gets a 5% commission on any of these sales. Many other diggers have the capability to sell directly to auction houses, brokers, and collectors. The names and telephone numbers of New York collectors are casually traded among allied diggers. Many have arrangements to call dealers collect or via toll-free numbers.

The participants in digging activities are not exclusively those in need of cash. Successful individuals and families, with economic, social, and political power, also dig at the sites. These people often have steady, full-time employment, are whaling captains and boat owners, and may hold or have held political office. Factors other than economic necessity, such as recreation, education, and tradition, apparently prompt these people. Excavation at the sites is often seen as family recreation that provides educational

opportunities. Artifacts are shown to children and are placed in a context of modern and traditional lifeways. They are also used to substantiate legends and local oral history. Tradition is also cited as a factor, since people have now been digging in these sites for over 50 years; it has been a socially acceptable activity for several generations.

The casual nature of some digging at least partially reflects recreational motivations. The activity provides opportunities to leave the household, enjoy the outdoors, socialize or find solitude, and get exercise. Digging, as a form of gambling or treasure hunting, provides a recreational thrill. The popularity of this type of recreation is manifested by frequent participation in sweepstakes, lotteries, bingo, and card playing. In Gambell, many games of chance are well established; community bingo and pull-tabs are especially popular. Expended pull-tabs, also known as "rippies" or "ripoffs," are often found in backdirt piles at the sites. Extremely worn, small bills commonly observed in circulation are attributed by locals to heavy use during card games. The largest potential payoffs, however, are found in another popular game of chance: digging.

Finally, the sites are common property, and all people in Gambell have the right to dig. Perhaps families with no economic pressures are motivated to dig in order to maintain their rights to this resource or to guarantee a share of the resource before it is gone. Whatever the non-economic motives, the economic gains from digging are an added bonus.

The Ethical Dilemma

Current strategies for curtailing the looting problem in the United States include legislation, law enforcement, education, and public involvement. Legislation and law enforcement alone have not been effective. Education and public involvement are the newest approaches to the problem and may eventually have a significant effect, although doubts remain (King 1991). All of these strategies or policies have been advocated by individual archae-

ologists and archaeological organizations. If these policies succeed in shutting down the demand for artifacts, quenching or deflecting collectors' desires to possess Native American artifacts, and protecting archaeological sites from looting, what will be the effect on the Native subsistence digger? Should archaeologists, as anthropologists, ignore the potentially substantial effects of archaeologist-influenced public policies regarding site looting on a group of Native Americans? How will they continue their "traditional" lifestyles which now include technology purchased and maintained by cash? Parallel dilemmas exist in Canada where policies have been generated by animal rights activists (Wenzel 1991: 175); native communities that once had their economic basis in seal hunting have been significantly disrupted by the seal fur ban. At present, there are no clear and easy solutions to the subsistence digger dilemma.

The introduction of alternate sources of cash income combined with present anti-looting strategies could stop site destruction and ameliorate any economic effects on Native groups. The Eskimos of St. Lawrence are extremely wary of large-scale natural resource development. They fear the land will be lost through sales to corporations or individuals who will become majority shareholders in the corporations (John Muir Institute, Inc. 1984: 125; Crowell 1985: 23). Elsewhere in the Arctic, non-indigenous development plans have not meshed with traditional subsistence pursuits and have not been productive (Wenzel 1991: 183). The people of St. Lawrence must have input into any development schemes if they are to be successful.

The two villages on St. Lawrence have joined together in a non-profit venture named St. Lawrence Economic Development Corporation (SLEDCO). Appointments to the 12 member board are evenly divided between the villages and represent Indian Reorganization Act (IRA) councils, City governments, and at-large members from both Gambell and Savoonga. The organization is intended to address all development issues (Don Smith, personal communication, 1991).

Several economic development plans currently are being considered for St. Lawrence Island, and short-term projects should continue to provide money to the local economy. The clean-up of World War II debris, airport runway expansions, and other government-sponsored public works projects will provide some employment, but not permanent, full-time jobs. Exploitation of other island-based resources might have more long-term effects. The feasibility of harvesting various seaweeds for sale to the health food and medical industries is actively being researched. The reindeer industry is being revived through herd expansions that may increase sales of meat and antler products to Asian markets. The expansion of eco-tourism, particularly birdwatching, is another possible development for the future (Don Smith, personal communication, 1991).

Alternatives must be found that will contribute cash to the local economy, decrease demands for ancient artworks and curios, promote conservation, and increase reverence for the island's antiquities. Hopi and Zuni artisans of the American Southwest use designs from ancient potsherds for inspiration (Stanislawski 1969: 13, 1978: 221–222), and St. Lawrence Island craftspeople could incorporate some of the aesthetic features of earlier works and use their own cultural heritage in a similar fashion. In this way, their traditional art and heritage would be continually revived and reinforced as something important and meaningful.

Summary

This case study reveals some of the behavioral aspects of looting, examines causal factors underlying site destruction, and illuminates the shadowy world of artifact trafficking. Mainly, however, this study has focused on Native subsistence diggers: their situation, attitudes, and motivations. As a group, subsistence diggers add a unique level of complexity to the site looting problem in Alaska and elsewhere in the world. The information

presented here contributes to a better understanding of the looting-trafficking/local economy dichotomy and may ultimately lead to appropriate solutions to the problem. As pointed out by Cheek (1991), what is lacking are Native perspectives on the subject. Further investigations in Gambell would doubtless identify a greater range of concerns and attitudes than those presented here and would more accurately represent the Native perspective. This study presents a complicated problem but does not provide solutions. Perhaps, however, it will stimulate professionals to apply some thought to this dilemma.

Acknowledgments
The anonymous Gambell diggers must be thanked for their candor in discussing this emotionally-charged issue. A number of scholars contributed useful comments, ideas, and information. In particular, I would like to thank Robert Ackerman, Stephen Braund, Aron Crowell, Steven Loring, Ken Pratt, and George Wenzel. Figure 1 is by Ray Norman.

REFERENCES

Anyon, Roger, 1991. "Protecting the Past, Protecting the Present: Cultural Resources and American Indians," in George Smith and John Ehrenhard, eds., *Protecting the Past*. Boca Raton: CRC Press, 215–222.

Burgess, Stephan, 1974. *The St. Lawrence Islanders of Northwest Cape: Patterns of Resource Utilization*. Ph.D. dissertation, University of Alaska Fairbanks. Ann Arbor: University Microfilms.

Cheek, Annetta, 1991. Review of Phyllis Messenger, ed., *The Ethics of Collecting Cultural Property: Whose Culture? Whose Property? American Antiquity* 56: 557–558.

Christensen, H., K. Maberry, M. McAllister, and D. McCormick, 1988. "Cultural Resource Protection: A Predictive Framework for Identifying Site Vulnerability, Protection Priorities, and Effective Protection Strategies," in J. Tainter and R. Hamre, eds., *Tools to Manage the Past: Research Priorities for Cultural Resource Management in the Southwest*. U.S. Forest Service, Southwestern Region and Rocky Mountain Forest and Range Experimentation Station, 62–67.

Collins, Henry, 1975. *Archaeology of St. Lawrence Island, Alaska*. (Originally published in 1937 as *Smithsonian Miscellaneous Collections* Vol. 96, No. 1.) Ann Arbor: University Microfilms.

Crowell, Aron, 1985. *Archeological Survey and Site Condition Assessment of Saint Lawrence Island, Alaska, 1984*. Report submitted to Department of Anthropology, Smithsonian Institution, Washington, D.C., and Sivuqaq, Incorporated, Gambell, Alaska.

Geist, Otto, and Froelich Rainey, 1976. *Archaeological Investigations at Kukulik, St. Lawrence Island, Alaska*. (Originally published in 1936 as Vol. 2 of *Miscellaneous Publications of the University of Alaska* by the U.S. Government Printing Office, Washington, D.C.). New York: AMS Press.

Gramann, J., and G. Vander Stoep, 1986. "Reducing Depreciative Behavior at Shiloh National Military Park," *Technical Report* No. 2. College Station: National Park Service Cooperative Park Studies Unit, Texas A&M University.

Hoffman, Teresa, and Shereen Lerner, 1988. "Arizona Archaeology Week: Promoting the Past to the Public," *Archaeological Assistance Program Technical Brief* No. 2. Washington, D.C.: U.S. Department of the Interior, National Park Service, Archaeological Assistance Division.

John Muir Institute, Inc., 1984. "A Description of the Socioeconomics of Norton Sound," *Technical Report* No. 99, Contract No. AA851-CT2-38. Prepared for the Minerals Management Service, Alaska Outer Continental Shelf Region, Leasing and Environmental Office, Social and Economic Studies Unit.

Keim, Charles, 1969. *Ahgvook, White Eskimo: Otto Geist and Alaskan Archaeology*. College: University of Alaska Press.

King, Thomas, 1991. "Some Dimensions of the Pothunting Problem," in George Smith and John Ehrenhard, eds., *Protecting the Past*. Boca Raton: CRC Press, 83–92.

Little, Ronald, and Lynn Robbins, 1984. "Effects of Renewable Resource Harvest Disruptions on Socioeconomic and Sociocultural Systems: St. Lawrence Island," Contract No. AA851-CTI-59. Prepared for The John Muir Institute, Napa, California, and Alaska Outer Continental Shelf Office, Socioeconomic Studies Program, Minerals Management Service, Anchorage, Alaska.

McAllister, Martin, 1991. "Looting and Vandalism of Archaeological Resources on Federal and Indian Lands in the United States," in George Smith and John Ehrenhard, eds., *Protecting the Past*. Boca Raton: CRC Press, 93–99.

McManamon, Francis, 1990. "A National Strategy for Federal Archaeology," *Federal Archeology Report* 3(1): 1, 13, 23. Washington, D.C.: U.S. Department of the Interior, National Park Service, Archaeological Assistance Division.

Messenger, Phyllis, ed., 1989. *The Ethics of Collecting Cultural Property? Whose Culture? Whose Property?* Albuquerque: University of New Mexico Press.

Morton, Susan, 1989. "The Archaeological Resources Protection Act and Alaska," *Federal Archeology Report* 2(3): 1–2. Washington, D.C.: U.S. Department of the Interior, National Park Service, Archaeological Assistance Division.

Neumann, Loretta, 1989. "Saving the Past for the Future: SAA Embarks on a Project to Prevent Looting," *Bulletin of the Society for American Archaeology* 6(1).

Nickens, Paul, 1991. "The Destruction of Archaeological Sites and Data," in George

Smith and John Ehrenhard, eds., *Protecting the Past.* Boca Raton: CRC Press, 73–81.

Nickens, Paul, S. Larralde, and G. Tucker, Jr., 1981. *A Survey of Vandalism to Archaeological Resources in Southwestern Colorado. Cultural Resources Series* No. 11. Denver: Bureau of Land Management, Colorado State Office.

Nichols, Deborah, Anthony Klesert, and Roger Anyon, 1989. "Ancestral Sites, Shrines, and Graves: Native American Perspectives on the Ethics of Collecting Cultural Properties," in Phyllis Messenger, ed., *The Ethics of Collecting Cultural Property: Whose Culture? Whose Property?* Albuquerque: University of New Mexico Press, 27–38.

Nowak, Michael, 1977. "The Economies of Native Subsistence Activities in a Village of Southwestern Alaska," *Arctic* 30: 225–233.

Parker, Patricia, 1990. *Keepers of the Treasures: Protecting Historic Properties and Cultural Traditions on Indian Lands.* A Report on Tribal Preservation Funding Needs Submitted to Congress by the United States Department of the Interior, National Park Service, Interagency Resources Division, Branch of Preservation Planning, Washington, D.C.

Rogge, A. E., ed., 1988. "Fighting Indiana Jones in Arizona," *American Society for Conservation Archaeology Proceedings 1988.*

Scott, Stuart, 1984. "St. Lawrence: Archaeology of a Bering Sea Island," *Archaeology* 37(1): 46–52.

Smith, George, and John Ehrenhard, eds., 1991. *Protecting the Past.* Boca Raton: CRC Press.

Staley, David, 1990. "Wait's Modest Proposal and Cultural Resource Reality in Alaska," *American Society for Conservation Archaeology Report* 17(1): 19–24.

Stanislawski, Michael, 1969. "What Good is a Broken Pot?" *Southwestern Lore* 35: 11–18.

———, 1978. "If Pots Were Mortal," in Richard Gould, ed., *Explorations in Ethnoarchaeology.* Albuquerque: University of New Mexico Press, 201–227.

U.S. Department of Commerce, Bureau of the Census, 1991. *1990 Census of Population and Housing. Summary: Population and Housing Characteristics, Alaska.* Washington, D.C.: Economics and Statistics Administration.

VanStone, James, 1960. "A Successful Combination of Subsistence and Wage Economies on the Village Level," *Economic Development and Cultural Change* 8: 174–191.

Vitelli, K., 1984. "The International Traffic in Antiquities: Archaeological Ethics and the Archaeologist's Responsibility," in E. L. Green, ed., *Ethics and Values in Archaeology.* New York: The Free Press, 143–155.

Wardwell, A., 1986. *Ancient Eskimo Ivories of the Bering Strait.* New York: Hudson Hills Press.

Wenzel, G., 1991. *Animal Rights, Human Rights: Ecology, Economy, and Ideology in the Canadian Arctic.* Toronto: University of Toronto Press.

Who Owns the Spoils of War?

As Germany and Russia spar over the return of wartime booty, historians and legal scholars take a fresh look at what really happened 50 years ago.

Karl E. Meyer

Karl E. Meyer is a member of the editorial board of The New York Times *and the author of* The Plundered Past *and* The Pleasures of Archaeology.

What Byron called the "fatal gift of beauty" is again sowing international discord, as it has since the Trojans abducted Helen. The latest dispute concerns a dazzling collection of Old Master and Impressionist paintings, recently exhibited for the first time in half a century in Moscow and St. Petersburg. It also concerns a royal ransom in the decorative arts; several million books, including two or perhaps three Gutenberg Bibles; whole storerooms of manuscripts and archival records; and the celebrated Treasure of Priam, the Bronze Age artifacts unearthed at Troy in 1873 by Heinrich Schliemann, a symbol and metaphor of the entire dispute (see ARCHAELOGY, November/December 1993).

Germany claims ownership of most of these prizes, all of which were removed by Russian forces in 1945. At first glance the German case seems airtight. The Soviet Union and Germany agreed in 1990 to exchange all works uprooted from either country during World War II, an agreement confirmed two years later by President Boris Yeltsin of the new Russian Federation. A joint commission was estab-

lished to compile lists of missing works and to preside over exchanges. But it soon became apparent that under such an agreement far more art would flow from Russia back to Germany than vice versa.

Hesitantly at first, then more boldly, the Russian government took up the refrain of militant nationalists and museum directors such as Irina Antonova of the Pushkin State Museum of Fine Arts in Moscow, whose vaults had hidden the Trojan treasure since 1945. Do not give back a thing, they argued, noting that Russia was still owed reparations for 20 million war dead and 400 looted museums. That Russia had approved a repatriation agreement with Germany, not to mention successive Hague conventions that bar use of cultural treasures as reparations, went unmentioned.

Hence the buzz of anticipation in New York early this year when a dozen Russians turned up at a conference on "The Spoils of War." The three-day event, sponsored by the Bard Graduate Center for Studies in the Decorative Arts, was literally an eye-opener. Delegates from Germany, France, Poland, Hungary, and elsewhere gaped at Russian slides of longmissing Old Master paintings, prints, and drawings seized by Soviet forces. And for the first time at a public forum, Russian cultural officials developed their case for keeping every-

thing. Mark M. Boguslavky of the Institute of State and Law of the Russian Academy of Science, a legal adviser to the Russian Ministry of Culture, claimed that all art removed from Soviet soil during World War II was taken illegally. "On that we all agree," he said, but as for the art removed from Germany by the Red Army, "we cannot agree it was illegal." He reasoned that with Hitler's defeat there was no German state, and since the Soviet Union was the legitimate governing authority in its occupation zone, it had every right to remove cultural property. Besides, in vaguely defined wartime declarations the Allies had accepted the idea of "restitution in kind," and Russia was merely applying that principle to Germany. It had indeed pledged to return what had been illegally removed from Germany, but, since everything was legally removed, Russia was not obliged to return anything.

This demarche was reminiscent of earlier times when Soviet diplomacy consisted of a thump on the table and a tirade in *Pravda*. What was different at the Bard conference, the Cold War being over, was the absence of unanimity among the Russian delegates. Not only did they differ with each other on the need for compromise and an end to secrecy, they differed openly and passionately. Resistance among younger scholars to official orthodoxy was borne home by the presence of Konstantin Akinsha, an art historian and journalist, and Grigorii Kozlov, a former inspector for Russia's Department of Museums and former curator of the Museum of Private Collections affiliated with the Pushkin Museum. Akinsha and Kozlov were the first to disclose, in a 1991 *ARTnews* article, that the Schliemann treasure, along with countless other works missing from German and European collections, had been hidden for decades in Soviet "special depositories." Their report encouraged similar exposés by other young researchers, notably Alexei Rastorgouev, an art historian at Moscow University, whose specialty is the "displaced" art of World War II. Thanks to their combined work, which appeared in Russian and international art journals, it is possible for the first time to piece together what really happened 50 years ago.

Russian passions concerning captured German artworks cannot be understood without recalling the rape of European cultural treasures during the Third Reich. A failed artist himself, Hitler dreamed of building a vast art museum in Linz, near his Austrian birthplace. He recruited a Dresden museum director, Hans Posse, to gather a collection by whatever means necessary and ordered the Wehrmacht to assist a special trophy unit commanded by Nazi ideologist Alfred Rosenberg. Posse and Rosenberg competed for spoils with the sybaritic Hermann Goering, with Himmler's SS, and with thousands of officers billeted in foreign castles and estates.

In France and the Low Countries art was harvested by seizing works from Jewish collections and state museums, or by forced sales, such as the "purchase" of superb Old Master drawings from Dutch collector Franz Koenigs. In the East, Polish museums were stripped and royal palaces destroyed. Slavs were deemed *Untermenschen,* their history worthless. In his first tour of the Royal Palace in Warsaw, Governor-General Hans Frank set the example by tearing silver eagles from the canopy covering the royal throne and pocketing them.

Poland's fate foreshadowed the devastation of the Soviet Union. Within weeks of Hitler's blitzkrieg of June 1941, German forces occupied czarist palaces on the outskirts of Leningrad. At the palace of Catherine the Great at Tsarskoye Selo, they dismantled the Amber Room, a great chamber whose walls were lined with precious amber, which had been given to Peter the Great by Frederick-William II of Prussia. The walls of the room were taken to Koenigsberg in East Prussia, where they disappeared, removed and hidden by the Germans or unknowingly destroyed in the Russian assault on the city. German depredations over a three-year period are graphically described in Lynn Nicholas' account of World War II plunder, *The Rape of Europa:* "They took anything they could pry loose from the myriad palaces and pavilions around Leningrad, right down to the parquet floors. They opened packed crates and helped themselves to the contents. Mirrors were smashed or machine gunned, brocades and silks ripped from the walls. At Peterhof . . . the gilded bronze statues of Neptune and Samson upon which the waters played were hauled off to the smelting furnace in full view of the distraught townspeople." Not since the Goths and Vandals had Europe witnessed so spiteful an assault on other people's cultural treasures. The ancient cathedral at Novgorod was ravaged, Pushkin's house ransacked, Tolstoy's manuscripts burned, and elsewhere museums, churches, libraries, universities, and scientific institutes were robbed and destroyed. Most of the Nazi plunder has never been recovered.

Small wonder that, as the battlefront shifted toward Germany, Soviet retribution was swift and all encompassing. In November 1943 an edict of an Emergency State Committee authorized the removal of state and private libraries and art collections to Russia. A Trophy Commission was formed to comb castles, bunkers, salt mines, and caves in which Germans had hidden their own treasures as well as looted foreign art. In Dresden the Russians removed everything portable, includ-

ing the jeweled contents of the famous Green Vault in the royal castle and more than 500 drawings from the Koenigs collection, which Hitler's agents had brought from Holland. By then a new vision had taken hold in Moscow: the postwar creation of a great Museum of World Art to be filled with works seized as compensation for Nazi vandalism. In January 1945 Stalin signed a directive authorizing massive removal of cultural property of all kinds, ostensibly for the supermuseum.

Four months later the trophy unit arrived in Berlin, where it seized the Pergamon Altar, with its celebrated Hellenistic frieze depicting the battle of the gods and giants, originally acquired by Germany in Turkish Asia Minor. From a bomb-proof bunker near the Berlin Zoo, it confiscated cases of Trojan gold that Schliemann had found at Hisarlik and presented to his native Germany in 1881. Romantically if erroneously dubbed by its finder the Treasure of Priam, the collection consists of hundreds of gold and silver objects, including a gold-beaded headdress once proudly modeled by Schliemann's young Greek wife, Sophia. The cases were flown to the Pushkin Museum, where a receipt was signed by 28-year-old curator Irina Antonova, a tiny woman with blazing eyes who had grown up in Berlin, where her father had been a Soviet trade official. Antonova has survived six Soviet leadership upheavals and the collapse of communism, and still reigns as Pushkin director and guardian of wartime spoils.

Soviet soldiers needed little encouragement in following the Trophy Commission's lead. General Vassily Chuikoff, having settled in the estate of Otto Krebs outside Weimar, saw to it that 98 Impressionist paintings in the Krebs collection were removed to Leningrad, where they were hidden until this year. Other commanders filled railroad cars with the contents of Prussian estates. At Schloss Karnzow, Lieutenant Victor Baldin came upon soldiers in the cellar shuffling through hundreds of Old Master drawings, placed there for safekeeping by curators of the Bremen Kunsthalle. Baldin crammed into his suitcase 364 drawings, including a Dürer that he acquired in a swap for a pair of boots. Baldin, an art historian, preserved the drawings, and years later tried vainly to have them returned to Bremen.

By all these routes, a flood of art reached Russia. Soviet plans for a supermuseum, however, were stalled in good part by the long-forgotten work of a handful of soldiers in the West known as "monuments men." That archaeologists, with an interest in ruins and their preservation, might play a useful military role was not at first obvious to the British War Office. Italy unwittingly caused a change of mind in 1941 when it accused British troops of vandalizing the classical ruins of Leptis Magna, Cyrene, and Sabratha in Libya. Lieutenant Colonel Mortimer Wheeler, the breezily self-assured excavator of Mohenjodaro, who happened to be serving in North Africa, was given the job of safeguarding the sites, which he did with éclat. Wheeler was supported in London by Sir Leonard Woolley, excavator of Ur, who headed the army's Archaeological Adviser's office (consisting of Sir Leonard, Lady Woolley, and a clerk).

When the United States entered the war, influential scholars soon began lobbying for a more ambitious American counterpart to Woolley's office. William Dinsmoor, then president of the Archaeological Institute of America, was among those who met with, and apparently convinced, Chief Justice Harlan Fiske Stone, an ex-officio trustee of the newly formed National Gallery of Art, that an art and monuments unit be formed. Stone sent his recommendations to the White House on December 8, 1942. What probably tipped the scales in favor of the recommendation was Roosevelt and Churchill's decision in January 1943 to invade Sicily, with its vulnerable Greek and Roman ruins and its famous Byzantine churches.

Months later in Sicily, Captain Mason Hammond, a Harvard classics professor acting as art adviser to the Supreme Allied Commander, appropriated a battered vehicle, organized rescue groups, posted off-limits signs,

and courted the annoyance of generals. Hammond was the first of several score monuments officers, men and women, most of them scholars and museum curators, who accompanied Allied armies through Italy, France, and Germany. There was little they could do about wartime devastation: Monte Cassino was destroyed; Pompeii was bombed, as was a church in Padua with frescoes by Mantegna. There were devastating aerial assaults on Dresden, Nürnberg, and other old German cities. Nor could they be held responsible for thousands of soldiers who pocketed spoils of war. In one memorable heist, a U.S. Army artillery officer from Texas, Lieutenant Joe Tom Meador, "liberated" the cathedral treasures of Quedlinburg in the Harz mountains of north-central Germany. He mailed home rock-crystal reliquaries, a jewel-encrusted silver casket, and the priceless *Samuhel Gospels,* written in gold ink and bound in a jeweled cover, part of a treasure associated with Henry I of Saxony, who is sometimes described as the founder of Germany. After Meador's death in 1980, his heirs tried to sell his booty, which to their astonishment was appraised at tens of millions of dollars. An enterprising *New York Times* reporter, William H. Honan, picked up rumors of the attempted sale, identified Meador, and helped bring about the repatriation of the Quedlinburg treasures, with the lubrication of a $3.75 million "finder's fee" to the heirs from the German Cultural Foundation.

The monuments officers were far more successful protecting the quantities of German art and Nazi booty hidden in castles, caves, and mines. At war's end they learned that senior American officials, abetted by covetous museum directors, had proposed sequestering German art as war reparations. The idea was opposed by General Lucius Clay, commander of U.S. forces in Germany, who favored the swiftest possible return of all booty to its rightful owners, though he did suggest that some German masterpieces might be exhibited temporarily in America.

To monuments officers, even that

was all too reminiscent of the Nazi policy of "temporary" removals, purportedly to "protect" other people's art. They drew up what became known as the Wiesbaden Manifesto, which soberly warned, "no historical grievance will rankle so long, or be the cause of so much justified bitterness, as the removal, for any reason, of a part of the heritage of any nation, even if that heritage may be interpreted as a prize of war." Signed in November 1945 by 25 officers and supported by five others not present, the manifesto came to the attention of Janet Flanner, whose account in *The New Yorker* was immediately cited by officials opposing any use of art as reparations.

President Truman rejected the reparation idea but did approve an exhibition of 202 masterpieces from Berlin museums. The National Gallery's first blockbuster show, it drew a million visitors in 1948, then traveled to New York and St. Louis. By then Europe was dividing into East and West, and General Clay was mounting an airlift to encircled West Berlin. Returned in 1955, the Berlin paintings were placed in the new Dahiem Museum in what was then the American sector, and there they remain today. Meanwhile, thanks to the monuments officers, some 500,000 cultural items looted by Nazis in Slavic countries and found in western Germany were repatriated, an unreciprocated restitution that is invariably ignored in Russian reckoning.

All this had its effect on Moscow. Nothing more was said about establishing a Museum of World Art, with its embarrassing resemblance to Hitler's plans for Linz. In 1945, Soviet prosecutors at Nürnberg agreed with Western victors in defining the plunder of art as a war crime. The Soviet Foreign Minister, Vyacheslav Molotov, even joined with Britain in censuring America's temporary removal of German art. But what truly complicated Soviet cultural diplomacy was the division of Germany and the emergence of a comradely ally, the German Democratic Republic. In 1958, as a goodwill gesture and to buttress the legitimacy of the new East German regime, Nikita

Khrushchev returned the Pergamon Altar to its old home in East Berlin and gave back to Dresden most of its Old Masters and the bejeweled objets d'art from the Green Vault. This wise and realistic gesture was opposed by museum officials such as Irina Antonova, who at the Bard conference in New York was still deploring a decision "dictated by politics." Curators come to believe they own what is in their care. Commenting on the fate of Priam's Treasure in an interview in ARCHAEOLOGY (November/December 1993), Valery Kulishov, a member of the Russian State Commission on Restitution, noted: "You must understand the feelings of the Pushkin Museum officials. If you have it, it's part of you. Psychologically, you're so much attached and bound to what you had, even secretly, in your repository. It's very hard now to give it back, regardless of any kind of agreements."

Trophy art, however, is not exhibited or cataloged. Anybody with access to storerooms can steal and sell it. Leakage has been considerable. Of 562 drawings in the Dutch Koenigs collection seized in Dresden, 33 remained in Germany. But in 1957, the Pushkin Museum's unpublished records listed only "337 sheets," and the total today is said to be 308. A similar attrition has taken place in the Krebs collection, which for five decades has been hidden in the Hermitage in St. Petersburg. At the Bard conference, Alexei Rastorgouev showed slides of drawings from Dresden now owned by unidentified Russian private collectors. Dealers in Europe and America routinely check the Koenigs catalog when offered drawings of suspiciously high quality.

Hence the urgent need to display and catalog all of Russia's wartime booty as soon as possible. It was this consideration that prompted the Hermitage director, Mikhail Piotrovski, to arrange the showing this past March of Impressionist and Post-Impressionist paintings from the Krebs and other private collections. A few weeks earlier Irina Antonova, not to be outdone, had quickly organized a comparable show of Old Masters from German

and Hungarian collections at the Pushkin. One hopes such competition will be contagious. In Piotrovski's sensible view, it is up to the courts to decide legal title, and up to the museums to make public what they hold. In a wider sense, though, the courts can only settle claims of heirs and museums when and if Russia and Germany reach a political settlement.

As for Russia . . . even those sympathetic to its cause will wonder whether five decades of concealment attest a confident claim of ownership.

In the early 1970s, I delved into the secretive antiquities market and its links with collectors and curators. The results were serialized in *The New Yorker* and published as The *Plundered Past.* If I learned any lesson, it was that on matters of acquiring cultural treasures, no art-consuming nation has truly clean hands. Consider the United States. As Lynn Nicholas recounts in *The Rape of Europa,* in 1939 the Nazis staged a scandalous auction at the Fischer Gallery in Lucerne at which allegedly "degenerate" art by Braque, Picasso, Van Gogh, and others was sold at derisory prices. The pictures had been taken from leading German museums. Among the bidders was a refugee German dealer, Curt Valentin of the Bucholz Gallery in New York, who acquired paintings by Derain, Kirchner, Klee, Lehmbruck, and Matisse. He was bidding on behalf of the Museum of Modern Art, whose director, Alfred Barr, exhibited the five works with no hint of their true provenance. No doubt the sale was legal, but it speaks volumes that the entire transaction was secret. By the same token, Harvard's acquisition of a major work by Max Beckmann, sold at the same auction, was also legal. But both institutions were extracting an advantage from a political calamity

that befell German museums, a fact not advertised in accession labels.

As for Germany, everyone repudiates the cultural barbarities and wholesale brigandage that marked the Third Reich. There will be no such unanimity on Germany's legal title to the Schliemann treasure, which was spirited from Ottoman Turkey in murky circumstances, provoking a criminal suit and cash settlement at the time, and leading to a formal claim by the present Republic of Turkey. Nor is anyone talking about the controversy surrounding the bust of Queen Nefertiti, Germany's single most celebrated antiquity. Acquired in a division of finds at Amarna in 1914, the statue was hidden for a decade; Egyptians cried foul from the moment it was finally put on display in Berlin. Like other European art-importing countries, Germany has yet to ratify the UNESCO convention barring the illegal importation of cultural property. Purchase of unprovenanced antiquities, many of them clearly smuggled from their country of origin, is widespread, as visitors to German museums can readily see.

As for Russia, it can indeed point to a traumatic past, but even those sympathetic to its cause will wonder whether five decades of concealment attest a confident claim of ownership. Certainly neither Poland nor Holland, Ukraine nor Hungary, ever invaded the Soviet Union, yet their claims for restitution have also gone unanswered. Ironically the Yeltsin government is seeking restitution of real estate and other properties owned by the czarist regime and its subjects in France, Italy, and Israel, appealing to the very norms of law and equity it declines to apply to its own wartime booty.

How sensible if Russia broke the ice by returning a set of rare books taken from Gotha in 1945, an act of restitution urged by a Moscow librarian speaking at the Bard conference. This gesture might be coupled with an offer to submit claims to the Trojan gold to the World Court for binding adjudication (as Germany has proposed) with the proviso that Turkey's claim also be given a full hearing. And how wise if Germany promoted an international

Limits of World Law

LIEBER

ROERICH

Two remarkable people helped write the laws meant to bar warring nations from destroying or looting each other's cultural treasures. One was the German American soldier and philosopher, Francis Lieber, author of a military code promulgated by Lincoln during the Civil War. The other was Nicholas Roerich, a Russian painter and mystic, who in 1935 persuaded the United States and 20 other countries to approve a treaty asserting the inherent neutrality of works of art in wartime.

The belief that cultural treasures need special treatment was expressed as early as 1758 by Emheric de Vattel, a legal scholar during the Enlightenment, whose treatise *The Law of Nations* spoke to the future: "For whatever cause a country is ravaged, we ought to spare those edifices which do honor to human society, and do not contribute to increase the enemy's strength—such as temples, tombs, public buildings and all works of remarkable beauty. . . . It is declaring one's self to be an enemy of mankind, thus wantonly to deprive them of these wonders of art." Napoleon, nonetheless, crammed the Louvre with wagonloads of conquered art. At the Congress of Vienna in 1815, the Allies ordered France to return the art, since looting, in the words of the Duke of Wellington, was "contrary to the principles of justice and the rules of modern law."

Yet those laws were unwritten. By chance, this was rectified by Francis Lieber, a Prussian-born soldier who in 1827 emigrated to America. He taught legal philosophy at Columbia College in New York and during the Civil War President Lincoln asked him to draft a military code. Issued as General Order 100 in 1863, it called among other things for the protection during wartime of "classical works of art, libraries, scientific collections or precious instruments, such as astronomical telescopes."

The Lieber code inspired a similar declaration in 1874 at the Conference of Brussels that was endorsed by the German kaiser. This declaration in turn inspired the Russian czar to promote a more ambitious conference at the Hague. In 1907, some 40 nations approved a series of conventions that expressly forbade the seizure or destruction in wartime of cultural treasures. The Hague codes proved of limited value during World War I, so in 1935 a fresh attempt was made. This was the work of Nicholas Roerich (1874–1947), a Russian artist who designed the sets for Stravinsky's ballet *Le Sacre du Printemps.* As an explorer, he had led a five-year expedition to central Asia, and had also served as vice-president of the Archaeological Institute of America. A friend of Secretary of Agriculture Henry Wallace, Roerich persuaded the Roosevelt Administration to support a new treaty to protect artistic works, scientific instruments, and historic monuments. He devised a special flag, with three globes in a mystic triad, to mark protected cultural treasures.

Since World War II, insurgents have targeted the great Khmer ruins at Angkor, the walled medieval city of Dubrovnik, and the Ottoman bridges of Bosnia, as well as thousands of churches, mosques, synagogues, temples, palaces, libraries, and memorials of every kind. Nobody has yet found a way of enforcing civilized aspirations; the worst enemy of humanity's noblest works is still humanity itself.—K.E.M.

effort to restore Russian museums and churches. Initiatives like these must be taken quickly, for it takes only a modicum of historical memory to know that it is later than the two governments think.

The Russian parliament has already given preliminary approval to legislation that would give Russia full title to all wartime booty. If that legislation is adopted, there will certainly be reper-

cussions. German aid to Russia is reckoned at more than $73 billion since 1990, including $40 billion in loans and $14 billion in direct grants. If Bonn cuts or conditions its aid to Moscow, a likely next move, there will be a Russian outcry over German bullying and a clamor for reprisals in the Russian parliament.

Back in 1945 American monuments officers, in their Wiesbaden declara-

tion, warned that disputes over captured spoils can sow enduring acrimony. That indeed is the theme of Homer's *Iliad,* which begins with Achilles' fury at the prizes of war that Agamemnon greedily bestows on himself. If no progress is made this year toward resolving the quarrel over Russia's wartime booty, positions will harden, and taking a modest step forward will be even more difficult. As evidence, consult the *Iliad.*

Troy's Prodigious Ruin

Almost one hundred twenty-five years after Heinrich Schliemann discovered the site of Troy on the northwest Anatolian coast, archeologists continue to dig in the dust of Priam's city, discovering new treasures and recovering lost chapters of Trojan history.

Caroline Alexander

Trained as a classicist, Alexander had never actually been to Troy before this assignment, but dates her interest in the Iliad *from age fourteen, when she read the great epic in an English translation. Since then, her involvement with the classics has persisted; she has even established a classics department at the University of Malawi in East Africa.*

> *The day shall come, the great avenging day,*
> *Which Troy's proud glories in the dust shall lay,*
> *When Priam's powers and Priam's self shall fall,*
> *And one prodigious ruin swallow all.*
>   Homer, Iliad, Book IV, Line 96

My interest in the Archaeological Museum of Istanbul lay, not in its world-class collection of Greco-Roman art, but in a single glass exhibition cabinet tucked away in a second-floor wing that is closed for approximately half of every week. The museum is short staffed, and this room is the most expendable. With no other visitor in sight, I crouched before the cabinet and focused on its contents: odds and ends of jewelry and ornaments—pins, hair fasteners, earrings, a bracelet, and a few lumpy ingots of gold—little to command a casual visitor's attention. Yet these objects were in their way legendary: they had been unearthed at Troy, the city immortalized by Homer in the *Iliad.*

The discovery in 1873, by the German archeologist Heinrich Schliemann, of a hoard of magnificent treasure within the ruins of Troy represented more than an incalculable gift to science; for many people, the "Great Treasure" proved that Troy, or Ilium—King Priam's city—was not mythological fiction but historical reality.

In every way as famous as the discovery of the treasure was its subsequent "loss." Donated by Schliemann to the Prehistory and Early History Museum in Berlin, it was transferred during the Second World War to one of the flak towers within the grounds of the Berlin Zoo for safekeeping. Despite this precaution, the treasure vanished in 1945, swept away to parts unknown by the chaos of war. Rumors abounded about its fate—it had been melted down, it was in the vaults of a Texas oil baron, it had been seized by the Russians. For decades, the only remnant of Troy's gold was the Istanbul Museum's sparse collection, which had been unearthed by Schliemann in a later excavation of the same site.

In August of 1993, however, the Pushkin State Museum of Fine Arts in Moscow dropped a bombshell and announced that the gold of Troy had long been hidden in its vaults, taken as booty by the Red Army during its occupation of Berlin. This spring will see the long awaited public exhibition of the treasure and the closure of an old and tantalizing mystery.

For archeologists, any artifact from the Bronze Age, whether of gold or common pottery, is cause for excitement. But for the layman, Schliemann's Great Treasure will inevitably be viewed not on its own merits but in the reflected glory of the *Iliad* and the Trojan War. In his own time, Schliemann's sensational discovery led streams of distinguished visitors to his excavation site. Similarly, today it is almost impossible to contemplate King Priam's treasure without longing for a glimpse of the bare bones of his fabled city.

The remains of Troy are scattered over the mound of Hissarlik, situated on the spur of a limestone plateau on the northwest coast of Turkey. From the height of Hissarlik, one looks down on a broad plain cut by two rivers—the Scamander and Simois of the *Iliad*—whose courses can be traced by the line of willows and tall cypresses that flank their banks. To the west, the plain is bounded by the Aegean; to the north by the racing waters of the Dardanelles (known in ancient times as the Hellespont), the narrow strategic strait that divides Europe from Asia.

Troy's wealth derived from its monopoly of the strait. Today, Hissarlik stands some three miles from the sea, but in ancient times, before the plain's two rivers silted it up, a deep bay protruded inland to within half a mile of Troy's walls. Another of the city's natural resources was the wind, the steady northeasterly so striking even to modern visitors: *Ilios ënemoessa,* "windy Ilium," as the city was called by Homer. The keelless boats of the Homeric Bronze Age were not equipped to sail against the wind, so any ship wishing to enter the Dardanelles would either have

An artist's view of Troy 4,500 years ago shows a well-defended citadel with ramps leading from two gates up to the king's palace.

to beach at Troy's harbor and wait for a favorable breeze or arrange to transport its goods overland. In either case, it would be prey to Troy's tribute collectors. Additional revenue would have come from the sale of supplies to the landbound crews, and perhaps also from the services of pilots and guides. At the crossroads of trade plied between east and west—Asia and Europe—this strategically placed maritime city might have experienced not one but many Trojan wars.

But for most people, the only war that counts is the one of which Homer sang—the subject of the *Iliad*. This epic was set down in approximately the first half of the eighth century B.C., some five centuries after the war it purportedly reports. Behind the poem lie several centuries of oral transmission. In bare outline, the *Iliad* is about the war that

the Greeks and Trojans fought over Helen of Sparta, the legendary Greek beauty who left her husband, Menelaus, for the Trojan prince Paris. The *Iliad* itself does not cover the elopement nor does it mention the famous and legendary wooden horse—other epics, some now lost to us, treated these events.

The poem is devoted to a critical, roughly two-week period in the tenth and final year of the war. It opens with the quarrel between Achilles, the greatest of the Greek warriors, and Agamemnon, his commanding officer. Subsequently, Achilles withdraws from the war, with disastrous consequences for the Greeks. Toward the end of the epic, Achilles allows Patroclus, his closest companion, to impersonate him by wearing his armor. Initially, this ploy works and the Trojans retreat in terror—until Patroclus

is killed by Hector, the great Trojan hero. From this point, the epic's theme is the vengeance of Achilles. Returning to the fray, Achilles confronts Hector and kills him before the Scaean Gates of the city and, with the dead man's horrified family looking on, drags Hector's body around Troy's walls behind his chariot. Some days later, Hector's aged father, Priam, creeps into Achilles' tent and pleads for the body of his son. Achilles relents, and the *Iliad* concludes with the burial of Hector.

Unlike other mortals, Achilles was born with a choice of two fates: he could either stay at home and live a long, undistinguished life or die young and win great glory. By returning to battle to avenge Patroclus, he consciously chose the fate he had earlier passionately resisted. In its speeches, which draw out the bitterness of war and of dying young, in its poignant use of similes from nature and peacetime, in its contrast of the lot of man with that of the undying gods, in grand theme and small detail, the *Iliad* unfurls its message—that man's greatest battle is with his own mortality. It is a battle he necessarily loses.

In 1871, when Heinrich Schliemann began to search for Troy, most scholars believed that it was a place solely of the imagination. Troy's general location should have been obvious from the *Iliad*'s descriptions, but few people before Schliemann had bothered to put a spade in the earth to find it. Schliemann, a peripatetic, forty-nine-year-old German businessman, had made a fortune in the indigo trade in Russia and had acquired Russian citizenship and a Russian wife. In 1850, during the gold rush, he moved to California, where he made a fortune in banking. Two years later, he moved back to Russia to make yet another fortune selling indigo and potassium nitrate to the Russian army. His worldly success assured, Schliemann now shed his Russian wife and married Sophia Engastromenos, a Greek woman thirty years his junior. Although he liked to say, after the fact, that he had decided to discover Troy at age eight, the more likely truth is that a visit to the Trojan plain, as part of a grand tour in 1868, aroused his interest. Here he met Frank Calvert, an Englishman who was acting American vice consul at Çanokkale and an enthusiastic Homerist. Calvert owned half of Hissarlik, where he had made exploratory and encouraging digs, and he drew Schliemann's attention to the site.

Under Turkish law, an official permit was required for all excavations, and any artifacts unearthed belonged to the owner of the land where it had been found. On April 9, 1870, Schliemann, with neither a permit nor the consent of the Turkish owners, had his hired men sink two long trenches west of Hissarlik's summit. Miscellaneous artifacts were unearthed—coins, pottery, bones, terra cotta objects—and, at a depth of about sixteen feet, "a wall two metres thick formed of stones of limestone and of great solidity and skillfully hewn," which Schliemann immediately concluded to be "clearly the walls of a pal-

(Illustration by Christoph Haussner)

Well-defended, free-standing houses from 3,500 years ago show that the people of Troy were advanced in engineering, masonry, and town planning.

ace or temple." The trial trenches also revealed that the site encompassed many levels of successive occupation, with walls built upon the foundation of earlier walls, forming a bewildering, multitiiered labyrinth.

Schliemann's attempt to bully the two Turks into selling their share of Hissarlik failed, and he left to deal directly with officials in Constantinople. Here, for once, he met his match. In January 1871, the Turkish Minister of Public Instruction, Safret Pasha, purchased from the Turkish owners their share of Hissarlik; thus, any artifacts found would belong to the government and to the newly established Imperial Museum in Constantinople (now the Archaeological Museum of Istanbul). Outmaneuvered, Schliemann offered to underwrite the cost of excavation in exchange for an equal share in any artifacts he unearthed. (Later, he came to a similar arrangement with Frank Calvert.) The bargain was struck, and in August of 1871, Schlie-

mann obtained his permit to excavate the ruins of Troy.

Schliemann returned to Hissarlik in September and for the next three years led a team of seventy to eighty workmen at the excavation. Digging with a vengeance, they extended his great trenches and sank new ones. Although the haste with which he proceeded has appalled many who came after him, at the time of Schliemann's work, archeology was a new science, and blame for the destruction of artifacts cannot be attributed exclusively to his impatient character. Nonetheless, precious levels of Hissarlik's complex strata were lost forever within a few short seasons. Schliemann's assumption was that the Troy he sought—Homer's Troy—would be found near bedrock because it appeared to him that the more desirable artifacts were being unearthed from the lowest levels.

The second season ended encouragingly with the discovery of some gold ornaments and a twenty-foot-high wall

(Illustration by Christoph Haussner)

A view of Troy as it might have looked in 1300 B.C., with people thronging its busy streets.

built on bedrock, which Schliemann immediately proclaimed to be the Great Tower of Ilium. In January 1873, the beginning of his third season, excavation continued on the "tower," which increasingly began to look like a wall. In April came the exciting discovery of a paved road running from the hill to the plain. Later, following the sinking of twenty exploratory shafts, a double gate was unearthed at the juncture of the road with the city wall, excitably identified by Schliemann as the Scaean Gates, outside of which some of the *Iliad's* most memorable and stirring actions take place.

Things began to move swiftly; two buildings were uncovered, one of which Schliemann declared to be Priam's Palace. Bones, a broken helmet, a copper sword, pottery, and two knives came to light. An old trench was extended, a new one begun, and on May 31, Schliemann

made what has fairly been called one of the most famous finds in the history of archeology. Within the structure he had identified as Priam's Palace, he came upon a large copper object, with a glint of gold behind. In his book, *Troy and Its Remains,* Schliemann writes that "in order to withdraw the treasure from the greed of my workmen, and to save it for archaeology," he called a break, and while the workmen were away, extracted "the Treasure" with a knife. While his "dear wife" held out her shawl, he piled in a copper shield, a caldron and vase, a golden cup, a sauceboat and bottle, an electrum cup, three large-lidded silver vases and two smaller ones, spearheads, battle-axes, daggers, two dazzling gold diadems, a gold headband, sixty gold earrings, and approximately 9,000 small gold ornaments.

Smuggling his booty out of Turkey amidst crates of his personal possessions, Schliemann brought it safely to Athens. Inevitably, Turkish officials learned of his deception and in March 1874, represented by the director of the Imperial Museum in Constantinople, the government filed a very public lawsuit for its agreed-upon half share of all finds. When the case was eventually decided in favor of the Turks, policemen were sent to Schliemann's residence to collect the disputed objects, only to find that the treasure was mysteriously absent—Schliemann had already taken the precaution of storing it in the French School at Athens. Finally, the Turkish government agreed to settle for the sum of 50,000 francs, the equivalent of about $3,000. Having estimated his hoard to be worth at least $80,000, Schliemann, in a calculated gesture of "goodwill," sent five times the amount requested, along with four sacks of stone implements from the same excavation. The treasure was his; but when in later years he was allowed to excavate the site again, it was in the presence of two Turkish overseers.

Priam's Treasure was first displayed in the South Kensington (now Victoria and Albert) Museum in London. Subsequently, depending on his mood and the political expediency of the moment, Schliemann either offered it for sale or promised it to museums in Athens, France, Britain, and Russia—he even dropped a hint to the United States government that he would like to be consul to Athens "and would of course amply reward the Smithsonian Hall in Washington by gifts of antiquities for the honor the govt. might bestow upon me." Germany, however, wooed him most successfully, and in 1880, in exchange for honors of various kinds, he committed his priceless treasure to his countrymen. According to his stipulations, the treasure was housed in a wing, bearing his name in gold letters, of the new Prehistory and Early History Museum in Berlin.

Systematic excavations of Troy continued after Schliemann's death in 1890 and were conducted until 1894 by the German archeologist and architect—and Schliemann's friend and supporter—Wilhelm Dürpfeld. Between 1932 and 1939, Carl Blegen, an American professor at the University of Cincinnati, made further advancements. The work of these two men established the chronology of Troy's different settlements and strata.

Dürpfeld's careful work established a riveting, if awkward, truth. Schliemann's Troy, which included Priam's Palace, the Scaean Gates, and the Great Treasure itself, belonged to what Dürpfeld identified as Troy II, the second-oldest discernible settlement on the site, dating as far back as 2500 B.C.—a good twelve hundred years before the estimated date of the Trojan War. There are other awkward truths. In a recent biography of Schliemann, David Traill's careful reading of Schliemann's various accounts of his discovery in his diary, correspondence, and published papers, together with the recollections of one of his servants, makes it clear that the Great Treasure was found in bits and pieces over an extended period of time. The majority of the hoard was found outside the city wall—not, as Schliemann had claimed, within the palace—and may well have been from a burial site; but a single treasure, a treasure worthy of King Priam, was what Schliemann needed to satisfy both his own romantic illusions and a skeptical scientific world, and so the various finds were condensed into one. Finally, since his "dear wife," Sophia, was in Athens, she could hardly have been at hand to hold out her shawl.

Such discrepancies did much to discredit Schliemann, and some critics went so far as to suggest that the entire treasure was a fake, pieced together from jewelry purchased in the local bazaar. The examination of the treasure by a panel of experts invited to Russia in 1994, however, has silenced that rumor, and in this respect, at least, Schliemann has been vindicated. The Great Treasure was stolen, misleadingly presented, and dates from the "wrong" era—but it is nonetheless real.

One would have thought that a site so famous would long ago have yielded all its secrets, but an international team of archeologists, under the direction of Manfred Korfmann, of Tübingen University in Germany (in association with the University of Cincinnati and the German Archaeological Institute), is currently exploring Hissarlik anew. The new archeological team has been excavating at Troy since 1988, nearly fifty years after Blegen's work ceased. Drawing on a battery of sophisticated sciences, such as paleobotany, geochemistry, metallurgy, carbon-14 dating, and geomagnetic prospecting, the current team has gone a long way toward reconstructing the many settlements that once flourished on the mound. Remains of at least nine distinct settlements, ranging from approximately 3000 B.C. to the sixth-century A.D. Roman city of New Ilium, lie cheek by jowl with one another; by turning a corner, one can literally step from one ancient age into another.

Inevitably, for nonspecialists, the Middle to Late Bronze Age settlements of Troy VI (circa 1700 to 1250 B.C.) and Troy VIIa (circa 1250 to 1000 B.C.) are the most compelling. The Trojan War (if indeed it happened) is usually dated between 1275 and 1240 B.C. Although most of the evidence for the levels immediately preceding Troy VI were destroyed by Schliemann, enough remains for archeologists to determine that Troy V was destroyed by fire, and that Troy VI saw the establishment of an entirely new principality. The citadel of this period exceeded in size and the quality of its masonry all that had gone before. Significant sections of its magnificent walls survive, and would be compelling even without their mythological pedigree. Constructed of large, beautifully dressed limestone, the strategically defensive, inward-leaning—or "battered"—walls are sometimes embellished with offsets that divide their outer face—an eye-pleasing feature that reflects a society with wealth enough to go beyond the basics. Within the walls, the citadel was divided into six sections by wide streets that radiated from each of its five gateways. Free-standing houses built on concentric terraces faced the acropolis and the palace of the king—a large, two-storied "megaron" building, built around an open hearth. From the main southern gate, flanked by a tower, a road with central guttering still slopes up into the ruins of the city.

In addition to physical artifacts, details of contemporary daily life have been revealed. The inhabitants of Troy VI probably spoke Luvian, an Indo-European language related to Hittite. The Scamander plain in the Bronze Age was marshy—perhaps alive with the bird life Homer describes—while the outlying areas were good for hunting fallow deer, leopards, wild boar, and even lions. The bones of domestic animals, such as sheep, cattle, pigs, and horses, have been unearthed. Herring and tuna caught in the Dardanelles may have been an important trade commodity, while the number of terra cotta spindle whorls indicates a thriving wool industry. Ironically, while excavators were led to Troy by an epic par excellence of men and war, the material artifacts the site has so far yielded are overwhelmingly feminine and domestic.

In 1992, a defensive trench some 1,300 feet south of the citadel was uncovered, indicating a previously unknown lower settlement area. This combination of citadel and lower city is characteristic of Anatolian and northern Syrian settlements of the same era. Perhaps the most exciting revelation comes from the plain. In Besik Bay, the sandy cove facing the island of Tenedos in the Aegean, a cemetery was found where a variety of foreign peoples were buried, suggesting that it had been used by crews of landbound ships waiting for following wind. Included were cremations from the thirteenth century B.C. It is here, then, that the Greek ships mustered under Agamemnon would have landed.

An earthquake brought an end to the thriving city of some five to six thousand people. The cracks it rent in the surviving walls are visible in several places, although the absence of human skeletons from this period suggests that the population had enough warning to escape. After the crisis passed, the same people returned to Troy and repaired their city. Renovations were made hastily, with numerous small houses crammed together, as if a larger population than before now sought safety within the city walls. This, combined with a number of enormous buried storage jars, suggests preparations for a long-time siege.

This renovated city, Troy VIIa, lasted for some seventy years and was then destroyed by a conflagration. Now, many human skeletons were found, along with evidence that not only fire but also an enemy's massacre destroyed the population. Was this the Trojan city, weakened by earthquake, that the invading Greeks finally sacked? Some scholars have suggested that the legend of the wooden horse of Troy is consistent with the earthquake since the Homeric epithet for Poseidon, god of the sea, is "earth shaker," and his popular symbol is the horse. Perhaps, after sacking the city they had attempted to storm for ten long years, the Greeks, grateful for the fatal weakening wrought by the earth shaker in the Trojan defensive walls, left a wooden horse as a votive offering. The site was abandoned, reoccupied, and then, in approximately 1000 B.C., destroyed by fire. For the next four centuries, Hissarlik lay deserted.

Over the ages, a number of distinguished visitors, inspired by the *Iliad,* have made pilgrimages to the site. The Persian king Xerxes sacrificed here in

480 B.C. on his way to his disastrous encounter with the Greeks. Alexander the Great, who slept with a copy of the *Iliad* under his pillow, came to Hissarlik on his way to conquer the world and paid homage to the alleged tomb of Achilles by running naked around it. Julius Caesar walked the plain and paced the hill, then overgrown with thorny scrub, and both Caesar and Constantine considered building a new capital at Troy on the mound of Hissarlik. In the winter of A.D. 354, the emperor Julian, that earnest pagan called the Apostate, came ashore and found a fire still burning on an altar to the Trojan hero Hector—apparently tended by none other than the resident Christian bishop. And surely Homer, too, paid homage to this site. Some vestige of the splendid walls of Troy VI would still have been visible on the city's landward side in his day.

Although the year's excavation season was over at the time of my visit, and the team had returned home, evidence of their labor was apparent: amid a confusion of leveled stone foundations and partial walls, the distinct strata of a cleanly cut trench had been neatly la-

beled with little flags, and one of the more ancient walls on the site showed signs of having been recently shored up and restored. South of the citadel, on level ground and hidden from general view by high, parched grass, rectangular pits indicated the team's most recent, and literally groundbreaking, work. Peering down into these sunken pits and trenches, deserted as they now were, I felt a pang of optimism—perhaps something new might still be wrung from these tired old stones.

Walking away from the hill of Hissarlik, I tried to recall how I used to imagine this land upon which the Greeks had camped and warriors had clashed. My recollected images were hazy—by night a dark field interspersed with campfires, and by day a dusty expanse stirred by sandaled feet. Nothing at all like the golden landscape I now walked over, with its parched grass shaded here and there by olive trees and small valonia oaks. Nor, unaccountably, had I ever considered the hard blue Aegean sky. Was it really on such pastoral, domesticated land, under the crinkled leaves of stunted oaks, that Achilles cut his enemies to pieces and Hector took his last stand?

(Joe Lemonnier)

Part 1

Lure of the Deep

James P. Delgado

James P. Delgado is director of the Vancouver Maritime Museum and the author of numerous books on nautical archaeology, including Great American Ships, *co-authored with J. Candace Clifford (Washington, DC: Preservation Press, 1991).*

"It is probable that a greater number of monuments of the skill and industry of man will in the course of ages be collected together in the bed of the oceans, than will exist at any one time on the surface of the continents."

Sir Charles Lyell
Principles of Geology (1932)

For thousands of years the oceans have been great highways for communication and commerce. Many vessels have been lost and now rest on the ocean floor. Until recently, these shipwrecks, and the incredible record of the past that they contain, were beyond our reach. Now, thanks to new technologies, scholars as well as treasure hunters can safely descend to great depths to explore or plunder them.

At stake are a host of ancient wrecks—trading ships scattered about the Mediterranean seabed; gold-laden Spanish galleons off the coasts of North, Central, and South America; and Spanish and Portuguese ships off the Azores, their cargo of treasure from Asia, Africa, and the East Indies still intact. Many of these sites are incredibly well preserved, with both ships and their contents in near pristine condition. Salvors have barely begun exploiting these cultural resources, but the potential for them to do so is increasing by the day, a cause for alarm among archaeologists.

Early technologies useful in the pursuit of sunken treasure were pioneered by the British adventurers John and Charles Deane, who in 1836 dove on Henry VIII's warship *Mary Rose,* which had sunk in 40 feet of water off England's southern coast in 1545. Wearing metal helmets and leather suits and breathing through tubes attached to an air pump on the surface, the brothers wrested huge cannon and well-preserved wood from the ship. Their quest was motivated in large part by financial gain from the salvage of the guns, but the age of the timbers and the history of the ship inspired them to preserve small pieces of wood as relics, which they used as covers for the souvenir books that accompanied a display of the cannon.

A century later, from 1918 to 1923, nearly $10 million in gold bullion was salvaged from the British ocean liner *Laurentic,* which sank in 120 feet of water after being torpedoed by the Germans in January 1917. This operation led to the development of the first decompression tables, which allow divers to calculate the time that can be spent at a given depth and the time needed between dives to avoid dangerous nitrogen buildup in the blood, a condition commonly known as "the bends."

After World War II the invention of scuba gear allowed forays as deep as 200 feet. Wartime technologies for locating enemy submarines, including sonar and magnetometers, were appropriated by treasure hunters searching for sunken ships. Recreational divers, souvenir hunters, and salvors quickly stripped wrecks in shallow coastal waters. Alarmed by such pillaging, many countries adopted legislation to protect wrecks within their jurisdictions, generally three to 12 miles out to sea. These laws have slowed the plundering of shipwrecks within national boundaries. Wrecks in deep international waters were protected by their inaccessibility.

The first breakthrough in deep-sea salvage came in June 1963, when a U.S. Navy crew using the bathyscaphe *Tri-*

este II searched for and recovered the American nuclear submarine *Thresher,* which had sunk more than one and one-half miles in the Atlantic after experiencing mechanical problems. In 1965 the Navy was able to locate a hydrogen bomb that had dropped into the sea after a midair collision between a bomber and its refueling tanker off Palomares, Spain, by sending a remotely operated vehicle (ROV) down some 3,000 feet. The following year the Navy recovered the bomb using the manned submersible *Alvin.* Within a few years such military technology would be used by civilians to find historically significant wrecks in far deeper waters.

Clive Cussler's novel *Raise the Titanic!,* published in 1976, described a futuristic salvage of the ocean liner *Titanic,* which sank with more than 1,500 passengers on her maiden voyage from Southampton to New York in 1912. Finding the legendary vessel in the deep waters of the North Atlantic was declared impossible after a series of well-publicized attempts to locate the ship by Texas oil millionaire Jack Grimm. He had searched for *Titanic* in the early 1980s using side-scan sonar, magnetometers, and a remotely operated camera towed 650 feet above the seabed, but missed the ship by more than a mile.

In 1985 Robert D. Ballard, then of the Woods Hole Oceanographic Institution, and Jean-Louis Michel, of the Institute Français de Recherche pour l'Exploitation des Mers, succeeded in finding *Titanic* in more than 12,000 feet of water off the Grand Banks of Newfoundland. Like Grimm, they had towed an array of instruments behind their research ship, including high-resolution sonar and a camera, but they had "flown" them closer to the seabed. The following year they visited the wreck in *Alvin* and investigated its interior using a camera-toting ROV named *Jason, Jr.* that brought ghostly images of intact chandeliers and grand staircases into homes worldwide.

There has been much debate over what to do with *Titanic.* Some, including Ballard, believe it should be left untouched as a memorial to the dead. Others want artifacts and parts of the wreck salvaged and put on display. Still others have recovered items from the

(COURTESY WOODS HOLE OCEANOGRAPHIC INSTITUTION)

Illustration depicts a research vessel being guided to a known wreck site by satellite. From such a vessel, archaeologists can document artifacts on the ocean floor using manned submersibles or remotely operated vehicles (ROVs) tethered to the research ship. ROVs and untethered autonomous underwater vehicles are guided to sites by shipboard magnetometers and side-scan sonar.

ship and are now selling them. In 1989 Congress passed the Titanic Memorial Act, urging that artifacts from the ship not be sold in the United States. The measure called for international discussions on preserving the wreck as a memorial, suggesting that plans be developed for "appropriate" recovery and salvage. Ignoring the act, Titanic Ventures, Inc., based in Connecticut, recovered some 1,800 artifacts from the ship in 1987, including dinnerware, bottles of champagne, and personal effects, using the French submarine *Nautile.* RMS Ti-

tanic, Inc., of New York, brought up still more artifacts in 1993, 1994, and 1995, including coal, the sale of which has been advertised in newspapers and magazines. While the Titanic Memorial Act expressed the wishes of Congress, the older Law of Salvage prevailed and RMS Titanic was awarded sole salvage rights to the wreck by the United States District Court for the Northern District of Virginia. The group has proposed exhibiting some of the artifacts in a floating museum that would visit ports around the world.

In 1987 the Columbus-America Discovery Group, a consortium based in Ohio, discovered the wreck of the American side-wheel steamer *Central America*, which sank in 1857 in 8,000 feet of water more than 260 miles off the coast of South Carolina. The salvors captured headlines with their recovery of gold bullion worth more than $2 million using an ROV named *Nemo*. One of *Nemo's* robot manipulator arms shot large quantities of epoxy onto the gold bars so they could be brought up en masse. In 1989 Seahawk, a company in Tampa, found and later recovered precious artifacts from a seventeenth-century Spanish galleon—possibly *Neustra Señora de la Merced*, which was lost in 1622—in 1,500 feet of water in the Gulf of Mexico. Recently, salvors discovered the American liberty ship *John Barry*, loaded with $26 million in Saudi silver dollars, in deep waters off East Africa. The ship had been carrying money to support the Soviet Union's efforts against the Nazis when it was torpedoed by a U-boat in 1944. The *I-52*, a Japanese submarine that had been carrying gold bullion now worth $15 million to Nazi Germany, was found last year by businessman Paul Tidwell and his Virginia-based company Au Holdings. Sunk by Allied forces on June 23, 1944, the submarine lies under more than 18,000 feet of water, making it the deepest wreck found to date.

Archaeologists have not been sitting idly by. In 1989 Ballard and archaeologist Anna Marguerite McCann, using *Jason, Jr.,* discovered and documented a fourth-century A.D. Roman wreck in 3,000 feet of water in the Mediterranean. Called *Isis,* the ship is the deepest known ancient wreck. Last summer Ballard, now president of the Institute of Exploration in Connecticut, began searching for more wrecks in the Mediterranean by retracing ancient trade routes—from Ostia to Carthage and along the coast of North Africa. At his disposal is the U.S. Navy's nuclear submarine *NR-1*. Launched in 1969, *NR-1* can dive to 3,000 feet and travel at a speed of more than ten knots. It can remain submerged for weeks, even months, its high-resolution side-scan sonar "seeing" more than 600 feet on

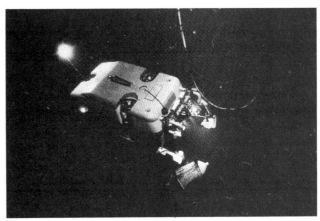

(COURTESY WOODS HOLE OCEANOGRAPHIC INSTITUTION)

The ROV *Jason, Jr.* collects an amphora from *Isis,* a fourth-century A.D. Roman ship that sank 100 miles north of Carthage.

either side of the vessel. Ballard and his team are mapping wrecks and pinpointing debris fields, all potential targets for archaeological research.

Such assistance from the Navy could give academic institutions and research professionals a competitive edge over commercial salvors, only a few of whom can afford such sophisticated technology. RMS Titanic estimates that it has spent some $50,000 per artifact recovered, and to date the company is unsure how it will recoup its investment. Paul Tidwell estimates that it will cost $8 million to recover the bullion from *I-52*, gold to which he may not be legally entitled. If it is determined that the gold was a payment for goods delivered to Japan, it might belong to Germany if that country should decide to assert a claim. If the gold is deemed a capturable asset the Allies may be entitled to it as war reparations.

Can or should archaeologists forge a working relationship with salvage groups? We should not participate in projects that profit from the sale of artifacts and salvors who promise not to do so will also have to guarantee that they will properly excavate and record a site, and that there will be adequate financing to carry projects beyond the retrieval of artifacts to conservation, publication, and curation of the finds.

Despite a few well-publicized for-profit excursions into the deep, there are not that many treasure hunters working on the ocean floor. But the potential is there for a rapid expansion of salvage operations. Archaeologists must draw some battle lines. Are *Titanic* and World War II ships significant archaeological sites? We currently assess the importance of a site or an artifact by what it tells us about the past, and by its potential to yield new information. Not all wrecks of the past 100 years may be archaeologically significant, though all wrecks should be evaluated. We should focus our efforts on using the new technology to find and study archaeologically significant sites such as *Isis,* and offer the public "profit" through knowledge, not plunder.

FURTHER READING

Recommended are William Hoffman and Jack Grimm, *Beyond Reach: The Search for the* Titanic (New York: Beoutom Books, 1982); Bartle Penrose, *Stalin's Gold: The Story of HMS* Edinburgh *and Its Treasure* (Nw York: Granada, 1982); Sarah Dromgoole and Nicholas Gaskell, "Who Has a Right to Historic Wrecks and Wreckage?" *International Journal of Cultural Property* 2:2 (1993), pp. 217–273; Robert D. Ballard, *The Discovery of the* Titanic (New York: Warner Books, 1987), and *The Discovery of the* Bismarck (New York: Warner Books, (1990); Flora Lewis, *One of Our H-Bombs Is Missing* (New York: McGraw-Hill, 1967); and George Bass, *Ships and Shipwrecks of the Americas* (New York: Thames & Hudson, 1988).

(continued)

Part 2

HIGH TECH TOOLS: SCUBA TO SUBMERSIBLES

Since the development of scuba following World War II, diving has become less expensive and easier to learn. Not only is equipment lighter, but small computers now tell users how long they may remain at a given depth, and the time they need between dives to avoid dangerous nitrogen buildup in their blood. Even with these developments, however, there are still depth and duration of dive limits beyond which underwater explorers take serious risks.

To go beyond these limitations, some divers use Heliox, a mixed gas that reduces the risk of decompression sickness, allowing them to descend more than 500 feet. Newtsuits allow divers to descend to 1,000 feet without fear of decompression sickness. These pressurized body-fitting suits use foot pedals to control a thruster pack that can propel a diver at a speed of four knots. Tethered to a surface ship, the Newtsuit diver can remain submerged for up to 48 hours.

Marine archaeologists and salvors in search of deep ocean wrecks are using manned submersibles and remotely operated vehicles (ROVS). One of the best known submersibles is *Alvin*, developed for the U.S. Navy in 1964 and used to explore the wreck of *Titanic*. While *Alvin* can descend to 14,764 feet, other submersibles—France's *Nautile,* Russia's *Mir 1* and *2*, the U.S.'s *Sea Cliff,* and Japan's *Shinkai 6500* can dive to depths of up to 20,000 feet. *Shinkai,* capable of reaching 21,325 feet, is currently the world's deepest diving craft. These vessels carry an array of sonars and cameras and a crew of three or four, and can remain submerged for up to eight hours. It can, however, take up to three hours to reach a mean ocean depth of 4,000 feet and three hours to return to the surface, leaving barely two hours of search time. Moreover, all such craft require support vessels able to launch them using a deckmounted crane. In most cases the support equipment costs more than the submersible.

ROVs are considerably less expensive to operate, and several models are commercially available. During the past decade, ROVs equipped with cameras, robot manipulator arms, and artifact retrieval baskets have descended deeper and performed increasingly complex tasks, including the collection of sediment samples and fragile artifacts. But even ROVs are limited by the fact that they are tethered to a surface ship and need to be monitored constantly as they perform their tasks. The latest development is the autonomous underwater vehicle (AUV), an "intelligent" robot that can search for shipwrecks and submerged artifacts without a link to the surface. AUVs are now being used to monitor seismic activity and water pollution, and one day could be parked on protected wrecks to monitor any intrusion by treasure hunters.—J.P.D.

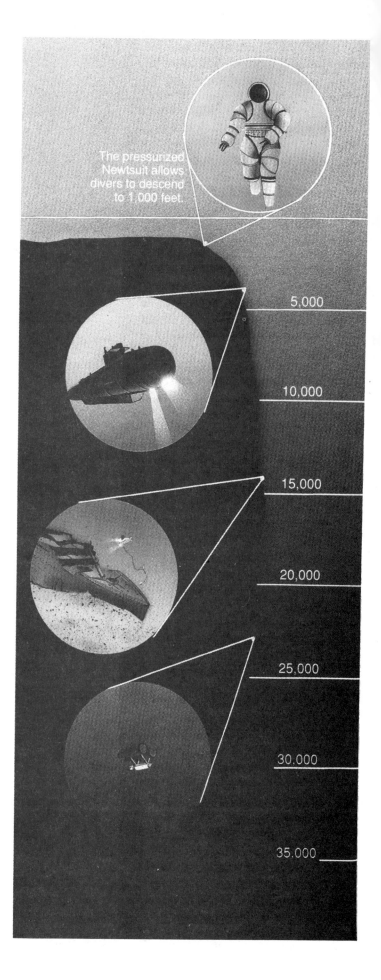

The pressurized Newtsuit allows divers to descend to 1,000 feet.

5,000
10,000
15,000
20,000
25,000
30,000
35,000

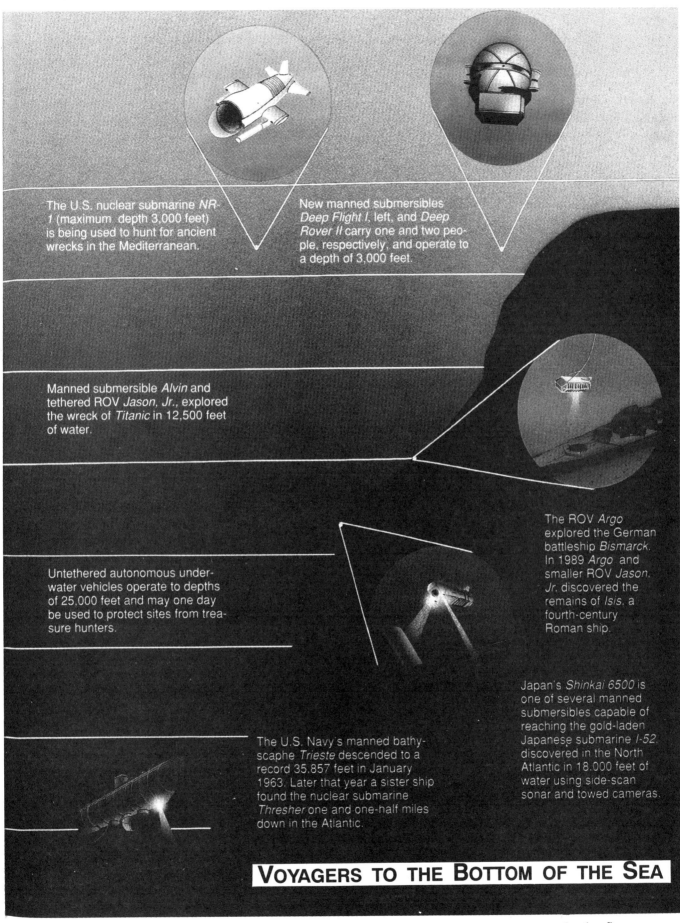

The U.S. nuclear submarine *NR-1* (maximum depth 3,000 feet) is being used to hunt for ancient wrecks in the Mediterranean.

New manned submersibles *Deep Flight I*, left, and *Deep Rover II* carry one and two people, respectively, and operate to a depth of 3,000 feet.

Manned submersible *Alvin* and tethered ROV *Jason, Jr.*, explored the wreck of *Titanic* in 12,500 feet of water.

The ROV *Argo* explored the German battleship *Bismarck*. In 1989 *Argo* and smaller ROV *Jason, Jr.* discovered the remains of *Isis*, a fourth-century Roman ship.

Untethered autonomous underwater vehicles operate to depths of 25,000 feet and may one day be used to protect sites from treasure hunters.

Japan's *Shinkai 6500* is one of several manned submersibles capable of reaching the gold-laden Japanese submarine *I-52*, discovered in the North Atlantic in 18,000 feet of water using side-scan sonar and towed cameras.

The U.S. Navy's manned bathyscaphe *Trieste* descended to a record 35,857 feet in January 1963. Later that year a sister ship found the nuclear submarine *Thresher* one and one-half miles down in the Atlantic.

VOYAGERS TO THE BOTTOM OF THE SEA

(continued)

Part 3
MURKY LEGAL WATERS

A large body of international law governs activity on the high seas, but few regulations apply specifically to cultural remains. According to the United Nations Convention on the High Seas of 1958, all nations have the freedom to fly over, sail upon, fish, and lay pipelines and submarine cables in the seabed of international waters. Article 8 of the convention states that "warships on the high seas have complete immunity from the jurisdiction of any State other than the Flag State." In recent years some nations have used this provision to retain jurisdiction over sunken warships in other nations' territorial waters, or in international waters, to protect them as war graves. Other nations have granted salvors permission to recover treasure from shipwrecks while retaining ownership of the vessels. In 1980 Great Britain's Ministry of Defence granted divers permission to recover $20 million in gold bullion from the cruiser *Edinburgh,* torpedoed by a German U-boat in 1942 in the Barents Sea. According to salvor Paul Tidwell, Japanese officials have granted similar permission for the deep-ocean recovery of $25 million in bullion from the submarine *I-52,* sunk by U.S. forces in the Atlantic while en route to Nazi Germany.

In other cases, to avoid ownership battles or conflicting claims, salvors have invoked the Law of Finds, or "finders, keepers." From time to time, however, legal challenges have been raised. The Columbus-America Discovery Group of Ohio squared off against insurance companies over the gold bullion cargo on the American side-wheel steamer *Central America,* which sank off the coast of South Carolina in 1857. Columbus-America was initially awarded custody of the cargo when the judge presiding over the case in Admiralty Court in the Northern District of Virginia ruled that the insurance companies had not kept accurate records of what they had lost or paid in claims, and had not actively pursued recovery of the cargo in the 130 years since the ship sank. A circuit court of appeals, however, reversed the decision, applying the Law of Salvage, which entitled the owners—in this case the insurance companies who paid out claims—to regain their lost cargo. They were, however, ordered to pay a salvage award of 90 percent of the gold to Columbus-America for its "services" in bringing up the treasure.

The United Nations Convention on the Law of the Sea, adopted in 1982, contains two articles (149 and 303) that deal with shipwrecks and other cultural materials in international waters. The convention, which must be ratified by individual nations, enjoins those that sign to "protect objects of an archaeological and historical nature found at sea." It also stipulates that "all objects of an archaeological or historical nature . . . shall be preserved or disposed of for the benefit of mankind as a whole, with particular regard being paid to the preferential rights of the state or country of origin." The convention, however, does not override Admiralty Law or the rights of identifiable owners. It did establish the International Seabed Authority, a tribunal responsible for matters concerning exploration and exploitation of natural resources, but the Authority was not charged with any responsibility for managing historical or archaeological resources. In short, the convention sets a noble goal of ensuring that wrecks are conserved for the "benefit of mankind," but does not provide a mechanism for doing so.

The International Law Association, a legal advisory body to the United Nations, has proposed a Convention on Underwater Cultural Heritage. Based on the two relevant articles of the Law of the Sea, it allows governments to extend their authority 200 miles out into international waters that have been designated a "cultural heritage zone," and asks signatory nations to control the maritime activities of their citizens by, for example, prohibiting treasure hunters from operating from their ports. The convention also allows the seizure of looted artifacts brought into a nation's territory and provides for sanctions against those who violate a designated cultural heritage zone. Even if such a convention is adopted, nations such as the United States may choose not to sign it because a final convention might undermine private ownership rights protected by Admiralty Law. This May UNESCO is holding a meeting of international experts to fine-tune the convention and recommend a course of action.

Archaeologists and legal scholars are now studying an agreement signed by Sweden, Finland, and Estonia this past February about the wreck of the ferry *Estonia,* which sank in the Baltic Sea on September 28, 1994, while sailing from Tallinn to Stockholm, drowning some 900 passengers. Under the terms of the agreement, the wreck and its surrounding area are regarded as a "final place of rest for victims of the disaster," and all three nations have passed laws prohibiting their citizens from any activities that would disturb the wreck, in particular the recovery of human remains or personal property. A similar agreement between the United States, Canada, France, and the United Kingdom concerning *Titanic* has just been drafted, providing guidelines for future archaeological investigation of the ship. This raises the possibility of nations cooperating in the future not only to prohibit salvage operations, but perhaps to find a forum for international cooperation, as was envisioned by Congress in its 1986 Titanic Memorial Act, which was intended to prohibit sale of the ship's artifacts in the United States. Clearly the last chapter has yet to be written on this subject.

—J.P.D.

Part 4

Wrecks within National Boundaries

In the early eighteenth century, the Dutch maritime lawyer Cornelis van Bynkershoeck wrote:

. . .wherefore on the whole it seems a better rule that the control of the land over the sea extends as far as cannon will carry; that is to say as far as we seem to have both command and possession. I have to say in general terms that the control from the land ends where the power of man's weapons end.

Such reasoning led to the establishment of territorial seas, traditionally defined as maritime belts extending three miles from a nation's coastline. More recently a number of nations, including the United States, have extended their territorial seas to 12 miles, while others have claimed a 200-mile limit, a distance not recognized in international law.

Beyond territorial seas there are continental shelves. The United Nations Convention of the Continental Shelf (1958) allows for "exploration . . . and exploitation of natural resources" found there to a depth of 600 feet. The International Law Association, a United Nations advisory group, has noted, however, that "it is clearly understood that the rights in question do not cover objects such as wrecked ships and their cargoes (including bullion) lying on the seabed or covered by the sands of the subsoil." Nonetheless some nations, including Cyprus, Australia, Norway, and the Seychelles, have passed laws claiming their right to shipwrecks and other cultural resources on the continental shelf.

Some nations—the United States, Canada, and Australia, for example—have delegated authority over territorial seas to subnational political units. The U.S. Submerged Lands Act of 1953 grants states control of such lands within the three-mile limit. The Abandoned Shipwreck Act of 1987 asserts federal ownership of submerged wrecks and then delegates ownership and authority to the states.

National archaeological and historic preservation laws must contend with Admiralty Law, an internationally accepted body of legal opinion pertaining to all things done upon and relating to the sea. In the United States admiralty jurisdiction is vested in the district courts, subject to appeal to a circuit court of appeals and the Supreme Court. Admiralty Law describes salvage as a "service voluntarily rendered in relieving property from an impending peril at sea by a person under no legal obligation to do so." There has been considerable debate, particularly in the United States, over whether culturally significant shipwrecks and antiquities should be viewed as in "impending peril" and hence subject to Admiralty Law. The debate is now moot in territorial waters since many nations have excluded antiquities and historic wrecks from provisions of Admiralty Law. The last two countries to allow such laws to apply to culturally significant or historic wrecks in their territorial waters were the United States and South Africa. The U.S. changed its position with the passage of the Abandoned Shipwreck Act. While archaeologists generally approve of the act, they would like to see it extended to America's recently established 12-mile limit, rather than the original three-mile boundary.

—J. P. D.

35,000-Year-Old Artifacts Repatriated in Tasmania

Claiming that materials recovered from Pleistocene and Early Holocene archaeological sites are of "great spiritual and psychological importance" to their community, the Tasmanian Aboriginal Land Council (TALC) has forced archaeologists at La Trobe U (Melbourne, Australia) to return 5 assemblages for possible reburial before scientific analyses were completed. According to the TALC, reburial of the assemblages in their respective sites would "heal the wounds" created by their excavation.

TALC took archaeologists Tim Murray and Jim Allen (School of Archaeology, La Trobe U) to court, but before the case could be tried the Tasmanian Minister for Environment and Land Management took possession under his authority and repatriated the excavated materials back to Tasmania. The sites—none of which was known to Tasmanian Aborigines prior to their excavation in 1987–89—consisted of "garbage discarded by humans" and materials "unassociated with human occupation"—animal bones found in the feces of Tasmanian devils, regurgitated owl pellets and the bones and shells of naturally deposited animals and snails. No human bones, ornaments or art that might be considered sacred were found among the human debris, which contained only the remnants of food, charcoal and discarded stone and bone tools, with the debitage from their manufacture. Discounting a single contact site (a white settlement farm that contained some Aboriginal tools made

of glass), only one of the other 4 sites involved in this suite has had any human occupation in the last 12,000 years. The whole region of Tasmania containing these sites has, in fact, been unoccupied by humans throughout this time, for at the end of the last ice age the region was covered by temperate rain forest, which drove out both the game and human inhabitants.

FIRST HUMAN ARRIVALS

One of the 4 sites studied by Murray and Allen was first occupied approximately 35,000 radiocarbon years ago, and two others about 30,000 years ago. Each is a limestone cave or shelter with excellent preservation of organic materials and rich with stone tools and faunal remains; although the excavated samples have been small in volume, some 400,000 items are now described in the database. Since all three sites were abandoned by 12,000 BP, they have also remained undisturbed by humans throughout the Holocene and represent 3 of the 6 earliest known in Tasmania (including the oldest). Despite the fact that the Tasmanian sites are located 43° south of the equator and at the opposite end of the northern shores of Australia that saw the first human arrivals, they are among the oldest sites in the continent. The speed with which the entire continent—about the size of the US—was colonized by hunter-gatherers, in addition to their

high latitudes, makes them particularly valuable to scientists. At the height of the last ice age these sites were only a few kilometers from glaciers and barely 1,000 km north of the permanent Antarctic ice cap. That hunter-gatherers had managed to adapt so quickly to periglacial conditions after arriving in Australia from tropical Southeast Asia—apparently without the benefit of sewn clothing and sophisticated tools and weapons—offers new insights into late Pleistocene human adaptability and may hold clues to understanding other colonizations, including that into the Americas.

PERMISSION AND EMPOWERMENT

The issue over repatriation surfaced in 1993 during the process of seeking extension of the La Trobe team's permit to hold the material interstate. Each of the 5 sites had been legally excavated under permits issued by the Tasmanian Department of Parks, Wildlife and Heritage (hereafter referred to as Parks). Prior to 1990, such permits were customarily issued for three years—to cover both excavation and analysis. The Aboriginal community was not only formally consulted before granting permits, all excavations employed at least one Aboriginal representative empowered to stop excavation should human skeletal material be found. After 1900 and the formation of TALC, permits were reduced to one year only. Although these time limits were placed on the permits, Parks had never enforced the limits, and many assemblages now out of permit time have yet to be returned by various university departments. La Trobe's request for extension was the first occasion any extension or renewal had been sought since the relevant act was promulgated in 1975. Parks referred the request to TALC, which recommended the minister not extend La Trobe's permit; in their view, sufficient time had elapsed for completion of the scientific analysis. In advising the minister, senior Parks officials claimed that "the advantages of empowering the Aboriginal community outweighed the scientific loss." Despite the minister handing these collections back to TALC last November, there has been no move by TALC or Parks to force the return of other Tasmanian archaeological collections from elsewhere in Australia. Allen rejects notions of personal victimization: "We were just in the wrong place at the wrong time. TALC wanted to demonstrate political power and Parks took the easy option to accede to their

demands. Whether this will change general Parks policy in terms of their responsibility to manage and safeguard Tasmanian sites and heritage is yet to be seen."

RESPONSIBLE OWNERSHIP

The Tasmanian case has generated extensive press, radio and television coverage in Australia, as well as discussion in the international scientific community (See V. Morrell, "Who Owns the Past?" *Science,* June 1995). Murray and Allen agree that the category of "culturally significant material heritage" should be extended—particularly in Tasmania, where all full-blood Tasmanians were gone within the first 80 years of European settlement—to include archaeological collections because "they provide the main cultural link between modern Tasmanian Aborigines and the Aboriginal past with which they identify." These archaeologists note, however, the vulnerability of scientific research in a politically charged environment. Murray

and Allen make the case for responsible ownership. "Irreversible decisions such as those to destroy cultural property should not rest with any organization which is responsible only to itself and subject to no legislative constraints." This case also raises the question of ownership when dealing with an interrupted time-depth of 30,000–35,000 years. Murray and Allen argue that materials from caves that have no evidence of human activity for the past 12,000 years but that provide information on some of the earliest human habitation in the Pacific become the "heritage of all living humans, not merely TALC." Moreover, they argue that destruction (through reburial) of these unique documents illuminating our common human history denies the future access to the past, and as such is a form of censorship. [*Based on "The Forced Repatriation of Cultural Properties to Tasmania," T. Murray and J. Allen. Antiquity 60(195):871–874. Interested readers may also wish to consult J. Allen, "A Short History of the Tasmanian Affair," Australian Archaeology, 41 (December):43–48, 1995.*]

Beirut Digs Out

Developers vie with archaeologists over the future of a 5,000-year-old city.

Marilyn Raschka

Marilyn Raschka is a journalist and writer who has lived in the Middle East for more than 25 years.

According to Lebanese folklore, Beirut was destroyed and rebuilt seven times during its 5,000-year history. When the recent civil war ended in late 1990, the Lebanese army took possession of the downtown or "old city," where much of the fighting had taken place. As a journalist, I was invited to document the city's eighth destruction.

When I first moved to Lebanon in 1970 to do graduate work in linguistics at the American University of Beirut, the city's huge Martyrs' Square, honoring those who had rebelled against Ottoman rule in 1915, teemed with vehicles, people, goods, and produce, and the din was deafening. In those days I gave little thought to the city's venerable buildings, captivated as I was by the color and energy of Beirut's commerce. The old city center was only a stage. By 1990 that stage, along with the social fabric of Lebanon, was in ruins, its historic churches, mosques, and public buildings ravaged by 15 years of war during which 150,000 people were killed, one-third of the population fled their homes, thousands were maimed, and thousands more simply disappeared. Survivors of the war were horrified at the destruction. "God what a loss," they would say, adding "Inshallah [God willing], we will rebuild." Some talked about a unique opportunity to excavate ancient Beirut, to locate its Phoenician roots and Roman past. Where were the city's Bronze Age ramparts? Where was the famed Roman law school mentioned by the eminent theologian Gregory Thaumaturgus in A.D. 239? For two centuries the law school flourished, and the reputation of Beirut's jurists spread through the provinces. Others spoke of the pressing need to create a city that once again would be the pride of the eastern Mediterranean. Last January, having been on family business in the United States for a year, I returned to Beirut to see firsthand how both sides, archaeologists and developers, were progressing.

I found both conservation and rebuilding in full swing. (Israel's bombing of targets on the outskirts of Beirut and brief blockade of the city's harbor had little effect on the rebuilding.) The bat-

(MARILYN RASCHKA)

Some of Beirut's buildings from the French Mandate period (1919–1943) are being restored.

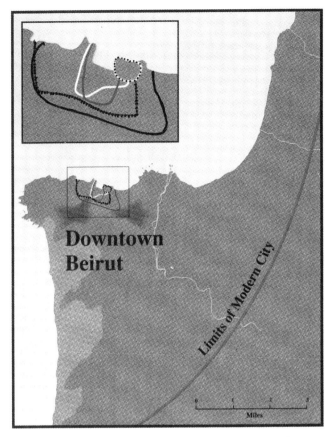

(LYNDA D'AMICO)

For most of its history Beirut has existed within the boundaries of its modern downtown, indicated by striped line, the area most affected by infrastructure work. Dotted line marks ancient tell, the earliest area settled; white line extent of the Middle Bronze Age city, an important trade center; black line the Roman and Byzantine periods when the city was known as Berytus; and gray line the medieval fortification walls.

tered facade of Lebanon's National Museum had been restored. The repository of the country's most prized antiquities, the museum had stood at the worst of all possible places—the city's Green Line, the infamous divide between warring factions (see ARCHAEOLOGY, January/February 1994). During the war the museum had to be abandoned. Smaller treasures were packed and hidden in safe houses such as the Central Bank of Lebanon. Cases of pottery and terracotta figurines were secured in the museum behind sealed doors. Statues and sarcophagi too heavy to be moved—a second- or third-century A.D. statue of Hygeia, a goddess of health, and the thirteenth-century B.C. sarcophagus of King Ahiram of Byblos—were encased in concrete blocks and cement. Today

they have been freed from their protective casings and await the museum's reopening.

I asked Helga Seeden of the American University of Beirut about her excavations. She told me of her finds in the extensive market or souk area of downtown Beirut: 3 to 4 million potsherds, 2,000 Roman lamps, some 7,000 coins of the Hellenistic through Ottoman periods, nearly 1,200 square yards of mosaics from both private and public Byzantine establishments, and 110 pounds of glass fragments from Roman to Ottoman times. She had also unearthed evidence of a flourishing silk industry: seven basins where the silkworm cocoons had been washed and threads reeled. According to nineteenth-century documents, Ottoman Beirut was sur-

rounded by mulberry trees on whose leaves silkworms fed. Seeden cleaned several of the basins for preservation in place while others were sacrificed as she dug deeper, exposing mosaic floors of Byzantine residences. Nearby she found Byzantine shop porticoes with alphabetic addresses worked into their mosaic floors. The "alpha" shop was found first. Beta, delta, gamma, and epsilon soon emerged.

At one point Seeden was approached by an onlooker with more than the usual curiosity. "I can help you when you excavate there," he said, pointing to where his own shop had once stood. In the 1960s he and his neighbor had found two Roman column drums while digging a basement storage room. One provided a convenient foundation for a wall; the other was put down an old well, where Seeden did find it.

In 1990 bulldozers clearing debris near this site uncovered the domed shrine of an eminent Mamluk religious scholar, Ibn 'Iraq al-Dimashqi, dating to 1517. A square, brick, arched sanctuary, it served as a hostel or inn for the followers of the scholar and as a private religious school, according to the sixteenth-century Arab historian Ibn Tulun. Today it is the only standing late Mamluk monument in Beirut. The Mamluks, an elite military corps, had overthrown their Egyptian masters in 1250 and ruled over Egypt and its territories, including Lebanon, until they were overcome by the Ottomans in 1517. Other buildings, constructed during Ottoman times, had hidden the shrine. Here Seeden also found elaborately constructed Ottoman water and drainage systems, neatly fitted ceramic pipes so efficient that some had remained in use until they were demolished during recent reconstruction work.

The war-ravaged area being rebuilt covers 282 acres of downtown Beirut. Another 114 acres of reclaimed land on the seafront will also be developed. To do this efficiently, the Lebanese Parliament in 1992 created the Lebanese Company for the Development and Reconstruction of Beirut Central District, or SOLIDERE, the French acronym for the giant real estate company. First on SOLIDERE's list of priorities was to clear out the rubble of war and raze hun-

(MARWAN NAAMANI)

Lebanese restorer mends ancient vessels found during recent excavations.

the French mandate in 1933, require archaeology before development. He described his dealings with SOLIDERE as "hard, hard discussions," adding "I told them, 'You have such an investment here, so if you want it done more rapidly you will have to pay for the archaeological survey and excavation.' "

To date SOLIDERE has spent $4 million for archaeological work. It has paid for backhoes and bulldozers to clear the modern rubble, for foreign archaeology teams, and for computer systems and programs with which to record the sites and finds. It has financed exhibits and publications, including a brochure called *Paths of History* that is given free to the many visitors the downtown project attracts. SOLIDERE has three guides who conduct tours of downtown archaeology for schools and the public. According to the Master Plan, on display at a kiosk downtown, sizable areas will be turned into archaeological parks. Parts of parking garages and building lots are earmarked for displaying finds in place. A museum dedicated to the history of Beirut is being discussed.

dreds of condemned buildings. Some 308 structures will be restored because of their architectural, historical, or religious significance, including ornate buildings from the French Mandate (1919–1943) and the Omari mosque (1291), a converted twelfth-century crusader cathedral. In November 1994 a contractor began working on new infrastructure—water mains, sewers, electricity and communications lines, and underground parking lots—part of SOLIDERE's vision of Beirut as a carefully planned modern city. In doing so the contractor dug into the city's ancient past.

I spoke about archaeology and the rebuilding program with Michel Eddé, Lebanon's minister of higher education and culture, whose ministry's responsibilities include making decisions about archaeological work in Beirut and throughout the country. A politician from a wealthy, well-connected family, Eddé has life-or-death power over the city's cultural heritage. Naturally he attracts his share of complaints. Critics say he wants control of the archaeology and credit for the finds but cannot finance much beyond exploratory excavations. He told me how no one had expected such important discoveries so soon in the downtown digs and how excited the Lebanese press and people were about their patrimony. His greatest

pride, he said, was reserved for "our young archaeologists who will be the most wonderful product of the archaeological work." When asked who was responsible for protecting archaeological remains, he responded that his country's antiquities laws, instituted under

(MARILYN RASCHKA)

This portion of a main thoroughfare, the *cardo maximus,* of Roman Beirut, center, will be preserved in place.

(MARILYN RASCHKA)

Archaeologists compete with backhoes as time runs out for Byzantine period shops.

The entire project is to be completed by the year 2018, when SOLIDERE's 25-year charter from the government expires. Its cost has been estimated at $2.4 billion, of which the $4 million expended on archaeology is a mere 0.17 percent. (In Athens, the Greek government spent about $19.5 million for salvage archaeology in advance of the city's new subway.) SOLIDERE raised most of its money through a sale of shares, which netted $650 million.

When SOLIDERE contracted out the huge infrastructure part of the project, it set a four-year deadline, placing archaeology and development on a collision course. To make matters worse, it offered a 20 percent bonus if the work was finished in three rather than four years. SOLIDERE hired Dutch archaeologist Hans Curvers to work on site, communicating with its in-house archaeologist, Harith Boustany, via two-way radio. If archaeological remains were found in the path of demolition equipment, Curvers would evaluate the finds, determine

how much delay, if any, to impose, and make final decisions with Boustany about excavation, preservation, or destruction of the site.

The UNESCO representative in Lebanon, Kacem Bensalah, like Eddé, assured me that archaeology takes precedence over development, and that "excavating Beirut will help change the mentality of the Lebanese" and heal the wounds of the war by restoring a sense of national unity. He recalled, however, a report issued after a visit by UNESCO secretary general Federico Mayor in 1995, which concluded that the archaeological "work was of good quality, but the overall plan was insufficient" to cope with the magnitude of the site.

As of last January some 50 sites, from Phoenician to Ottoman, had been identified. When I visited Helga Seeden's site I was astonished to find that the Mamluk shrine was there but everything else was gone. No cocoon basins, no reused Roman columns, no walls, no hint of the Ottoman drainage

system whose pipes had appeared on the cover of a SOLIDERE-funded brochure on downtown archaeology. All had been bulldozed during infrastructure work. Nearby a team of archaeologists was removing the Byzantine alpha shop mosaic. They said they were seven days behind schedule. Whose schedule? The contractor's. Delay was costing him money. As if to spur them on, a backhoe tore at the earth just yards away. A few days later I returned to the site. No trace of the shops remained. The bulldozers had been given the go-ahead.

Only one site had enjoyed immunity from this fate—the area thought to contain the Roman law school and dug by Muntaha Saghieh of Lebanese University. Funding for its excavation has come from SOLIDERE, UNESCO, and Prime Minister Hariri. A well-preserved set of Roman Corinthian columns was found in the 1950s in this area, a short distance from historic Greek Orthodox and Greek Catholic churches. It was here that one of the main Roman thoroughfares, the *cardo maximus,* was discovered. The archaeology here is meticulous—urban archaeology at its finest. If anything remains of Beirut's once-famous fifth-century A.D. law school, it will be found here. The high quality of the remains—columns, a Roman cryptoporticus (removed last fall to make room for an underground parking lot), and a Roman-Byzantine basilica excavated in 1927—suggests buildings of consequence. In 1906 a funerary monument with an inscription naming Patricius, a sixth-century A.D. professor at the law school, was found here. Artifacts are stored on site in a secure building, and information on the finds is archived on computer data bases as fast as the students can feed it in. Warned in advance of the existence of major sites, SOLIDERE is glad to have them remain as archaeological parks. But just yards from this model site is a pile of Roman column shafts yanked from the earth during infrastructure work. When I asked about them, the archaeologists working at the site only shrugged their shoulders.

The location of Bronze Age Beirut, near the modern port, has been known since the 1950s, when the foundation

5. THE NEW POLITICS OF ARCHAEOLOGY

(MARILYN RASCHKA)

Archaeologists removed mosaic from a Byzantine shop before bulldozers and backhoes moved in. The site was later demolished.

(MARILYN RASCHKA)

Shops in Beirut's Byzantine market were identified by alphabetic addresses in their mosaic floors. This mosaic is from the "alpha" shop.

was dug for the first multistory department store in the downtown area. At the time four Canaanite rock-cut tombs were unearthed by bulldozers, studied and then destroyed. The Bronze Age city lies nearby and is being excavated by Leila Badr, curator of the Archaeological Museum of the American University of Beirut. Finds there include huge amounts of pottery, murex shells from the purple dye industry, Canaanite and

Phoenician city ramparts, a Bronze Age tomb, and the remains of a crusader fortress. Winter rains were pounding sections of a 3000 B.C. mud-brick wall found near the site when I visited. Little time, money, or energy is available to maintain and preserve exposed remains. One section of wall had been covered with plastic sheeting that tore loose in the first winter storm. Obviously heritage management is more than plastic

sheeting, but the question of who will manage and finance this aspect of Beirut's archaeology has gone unanswered. Happily, the Canaanite-Phoenician city site was given protected status this past April. No further urban work will be done on the site and SOLIDERE's Master Plan will be amended to preserve it in place.

Early this year the seawall of the Ottoman port was uncovered by bulldozers as they dug a trench for more infrastructure. Only salvage archaeology was carried out there, and the wall was later demolished. The Canaanite (Bronze Age) and Phoenician (Iron Age) city walls on George Haddad Street suffered a similar fate. The street appears on old maps as two blocks long and running through the red-light district. SOLIDERE's Master Plan called for a highway connecting the city with what will be the new seafront, and George Haddad Street was chosen as the route. In November 1994 bulldozers dug a trench as they worked their way from the sea toward the street's original two blocks, cutting into large wall-like structures. Digging stopped but was resumed in February by which time Lebanese University archaeologist Naji Karam had been assigned to the site. On February 24 at 2:30 P.M. archaeologists left the site having told the bulldozer operators not to come close to the wall they were excavating. Representatives of both UNESCO and the Department of Antiquities reiterated the warning, which was in accordance with the law. When the archaeologists returned the next morning they found that a 20-foot stretch of the Canaanite wall had been destroyed.

The finds in Beirut have been fantastic, providing an unbroken archaeological record of the city's past. A proposed City of Beirut Museum may one day house a Canaanite jar burial with the skeleton of a young girl wearing a necklace of gold and carnelian beads; local Canaanite pottery and ancient imports, including an Egyptian jar with the name of Ramses II; a Hellenistic sculpture thought to represent a deity; a bronze coin of Roman Emperor Galerius Maximianus (A.D. 305-311); Byzantine pilgrim flasks for holy water; and Mamluk and Ottoman glazed pottery.

But the losses have been staggering. Crusader fortress walls were bulldozed even though the site was earmarked as a candidate for preservation in place. Ten Iron Age shaft tombs, two of which were found intact, stand in the way of infrastructure and will be removed. Archaeologists have found piles of crushed murex shells, industrial waste from Phoenician purple-dye extraction. The stone chute where the crushed shells were thrown after processing was excavated but will now be bulldozed. Groups of young student archaeologists talked to me in private about their concerns, but not until the day before I left did I hear criticism from anyone directing excavations. Naji Karam had written an article in the Arabic daily *An-Nahar* (January 17, 1996) criticizing the government for letting SOLIDERE, a private company, take over the downtown area, and accusing SOLIDERE of rushing the work to increase its profits. "The endless struggle between the developer and the archaeologist," he wrote, "has been faced by other countries before us and was solved in an acceptable way. More than once SOLIDERE has told us that the archaeology that they have come across is not of a high enough cultural quality, and that archaeologists will not be allowed to put up obstacles to development. We must condemn archaeology by bulldozer. . . ." Karam called for a temporary halt to the development work to provide adequate time and resources for archaeologists to conduct proper excavations, and to allow the Master Plan to be redesigned to preserve more sites and monuments in place.

It is unlikely that anyone will pay much attention to Karam. After the infrastructure is complete, individual developers will buy lots and begin building. While Eddé and others insist that archaeology will come first, the reality is that politics and money are playing a disproportionate role in the rebuilding of Beirut, and will continue to do so.

FURTHER READING

Recommended are M. Raschka, "Salvaging a Scarred Land," ARCHAEOLOGY 47:1 (January/February 1994), pp. 64–67, and "Beirut Discoveries," ARCHAEOLOGY 48:2 (March/April 1995), p. 18; and W. A. Ward, "Archaeology in Lebanon in the Twentieth Century," *Biblical Archaeologist* 57:2 (June 1994), pp. 66–85.

Germany's Nazi Past
The Past as Propaganda

*How Hitler's archaeologists distorted European prehistory to
justify racist and territorial goals.*

Bettina Arnold

The manipulation of the past for political purposes has been a common theme in history. Consider Darius I (521–486 B.C.), one of the most powerful rulers of the Achaemenid, or Persian, empire. The details of his accession to power, which resulted in the elimination of the senior branch of his family, are obscured by the fact that we have only his side of the story, carved on the cliff face of Behistun in Iran. The list of his victories, and by association his right to rule, are the only remaining version of the truth. Lesson number one: If you are going to twist the past for political ends, eliminate rival interpretations.

The use of the past for propaganda is also well documented in more recent contexts. The first-century Roman historian Tacitus produced an essay titled "On the Origin and Geography of Germany." It is less a history or ethnography of the German tribes than a moral tract or political treatise. The essay was intended to contrast the debauched and degenerate Roman Empire with the virtuous German people, who embodied the uncorrupted morals of old Rome. Objective reporting was not the goal of Tacitus's *Germania;* the manipulation of the facts was considered justified if it had the desired effect of contrasting past Roman glory with present Roman decline. Ironically, this particular piece of historical propa-

ganda was eventually appropriated by a regime notorious for its use and abuse of the past for political, imperialist, and racist purposes: the Third Reich.

The National Socialist regime in Germany fully appreciated the propaganda value of the past, particularly of prehistoric archaeology, and exploited it with characteristic efficiency. The fact that German prehistoric archaeology had been largely ignored before Hitler's rise to power in 1933 made the appropriation of the past for propaganda that much easier. The concept of the *Kulturkreis,* pioneered by the linguist-turned-prehistorian Gustav Kossinna in the 1920s and defined as the identification of ethnic regions on the basis of excavated material culture, lent theoretical support to Nazi expansionist aims in central and eastern Europe. Wherever an artifact of a type designated as "Germanic" was found, the land was declared to be ancient Germanic territory. Applied to prehistoric archaeology, this perspective resulted in the neglect or distortion of data that did not directly apply to Germanic peoples. During the 1930s scholars whose specialty was provincial Roman archaeology were labeled *Römlinge* by the extremists and considered anti-German. The Römisch Germanische Kommission in Mainz, founded in 1907, was the object of numerous defamatory attacks, first by Kossinna and

later by Alfred Rosenberg and his organization. Rosenberg, a Nazi ideologue, directed the Amt Rosenberg, which conducted ethnic, cultural, and racial research.

Altered prehistory also played an important role in rehabilitating German self-respect after the humiliating defeat of 1918. The dedication of the 1921 edition of Kossinna's seminal work *German Prehistory: A Preeminently National Discipline* reads: "To the German people, as a building block in the reconstruction of the externally as well as internally disintegrated fatherland."

According to Nazi doctrine, the Germanic culture of northern Europe was responsible for virtually all major intellectual and technological achievements of Western civilization. Maps that appeared in archaeological publications between 1933 and 1945 invariably showed the Germanic homeland as the center of diffusionary waves, bringing civilization to less developed cultures to the south, west, and east. Hitler presented his own views on this subject in a dinner-table monologue in which he referred to the Greeks as Germans who had survived a northern natural catastrophe and evolved a highly developed culture in southern contexts. Such wishful thinking was supported by otherwise reputable archaeologists. The *Research Report of the Reichsbund for German Prehistory,*

July to December 1941, for example, reported the nine-week expedition of the archaeologist Hans Reinerth and a few colleagues to Greece, where they claimed to have discovered major new evidence of Indogermanic migration to Greece during Neolithic times.

This perspective was ethnocentric, racist, and genocidal. Slavic peoples occupying what had once been, on the basis of the distribution of archaeological remains, Germanic territory, were to be relocated or exterminated to supply true Germans with *Lebensraum* (living space). When the new Polish state was created in 1919, Kossinna published an article, "The German Ostmark, Home Territory of the Germans," which used archaeological evidence to support Germany's claim to the area. Viewed as only temporarily occupied by racially inferior "squatters," Poland and Czechoslovakia could be reclaimed for "racially pure" Germans.

Prehistoric archaeologists in Germany, who felt they had been ignored, poorly funded, and treated as second-class citizens by colleagues specializing in the more honored disciplines of classical and Near Eastern archaeology, now seemed to have everything to gain by an association with the rising Nazi party. Between 1933, the year of Hitler's accession to power, and 1935, eight new chairs were created in German prehistory, and funding became available for prehistoric excavations across Germany and eastern Europe on an unprecedented scale. Numerous institutes came into being during this time, such as the Institute for Prehistory in Bonn in 1938. Museums for protohistory were established, and prehistoric collections were brought out of storage and exhibited, in many cases for the first time. Institutes for rune research were created to study the *futhark*, or runic alphabet in use in northern Europe from about the third to the thirteenth centuries A.D. Meanwhile, the Römisch Germanisches Zentral Museum in Mainz became the Zentral Museum für Deutsche Vor- und Frühgeschichte in 1939. (Today it has its pre-war title once again.)

Open-air museums like the reconstructed Neolithic and Bronze Age lake settlements at Unteruhldingen on Lake Constanz were intended to popularize prehistory. An archaeological film series, produced and directed by the prehistorian Lothar Zotz, included titles like *Threatened by the Steam Plow, Germany's Bronze Age, The Flames of Prehistory,* and *On the Trail of the Eastern Germans.* The popular journals such as *Die Kunde (The Message),* and *Germanen-Erbe (Germanic Heritage)* proliferated. The latter publication was produced by the Ahnenerbe ("Ancestor History") organization, run as a personal project of Reichsführer-SS and chief of police Heinrich Himmler and funded by interested Germans to research, excavate, and restore real and imagined Germanic cultural relics. Himmler's interests in mysticism and the occult extended to archaeology; SS archaeologists were sent out in the wake of invading German forces to track down important archaeological finds and antiquities to be transported back to the Reich. It was this activity that inspired Steven Spielberg's *Raiders of the Lost Ark.*

The popular journals contained abundant visual material. One advertisement shows the reconstruction of a Neolithic drum from a pile of meaningless sherds. The text exhorts readers to "keep your eyes open, for every *Volksgenosse* [fellow German] can contribute to this important national project! Do not assume that a ceramic vessel is useless because it falls apart during excavation. Carefully preserve even the smallest fragment!" An underlined sentence emphasizes the principal message: "Every single find is important because it represents a document of our ancestors!"

Amateur organizations were actively recruited by appeals to patriotism. The membership flyer for the official National Confederation for German Prehistory (*Reichsbund für Deutsche Vorgeschichte*), under the direction of Hans Reinerth of the Amt Rosenberg, proclaimed: "Responsibility with respect to our indigenous prehistory must again fill every German with pride!" The organization stated its goals as "the interpretation and dissemination of unfalsified knowledge regarding the history and cultural achievements of our northern Germanic ancestors on German and foreign soil."

For Himmler objective science was not the aim of German prehistoric archaeology. Hermann Rauschning, an early party member who became disillusioned with the Nazis and left Germany before the war, quotes Himmler as saying: "The one and only thing that matters to us, and the thing these people are paid for by the State, is to have ideas of history that strengthen our people in their necessary national pride. In all this troublesome business we are only interested in one thing—to project into the dim and distant past the picture of our nation as we envisage it for the future. Every bit of Tacitus in his *Germania* is tendentious stuff. Our teaching of German origins has depended for centuries on a falsification. We are entitled to impose one of our own at any time."

Meanwhile archaeological evidence that did not conform to Nazi dogma was ignored or suppressed. A good example is the controversy surrounding the Externsteine, a natural sandstone formation near Horn in northern Germany. In the twelfth century Benedictine monks from the monastery in nearby Paderborn carved a system of chambers into the rock faces of the Externsteine. In the mid-1930s a contingent of SS Ahnenerbe researchers excavated at the site in an attempt to prove its significance as the center of the Germanic universe, a kind of Teutonic mecca. The excavators, led by Julius Andree, an archaeologist with questionable credentials and supported by Hermann Wirth, one of the founders of the SS Ahnenerbe, were looking for the remains of an early Germanic temple at the Externsteine, where they claimed a cult of solar worshipers had once flourished. The site was described in numerous publications as a monument to German unity and the glorious Germanic past, despite the fact that no convincing evidence of a temple or Germanic occupation of the site was ever found.

So preposterous were the claims made by Andree, Wirth, and their associates that numerous mainstream archaeologists openly questioned the findings of the investigators who became popularly known as *German omanen* or "Germanomaniacs." Eventually Himmler and the Ahnenerbe organization disowned the project, but not before several hundred books and pamphlets on the alleged cult site had been published.

By 1933 the Nazis had gone a step further, initiating a movement whose goal was to replace all existing religious denominations with a new pseudo-pagan state religion based loosely on Germanic mythology, solar worship, nature cults, and a Scandinavian people's assembly or *thing,* from which the new movement derived its name. Central to the movement were open-air theaters or *Thingstätten,* where festivals, military ceremonies, and morality plays, known as *Thingspiele,* were to be staged. To qualify as a Thingstätte, evidence of significant Germanic occupation of the site had to be documented. There was considerable competition among municipalities throughout Germany for this honor. Twelve Thingstätten had been dedicated by September 1935, including one on the summit of the Heiligenberg in Heidelberg.

The Heiligenberg was visited sporadically during the Neolithic, possibly for ritual purposes; there is no evidence of permanent occupation. It was densely settled during the Late Bronze Age (1200–750 B.C.), and a double wall-and-ditch system was built there in the Late Iron Age (200 B.C. to the Roman occupation), when it was a hillfort settlement. Two provincial Roman watchtowers, as well as several Roman dedicatory inscriptions, statue bases, and votive stones, have been found at the site.

When excavations in the 1930s failed to produce evidence of Germanic occupation the Heiligenberg was granted Thingstätte status on the basis of fabricated evidence in the published excavation reports. Ironically, most of the summit's prehistoric deposits were destroyed in the course of building the

open-air arena. The Heiligenberg Thingstätte actually held only one Thingspiel before the Thing movement was terminated. Sensing the potential for resistance from German Christians, the Ministry of Propaganda abandoned the whole concept in 1935. Today the amphitheater is used for rock concerts.

Beyond its convenience for propaganda and as justification for expansion into countries like Czechoslovakia and Poland, the archaeological activities of the Amt Rosenberg and Himmler's Ahnenerbe were just so much window dressing for the upper echelons of the party. There was no real respect for the past or its remains. While party prehistorians like Reinerth and Andree distorted the facts, the SS destroyed archaeological sites like Biskupin in Poland. Until Germany's fortunes on the eastern front suffered a reversal in 1944, the SS Ahnenerbe conducted excavations at Biskupin, one of the best-preserved Early Iron Age (600–400 B.C.) sites in all of central Europe. As the troops retreated, they were ordered to demolish as much of the site's preserved wooden fortifications and structures as possible.

Not even Hitler was totally enthusiastic about Himmler's activities. He is quoted by Albert Speer, his chief architect, as complaining: "Why do we call the whole world's attention to the fact that we have no past? It's bad enough that the Romans were erecting great buildings when our forefathers were still living in mud huts; now Himmler is starting to dig up these villages of mud huts and enthusing over every potsherd and stone axe he finds. All we prove by that is that we were still throwing stone hatchets and crouching around open fires when Greece and Rome had already reached the highest stage of culture. We should really do our best to keep quiet about this past. Instead Himmler makes a great fuss about it all. The present-day Romans must be having a laugh at these revelations."

"Official" involvement in archaeology consisted of visits by Himmler and various SS officers to SS-funded and staffed excavations, like the one on the

Erdenburg in the Rhineland, or press shots of Hitler and Goebbels viewing a reconstructed "Germanic" Late Bronze Age burial in its tree-trunk coffin, part of the 1934 "Deutsches Volk—Deutsche Arbeit" exhibition in Berlin. Party appropriation of prehistoric data was evident in the use of Indo-European and Germanic design symbols in Nazi uniforms and regalia. The double lightning bolt, symbol of Himmler's SS organization, was adapted from a Germanic rune. The swastika is an Indo-European sun symbol which appears in ceramic designs as early as the Neolithic in western Europe and continues well into early medieval times.

German archaeologists during this period fall into three general categories: those who were either true believers or self-serving opportunists; those (the vast majority) who accepted without criticism the appropriation and distortion of prehistoric archaeology; and those who openly opposed these practices.

Victims of the regime were persecuted on the basis of race or political views, and occasionally both. Gerhard Bersu, who had trained a generation of post–World War I archaeologists in the field techniques of settlement archaeology, was prematurely retired from the directorship of the Römisch Germanische Kommission in 1935. His refusal to condone or conduct research tailored to Nazi ideological requirements, in addition to his rejection of the racist Kossinna school, ended his career as a prehistorian until after World War II. The official reason given for the witch-hunt, led by Hans Reinerth under the auspices of the Amt Rosenberg, was Bersu's Jewish heritage. By 1950 Bersu was back in Germany, again directing the Römisch Germanische Kommission.

It should be noted that some sound work was accomplished during this period despite political interference. The vocabulary of field reports carefully conformed to the dictates of funding sources, but the methodology was usually unaffected. Given time this would have changed as politically motivated terms and concepts altered the intellectual vocabulary of the discipline. In 1935, for example, the entire prehistoric and early historic chronologies were officially renamed: the Bronze and pre-Roman Iron Ages became the "Early Germanic period," the Roman Iron Age the "Climax Germanic period," the Migration period the "Late Germanic period," and everything from the Carolingians to the thirteenth century the "German Middle Ages."

It is easy to condemn the men and women who were part of the events that transformed the German archaeological community between 1933 and 1945. It is much more difficult to understand the choices they made or avoided in the social and political contexts of the time. Many researchers who began as advocates of Reinerth's policies in the Amt Rosenberg and Himmler's Ahnenerbe organization later became disenchanted. Others, who saw the system as a way to develop and support prehistory as a discipline, were willing to accept the costs of the Faustian bargain it offered. The benefits were real, and continue to be felt to this day in the institutions and programs founded between 1933 and 1945.

The paralysis felt by many scholars from 1933 to 1945 continued to affect research in the decades after the war. Most scholars who were graduate students during the 12-year period had to grapple with a double burden: a humiliating defeat and the disorienting experience of being methodologically "deprogrammed." Initially there was neither time nor desire to examine the

reasons for the Nazi prostitution of archaeology. Unfortunately prehistoric archaeology is the only German social-science discipline that has still to publish a self-critical study of its role in the events of the 1930s and 1940s.

The reluctance of German archaeologists to come to terms with the past is a complex issue. German prehistoric archaeology is still a young discipline, and first came into its own as a result of Nazi patronage. There is therefore a certain feeling that any critical analysis of the motives and actions of the generation and the regime that engendered the discipline would be ungrateful at

---

The reluctance of German archaeologists to come to terms with the past is a complex issue.

---

best and at worst a betrayal of trust. The vast majority of senior German archaeologists, graduate students immediately after the war, went straight from the front lines to the universities, and their dissertation advisers were men whose careers had been determined by their connections within the Nazi party.

The German system of higher education is built upon close bonds of dependence and an almost medieval fealty between a graduate student and his or her dissertation advisor. These bonds are maintained even after the graduate student has embarked on an

academic career. Whistle-blowers are rare, since such action would amount to professional suicide. But in the past decade or so, most of the generation actively involved in archaeological research and teaching between 1933 and 1945 have died. Their knowledge of the personal intrigues and alliances that allowed the Nazi party machine to function has died with them. Nonetheless, there are indications that the current generation of graduate students is beginning to penetrate the wall of silence that has surrounded this subject since 1945. The remaining official documents and publications may allow at least a partial reconstruction of the role of archaeology in the rise and fall of the Nazi regime.

The future of prehistoric archaeology in the recently unified Germany will depend on an open confrontation with the past. Archaeologists in the former East Germany must struggle with the legacy of both Nazi and Communist manipulation of their discipline. Meanwhile, the legacy of the Faustian bargain struck by German archaeologists with the Nazi regime should serve as a cautionary tale beyond the borders of a unified Germany: Archaeological research funded wholly or in part by the state is vulnerable to state manipulation. The potential for political exploitation of the past seems to be greatest in countries experiencing internal instability. Germany in the years following World War I was a country searching for its own twentieth-century identity. Prehistoric archaeology was one means to that end.

Contemporary Archaeology

The origins of contemporary archaeology may be traced back to the nineteenth century. Several currents of thoughts and beliefs coalesced in that unique century. Some say it started with a Frenchman named Boucher de Perthes who found odd-shaped stones on his property, stones that could comfortably be held by a human hand. Undoubtedly, thousands of other people made such finds throughout history. But to Monsieur de Perthes, these stones suggested a novel meaning. He wondered if these odd rocks might not have been tools made by long-ago humans lost in the mists before history.

Other exciting changes were occurring in the epistemology of the nineteenth century that would soon lend credibility to this hypothesis. There was the publication of *On the Origin of Species* by Charles Darwin in 1859. In this book, which, by the way, never mentioned humans or any implied relationship they might have to apes, Darwin suggested a general process that became known as *natural selection*, wherein species could change gradually through time. This was a revolutionary idea because then even biologists believed that species were immutable. Now if species could change, the implication was that maybe even human beings (who were considered above nature) could change.

There was the concurrent emergence of the idea of *uniformitarianism,* which implied that Earth was old, very old, perhaps hundreds of thousands of years old. (It is, in fact, about 5 billion years old). With this idea, the revolutionary possibility that human beings could have existed before history became more plausible. Such a serious challenge to the established wisdom that Earth was only about 6,000 years old gave rise to a new age of speculation on the very meaning of being human.

The newly emerging science of paleontology and the discovery and recognition of extinct fossil species further challenged the elevated status of human beings. Nineteenth-century (and earlier) philosophers challenged the nature of humanity. Among the intellectuals of the Western world, the long held anthropocentrism of the Christian view gradually shifted to a more secular view of humankind as part and parcel with nature and, thus, subject to the rules of nature and natural events, without reference to a theology.

In was within the juxtaposition of these new philosophies and sciences in the nineteenth century that Boucher de Perthes let his hypothesis on the antiquity of his stone tools be known. Throughout the world, others answered that they too had found these same odd-shaped stones and had thought similar thoughts. The study of archaeology had begun.

As a science evolves, it naturally diversifies. In the case of archaeology, there is some concern now that as archaeologists continue toward greater diversity, they will specialize themselves right out of the mainstream of archaeology. However, as discussed in the overview of Unit 1, archaeology is a subfield of cultural anthropology, and the shared cultural concept keeps the field of archaeology united. That is not to deny that mainstream archaeology is now being pulled in many different directions.

However, these different directions may be viewed as an expansion of traditional archaeological pursuits.

In this unit, selections deal with the interest in the preservation, conservation, reconstruction, and transformation of archaeological sites into the present for the educational and aesthetic value of the sites themselves. Such is the direction of contemporary archaeology. Serious attention must be directed toward the practical aspects of the financing of archaeological endeavors and the incorporation of alternate sources of labor in these new political times.

Finally, who makes the moral judgments? What of the rights of developers, dam builders, and road builders? It is their livelihood to do their work even if it means destroying archaeological sites. Archaeology itself is also a potentially serious threat to archaeological sites. An archaeological site is a *nonrenewable* resource. Archaeological excavation is the systematic destruction of sites and their total ecological context. Anything overlooked, mislaid, not measured, or in some way not observed is a lost piece of the past. If the information is never shared (published), it is a complete loss. But unlike dam builders or those who construct roads, the goal of archaeologists is the recovery, comprehension, and preservation of these sites. From the time human beings picked up stones and made them into tools, we were holding microchips in our hands. And we have only just begun.

Looking Ahead: Challenge Questions

Why is an archaeological site defined as a *nonrenewable resource*?

What is conservation archaeology? Give several examples.

How do dams destroy archaeological sites and their ecological context?

Should dam building be stopped? Why or why not?

Discuss salvage archaeology. Give an example.

Should spectacular archaeological sites be preserved? Why or why not?

Discuss public archaeology. What motivates people to volunteer for archaeology digs?

The Preservation of Past

Conservators are racing to save monuments threatened by development, pollution, looting and neglect. In the process, they are transforming the field of archaeology into a new science

Marguerite Holloway

Staff Writer

Just before sunset, the stones of Pueblo Bonito in Chaco Canyon, New Mexico, glow golden, and their varied patterns stand out like friezes. The ruin—an elaborate city built and inhabited by Anasazi Indians between A.D. 850 and 1150—becomes empty of the day's tourists, and the cold of the desert night begins to settle in the shadowy rooms and kivas, circular ceremonial centers sunken in the ground. The small vents and tapered doors grow black.

One of these dark entrances—a high, squat door sitting at the junction of two walls—captures the attention of Dabney Ford, an archaeologist with the National Park Service who has worked at and studied Chaco Canyon for more than 10 years. She explains that the opening is aligned to catch sunlight only on the winter solstice. On that day, rays of light reflect on a specially built wall corner on the opposite side of the room. Although archaeologists understand relatively little about Anasazi culture, some have recently come to believe that the design of Pueblo Bonito—like that of Teotihuacan in Mexico, Machu Picchu in Peru and many other ancient cities—reflects astronomical cycles. The door is just one example of an architecture oriented by solar and lunar fluxes—one that perhaps embodies Anasazi political and social hierarchy.

"Architects and archaeologists have had a hard time perceiving the complexity of this society," Ford notes, as she moves through tiny doorways, pointing out wood beams that have survived intact for hundreds of years. Chaco Canyon "is pretty humbling."

It is also falling apart. Being able to reinterpret Anasazi culture (if one is an archaeologist), visit the site (if one is a tourist) or pray in the sacred kivas (if one is a tribal descendant) depends on the walls' not buckling or collapsing as water seeps into the aging rocks and mortar. It depends on preventing salt crystals from growing in the stones and breaking them apart, vandals from digging up artifacts and visitors from climbing on walls or wood beams, splintering in minutes what endured for a millennium. Preserving Chaco Canyon entails solving a series of problems posed by archaeological sites around the world.

These concerns have, in the minds of many archaeologists, art historians and preservationists, reached crisis proportions. All 440 places designated by UNESCO as World Heritage Sites (including Chaco Canyon) are threatened, explains Bernd von Droste, director of the World Heritage Center in Paris. Angkor in Cambodia, the Pyramids in Egypt, the Parthenon in Athens, the old city of Dubrovnik in Croatia, the earthen bas-reliefs of the Royal Palaces of Abomey in Benin and the homind fossil footprints found by archaeologist Mary Leakey in Tanzania

are among hundreds of cultural and anthropological icons in danger of destruction. "In another 20 years, most of the archaeology of Egypt is going to be in museums," remarks Fred Wendorf of Southern Methodist University, who has been working in Egypt since 1962. "Everything else is going to be covered by water or plowed up in fields or coated with asphalt."

The principal threats to archaeological sites are the same ones cited by environmentalists as endangering biodiversity: development, population growth, tourism, illegal traffic, air pollution, war, neglect and, in some cases, botched efforts at conservation. Nevertheless the dangers stalking the world's cultural patrimony have not catalyzed any grassroots campaign to rival that of the green movement. (Some archaeologists speculate that, despite the public's fascination with Indiana Jones, roofless buildings do not have the same appeal as baby seals. Degradation also can be too slow to engage general interest: the fading looks of a sculpture may be seen only by comparing a contemporary photograph with one taken 30 years ago.)

Within the archaeological community, however, the growing perils are fostering a reevaluation of the entire field. "The whole attitude of archaeologists has been to plunder, then leave," notes Pamela Jerome, a professor at Columbia University, who is teaching one of the first courses exclusively on site conservation given at a graduate school. Typically archaeologists have excavated and then moved on—sometimes covering ruins over again to preserve them, a process called backfilling. Their training has not included work in conservation. That effort has instead been the province of museum-trained conservators, who restore only portable artifacts and collected objects. The two groups have often been at odds, Jerome says: one trying to push ahead with a dig, the other saying slow down, save this.

WASTING AWAY

But field archaeologists are now facing many of the challenges that have always confronted object conservators: disintegration and loss. They "have begun to realize that the rate of site destruction is pretty sizable and that archaeology is a nonrenewable resource. They have become more interested in preserving sites in situ," describes Francis P. McManamon, an archaeologist at the National Park Service. "That awareness has been reinforced by the recognition that you still have to take care of all the material that was excavated." Park Service collections alone hold an estimated 24.6 million objects, of which 16.8 million have not yet been catalogued. (Renovating facilities to care for these artifacts properly, something required under 1990 regulations, could cost more than $59.8 million.) The staggering amount of material that has been amassed worldwide has led some researchers to call for moratoriums on excavations until collections have been thoroughly researched; in many cases, recovered objects waste away in dusty vaults, unstudied and ill cared for.

The artifact crisis and the site crisis together have led to a new ethic and science. Borrowing from the wealth of knowledge about conserving artifacts and from materials science, scientists at several institutions—including the Getty Conservation Institute (GCI) in Marina del Rey, Calif., the International Centre for the Study of the Preservation and the Restoration of

Cultural Property in Rome, the International Council on Monuments and Sites in Paris, UNESCO, the World Monuments Fund in New York City and various laboratories and universities—are formalizing the discipline of site conservation. Symposiums and courses such as Jerome's are beginning to appear. The International Institute for Conservation of Historic and Artistic Works will hold its 1996 meeting on archaeological preservation. A journal, *Conservation and Management of Archaeological Sites,* to be published in London, is slated to start this year.

The primary goal of this burgeoning area of research is to slow deterioration. Buried ruins can survive for eons because they reach equilibrium with their stable surroundings. When dug out of sand or a mat of jungle growth or opened to air, their components

begin to fall apart. "You are exposing it to sun, to rain, to dewfall, to oxygen, to all these things," describes Neville H. Agnew, associate director of programs at the GCI. "You catalyze a whole assemblage of degeneration that just springs into action—sometimes even within hours of excavation you can see deterioration starting." Some protective strategies being investigated include determining how to backfill ruins correctly, how to monitor caves or tombs for changes in humidity that could cause wall paintings to flake off, how to treat stones of tropical ruins with biocides and how to protect adobe, or earthen, buildings from the ravages of earthquakes.

Although backfilling has been practiced casually by archaeologists for years, it has never been tested rigorously. Conservationists view reburial as the best solution for many places,

YUNGANG GROTTOES in China are threatened by pollution, arid climate, and water seepage. These factors are causing the 1,500-year-old sculptures to deteriorate, as is evident in a comparison of the same statue in 1933 (*below, left*) and in 1991 (*below, right*). Conservators are working to drain water from the site and to construct shelters to protect certain caves.

but the procedure remains controversial because researchers want their sites left uncovered so they, or the public, can wander around. This concern is evident at Chaco Canyon, where the GCI is collaborating with the Park Service on a backfilling experiment. Every year the park receives 80,000 visitors, who, presumably, want to see most of the site.

Even in Chetro Ketl, one of the great houses of Chaco, it is clear that some effort is needed to stanch further deterioration. The effects of wind, rain and a failed attempt at stabilization are all apparent. Heavy cement applied to the top of walls in the 1960s to keep out moisture has broken the lighter, underlying stone. Erosion around the base of many walls has destabilized them to the verge of collapse. Water has entered the crowns of other walls, frozen and subsequently forced apart the stones below. And water has caused salt to effloresce, or leach out, from the structure. Once such saline crystals form, they grow or shrink depending on the availability of moisture—and when they grow, they, too, push apart the stones, ultimately crumbling them.

Ford points out the white salt stains along the walls as she walks through the building, explaining the setup. Only 10 of 60 targeted rooms at Chetro Ketl have been backfilled, because reburying

the rest would cost about $150,000—the annual maintenance budget for the entire 10-mile-long section of canyon and its thousands of ruins. Some rooms have been refilled only a few feet, with drains installed to pull moisture away from the walls and out of the site into drainage ditches. In other places, troughs buried in the center of the chambers collect and evaporate water.

In one room with wood beams, back-filling has been quite extensive and includes what are called geo-synthetic materials—in this case, a sheet of black knotted plastic, which holds the soil firmly in place. Keeping the soil stable and getting the damp away are crucial so that the reburied wood does not rot, Ford says, and this test is being carefully monitored. She scrambles over to a nearby kiva and gestures toward a lunar probe look-alike standing, ungainly, in the middle of the sacred space, recording fluctuations in moisture and temperature.

Although the experiments are not finished, in some chambers the system seems to be stabilizing the walls. In other places, the attempts are not so successful, and the right strategy remains elusive. "It may be a real mess," Ford shrugs, "but, hey, that's science."

Unforeseen results are inevitable because every location is different and because site conservation technology

NEFERTARI'S TOMB in Egypt houses wall paintings that were damaged when the site was entered in 1904 (*left*). To preserve the recently cleaned and protected murals, researchers argue that tourism should be limited. A virtual-reality guide could offer visitors an alternative (*below*).

is just emerging. Agnew of the GCI recalls being called in to help preserve fossilized dinosaur tracks in Lark Quarry, a remote region of Australia. A shelter designed to protect the prints had also protected kangaroos from the hot sun, and so they would congregate there, cooling off and defecating, which did little to help preserve the tracks. Agnew concludes that the best approach if one does not have the resources needed to maintain a monitoring crew—which Lark Quarry management did not—is just "to rebury the site until that time when it can be opened for public display."

That lesson is being applied to fossil footprints in Tanzania that are more than 3.5 million years old. The GCI is evaluating how best to cover the famous Laetoli tracks that established bipedalism in hominids of that era. Although Leakey covered the site with dirt in 1979, tree roots have destroyed part of the trackway. Researchers are now considering how water flows in and around the site, whether they should use biocides to control the growth of weeds and trees, how they should signal future excavators that these levels of dirt and other materials are not original, how deep the prints should be buried and what kinds of geosynthetic materials should be incorporated. Once covered, it is unclear when, or if, the prints will be unearthed—or how it would be determined that experts should reinterpret the site or that the public should view the prints.

"There are challenges at many levels—they are not just scientific and technological," Agnew remarks. "We have to understand the mechanisms of deterioration of material and sites from a scientific point of view; that is critical. But it goes well beyond that as well." The issue of access, for instance, is pivotal. Archaeologists have the privilege of excavating places that belong to all of humanity. But what if strangers love the site to death?

The Egyptian Antiquities Organization is grappling with that concern at Nefertari's tomb in the Valley of the Queens. Originally opened in 1904, the tomb of the favorite wife of Ramses II houses magnificent wall paintings de-

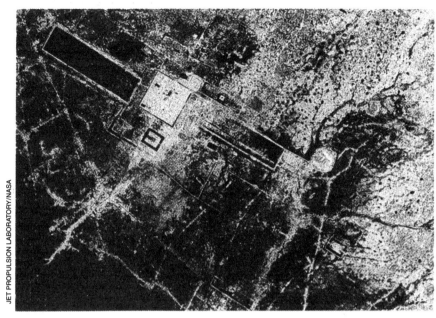

ANGKOR BY SATELLITE offers a fresh perspective for archaeologists studying the ancient Khmer city in Cambodia. Conservators hope data on vegetation growth and hydrology can aid them in protecting the site from further degradation and, perhaps, in restoring some of the original canals and reservoirs.

picting Nefertari's voyage to the afterlife. The luxurious red, yellow, white and green murals were destabilized during discovery and after the introduction of desert air: plaster was damaged, and salts crystallized, sometimes an inch thick, pushing off the mud plaster and growing through the pigment. Before the 1980s it was clear that the paintings would not survive much longer. Between 1988 and 1992 some of the paintings were painstakingly removed and cleaned, and flakes of paint were reattached. The paintings were then put back in place.

The past two years have been devoted to monitoring humidity and changes in temperature to see how stable the internal environment is and whether it could support visitors. Shin Maekawa, head of environmental sciences at the GCI, tried to determine what the original state of the tomb was before it was opened because that condition had preserved the paintings perfectly for about 3,200 years. Through a series of experiments he found that the tomb had been quite humid through the centuries. In fact, humidity probably reached 50 percent in the summer months.

"Until that time, people thought that in order to conserve wall paintings it had to be drier, but that is not true," Maekawa explains. What turns out to be most critical is keeping such levels stable, something that can be achieved only if the number of visitors is strictly limited. "It took the tomb three days to recover from having 20 people inside for half an hour in the summer," Maekawa reports. Other popular tombs—such as Tutankhamen's, which already shows extensive deterioration—may have more than 3,000 visitors a day. "Despite all that effort we put in, if unregulated numbers of tourists are allowed into the tomb again, the wall paintings will be placed in danger," Maekawa warns.

Nevertheless, the government is under great pressure to open it. Tourism brings Egypt about $3 billion annually, and the reopening of Nefertari's tomb could boost the number of visitors. Indeed, although it can be beneficial, tourism is cited as one of the gravest threats to sites everywhere. According to von Droste of UNESCO, there were 500 million international tourists in 1994; about 40 percent of them traveled to see monuments such as the

Sphinx, the Mayan temples of Tikal in Guatemala or the city of Petra in Jordan. Unfortunately, von Droste says, tourism often produces money for operators outside the countries being visited, so "revenues rarely go to the protection of the site." To address this problem, the GCI and others are trying to devise sustainable site management plans—as well as plans for historic centers within cities—that involve the local community, scientists, the government and the tourist industry.

In some cases, replicas can serve as proxies, protecting originals from the touch of tourists. The cave paintings of Lascaux in France were nearly destroyed by visitors brushing up against the walls. So the government built a replica nearby. The original caves are now viewed only by scholars, and the facsimile has become so popular that the number of tourists has to be limited. The GCI and Infobyte in Rome developed a virtual-reality guide to Nefertari's tomb—an alternative to visiting the real thing that may become common. But such solutions do not convey the power of a place. Nor do they resolve the question of who has the right to visit a site, whether sacred places should be left untouched or whether something should be preserved if no one can see it.

LIMITED ACCESS

It is worth saving sites, even if no one can get in there other than a few select scholars and other people," Agnew states energetically. "Of course, one does not like to be elitist and exclude the visiting public, but in fact, 90 percent of most tourists are not interested in art history. They come ill prepared: they wander in, and they wander out. Those people can go see other tombs in Egypt or other sites that are not threatened. I do not believe everyone has an inalienable right to see everything they want to see, any more than everyone can get into a Pavarotti concert—there are a limited number of seats. That is the reality of life."

Most preferable to conservators would be to extract archaeological information without touching the site at all. Consequently, researchers are increasingly using remote sensing—that is, recording information with cameras, radar, magnetometers—in short, any technology that will reveal aspects about a site from afar. "We are trying to develop the tools for conservation," says Farouk El-Baz, director of the Center for Remote Sensing at Boston University. El-Baz and his colleagues have used one of the techniques to determine how moisture was entering Nefertari's tomb as well as to extract air from a sealed chamber at the base of the Great Pyramid of Giza and to photograph the room's contents.

Remote sensing by satellite was recently used to map Angkor in Cambodia, and conservators are attempting to figure out how to apply the information. Angkor was the capital of the Khmer Empire from the ninth until the 15th century. Because each king would build a new capital, Angkor has more than 60 major monuments. The site is overgrown, stones have fallen out of place and the details of many sculptures have faded. Teams from several countries are working on various temples, each following its own distinct approach.

Preserving monuments in tropical environments is an unruly task because the jungle keeps taking over. Conservators have to decide whether to use biocides to kill vegetation and whether to shelter sites. Angkor gets 12 feet of water a year. "That much water is going to support plant growth, no matter what you do," says John Stubbs of the World Monuments Fund, which is preserving the compound of Preah Khan.

Stubbs has decided not to use biocides. Instead the team is removing heavy plant growth by hand, documenting many of the statues and performing anastylosis—replacing stones from where they have landed on the ground to what is assumed to be their original position in the ruin. On the whole, the World Monuments Fund approach is hands-off and reflects the growing consensus among archaeologists that sites should not be reconstructed, because that activity entails a potentially incorrect reinterpretation of the past.

Nevertheless, Stubbs does favor a certain kind of reconstruction and hopes to use the satellite data from the National Aeronautics and Space Administration to that end. "I would like to restore water features because I am quite convinced that the architecture was supposed to be seen in reflection," he explains. "The whole culture is about capturing and manipulating water." The image shows the reaches of the estuary, which covers the area from the Mekong River up to Angkor during the rainy season. The information could help conservators understand the region's hydrology, knowledge that could, in turn, help them determine how and whether to drain parts of the site to preserve it.

Stubbs's biggest fear about Angkor—and he is not alone—is that looting will leave it barren. "The popularity of the site, the new access, the hunger for Khmer art and the lawlessness of the place are all a recipe for pillaging," he notes. Stubbs says he has visited shops in Bangkok, inquired about buying Khmer antiquities and been shown pictures of objects taken from Preah Khan—and even some photographs of statues still in place.

Many archaeologists single out looting as the major threat to ancient sites and objects. It is impossible to get good numbers on the value of the stolen objects, but estimates run from $2 billion to $6 billion annually. From 80 to 90 percent of antiquities, including those sitting in museums, are considered "hot." The scale of seizures intensified in the mid-1980s, when people began to look at antiquities as investments, explains Ricardo J. Elia of Boston University. All the more horrible, he fumes, is that an artifact obtained as a spoil of plunder, at the expense of a destroyed site, comes to be seen as an art object when it is bought by a wealthy collector and ends up in a museum: "It starts out real dirty and ends up real clean."

For conservators, stopping illicit traffic and using science and technology to protect monuments and ruins are, in many ways, easier tasks than answering questions that are raised about saving sites. Given limited resources and conflicts of interest, what should be saved? "It used to be that time made the choice," reflects Miguel Angel Corzo, director of the GCI. "War came, and people used houses and monuments as quarries. It was just the natural evolution of things that brought us to where we are today. But now we have an extraordinary capacity to save whatever we want; the technology is there. What are we going to leave behind? Are we going to take the same attitude, 'Time will tell'? Or are we going to be people of the 21st century and say, 'This is who we are going to be remembered as'?"

It is tragically clear that wiping out a site can wipe out cultural identity—something that happens when ethnic groups clash, each trying to obliterate the culture of the other. China's razing of the monasteries of Tibet is but one example. The interpretation of archaeological remains powerfully shapes the outlook of an entire people, as can be seen in the evolving view of the Great Zimbabwe, a series of majestic granite structures constructed between A.D. 1400 and 1600. British colonialists claimed that the circular compound could not have been built by native Africans: northern invaders from either Greece, Egypt or the Middle East

must have swept down and built the sophisticated enclosure. It has been established, however, that it was the ancestors of regional Shona people who built the Great Zimbabwe. The cultural identity and independence of Zimbabwe (formerly Rhodesia) are closely linked to this monument.

African countries, in particular, could lose a profound part of their cultural identity if their sites are not conserved. The continent has a dearth of native archaeologists, and many places have not yet been excavated. According to a 1992 World Bank conference report, *Culture and Development in Africa,* there is only one archaeology program in 11 central African countries, and the total annual budget for the entire region is $20,000.

Despite the vast challenges and many unresolved ethical questions, the archaeological community is developing a philosophy of conservation. This shift could be seen in the response to the recent discovery of some 300 Cro-Magnon paintings in a cave near Avignon, France. Immediately after its discovery, the cave and its 20,000-year-old masterpieces were sealed off. "The cave should be left as it is. It must be studied, of course, but bearing in mind that the collecting of the information must not be destructive," says Jean Clottes, a prehistorian and adviser to the French Culture Ministry.

"It is out of the question to start excavating all over the place." As Clottes points out, ever smaller samples of materials are needed to date paintings, and so the investigations of archaeologists present may seem like ravages to those to come. Furthermore, "theories change," Clottes notes. "Everyone believes in one for 10 or 15 years, then there is another theory."

It is for the sake of these theories and for the awe of place and time that people want to hold on to their past. Multiculturalism—the celebration of any culture, no matter how small—as well as the movement toward the next millennium may be contributing to a growing nostalgia or, as some archaeologists put it, a need to reconnect with history. For others, though, the attempt to hold on to everything makes little sense. We Westerners tend to feel that it is massively important to preserve," comments Marian A. Kaminitz, a conservator at the National Museum of the American Indian. Others "have a strong sense of allowing things to return, of not holding on to them."

In the gathering dark of Chaco Canyon, Pueblo Bonito returns to the desert. An absolute stillness settles around the ruins. "It is beneficial that they are protecting it," says Petuuche Gilbert, a descendant of the Anasazi. But we could also let it go, he adds: "It would be part of the natural cycle."

217

Saving Our World's Heritage

Ellen Hoffman

On a potholed, dusty road a few miles south of the Mayan ruins of Tulum on Mexico's Caribbean coast, a crudely executed wall painting of a turtle advertises a primitive seaside bungalow camp. *PESCA, BUCEO, PATRIMONIO UNIVERSAL,* it says in Spanish. In English, its "FISHING, SKIN DIVING, WORLD HERITAGE." The causal tourist might never focus on or question the meaning of "WORLD HERITAGE." But to the diligent travel researcher or member of the eco-cognoscenti, that phrase signals a specific message: You are in or near a natural or cultural site "of outstanding universal value to mankind." In this case, the site a few miles down the road is the Sian Ka'an Biosphere Reserve, a 1.3-million-acre landscape of tropical forest, savannas and mangrove, and coastal and marine habitats that abound with white ibis and roseate spoonbills, manatees and monkeys, sea turtles, and the living corals of the world's second largest reef system.

Several hundred miles away, in the dense, vine-clogged jungle of Mexico's Chiapas state, the imposing stone temples of the Mayan city of Palenque attract thousands of visitors every year. But unless they search out the now-closed museum on the fringe of the site and read the plaque attached to the facade, they might never know that here—as in Sian Ka'an—they are in the presence of a monument that belongs to an elite club whose other "mem-bers" include the Great Wall of China, the Tower of London, Africa's Victoria Falls, and our Statue of Liberty.

The "club" is the World Heritage List, created by the World Heritage Convention, an international treaty approved in 1972 and since then signed by 134 of the world's 188 nations. The List consists of natural and cultural sites and monuments that meet specific criteria designed to verify their "outstanding universal value."

To get on the List, a site or monument must meet at least one of several criteria that emphasize both uniqueness and superlative qualities. A natural site, for example, might qualify because it is an "outstanding example" of a stage of the earth's evolutionary history or the habitat for an important threatened animal or plant species. A man-made site or monument, such as a building or a group of buildings, might make the List because it is a "unique artistic achievement" or because it represents a civilization that has disappeared.

"If we want to protect the world for future generations so they can enjoy the benefits of the work of nature, of millennia, the diversity of plants and species, the World Heritage List can help us do that," says Bernd von Droste, a German ecologist who directs the program from the World Heritage Centre at UNESCO headquarters in Paris.

A sedate, systematic bureaucrat on the podium when he was conducting business at the World Heritage Committee's annual meeting in Santa Fe, New Mexico, last December, in an interview von Droste revealed himself as a passionate advocate for the World Heritage Convention as a tool for nothing less than saving the world.

"Why do we need diversity of species? Of culture?" He answered his own question. "We need them for human survival. Since we don't know about the future, it's better to keep all the knowledge we have about how to adapt."

One purpose of the Santa Fe meeting was to celebrate 20 years of the World Heritage Convention—which the delegates did at a series of festive receptions and dinners sponsored by local officials and cultural institutions. But they also heard a clarion call from von Droste, who reported, "This year many more World Heritage sites are severely damaged or under threat than ever before in the history of the Convention," and cited examples including earthquake damage to the pyramids and other Egyptian monuments and war damage to the medieval city of Dubrovnik.

Population growth, widespread poverty and lack of education, global warming and acid rain ("It creates stone degradation that affects monuments"), climate change, the rising of the sea level—von Droste ticked off a series of physical threats to sites on the List. "If we believe what most scientists are saying," he said, "conservation will be in for a hard time."

To understand not just the physical but also the thorny political and finan-

LIST OF ENDANGERED PLACES

The following World Heritage sites have been inscribed on the Danger List because of threats to or deterioration of the characteristics for which they were placed on the List. The date signifies the year the site was placed on the List.

Benin: Royal Palaces of Abomey; damaged caused by tornado (1985).

Bulgaria: Srebarna Biosphere Reserve; drainage of wetlands has damaged the ecosystem and threatened bird habitats (1992).

Cambodia: Angkor; the former Khmer capital has suffered severe war damage and lacks a comprehensive plan for rehabilitation (1992).

Croatia: Plitvice Lakes National Park; near the border with Serbia, left without a comprehensive management structure and, due to the war, a total loss of tourism income (1992).

Ecuador: Sangay National Park; heavy poaching of wildlife, illegal livestock grazing, and a proposed road-construction project (1992).

Guinea and Cote d'Ivoire: Mount Nimba; lack of effective management, possible uncontrolled mining, and an influx of refugees from Liberia (1992).

Hashemite Kingdom of Jordan: Old City of Jerusalem; concern over the archaeological methods used to document the Old City and its walls (1982).

India: Manas Wildlife Sanctuary; damage to park infrastructure from invasion of Bodo tribespeople, including "illegal cultivation" (1992).

Mali: Timbuktu; enroachment of desert sand (1990).

Niger: Aïr-Ténéré National Nature Reserve; fighting between government forces of Niger and the Tuareg rebels. Six members of the park staff were held hostage for more than a year and a half. Four were released; two were killed (1992).

Oman: Bahia Fort; general deteriorating conditions and poor restoration practices (1988).

Peru: Chan Chan Archaeological Zone; damage from excavation work and plundering (1986).

Poland: Wieliczka Salt Mine; deterioration of salt carvings (1989).

Yugoslavia: Kotor and its Gulf; earthquake damage (1979). Old City of Dubrovnik; war damage to city walls and old buildings, especially their roofs (1991).

Zaire: Garamba National Park; alarming reduction in population of northern white rhinoceros (1984).

---

cial threats the sites on the List face, it's necessary to understand how the World Heritage Convention works. Individual governments nominate sites within their borders. They must convince the 21-member international World Heritage Committee (the group that met in Santa Fe) that each proposed site meets the criteria of "universal value to mankind," and pledge to conserve it.

'There is no way to ensure that sites are protected from environmental degradation, war, neglect, tourism, urbanization, and development.'

The Committee accepts or rejects nominations to the List on the basis of information supplied by two nonprofit organizations: the International Council on Monuments and Sites (ICOMOS) in the case of cultural or manmade sites, and the World Conservation Union

(IUCN) in the case of natural sites. Although neither of these groups is an official organ of UNESCO, their role is written into the Convention's guidelines.

Twenty years after its creation, the still-growing List consists of 378 sites. With an annual budget of around $2 million to implement the Convention, some sites have been named to the List without even being visited by impartial evaluators. And, although it's being discussed, there is no routine program of monitoring to ensure that all sites are protected from threats of environmental degradation, war, urbanization, tourism, and "development."

Once on the List, a site or monument the Committee believes faces "serious and specific dangers"—such as war damage, as in Dubrovnik, or in the case of Sangay National Park in Ecuador, "suffering from heavy poaching of wildlife, illegal livestock grazing, and encroachment"—may be placed on the World Heritage In Danger List, signifying the need for dramatic intervention or major financial or technical assistance. As of press time, the Danger List consisted of 15 sites, including six added at the December meeting.

The United States has 18 World Heritage sites, including Grand Canyon and Yellowstone national parks, Independence Hall in Philadelphia, and the Everglades. They are managed by the National Park Service and supported by tax dollars as well as admission fees. But many sites are in the developing world, where there is less tourism and a commitment to conservation poses wrenching decisions. "When people are living hand to mouth" as they do in some African game-reserve areas, for example, "you can't expect them not to poach," says Jim Thorsell, who evaluates natural sites for IUCN.

The Committee spends some of its funds on technical cooperation and training—restoring earthquake-damaged sites in Egypt or training natural-park managers, for example—but lacks the resources to support large-scale conservation projects.

During the week-long Santa Fe meeting, the delegates—some clad in colorful African robes or gauzy saris, others in the more severe attire of international diplomacy—attended marathon sessions in a hotel ballroom. UNESCO staff hurried up and down the aisles, distributing a blizzard of French- and English-language documents while the Committee discussed reports, guidelines, and budgets and made decisions via simultaneous translation, which were offered in French and English.

In addition to expanding the Danger List, the Committee added 21 new sites to the World Heritage List, including the Kasbah of Algiers and Angkor, the ancient Khmer capital of Cambodia. The tone of these sessions was primarily bureaucratic and politely diplomatic. Yet throughout this twentieth-anniversary meeting, there was a persistent undercurrent of urgency—of concern about the future of the World Heritage List. "The Convention is at a crossroads," said Andy Turner, who is involved with the World Heritage program in Australia. "It has got to deal with the difficult issues."

By the end of the week, the Committee's discussions had illuminated not only the physical threats facing the monuments, but also some of the thorny philosophical, political, and financial issues clamoring to be resolved. For example:
• How can the List be more "balanced"? Only 88 of the 378 sites are natural; 291 are cultural. Europe has a heavy concentration of sites, while other continents have only a few. The Committee has begun to address this by encouraging all countries that have signed the treaty to inventory sites they believe are eligible and want to nominate and by offering some funding to help prepare the nominations.
• Should the List even distinguish between natural and cultural sites? Too often, von Droste says, "culture and nature are artificially separated. They belong together. If you destroy the tropical forest, you also destroy the culture of the people who live there." To address this issue, the Committee has been trying to define a new category of sites called "cultural landscapes," which would recognize "combined works of nature and man."
• How can the World Heritage Centre find the resources to offer protection to so many sites? Publications sales and voluntary contributions by countries or individuals add to the budget, but von

Droste reported that as needs for both emergency funds and regular monitoring and technical assistance grow, the "overall budget at the disposal of the Committee is stagnating or even decreasing in real terms." A key reason for the decrease is that many countries lag far behind in their mandatory contributions. Argentina, for example, owed more than $65,000 for the years 1986 through 1993 as of last December.

Given these limitations, does the World Heritage Convention really have an impact on the future of the earth's most important, often threatened, monuments, natural habitats, and cultural sites? What has it accomplished? What challenges does it face, and what are its prospects for the future?

IUCN's Thorsell has compiled a list of 22 cases in which World Heritage Committee intervention, he says—through political pressure, funding, technical assistance, and the like—has helped protect or improve threatened sites. The success stories include Ecuador's Galápagos islands, where "tourism-control policies were introduced," and Tanzania's Ngorongoro conservation area, which received equipment needed for park management and was removed from the Danger List.

But these accomplishments seem like a drop in the bucket when compared with the size and needs of the entire List and von Droste's gloomy appraisal of the current state of World Heritage efforts.

One case in point—discussed at length in Santa Fe because of the difficulty of agreeing on what to do about it—is that of Mount Nimba, a natural reserve that straddles the borders of Guinea and Ivory Coast in West Africa. In 1980, Mount Nimba—which is described in a book about World Heritage as a "beautiful and isolated environment," the habitat of "rare species of bats, lichens, and other plants and animals"—was put on the List.

Twelve years later, at the Santa Fe meeting, the Committee placed Mount Nimba on the World Heritage In Danger List, citing two major threats to its integrity: a proposal by the Guinea government to open an iron mine adjacent to the site, and the presence of as

many as 60,000 "extremely poor Liberian refugees" in the region, who, von Droste told the Committee, "if not helped, will destroy the whole area."

Despite diplomatic conversations and meetings, technical missions to the reserve, and extensive debate at Santa Fe and previous meetings, the Committee can't even agree on the boundaries of the World Heritage site—and whether the proposed mine really is inside them. The Guinea government's delegate told the Committee in Santa Fe that the proposed mine—which the government has been developing for more than 20 years—"was never protected under World Heritage" because, he said, it was outside the site.

At the same time it put Mount Nimba on the Danger List, the Committee decided to send another mission to study the boundaries, determine the impact of the threats to its "universal values," and work toward development of a management plan to protect the reserve. The mission was successful. Participants generally agreed on new boundaries for the site. The Mount Nimba example illuminates several dilemmas that the World Heritage Convention confronts in its role as protector of our collective future:
• The Convention has lofty principles, but the Committee has limited ability to enforce them. Sites are put on the list because they're considered to be of great value and because individual governments agree to protect them. But, other than mobilizing world opinion, the Committee can do little to protect a site that's threatened by a government policy, such as the proposed iron-mine development, or by unforeseen events, such as the turmoil that led so many Liberians to seek refuge in another country. The case of Mount Nimba illustrates the difficult political and financial issues the Convention faces: The potential value of the iron mine to the country of Guinea is approximately $8 billion—money that could be spent to build an infrastructure and resolve pressing social problems.
• The Convention has lofty operational goals but few resources for implementing them. Even if contributions were

paid up, the budget cannot support thorough investigation of proposed nominations or regular monitoring of 378 sites, let alone keep pace with demands generated by adding to the List. This dilemma also emerged in debates on whether to add sites to the Danger List. As long as the Committee cannot provide funds for conservation programs or compensate governments for what they see as an economic loss—not mining in the Mount Nimba reserve—placement on the Danger List appears more like a reprimand than a positive call for protection.

•The structure for implementing the Convention is sensitive to political pressures. The World Heritage Centre is physically located in UNESCO headquarters and receives some funding and other support from the agency. The Convention and the Committee, however, are independent of UNESCO. (The director of the World Heritage Centre reports to and is responsible to the director general of UNESCO.) The entire Committee, which takes action on all nominations as well as makes program policy decisions, meets only once a year. As the Mount Nimba case illustrates, development and enforcement of effective conservation plans may require a long-term perspective as well as technical knowledge. But many delegates who attend the Committee meetings are diplomats rather than substantive experts—with a short-term assignment.

Despite the structural issues confronting the Convention and the continuing problems surrounding Mount Nimba, halfway around the world from West Africa, Australia offers a different, more positive model of the World Heritage system: an example of how environmentalists used the international treaty to safeguard sites in their own country and to stimulate public debate and awareness of environmental issues.

"Australians have a history of fighting in public about these things," says Andrew Turner, then-assistant secretary of the Commonwealth's (federal government's) Nature Conservation Branch, over breakfast one morning before the Committee went into session.

When the government proposed a logging ban in the Wet Tropics of Queensland, a World Heritage site, he recalled, "You couldn't walk into a pub without someone picking a fight about it, with someone else or with you."

Australia's constitution gives land-management power to the states, not to the central government. "In the early 1980s," Turner recounted, "the Tasmanian Hydroelectric Commission wanted to build a dam that would have flooded the valley of the Gordon River, including a lot of aboriginal caves with evidence of early habitation." The proposed dam was in the Tasmanian Wilderness, a World Heritage area that now encompasses about 10 percent of the state.

The Australian High Court set an important precedent in the 1980s in two decisions when it cited the national government's commitment to an international treaty—the World Heritage Convention—as grounds for approving the Commonwealth government's power to impose the logging ban in Queensland and prohibiting the proposed dam project in Tasmania.

Unlike most countries, the Australian government publishes a regular monitoring report on all of its World Heritage sites, describing the nature of the property; current issues, such as proposed construction or tourism growth; management plans; and the number of people who visited the site.

Most observers and participants in the World Heritage process agree that an important key to its future effectiveness is increasing awareness of the concept and the reasons for protecting natural and cultural monuments.

The United States played a key role in creating the Convention and makes the largest contributions to the program budget. But it took the meeting of the Committee in Santa Fe, 20 years after the formation of the treaty, to spur the National Park Service to commit itself to providing information about World Heritage to the millions of people who visit our sites every year.

In contrast, Spain, which has 15 sites, ranging from the prehistoric caves of Altamira to a twentieth-cen-tury Barcelona house designed by architect Antonio Gaudí, publishes a glossy, illustrated pamphlet describing each site and the purpose of the World Heritage Convention.

It may or may not be coincidental that one of World Heritage's most passionate advocates is a Spaniard, Federico Mayor, who is UNESCO's director general. "Each citizen of the world should become a defender of our world heritage," he said. "I like to imagine that the World Heritage message is a message of solidarity, of sharing, but that must come from the world level to the national and municipal levels."

Mayor said he's encouraged by the publicity given to conservation of the environment by the Rio conference and the possibility of increasing funding through the new Global Environmental Facility starting in 1994.

His vision for a vigorous, effective World Heritage program a decade from now emphasizes education and public awareness: "In Paris, at UNESCO headquarters, we have a clearinghouse for information, with publications from all over." In addition to the Paris Centre, he hopes to see five or six regional centers and national non-governmental organizations, which would actively promote an understanding of the Convention and suggest actions to help preserve World Heritage sites. "In children's textbooks, World Heritage would be a symbol of sharing and general awareness of what is precious in one's own and other cultures."

'Will our grandchildren be able to visit the Taj Mahal or the Galápagos Islands? The rock churches of Ethiopia or the lagoon of Venice?'

The person most on the spot now to shape the future of World Heritage is Centre director Bernd von Droste, who became director in May of 1992. Equipped with his meager budget and the energy that comes from knowing you're right, von Droste has begun to address issues of public awareness and funding by negotiating for a major television series on World Heritage and seeking private-sector funding.

Von Droste also has a sheaf of dreams for the future. Stressing that these are his personal ideas, not official UNESCO or Committee policies, he offered the following vision of an effective World Heritage program 20 years down the road:

• A World Heritage Fund of $2 billion or more, with new mechanisms to fund it, such as an energy tax.

• Formation of an academy of "the world's leading personalities—beyond any suspicion—to see that World Heritage is defended on the highest levels."

• Communication networks that will spread the World Heritage message.

• Proper management of tourism at all sites so that they continue to be protected at the same time that they contribute to economic development.

Will our children or grandchildren be able to visit and appreciate the sublime architecture of the Taj Mahal? Will they see the blue-footed boobies of the Galápagos? The rock churches of Ethiopia? The lagoon of Venice or the monoliths of Stonehenge? Or will they only be able to read about them in books?

In an ideal world, where we all recognize and appreciate natural phenomena and the achievements of humankind, where resources abound and protection of the planet is a shared value, our progeny would visit, learn from, and enjoy all of these World Heritage sites—and more. In the real world, points out IUCN's Thorsell, "World Heritage is a small player, taking in a small portion of the world's protected areas and the world's problems." But, he emphasizes, it's worth doing. "One thing that this world needs is more bridges. World Heritage helps build bridges."

Largest Pueblo Ruin to be Saved

New Mexico's Pueblo San Marcos offers enormous research potential

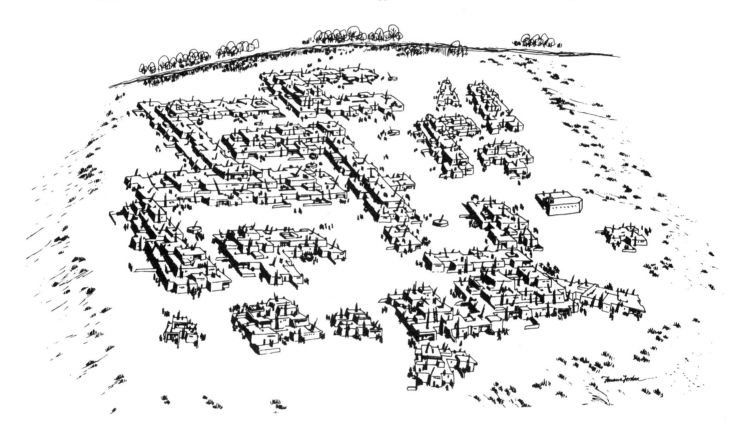

Artist's depiction of Pueblo San Marcos, including the misson church, as it may have appeared in 1620

The Archaeological Conservancy has entered into an option agreement to acquire an additional 40 acres of Pueblo San Marcos, the largest pueblo ruin in the United States, and perhaps the most important privately-owned ruin in the Southwest. The site has enormous research potential, with 22 blocks of rooms, 9 plazas, acres of middens, and a mission church. The first 20-acre parcel was acquired by the Conservancy in 1981.

THE SETTLEMENT OF GALISTEO BASIN

As early as A.D. 1100, numerous small pueblos in the Galisteo Basin of New Mexico, just south of Santa Fe, coalesced into a number of very large pueblo villages. New immigrants, perhaps from the collapsing centers of Chaco Canyon and Mesa Verde, swelled the towns to unprecedented size. These

pueblos flourished, dwindled, and then mysteriously disappeared, leaving only large ruins of adobe and stone, millions of pottery sherds and thousands of graves. The Spanish called these pueblos San Cristobal, Galisteo, San Lazaro, Pueblo Blanco, and San Marcos—the largest of all the pueblos.

Situated just south of Santa Fe and adjacent to the Cerrillos turquoise mines, Pueblo San Marcos was occupied from about A.D. 1100 until its abandon-

Reprinted by permission from *The Archaeological Conservancy Newsletter*, Fall 1996, pp. 1, 2, 7. The Archaeological Conservancy, 5301 Central Avenue NE, Suite 1218, Albuquerque, NM 87108.

ment at the time of the Pueblo Revolt in A.D. 1680.

The pueblo was at least two stories high in places and perhaps as high as three stories or more in others. There are a total of 22 room blocks surrounding nine large plaza areas containing an estimated 2,000 ground floor rooms. During the pueblo's height, the number of rooms probably reached 5,000, although not all were occupied at the same time.

Pueblo San Marcos, known as the "Turquoise Pueblo," controlled the turquoise mines in the nearby Cerrillos hills.

It is likely that San Marcos controlled the turquoise mines in the adjacent Cerrillos hills. Turquoise was traded throughout the Southwest and as far away as the Valley of Mexico. It has also been found in great quantities at Chaco Canyon. What commodities the turquoise was traded for is still not entirely clear.

Spanish accounts describe the pueblo as a thriving community when Coronado arrived in A.D. 1541. The village was visited by Castaño de Sosa in A.D. 1591, who gave it the name of San Marcos. Juan de Oñate, New Mexico's first governor, visited there in 1598 and noted the decline in the population, perhaps as a result of the effects that European diseases had on the native population. A mission church was established at San Marcos in the early 1600s.

In 1680, the pueblos rose in revolt against the Spanish. Haciendas were destroyed, priests were martyred, and the Spanish were forced to flee to El Paso. Santa Fe was occupied by Native American warriors. At San Marcos, the mission church was destroyed and the Catholic priest was executed when he fled to nearby Galisteo. Some reports have the warriors of San Marcos leading the assault on Santa Fe. Others have them backing out of the revolt and supporting the Spanish.

At the time of the Pueblo Revolt, San Marcos had a population of about 600. When the Spanish returned under Diego de Vargas in 1692, it was reported that Pueblo San Marcos was in ruins. Although there may have been a brief re-occupation of San Marcos following the re-conquest, the pueblo was completely abandoned by 1700.

RESEARCH AT SAN MARCOS

Pueblo San Marcos, which is listed in the National Register of Historic Places, holds the key to some of the most important questions in the Southwest, including the mystery of whether or not people from Chaco Canyon and Mesa Verde found refuge at San Marcos after the collapse of their communities. The site offers researchers valuable information about how past cultures adapted to drought and changing climates—an issue that is certainly important in today's era of dwindling natural resources. The site also provides an invaluable source of information about the pre-Revolt, Spanish colonial period.

A variety of research has been conducted at the site during the last 80 years. The earliest archaeological excavations at Pueblo San Marcos began in 1914 when Nels Nelson of the American Museum of Natural History in New York excavated four to six rooms in each of the pueblo's 22 room blocks. The artifacts were shipped to the mu-seum in Central Park where they remain to this day.

In the early 1980s, a Conservancy team under the direction of Dr. Curtis Brennan salvaged rooms damaged by the erosive forces of an arroyo.

In a 1989 survey completed by the University of Colorado under the direction of Dale Lightfoot and R. W. Lang, hundreds of agricultural features surrounding San Marcos were revealed—some of them more than a mile away from the pueblo. These agricultural features include pebble mulch fields, bordered gardens, agricultural terraces, and check dams designed to channel runoff water into agricultural fields.

In 1994, Dr. Judith Habicht-Mauche of the University of California at Santa Cruz conducted a field analysis project to study the surface ceramics at San Marcos in order to better understand the population dynamics of the protohistoric occupation period.

Today, Pueblo San Marcos is much like it was at the time of the Pueblo Revolt in 1680. The Spanish mission lies untouched since its destruction. The room blocks have collapsed into large mounds, preserving the lower floors. The plazas are covered with a protective layer of soil, and the middens are filled with broken pottery, bones, and other artifacts. The permanent springs still flow with clear, cool water.

To protect the site's valuable resources, management steps are being taken, including the development and implementation of a 100-year management plan for the preserve, in accordance with the guidelines of conservation archaeology.

Fundraising efforts for the site are under way. A total of $350,000 is needed to acquire the property and manage it as a permanent archaeological preserve.

Damming the Past

Are reservoirs destroying our archeological heritage? Scuba divers give us an answer

Daniel J. Lenihan

Trained as both a diver and an archeologist, Daniel J. Lenihan is chief of the National Park Service's Submerged Cultural Resources Unit. Recently his team mapped and photographed various American, German, and Japanese ships sunk in the 1946 atomic bomb testing at Bikini Atoll.

The movie light I hold in one hand plays over a graffiti-covered wall in the dark, concrete building. A scrawl in balloon letters, "The Lord Cometh," reminds me of spray-can wisdom I have seen on a hundred subway cars. I float slowly through the flooded hallway, walking on the index and middle finger of my free hand. Tiny clouds of silt puff up as I leave my odd paw prints. Another ghostly form, that of my diving partner, rises effortlessly toward the ceiling. He prepares to snap a picture of the illuminated words.

The building was probably a foundry. The Lord may have been here, but he's gone now. We linger for a second photo, then we too move on. Gently, silently but for the sound of our exhaled breaths splashing on the ceiling, we glide through a series of doorways devoid of doors and propel ourselves through a glassless window. On emerging, we are in the light of day, subdued by the twenty feet of water between us and the air above.

What does it take to cover sixty square miles of New Mexico desert with water? Sometimes, an act of God,

but in this case it was the Bureau of Reclamation. In 1911, Burec cameth and made rise the waters of the Rio Grande to create the Elephant Butte Reservoir and Recreation Area. The Southwest is full of these improvements on nature. They harness indolent rivers for electrical power, allow people to live in flood plains, and convert desert scrub into profitable farmland. Regaining the surface, I am reminded that they also insure the popularity of the outboard engine. Protective of the student divers under my supervision, I make obscene gestures at boaters who come too close to our diver warning flags.

I have visited many of these watery worlds. From 1975 to 1980, I led a National Park Service study of major water-impoundment areas in the United States, mainly in the arid Southwest. Other researchers were charged with assessing loss of habitat and scenic values. My task was to determine if the federal money allocated for salvaging archeological sites was being prudently spent.

The dozens of large reservoirs built by the Army Corps of Engineers, Bureau of Reclamation, Tennessee Valley Authority, and others throughout the country impact river valleys, usually the locus of past human activity. The scope of this phenomenon is hard to convey. The combined surface area of just two of the artificial lakes on the Colorado River, lakes Mead and Powell, for example, is more than 500 square miles, or about half the size of

Rhode Island. Sizable portions of these two lakes are deep enough to cover the Washington Monument. Beneath them now lie some 2,000 known sites of the Anasazi—the ancient ones—ranging from the ruins of pueblos to scatterings of stone tools. The sites identified in surveys before the valleys were flooded probably represent only a fraction of those actually present. Apart from the value archeologists attach to these remains, one can only imagine what living Indian peoples must feel when they see their heritage, including sacred sites and ancient landscapes, obliterated.

Even as the dams were being built, the American preservation community managed to impress upon Congress that archeological remains are irreplaceable. This sometimes elusive point was easiest to establish with politicians from regions where the loss of impressive ruins would be noticed by their constituents. One piece of legislation in the early 1970s authorized the spending of up to one percent of the entire cost of a new reservoir on salvage archeology. Large-scale excavations of the most dramatic sites in the deepest parts of the about-to-be lakes seemed the remedy of choice.

The result, however, was warehouses full of artifacts needing expensive curating, from sites dug for the wrong reasons. A reaction to this process was taking shape in the archeological profession about the time our study began, culminating in the formation of the American Society for Conservation Archeology. These archeologists argued for more focused use of available human and monetary resources—in essence, elegance of research design instead of energetic shoveling. Terms such as "partial-site excavation," "minimal impact archeology," and "problem-oriented research designs" started to replace "dig we must."

Were history and prehistory destroyed when covered by impounded river waters? Or were they preserved forever in an underwater data bank for future generations? Environmental impact statements authoritatively supported these two contradictory positions. With public funds going toward some very comprehensive and expensive archeological projects, federal reservoir managers wanted some definitive answers fast. The National Park Service was given the ball, and I, a diving instructor with a degree in anthropology, got to be quarterback. I moved to Santa Fe, where at the behest of Calvin R. Cummings, regional archeologist for the service's Southwest region, I assembled a team.

With more than a little dismay we realized that we had to define what was of archeological value before we could decide whether or not it was being destroyed. Is the stuff of archeology made up of only artifacts and bones and their relative locations? What about the texture and color of the soil they are found in—how does flooding affect such archeological clues? What of the soil chemistry, which helps to establish where humans performed different daily activities? What of the subtle properties of materials dated through arcane laboratory tricks? Heady fare for a handful of archeologists just out of graduate school, selected for the job largely because we could dive.

This foundry dive is a training exercise for a group of sport divers wishing to refine their underwater recording skills. As I struggle to remove my wet suit, however, I dredge up memories of reservoir dives past. My mind's eye takes me momentarily from the nearby shore of the placid Rio Grande to the mighty Colorado. It gives one pause to stand on the brink of Glen Canyon Dam and look down at the Colorado River on one side and Lake Powell on

the other. A raging river, a piece of raw wilderness, has been molded into a huge pond. At the bottom of the sixty-story concrete megalith, a reconstituted Colorado seems to shrug off the insult and strive to regain its personality. By the time it hits the Grand Canyon, it has become a serious river once more. Farther downstream it is dammed again to form Lake Mead, then Lake Mohave, and yet again to become Lake Havasu.

Hundreds of speedboats zooming in what seem to be long lanes of traffic give Lake Havasu the appearance of an aqueous turnpike. To cap the impression of some sort of surreal theme park, an entrepreneurial genius has placed the reconstituted London Bridge across a side channel of the impounded Colorado River. Moved stone by stone for the Thames, the bridge now stands as a monument to the general level of intelligence involved in our use of human energy and natural resources in the great American Southwest.

Below Lake Mead, released through the turbines of Hoover Dam, the Colorado rages through a narrow, steep canyon for several miles. For scuba divers, this is a challenging stretch. At Ringbolt Rapids the current drags divers down into a hole almost seventy feet deep before disgorging them back to the twenty-foot depth. Here, in the shallower reaches below the rapids, we tried to document the remains of an old river boat (such boats would winch themselves upriver using iron bolts set in the canyon walls). One of our group would try to take a photograph while holding on to the wreck with one hand, but if he relaxed his grip even slightly, the current would sweep him away, leaving behind only a swirl of sand and silt. And if he glanced back upstream, his mask would be ripped off. We eventually decided that a "preliminary evaluation" was sufficient, declared victory, and headed for more convenient sites to document.

The presence of historic shipwrecks in 'the desert is always cause for wonder. A few miles below Glen Canyon Dam, the *Charles H. Spencer* lies near Lee's Ferry, a popular point for rafters to begin their run through the

Grand Canyon. Near the ruins of the old mining camp, the craft lies in shallow water with most of its lower hull well preserved. At most water levels, the smooth, metal boiler is partly exposed, and Navajos fish from the perch it offers. Prefabricated in San Francisco, the *Spencer* was assembled at Lee's Ferry to carry coal to a gold mine. After the craft was launched more than a thousand miles from the ocean, its owners discovered it took more coal to fight the river than the vessel could carry as cargo. The craft was left to rot on the riverbank—a long-term proposition in this part of the world.

Newly impounded waters hold special surprises. I recall the hull of our small aluminum boat scraping over the tips of branches above Cochiti Dam, as Cochiti Lake filled just west of Santa Fe. These were the tops of ponderosa pines, their roots still embedded in the drowned soil sixty feet below us—New Mexico's high desert converted into an evergreen swamp. The Anasazi pueblos, which we had found on our foot survey through this valley years before, would know a strange requiem. While their descendants struggle to maintain an identity, selling their traditional wares on the plaza in Santa Fe, the Anasazi lie buried in earthen house floors, sleeping with the fishes.

Hiking along the ridgetops above Cochiti Dam, I have rested on smooth white logs hundreds of yards above the river. These convenient seats are driftwood, piled there when melts from heavy snowpacks in the Rockies raised the waters to levels unthinkable before impoundment.

During droughts in California's Folsom Reservoir, nature temporarily overrules the dam builders, as rivers fall to their original levels. Here, prehistoric house floors compacted from years of trampling resist the erosion of the receding waters better than the surroundings soils can. The curious result is that once-buried archaeological treasures are left pedestaled above the adjacent terrain. Stumps of oak trees stand beside them on their tap roots. Raccoons, nature's opportunists, have done their own excavating in the hardened house floors, placing snail shells and potsherds in neat piles outside their burrows. One suspects they are less interested in scientific analysis than in extracting the mollusks that took up residence in the house floors during inundation, but their precise digging technique would put some archeologists to shame.

Underwater in Texas, I have flutter-kicked through old ranch houses, cut my way through barbed-wire fences, trailed old railroad tracks into the depths, and followed asphalt highways (still feeling some compulsion to keep to the right of the yellow line). In some places I have even seen old dams that have been covered by the waters backed up by new dams. These reinforced concrete monsters that gobble up river valleys devour their own with equal indifference.

Several tense, cold winter days spent searching for a drowned diver in the submerged powerhouse of a dam near the Mexican border will stay with me always. A hundred feet below the surface, my colleague Larry Murphy and I entered through glassless windows much more forbidding than the ones in the Elephant Butte foundry and felt our way cautiously through murky water. Our tanks scraped against hazardous wires and steel bars hanging from the ceiling. Blinded by disturbed sediment that even our powerful lights couldn't penetrate, we felt our way down a flight of stairs, ran our hands over commodes, and searched restroom stalls. With equal caution we made our way back out before our double tanks emptied of their precious air.

We found the young man's body a day later, wedged in a corner between a glass partition and the electrical switch cage. Larry and I felt especially compelled to remove a fellow diver from this alien environment. Muttering words of encouragement to the lifeless form, we maneuvered him through the many obstacles to the surface.

The official conclusions of our National Reservoir Inundation Study, while voluminous, can be boiled down to a few general observations. The most surprising is that one of the lowest impact zones is in the bottom of a lake, particularly if it has been flooded quickly. Most of what has archeological value is preserved intact, except for soil chemistry, which loses its analytical use after inundation. Access, of course, is compromised, but the findings are reassuring, at least if the goal is to bank sites for future research.

The places worst hit turn out to be the zones where the water level varies up and down, subjecting sites to alternate wet and dry cycles. Little of archeological value survives that sort of treatment. In addition, this is where park goers have their greatest impact. As reservoir levels fluctuate seasonally or over the years, campers follow the beach line, parking their RVs side by side. At Roosevelt Lake in Arizona, for example, stones that marked the ancient house outlines of Hohokam and later Salado peoples for hundreds of years are piled helter-skelter by unknowing tourists to form campfire pits. Even areas outside the maximum flood pool are highly affected, as sites formerly exposed only to occasional visits of Native Americans and backpackers become available to anyone with a bass boat and a sixpack.

Our inundation project also taught us something about American values. Underlying the whole program was the premise that reservoirs were going to be built, archeological sites or endangered snail-darters notwithstanding. Society had already made its fundamental choices; we were providing answers that would improve the efforts to mitigate the impact.

Many reservoirs are beautiful places, although those who love wild rivers may find that hard to swallow. Some people, like the late writer and "eco-warrior" Edward Abbey, have such an intense hatred for dams that they would take satisfaction in seeing them blown up. The heroes of Abbey's *Monkey Wrench Gang* attempt just that, to the vicarious delight of many readers. They could just as well take solace, however, in contemplating the fragility of human-made structures. The ghosts of drowned rivers stir restlessly beneath the placid waters of reservoirs. In the eye-blink of a few thousand years, they will sweep away the concrete and earthen plugs that hamper their quest for the sea.

As I cram the last of the dive gear into our van at Elephant Butte, one of our students approaches me to ask a parting question. She points across the lake at the white line that runs along the steep shoreline just above the present water level—the bathtub ring common to many water impoundments. "What is that anyway?" she wants to know. I tell her it's blue-green algae bonded with calcium carbonate, and if she'd like a closer look, she can glance down at her feet, because she is standing in it. Like many of the things that affect us most, it isn't noticeable until we're removed enough to gain perspective.

Before the Deluge

Dam Construction in Turkey Threatens Invaluable Archaeological Sites

Karen Fitzgerald

The fifth-largest rock-and-earth dam in the world, the Ataturk is the third of 21 dams the Turkish government intends to build on the Tigris and Euphrates rivers. Supplying irrigation water and hydroelectricity, the dam promises to transform the vast dust bowl of southeast Turkey into a breadbasket that could feed all of the Middle East and Europe, too, according to Vassar College geologist Yildirim Dilek, who has studied the dam's impact.

But to make way for the future, pieces of the past must be sacrificed. The dam project has already flooded hundreds of archaeologically significant sites along the Euphrates and will affect hundreds more before completion. The clock is ticking for the archaeologists scrambling to excavate these potentially invaluable sites before the water rises. Much of the region is virgin territory to archaeologists.

Samsat, near the Euphrates, was one of the first victims of the dam project. A bustling city of 50,000 during the Roman Empire, Samsat goes as far back as the Neolithic Period. A rich site like this would normally take decades to excavate, but archaeologist Nimet Özgüç of the Turkish Historical Society and her team had only 11 years to work before the water came rushing in in the late 1980s.

Archaeologists from Ankara University, working under the direction of Olus Arik, have begun another emergency excavation at a town called Hasankeyf, due to be submerged upon the completion of the Tigris's Ilisu Dam in about six years. Many archaeologists consider Hasankeyf the most wrenching loss because of its striking buildings. "Hasankeyf is filled with masterpieces of Islamic architecture," says archaeologist Guillermo Algaze of the University of California, San Diego.

The dam region holds the only clues to the intersection of the Mesopotamian cultures to the south and the Anatolian cultures of ancient Turkey to the north, Algaze explains. Only four known sites record the incursion of the Sumerian culture of Mesopotamia into Anatolia, he says. The Carchemish Dam, planned for the Euphrates River, will put three of them under water.

Yet another threatened site, Kazane Hoyuk, may contain artifacts that overturn conventional notions of how and where civilization began. A tablet found there recently is written in cuneiform, the first system of writing, devised by the Sumerians. Some archaeologists consider it another example of Sumerian culture spreading into Turkey, but University of Virginia archaeologist Patricia Wattenmaker, a director of the excavation, says the artifacts found so far reflect a culture distinct from the Sumerians. The great size of the site—100 hectares—suggests it was a city of a population unheard of before the development of agriculture and civilization. Wattenmaker believes the prehistoric city was an independent seed of civilization, perhaps one of many independent city-states throughout the Middle East that nurtured cultural advances at about the same point in history.

Her team has excavated Kazane Hoyuk for only two summers, and only five to seven more years remain before irrigation construction concludes there. Then the land will be devoted to agriculture year round, making archaeological excavation too expensive to continue. Ironically, archaeologists would probably never have discovered the Kazane Hoyuk site if not for the large irrigation channel that now cuts through the modern town. During its construction, bulldozers kicked up prehistoric pottery that tipped off Wattenmaker to the importance of the site.

Although she knows her days at Kazane Hoyuk are numbered, Wattenmaker has only praise for the Turkish government's efforts to excavate the sites before flooding. She and other archaeologists point out that other countries, including the United States, do much less when technology encroaches upon archaeological material, a not-uncommon occurrence. "It happens literally every day everywhere in the world," Algaze says.

Regardless, the massive scale of the dam projects in a country so rich in antiquities makes Turkey's case particularly poignant. Turkey boasts more than 40,000 recorded archaeological sites, and half the country hasn't even been explored.

Dam construction imperils sites such as Kazane Hoyuk, which boasts pottery (above) dating back to 5000 B.C., and Harran, home of ancient Harran University (below).

Tales from a Peruvian Crypt

*The looting of a prehistoric pyramid stimulates an operation in salvage
archeology, with unexpected scientific dividends*

Walter Alva and
Christopher B. Donnan

*Walter Alva, a native of Peru, has
participated in numerous excavations
on that country's north coast and is the
director of the Museo Brüning at Lambayeque. Coauthor Christopher B.
Donnan is a professor of anthropology
and director of the Fowler Museum of
Cultural History at the University of
California, Los Angeles. They are the
coauthors of* Royal Tombs of Sipán
*(Los Angeles: Fowler Museum of Cul-
tural History, University of California,
1993).*

In the fertile river valleys that relieve
Peru's arid coastal plain, mud-brick
pyramids stand as the most visible evidence of the prehistoric Moche civilization, which flourished between the
first and eighth centuries A.D. Rising
out of agricultural fields in the Moche
River valley, the massive Pyramid of
the Sun was the largest structure ever
built in South America. With a ramp
that led up to small buildings on its flat
summit, it stood about 135 feet high
and sprawled over 12.5 acres at its
base. It once contained more than 130
million sun-dried bricks. Some of it
has eroded away naturally, while part
was demolished in the seventeenth century by Spanish entrepreneurs in search
of rich burials or other treasures.

About ninety-five miles north of the
Pyramid of the Sun, in the Lambayeque River valley, the Moche ceme-
teries and three pyramids near the
village of Sipán have long been the
target of looters. Over the years they
have dug many deep holes with picks
and shovels in hopes of locating intact
tombs containing ceramic vessels, shell
and stone beads, and rarer ornaments
of silver and gold. By November 1986,
they had nearly exhausted the ceme-
teries, and one group of treasure
seekers decided to focus on the smallest pyramid. Working at night to avoid
police detection, they dug a series of
holes, but found little of value. Then,
on the night of February 16, 1987, at a
depth of about twenty-three feet, they
suddenly broke into one of the richest
funerary chambers ever looted, tne
tomb of an ancient Moche ruler.

The looters removed several sacks
of gold, silver, and gilded copper artifacts. They also took some ceramic
vessels, but they broke and scattered
many others in their haste. Almost
immediately, the looters quarreled over
the division of the spoils, and one of
them tipped off the police. The authorities were able to seize some of the
plundered artifacts, but only a pitiful
amount was salvaged from the find.
The rest disappeared into the hands of
Peruvian collectors or was illegally
exported for sale in Europe, Japan, and
the United States.

Building on civilizations that preceded them in coastal Peru, the Moche
developed their own elaborate society,
based on the cultivation of such crops
as corn and beans, the harvesting of
fish and shellfish, and the exploitation
of other wild and domestic resources.
They had a dense, socially stratified
population, with large numbers of
workers devoted to the construction
and maintenance of irrigation canals,
pyramids, palaces, and temples. Their
lords apparently received food and
commodities from their subjects and
distributed them to lesser nobles and to
the potters, weavers, metalworkers,
and other artisans who created luxury
objects for the elite. In sculptures, decorated ceramics, and murals, archeologists have glimpsed many complex
scenes of Moche life, including hunting, combat, and ceremonial practices.

The luxury items from Sipán that
were confiscated by the police, including hollow gold beads of various
shapes and sizes, hinted at the magnifi-
cence of the plundered burial, which
must have belonged to one of the Moche elite. More fortune-hunters descended on the site in search of
overlooked valuables. They hacked at
the tomb walls and sifted through the
excavated dirt. By the time the police
secured the area, little was left except a
boot-shaped hole. Nevertheless, with
armed guards stationed around the
clock, we hastily organized an archeological survey to learn everything
possible of scientific value (author
Walter Alva directed the project;
coauthor Christopher B. Donnan was
one of the many participants.)

We began by making a contour map
of the three pyramids and what remained of their ramps and adjacent
plazas. The small pyramid, where the

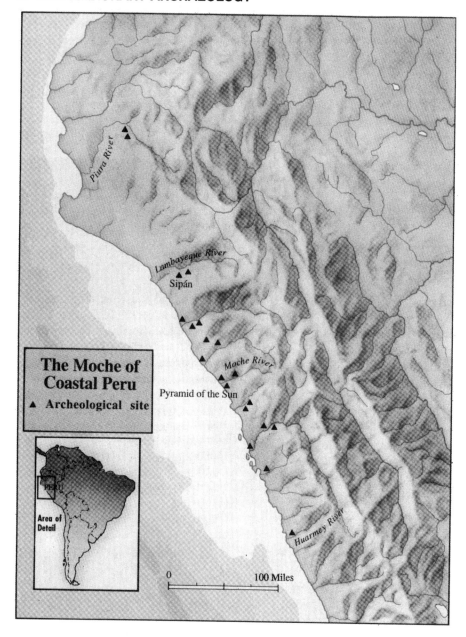

The Moche of Coastal Peru

▲ Archeological site

PERU

Area of Detail

Piura River

Lambayeque River

Sipán

Moche River

Pyramid of the Sun

Huarmey River

0   100 Miles

tomb had been found, was riddled with looters' tunnels, but in some places, the piles of dirt they had excavated helped preserve the original contours. The tunnels also enabled us to examine the internal construction. The pyramid and the rest of the complex evidently had been built and rebuilt over a long period of time, undergoing many changes as the various parts were enlarged. The small pyramid seems to have gone through six phases, beginning in the first century A.D. and ending about 300.

Although the burial chamber had been gouged out of shape, we were able to determine that it had originally

been roofed with large wood beams, which had decomposed. To our great surprise, we were able to uncover some of the tomb's contents that had been missed by the original looters and the subsequent gleaners. Clearing along one side of the chamber, we found the remains of a large, gilded copper crown decorated with metal disks; four ceramic jars modeled in the shape of human figures; and a copper mask with inlaid turquoise eyes. In excavating these, we also discovered a heavy copper scepter forty inches long, pointed at one end and bearing a three-dimensional architectural model on the other. The model depicted a

platform with a balustrade, surrounding an open-front building with one back wall and a peaked roof supported by posts. Seventeen double-faced human heads decorated the roof ridge, while depicted in relief on the wall was a supernatural creature, half feline and half reptile, copulating with a woman on a crescent moon.

Knowing that the pyramid would be further plundered once we left, we decided to open up a new section to methodical excavation, choosing a ten-by-ten meter (1,076-square-foot) area near the summit. Here we came upon a place where the mud brick had been carved out and refilled in ancient times. Digging down, we found eight decomposed wood beams, similar to those that had roofed the looted burial chamber. Buried beneath these, in the debris of what had been a small rectagular chamber, we found 1,137 ceramic bowls, jars, and bottles. They portrayed a variety of human figures: warriors holding war clubs and shields, nude prisoners with leashlike ropes around their necks, musicians with drums, and seated figures wearing beaded pectorals (biblike coverings). Some were arranged in symbolic tableaux, for example, musicians and prisoners ringing and facing noble personages.

As we removed the ceramics, we found several pieces of copper and, finally, a man's skeleton lying jackknifed on its back, with chin, knees, and arms pulled in toward the torso. Since the Moche customarily buried their dead in a fully extended position, we interpreted this individual to be a sacrificial victim, whose body had been shoved into the small chamber as part of the ritual offering.

Even as these offerings were being excavated, we discovered a second, larger rectangular area that appeared to have been carved into the pyramid and refilled. As we carefully excavated this, we found, about thirteen feet below the original surface of the pyramid, the skeleton of a man wrapped in a cotton shroud. He lay stretched out on his back and wore a gilded copper helmet. Over the right forearm, which rested on his chest, was a round copper shield. A little below we found the remains of seventeen parallel beams that, we dared hope, lay over a major, undisturbed burial chamber.

The discoveries that subsequently emerged surpassed our dreams. Buried in the chamber were the remains of a wood coffin that contained the richest grave offerings ever to be excavated scientifically in the Western Hemisphere. The body of a man between thirty-five and forty-five years of age had been laid to rest with a feathered headdress, banners of cloth with gilded copper decorations, beaded pectorals, nose ornaments and necklaces of gold and silver, ear ornaments of gold and turquoise, face coverings of gold, a gold backflap and a silver backflap that would have been hung from the belt, and countless other precious objects. In his right hand the deceased had held a gold and silver scepter topped with a large rattle, and in his left hand, a smaller scepter of cast silver. In relief on the rattle, which was shaped like an inverted pyramid, were scenes of an elaborately dressed warrior subjugating a vanquished opponent. The sculpted head of the smaller scepter echoed this theme.

Working six days a week, it took us four months to document and safely empty the delicate contents of the tomb. As our original budget became exhausted, we received some partial funding from a brewery and a truckload of noodles donated by a pasta manufacturer. At one point we were paying the fieldworkers with a combination of cash and noodles. We eventually secured new support from the Research Committee of the National Geographic Society and were able to proceed with further excavation.

All the while we had been working and moving equipment around the coffin burial, we had been walking only inches above hundreds of ceramic vessels, two sacrificed llamas, a dog, and the burials of two men, three women, and a child of nine or ten. Although we do not know this for sure, the men and the child might have been buried as sacrifices to accompany the principal figures. The remains of the females, however, were partly decomposed at the time they were placed in the tomb,

as evident from the way the bones were somewhat jumbled. They had probably died years earlier and their remains maintained elsewhere until this final interment.

As we excavated the tomb and cataloged its contents, we couldn't help wondering who was the important personage buried there. The key to the answer was a major photographic archive of Moche sculpture and drawings at the University of California at Los Angeles. As the tomb was being excavated, photographs of the objects were sent to UCLA for comparative study.

Many of the objects in the coffin suggested the man buried there was a warrior. The archive of Moche art contains hundreds of depictions from which we can reconstruct a sequence of Moche militarism and ceremonial activity. We can see processions of warriors carrying war clubs, spears, and spear throwers, perhaps on their way to battle. We can see warriors in combat, apparently away from settled areas. The essence of Moche combat appears to have been the expression of individual valor, in which warriors engaged in one-on-one combat, seeking to vanquish, rather than kill, an opponent. The victor is often shown hitting his opponent on the head or upper body with the war club, while the defeated individual is depicted bleeding from his nose or losing his headdress or other parts of his attire. Sometimes the victor grasps his adversary by the hair and removes his nose ornament or slaps his face.

As far as we can tell, the Moche warriors fought with one another, not against some foreign enemy. Once an opponent was defeated, he was stripped of some or all of his clothing and a rope was placed around his neck. The victor made a bundle of the prisoner's clothing and weapons and tied it to his own war club as a trophy. After a public parading of the spoils, the prisoners were arraigned before a high-status individual and finally brought back to the Moche settlements or ceremonial precincts. There the priests and their attendants sacrificed them, cutting their throats and drinking the

blood from tall goblets. The bodies were then dismembered and the heads, hands, and feet tied individually with ropes to create trophies.

Many representations of the sacrifice ceremony exist in Moche art. Although they vary, not always depicting all personages in the ceremony, apparently three principal priests and one priestess were involved, each associated with specific garments and ritual paraphernalia. The most important was the "warrior priest," generally depicted with a crescent-shaped nose ornament, large circular ear ornaments, a warrior backflap, a scepter, and a conical helmet with a crescent-shaped ornament at its peak. A comparison of these and other details with the contents of the tomb convinced us that the individual buried there was just such a warrior priest.

When the sacrifice ceremony was first identified in Moche art, in 1974, no one could be sure it was a real practice, as opposed to a mythical event. Now we had archeological evidence that this was an actual part of Moche life. Here was one of the individuals who presided over the sacrifices. Further, because the limited numbers of objects salvaged from the looted tomb were similar to some of those we had excavated, we could conclude that the looted tomb also must have belonged to a warrior priest.

As if this were not enough, during the excavation of the warrior priest's tomb, we located another suspected tomb elsewhere on the pyramid. We held off excavation until work on the earlier find was nearly complete. The knowledge we gained made it easier to anticipate the sequence of excavation. Again we found the residue of a plank coffin containing the rich burial of a man between thirty-five and forty-five years old. Among his grave goods was a spectacular headdress ornament of gilded copper, in the form of the head and body of an owl from which arched long banks with suspended bangles, representing the feathered wings. Nearby we found the remains of four other individuals: a male between fourteen and seventeen years of age, two females in their late teens or early twenties, and an eight- to ten-year-old child. Buried with the child were a dog and a snake.

The contents of this tomb were only a little less lavish than those of the warrior priest. They suggest that the principal individual was another of the priests depicted in the sacrifice ceremony—one we call the "bird priest." The major clue was the large owl headdress. He was also buried with a copper cup near his right hand, similar in proportion to the cups portrayed in pictures of the sacrifice ceremony.

Having identified these individuals as participants in the sacrifice ceremony, we began to wonder if such ceremonies took place in Sipán itself. The answer was soon revealed when, about eleven yards from the bird priest's tomb, we found several small rooms that contained hundreds of ceramic vessels, human and llama bones, and miniature ornaments and implements, mixed with ash and organic residues. Among the human remains were hands and feet, quite possibly the trophies taken from dismembered sacrificial victims. Altogether these looked to be the residue of sacrifice ceremonies, which the Moche apparently carried out at Sipán, as no doubt they did at their other centers.

The looted tomb, the two excavated tombs, and the sacrificial offerings all seem to date to about A.D. 290. While excavating the offerings, we found a fourth, somewhat earlier tomb containing the remains of a man between forty-five and fifty-five years old, also richly endowed with grave goods, including a necklace of gold beads in the form of spiders on their webs, anthropomorphic figures of a crab and a feline, scepters, an octopus pectoral with gilded copper tentacles, and numerous other ornaments and objects. Nearby we found the body of a young, sixteen- to eighteen-year-old woman next to a sacrificed llama. This tomb may also have belonged to a warrior priest, but not all the identifying elements are there. Possibly, this is simply because it dates to an earlier period than the depictions we have of the sacrifice ceremony, which are all from after A.D. 300.

Moche civilization collapsed suddenly, probably as a result of one or more of the natural cataclysms that periodically devastate coastal Peru—earthquake, flooding, or drought. The Moche had no writing system, so they left no records we can hope to decipher. They disappeared before Europeans reached the New World and could leave us eyewitness accounts. Yet with the scientific excavation of these royal tombs, we have gained an intimate portrait of some of their most powerful lords. Work at Sipán continues, now at a promising location near the tomb of the bird priest. As we dig more deeply, we look forward to our next encounter.

Maya Resurrection

After a millennium of decay, the buildings of Copán come back to life in Honduras's new museum of Maya sculpture

Barbara W. Fash and William L. Fash

A research associate at Harvard's Peabody Museum, Barbara W. Fash serves as artist and sculpture coordinator for the Copán Acropolis Archaeological Project (CAAP). She is responsible for the concept of Copán's new sculpture museum and supervised the reconstruction of the façades on display. Her husband and coauthor, William L. Fash, is the director of CAAP and the Bowditch Professor of Central American and Mexican Archaeology and Ethnology at Harvard. He is also the author of Scribes, Warriors, and Kings *(London and New York: Thames and Hudson, 1991).*

The older residents of the modern town of Copán Ruinas remember the earthquake that shook western Honduras in April 1934. The church in the town square was nearly destroyed, and dozens of houses were leveled. The nearby Maya ruins themselves suffered damage: four of the buildings on the acropolis, already undercut by river erosion, collapsed into heaps of rubble and what few sculptures remained on the other nine major buildings toppled. When Carnegie Institution archaeologist Gustav Stromsvik arrived shortly thereafter, he found people living in temporary lean-tos on the patios of their houses as they weathered the aftershocks of the following week. Cleanup work left ancient sculptures stacked in piles around the site.

The earthquake only added to the disarray created over the past centuries, during which local people and foreign visitors scavenged through the rubble of the Maya ruins and took attractive pieces for their own. This process began in the years following the collapse of the ruling Classic period dynasty in Copán, in about A.D. 820. Postclassic people removed sculpture from the temple that housed the tomb of the last ruler, Yax Pasah (New Dawn), and carried it off to their own homes. They buried their children and other loved ones in the east court of the acropolis, using the carved blocks from what had been a funerary temple to line the bottoms of the graves. They carried broken fragments of stone incense burners high into the mountains and left them in caves and crevices of the sacred mountains where they revered their ancestors.

Collectors of a different kind later scattered Copán sculpture all over the world: to museums in Brussels, Cambridge, Chicago, Cleveland, Esquipulas (Guatemala), Genoa, London, New Orleans, New York, Philadelphia, San Diego, Seville, Tegucigalpa (Honduras), the Vatican, and Washington, D.C. Meanwhile sun, wind, rain, and temperature change assaulted those sculptures that remained. As the great Mayanist Tatiana Proskouriakoff observed, "As if jealous of this superb creation of man, all the most violent forces of nature seem to have conspired to destroy it."

This history presents a challenge for those seeking to study the ancient sculptures. As a result of major research and conservation efforts by archeologists from the United States and Central America (working under the auspices of the Honduran Institute of Anthropology

and History), in the past decade more than 25,000 stone sculpture blocks from Copán's fallen temples and palaces have been studied and cataloged, and indoor storage areas have been created to protect them from the elements. Now we and our Central American colleagues (including Honduran archaeologist Ricardo Agurcia, the executive director of the Copán Association, and Guatemalan architectural restorer Rudy Larios, the codirector of the Copán Acropolis Archaeological Project) have embarked on another ambitious mission: to create a new sculpture museum in Copán.

Built by the Honduran government, the museum will insure the safekeeping of the monuments and unveil restored façades that once covered the larger buildings throughout the ancient city. Although less familiar to the public than Copán's free-standing stelae and altars, these façades contained the most plentiful, and often the best, stone sculptures in the city. The carvings fit together like mosaics to depict human figures, gods, animals, flowers, crops, and other motifs.

Set within the Copán National Park, the museum will consist of one main building and several smaller ones connected by outdoor trails. Construction of the main building is complete and installation of its exhibits is well under way, with the opening scheduled for July 20, 1996. Designed by Honduran architect Angela Stassano, the building is two stories high, broader at the second story. A large mound around the base is planted with trees native to the area to help the museum blend with its mound- and tree-filled surroundings. Natural light illuminated the Copán monuments and buildings for centuries, and every attempt has been made to use natural light within the museum. In addition to skylights, the museum has a large opening in the center of its roof, so that at any given time, the daily and yearly movements of the sun will highlight some exhibits more clearly than others, just as they do at the archeological site.

The building was planned to reflect the central concepts of the Maya worldview. The entrance is a stylized mouth of a mythical serpent, symbolizing a portal from one world to the next. As people proceed through the tunnel, they have a sense of entering another place and time. The entrance also evokes the tunnels that archeologists dig to reveal the earlier constructions buried inside the pyramidal bases of Maya buildings.

Aligned with the compass points, the four-sided building reflects the horizontal ordering of the ancient Maya world, to which the four cardinal directions and the yearly path of the sun were fundamental. Four was the number associated with both the sun god and the perimeters of a *milpa*, or cornfield.

In addition to the horizontal directions, the Maya envisioned an axis through a center point connecting the human plane to the supernatural worlds above and below. This vertical axis is also reflected in the museum. Images of deities and denizens of the underworld appear on the first floor. These include killer bats, skulls and long bones of the dead, portraits of deceased ancestors, and stingray spines. The spines were used in rituals by rulers, nobles, and commoners alike to draw blood from fleshy parts of their bodies as a sacrificial offering for gods and ancestors.

On the second floor, the world of the living is represented by pieces from eighteen different buildings, including seven complete façades. These illuminate a series of important themes in the lives of Copán's ancient inhabitants: agriculture and fertility, the ballgame and natural cycles, mountain deities, ritual sacrifice, warfare and the ruler as paramount warrior, links to other cities, the role of the scribe, the patron of sculptors, the royal residence and shrines, residences of the nobility and the role

of nobles in the collapse of the king's divine authority, and the council house. The second floor also presents celestial deities, including sun disks surrounded by clouds and a throne decorated with a sky band. The ceiling that frames the opening in the roof is decorated with Maya symbols for the celestial bodies and constellations of the night sky. These tricolored paintings are based on carvings from Copán.

The centerpiece of the museum, rising through both floors and piercing the open ceiling, is a reconstruction of an early Classic temple—a terraced, two-story building dubbed Rosalila (rose-lilac) by its excavators. The original, discovered beneath Structure 16 of the acropolis by Honduran archeologist Ricardo Agurcia, is the most intact structure ever found in Copán. A hieroglyphic step carved on its front stairway describes it as the work of Copán's tenth ruler, Moon-Jaguar, who reigned from A.D. 553 to 578. Unfortunately, it is only accessible by narrow tunnels, making it impossible to move and very difficult to observe. The full-scale replica will show it off in all its multicolored splendor. (When the ancient Maya stopped using the original structure, they painted over its modeled plaster decorations in white. Careful probes beneath this white layer have revealed several levels of paint, each colored differently, often with numerous repaintings. The museum replica duplicates the final color scheme.)

As a whole, the temple represents a deified mountain—a place of creation, a source of life-giving water (such as a cave, spring, stream, or waterfall), and birthplace of the sacred maize plant. The head of this mountain deity, which combines the attributes of both mother and father, is depicted on the lower central part of the roof crest, with a cleft in its forehead from which maize sprouts. Draped over the sacred mountain images and framing the image of a cave in the upper story are two-headed celestial dragons. These mythical creatures combine attributes of snakes and crocodiles.

Representations of the sun god adorn the lower parts of the temple. The sun's daily journey and the life cycle of maize

were linked together in veneration of the process of birth, life, death, and rebirth. Some of the images of the sun god are humanlike; others show him as a mythical bird. With his serpent-shaped wings outstretched, the sun as a celestial bird soars in four directions around the building. On the lowermost façades are seven serpent-winged birds, from whose open mouths emerge the head of the sun god.

Within the many chambers on both Rosalila's ground level and second story, the Maya rulers held rituals that put them in touch with their universe and their ancestors. When the building was closed and covered over, in about A.D. 650, a ritual bundle with nine elaborately shaped flints, three flint knives, stingray spines, and marine animals was deposited on the first floor in a small room. Other offerings were left in large clay vessels in the central room and altar. A portion of the lower rooms has been reconstructed in the museum replica so that visitors will be able to see where the offertory caches were found and will be able to experience what a temple was like on the inside.

Two important goals of the museum are to give Copán's modern inhabitants greater insight into the importance of the ancient sculpture and to train local workers in its conservation and restoration. Like the sun on its daily journey, or the maize through its yearly cycle, the Maya buildings and sculptures—and their meaning—are being resurrected. The sculptors who replicated the reliefs of Rosalila, together with all the other participants in the project, have shared the joy of renewing their ties to their heritage, and they take pride in returning Copán and its artistry to its proper place among the world's cultural treasures.

The Copán acropolis and its surrounding urban core and rural settlements lay in a pocket of the Copán River valley, whose fertile bottom land attracted agriculturists to the region more than 3,000 years ago. At the city's height, about A.D. 800, some 20,000 people occupied the Copán pocket, and the urban concentration displaced most farming to outlying lands. The city was a huge machine at work at the center of a civilization with hieroglyphic writing, an advanced calendar, and complex astronomy. The gradual collapse of that civilization—as a result of such stresses as overpopulation, contaminated water sources, political unrest, and warfare—is a common theme in the story of human life on earth.

In the modern-day town of Copán Ruinas, people speak Spanish, worship the Christian God, and attend schools that emphasize history after 1492. They partake of many aspects of Western "civilization," such as the telephone, electricity, MTV and CNN, and a diet enriched by Old World products. But the inhabitants of the town, as well as the poor farming families that eke out an existence in the mountains, still carry on many ancient Maya traditions. Their love of the Mesoamerican trinity of crops—corn, beans, and squash—is unchanged. Corn, prepared in myriad ways, is still the diet mainstay of everyone, rich and poor, rural and urban. *Pom,* the incense used by the ancient Maya in household and royal ritual, is still a prized commodity in the local market.

In rural areas, dwellings are still designed and constructed as they were two millennia ago. Wattle-and-daub walls are covered by thatch or palm roofs, and each family's compound consists of three or four small buildings grouped around a central courtyard. One structure serves as the bedroom; another is the kitchen; a third serves as a storage room for maize, beans, and other goods; and a fourth houses a shrine. Atop the shrine is a cross, but even this quintessential Christian symbol has pre-Columbian counterparts in the art, writing, and cosmology of the ancient Maya. Incense is burned on the altar in ceramic censers not unlike those found with the ancient altars and shrines.

Other aspects of traditional culture include beliefs in spirits that reside in the mountains and streams, even in the ruins of the dynastic center of the Copán acropolis. Some of these spirits, which bear Maya and Nahuatl (Aztec) names, can be recognized in ceramic and stone sculptures recovered in the archeological excavations. As in more traditional Maya communities elsewhere, the people of Copán take these supernatural and ancestral spirits very seriously. They sacrifice chickens at house dedication ceremonies and when they plant their fields of corn, beans, and squash each May. On May 3, the Day of the Cross, a superficially Catholic procession goes up to a concrete cross on the top of the nearest high mountain, in hopes that the devotion will bring the life-giving rains.

In years gone by, the more hispanicized, Ladino members of the community ridiculed the traditional beliefs and life ways of the more humble, Indian segments of the population who lived in the rural areas. This is beginning to change, as the work in the ruins and at the sculpture museum have shown the breathtaking works of art and architecture left by the ancient inhabitants of the Copán Valley. The work on the council house has struck a particularly resonant chord, showing as it does that the ruler acted in harmony—or at least in consultation—with the representatives of the families who lived outside the dynastic center. In 1994, to commemorate the 100th anniversary of the founding of the town of Copán Ruinas, the past was made present when a replica of the ancient council house was constructed in the courtyard of the modern municipal complex.

The Boom in Volunteer Archaeology

Richard A. Wertime

Richard A. Wertime is a Contributing Editor to ARCHAEOLOGY.

Americans of all ages and from all walks of life suddenly want to get involved in archaeology. In a poll of more than 50 federal, state, and local organizations, ARCHAEOLOGY has found a dramatic surge in volunteer participation coast to coast. One federal initiative, the Forest Service's "Passport in Time" program, which oversees volunteer archaeology in 107 of the 125 national forests, reports a 550 percent increase in volunteer applications since its original two-state program went national in 1991.

State "Archaeology Week" initiatives, which help garner volunteer support for statewide archaeological projects through museum exhibits, tours of active sites, and demonstrations of ancient practices, report major increases in amateur involvement in the past two years: up 300 percent in Virginia, 30 percent in Texas, and 100 percent in California. Urban-centered programs

also report surprising growth in volunteer participation—since 1992, up 200 percent in Fairfax County, Virginia; 75 percent in Portsmouth, New Hampshire; 30 percent in St. Augustine, Florida. Whatever induces people to get involved in archaeology—and there is a host of intriguing motives—one thing is certain: amateur participation couldn't come at a better time, for there are far too few professionals to deal with all of the sites that are being discovered or that need to be protected.

What do amateur archaeologists do? What kinds of training and supervision do they get? And why has their interest in digging into the past blossomed so suddenly in so many parts of the country?

Some of the answers to these questions lie in the scores of federal, state, and local programs that both feed and benefit from the public's hunger for archaeology. Major national organizations like the Archaeological Institute of America, the Society for American Archaeology, and the Society of Historical Archaeology have created independent and sometimes interlocking

programs that seek to educate the public about proper methods of archaeological investigation as well as site management and protection. In an effort to broaden public awareness and support, some 30 states now have an annual "Archaeology Week," and some, like Arizona and Virginia, an "Archaeology Month." Local enterprises like Alexandria Archaeology in Alexandria, Virginia, and Strawbery Banke in Portsmouth, New Hampshire, provide a wealth of opportunities for the avocational archaeologist, as do study centers such as the Crow Canyon Archaeological Center in Cortez, Colorado; the Four Corners School of Outdoor Education in Monticello, Utah; and the Center for American Archaeology in Kampsville, Illinois.

The federal government has long been a leader in site protection and preservation. In 1892 it set aside for preservation the prehistoric ruins at Casa Grande in Arizona. The 1906 Antiquities Act specified the protection of antiquities on all lands owned or controlled by the government and required permits to excavate them. More recent federal efforts have focused on public archaeology. Visionary professionals like Charles R. McGimsey, III, and Hester Davis in Arkansas helped steer through Congress the Archaeological Resources Protection Act (ARPA) of 1979 and its 1988 amendments, including Section 10(C), which mandates that federal agencies develop programs to increase public awareness about cultural resource significance and protection.

The Bureau of Land Management, the Forest Service, the National Park Service, the Army Corps of Engineers, the Fish and Wildlife Service, and the Bureau of Reclamation today administer some 700 million acres of public land. In response to ARPA these federal agencies and others have developed an array of research and stewardship programs designed to involve the public in the management of archaeological sites on these lands. The National Park Service's "Volunteers in the Parks" embraces a range of initiatives and volunteer possibilities, as does the Bureau of Land Management's "Adventures in the Past." The Forest Service's "Passport in Time" program, started in 1989 in four national forests in Wisconsin and Minnesota, was conceived by archaeologists Gordon Peters, Christy Caine, and Mark Bruhy, who needed help with site surveys, excavation, and lab work. They began recruiting volunteers under what was then the agency's cultural resource management program. "At the time," recalls Bruhy, "the program was a well-kept secret. We had no inkling that it would become a nationwide effort by 1991."

But for all the federal government's involvement in public archaeology, it is the regional, state, and grassroots efforts that constitute the wellspring of nonprofessionals in archaeology. Avocational societies across the United States identify, study, and protect sites; conduct public outreach programs; publish newsletters, scholarly bulletins, and monographs; and oversee museum collections. They are often headed by deeply committed nonprofessionals who may have spent years studying the archaeology of their region. David A. Andreozzi of Bar-

rington, Rhode Island, and Kathleen Joyce-Bassett of Roanoke, Virginia, are cases in point. Andreozzi, a cabinetmaker, has been president of the Narragansett Archaeological Society for five years. "People are amazed that Precolumbian activity occurred in our area," he says. "They're especially amazed by the lithics, and want to become more involved."

In the fall of 1992, while walking near a kettle hole (a symmetrical depression left by an ancient glacier) in the wooded part of a local golf course, Andreozzi spotted three stone flakes, each about the size of a dime. The kettle hole, 25 feet deep and 100 feet across, contained two to three feet of water. "It seemed an ideal prehistoric water source for the big game that Stone Age inhabitants relied on," he recalls. "I suspected that there might be a lithic workshop nearby and proposed to the board of governors of the Rhode Island Country Club that we excavate it. The board approved and we went out and found four Late Archaic hearths at least 4,500 years old with a wealth of lithics. We had hit the nail right on the head." The C-shaped hearths were well preserved, and stuck professional archaeologists who visited the site as unique. The excavation became the subject of the largest story the local newspaper had ever run, and Andreozzi began to hear from area teachers who wanted to bring their students to the site. "One hundred and eighteen students hiked over from Barrington Middle School," he remembers with pride. "We set up tables for the artifacts and even had some students participate in the fieldwork by digging and sifting for lithics." Before long, he developed a slide show for students who could not visit the site. Now, he says, "I've turned on 1,200 to 1,400 kids. We let them form their own teams, and they are helping us excavate test pits."

Andreozzi has just received a $2,000 grant from a Rhode Island philanthropist to pay for carbon dating and aid his outreach effort. About one-fiftieth of the potential site area has been excavated with the assistance of Paul Robinson, Rhode Island's state archae-

ologist; Barbara Hall, curator of the Haffenreffer Museum of Anthropology at Brown University, and her assistant David Gregg; and Carol Barnes Fidler and E. Pierre Morenon, Rhode Island College anthropologists. Material recovered at the site is being held by the Narragansett Society. After it is analyzed and cataloged, a representative collection will be presented to the country club. The remainder will be kept by the society and periodically made available to the public at the Barrington Preservation Society Museum.

Kathleen Joyce-Bassett, who works for the Virginia Department of Corrections, is president of the Archaeological Society of Virginia (ASV), which has 15 chapters statewide. "One of the most important concerns of our group," she says, "is providing education about preservation issues and about archaeology, both historic and prehistoric." Accordingly, the society publishes a quarterly bulletin, which contains articles by professionals and nonprofessionals, and recently received an award from the Society for Historical Archaeology for publishing seminal work. The society has also cosponsored with the Council of Virginia Archaeologists a series of symposia on Virginia archaeology, and is now engaged in an ambitious fundraising program known as the ASV 2000 Development Fund, whose objective is to raise $250,000 to establish an ASV center with a library and exhibitions. "Right now," says Joyce-Bassett, "everybody in our organization is a volunteer. The work we're doing has gotten so extensive that we need an executive director to handle all of the paperwork."

In many state societies avocational archaeologists work closely with professionals. In Texas, for example, archaeological societies are open to both professionals and amateurs. Thomas Hester, director of the Texas Archaeological Research Laboratory and a two-time president of the Texas Archaeological Society says, "the tie between avocationals and professionals goes back to the 1920s when the society was organized. There were not many professionals at that time, and

Educating the Volunteer

There are dozens of field schools and certification programs that train non-professionals, but how well-trained do they need to be? Many archaeologists feel that close supervision and a low ratio of professionals to amateurs are crucial to effective training. David Starbuck, who has directed or participated in at least 25 field schools, believes that one professional for every six amateurs is about right. He offers no formal certification, in part because "it is impossible to tell from a certificate whether someone is well trained." How does one tell? "Call up the previous instructor and simply ask him or her whether the trainee knows what to do," says Starbuck.

Others who work with volunteers take an even more flexible approach. "There are many jobs that untrained people can do," says KC Smith, a Museum of Florida History educator experienced in introducing archaeology to the lay public. "You can train people to do basic field-assistance activities—screening, washing of artifacts—in two hours, and that satisfies them perfectly. Not everybody needs extensive training."

Texas state archaeologist Robert J. Mallouf believes "professionals must accept the fact that it may not always be possible to instill professional attitudes in avocationals to the degree that one is comfortable turning them loose on a problematic undertaking. Most avocationals can reasonably be expected to fall short of expectations when it comes to the difficult, tedious requirements of scientific reporting."

In some states archaeologists do offer certification programs aimed at turning nonprofessionals into highly skilled colleagues. One such program is run by the Arkansas Archaeological Survey under the direction of state archaeologist Hester Davis. Widely emulated by states such as Kansas, South Carolina, New Mexico, Oklahoma, New Jersey, and Virginia, the program affords the nonprofessional a multitiered training experience, with everything from a two-and-one-half week program of lectures, lab, and fieldwork to opportunities to assist archaeologists in labs around the state. The strength of the Arkansas program is in the number of professionals who participate, as many as one archaeologist for every six volunteers. Kay McCarron, Fairfax County archaeologist in northern Virginia, has adapted the Arkansas model to serve the needs of the Washington, D.C., region. McCarron's program offers a technician certification upon completion of one year of lab work, excavation, and fieldwork, and a paraprofessional certification requiring at least three years of study.

The cost of archaeological training for avocationals is also an issue much discussed among professionals. For its teenage summer camp, which lasts two weeks, Alexandria Archaeology charges $475 per person per week, and acknowledges that it uses the money to support ongoing work. Similarly, the Colonial Williamsburg "Learning Weeks in Archaeology" program costs $550 for a two-week session. The Andover Foundation for Archaeological Research in Andover, Massachusetts, requests a hefty tax-deductible donation of $1,600 from those who volunteer to work at its rock-shelter site in southwestern New Mexico. By contrast, the Fairfax County, Virginia, certification programs costs $30 for technician certification and $50 for papaprofessional certification. Richard Boisvert, New Hampshire deputy state archaeologist and coordinator of the State Conservation and Rescue Archaeology Program, offers an innovative program for adults in archaeological recording, management, and education that is funded by the state's Historic Preservation Fund and hence costs nothing—although the program accepts donations for the rental of port-o-potties. "The public has a responsibility for its heritage," says Boisvert, "and archaeology has an obligation to include the public where it's appropriate. It's a two-way street. A great deal of archaeology can be taught to anyone who is reasonably intelligent and reasonably healthy." On the other hand, he adds, "If archaeology is available only to people who can afford it, that's wrong. It shouldn't become an exclusionary thing."

The cost of training goes hand in hand with the question of program quality. Not every avocational is satisfied with the preparation he or she receives. A case in point is the mixed experience of Joseph Illick, a professor of history at San Francisco State University. In 1991, Illick responded to an ad for volunteers in the Sierra Club magazine. He traveled to the mountain town of Blanding, Utah, to help locate, map, and photograph Anasazi Indian sites in the Abajo Mountains under a program jointly sponsored by the Sierra Club, the Bureau of Land Management, and the Forest Service. Having paid several hundred dollars for the privilege, he joined some 30 other volunteers mapping vast stretches of territory for days at a time. While his first day was devoted to a "reasonably comprehensive" series of orientation sessions, he felt that "there wasn't sufficient follow-up once we got out there," and that he and his fellow participants were covering a lot of territory "with only occasional glimpses of what this was all about." His frustration was compounded when the entire project was later abandoned, apparently because of disagreements among the project sponsors. Illick says he would volunteer again, but would check more carefully the manner in which participants were prepared and kept in touch with the general goals of the project. "I accept the fact that volunteers are expected to carry out the most mundane tasks," he notes, "but that labor should be accompanied by daily, or nightly, discussions of topics that elevate the experience. After all, that's why we contribute ourselves."

—R.A.W.

How to Volunteer

The National Park Service offers an informative brochure, *Participate in Archeology,* that lists titles of books, movies, television programs, and videos on archaeology, as well as a selection of titles for people who need a basic introduction to the discipline. Write: Publication Coordinator, Archaeological Division, National Park Service, P.O. Box 37127, Washington, DC 20013-7127.

The Forest Service publishes *PIT Traveler: Passport in Time Newsletter,* which lists volunteer opportunities. Write: Jill Schaefer, Volunteer Services Manager, Passport in Time Clearing House, P.O. Box 183664, Washington, DC 20036 (telephone: 202-293-0922; fax 202-293-1782).

The broadest annual listing of volunteer opportunities is the *Archaeological Fieldwork Opportunities Bulletin,* published by the Archaeological Insti-

tute of America. Write: Kendall/Hunt Publishing Company, Order Department, 4050 Westmark Drive, Dubuque, IA 52002 (telephone: 800-228-0810). The cost is $9.00 for AIA members, $11.00 for nonmembers. It also contains the names, addresses, and phone numbers of all state archaeologists and historic preservation officers, as well as regional societies of the Institute.

Earthwatch, published bimonthly by Earthwatch and sent to its members, also lists volunteer opportunities. Write: Earthwatch Membership Service, P.O. Box 8037, Syracuse, NY 13217 (telephone: 800-776-0188; fax 617-926-8352).

Nonprofessionals interested in opportunities available through private organizations and archaeological study centers should write directly to them. These include Crow Canyon Archaeological Center, 23390 County Road K, Cortez,

CO 81321 (telephone: 800-422-8975); Center for American Archeology, Department B, Kampsville Archeological Center, P.O. Box 366, Kampsville, IL 62053 (telephone: 618-653-4316); Four Corners School of Outdoor Education, East Route, Monticello, UT 84535 (telephone: 801-587-2156); Anasazi Heritage Center, Bureau of Land Management, 27501 Highway 184, Dolores, CO 81323 (telephone: 303-882-4811); University Research Expeditions Program, Department J-4, University of California, Berkeley, CA 94720 (telephone: 415-642-6586); Foundation for Field Research, P.O. Box 2010, Alpine, CA 91001 (telephone: 619-445-9264); and The Smithsonian Institution, Smithsonian National Associates, Research Expedition Program, Suite 4210, 490 L'Enfant Plaza SW, Washington, DC 20560 (telephone: 202-357-1350).

—R.A.W.

the few that we had worked closely with the amateurs." Texas is distinguished from many other states by the sheer number of its avocational archaeologists and by the independence of its 32 regional societies, which are not to be confused with the ten regional chapters of the statewide archaeological organization. Many members of the regional groups also participate in state chapter activities. Cities like El Paso, Fort Worth, Houston, and Dallas have their own societies.

In 1962 the Texas statewide organization started a summer field school that annually attracts 450 to 500 participants and moves around the state to endangered sites or locations where professionals need help with long-range regional studies. The field school is run by professionals, but is organized and managed by avocationals, who, says Hester, "provide the crew chiefs and the training." Texas, along with Arizona, has one of the oldest and best managed "site steward" programs in the country. Site stewards are avoca-

tionals who monitor and maintain sites, reporting damage or looting when it occurs. The stewards are appointed and administered by an advisory board representing the state's archaeological community, including academic and contract archaeologists as well as amateurs.

Nonprofessionals are attracted to archaeology for a number of reasons. Some want escape from their daily routines, others like the experience of new places, the mingling with new people, the challenge of the work. Affording as it does a material record, archaeology also offers *tangible* evidence of the past. Museum of Florida History educator KC Smith observes: "While the thrill of unearthing or working with ancient objects initially may draw volunteers to archaeological projects, they quickly appreciate that sites and artifacts are the keys to unlocking the past. Inevitable, their excited focus on 'things' evolves into an intense curiosity about the people who made those things."

Just as the motives vary, so do the talents that nonprofessionals bring to the field. Jill Osborn, who coordinates "Passport in Time" in Washington, D.C., insists that the central function of public archaeology is not to furnish professionals with free labor, but rather to enfranchise the public in the task of preserving the nation's heritage. Avocationals bring an array of talents to their work: skills in organization, management, and public relations; technical training in draftsmanship, cartography, and photography; and curatorial abilities.

Perhaps the most precious resource that people bring is curiosity. Janel Kerby was a 17-year-old high-school student from Canyon, Texas, when she traveled to Tallahassee to participate in a two-week program called "Florida Findings." Sponsored by the Girl Scout Council of Apalachee Bend and the Museum of Florida History, the program introduces newcomers to the field of archaeology. What led Janel to Florida is instructive: "When I was younger," she says, "my dad and grandfather would take me arrowhead hunting down in Plains, Texas. They were interested in the past—nothing scientific—they'd just talk about how things used to be." When she was 15, Janel joined the Panhandle and Texas archaeological societies. She learned about "Florida Findings" through the Girl Scout Wider Ops (for "wider opportunities") Program, which affords scouts the chance to participate in enrichment programs across the country. In Tallahassee, she worked on land and underwater sites. What made the experience so special? "There was something different to it," she says. "Other teachers I'd known knew the answers to questions they asked. In Florida, we helped find the answers."

Alexander Munton of Portsmouth, New Hampshire, is a 78-year-old retired expert in industrial hygiene, a field, he says, in which "accurate measurement is extremely important." To his volunteer work at Strawbery Banke in downtown Portsmouth, Munton brought his passion for precision. To measure the bases and rims of ceramics, he devised an ingenious transparent plexiglas measuring board with a series of concentric circles and a rule on it. The device measures pots, even large ones, quickly and accurately. He also devised excavation data sheets and drew maps recording various excavations at the site.

The first settlers to sail into Portsmouth Harbor in the early seventeenth century encountered an embankment covered with strawberry plants. Now a ten-acre historic urban neighborhood, Strawbery Banke encompasses a part of the old waterfront known as Puddle Dock (largely silted in by the turn of the century and land filled today), and nine furnished houses dating from 1695 to the 1950s. Munton got involved with Strawbery Banke in 1981, when he joined "Project Discovery," a program that trained volunteers for exploratory excavations at an historic home. In 1990 he joined his teenage grandson in a field school at another historic site. To his surprise, his grandson was "treated as one of the volunteers—as an adult" by director Martha

Pinello. "We were blessed at having an opportunity to be involved in an archaeological project together," says Munton. "It's not always easy to find sites available to amateurs." What hooked the senior Munton on archaeology? "Several things," he says. "Strawbery Banke has a high caliber of staff. They're very professional, very friendly. They take a lot of time with you. They're not set in their ways; they're anxious to progress. It's just an exciting place to be!" His first excavation, he said, "was like being a child at the seashore." His expertise has deepened with time. An archivist of considerable experience, he is writing an article for the New Hampshire Archaeological Society on deeds, probates, and early maps of Portsmouth.

Where is avocational archaeology headed? Most observers agree that the full potential has barely been tapped. The Forest Service, for one, plans to incorporate people with disabilities into its outreach programs. Special needs participants in the "Passport in Time" programs will have the same spectrum of challenges available to them as people without disabilities. Says Jill Osborn, "People with disabilities want those levels of challenge. A person in a wheelchair may want to push himself to the limit" in tackling archaeology in a wilderness setting. While she says that there are no plans to try to make all programs and sites accessible to people with disabilities, it is the government's intention to create avocational opportunities for them wherever they are reasonable. "It makes good business sense," says Osborn. "Forty-three million Americans have a permanent disability, and they are more active today than at any time in the past. If 30 percent of the total population is interested in heritage, 30 percent of the population with disabilities is also interested. In addition, Passport in Time is a family activity. If the experience excludes one person in the family with a disability, chances are, the rest of the family won't participate either."

This past September, the Society for American Archaeology convened its second "Save the Past for the Future"

conference in Breckenridge, Colorado. As they had done five years earlier at a gathering in Taos, New Mexico, conferees representing federal, state, and local agencies issued a plea for intensified efforts to educate the public about the widespread looting of sites and the need for greater public participation in site maintenance and protection. "Public education increases the public's understanding of and appreciation for the past," says George Smith, a National Park Service archaeologist based in Florida and a cochairman of the conference. "This translates into more volunteers and more effective site stewardship. The more people we can get involved the better the chance we will have to get this looting crisis under control."

Public archaeology is in some ways a uniquely American phenomenon. KC Smith believes "Americans have inherited something from their elders—a congenital fascination with people, places, events, and things of the past." As an observer of the archaeological scene for a generation, this writer would add his own perspective: archaeological activity—particularly that of unearthing what has been buried—affords citizens an especially potent metaphor for self-realization. Indeed, the pull that archaeology exerts seems almost mystical, inasmuch as it affords an opportunity to become grounded in the past. For Native Americans, this becomes an act of recovery, an reclaiming of ancient identity; for Americans with immigrant pasts, it is a strengthening of cultural and national affiliation.

Archaeology can be hot, cold, tedious, frustrating, unglamorous, and dirty work. For volunteers, the privilege of participating can be an expensive one. What draws people into such work? Archaeology is a field of great diversity. By virtue of its mission—recovering the past and articulating it to the present—it embodies the concept of the common good. Archaeology is a mirror held up, not to nature, but to humanity. To excavate the past is to polish that mirror, that we may better see ourselves and know more clearly who we are.

Index

Credits/Acknowledgments

Cover design by Charles Vitelli

1. About Archaeology
Facing overview—Illustration by Mike Eagle for DPG. 14—Courtesy of the Library of the University of Virginia. 15—Courtesy of Jeff Hantman. Map source: David Bushnell, "The Five Monacan Towns in Virginia, 1607," Smithsonian Miscellaneous Collections, Vol. 82, No. 12, 1930, a reprint of a section of the 1624 original.

2. Problem-Oriented Archaeology
Facing overview—WHO/photo. 57-59—Photos by Neal Brown. 93—Map by Joe LeMonnier for Natural History.

3. Experimental Archaeology
Facing overview—© 1985 by David Weintraub/Photo Researchers. 114—Jim Wagner (left), courtesy of Sophie de Beaune (right).

115—Courtesy of Sophie de Beaune (left), Johnny Johnson (right). 116—Johnny Johnson. 120-122—Photographs by Michel Lorblanchet. 128-129—Illustrations by Jean Wisenbaugh. Reprinted by permission of Lindgren & Smith, Inc., N.Y.

4. History and Ethnoarchaeology
Facing overview—United Nations photo.

5. Politics and Archaeology
Facing overview—Courtesy of York Archaeological Trust. 194-195—Illustration by Brian Sullivan.

6. Contemporary Archaeology
Facing overview—United Nations photo. 230—Map by Joe LeMonnier for Natural History.

ANNUAL EDITIONS ARTICLE REVIEW FORM

■ NAME: _____ DATE: _____

■ TITLE AND NUMBER OF ARTICLE: _____

■ BRIEFLY STATE THE MAIN IDEA OF THIS ARTICLE: _____

_____

■ LIST THREE IMPORTANT FACTS THAT THE AUTHOR USES TO SUPPORT THE MAIN IDEA:

_____

_____

_____

_____

■ WHAT INFORMATION OR IDEAS DISCUSSED IN THIS ARTICLE ARE ALSO DISCUSSED IN YOUR
TEXTBOOK OR OTHER READINGS THAT YOU HAVE DONE? LIST THE TEXTBOOK CHAPTERS AND
PAGE NUMBERS:

_____

_____

_____

_____

■ LIST ANY EXAMPLES OF BIAS OR FAULTY REASONING THAT YOU FOUND IN THE ARTICLE:

_____

_____

_____

_____

■ LIST ANY NEW TERMS/CONCEPTS THAT WERE DISCUSSED IN THE ARTICLE, AND WRITE A SHORT
DEFINITION:

_____

_____

_____

_____

*Your instructor may require you to use this ANNUAL EDITIONS Article Review Form in any
number of ways: for articles that are assigned, for extra credit, as a tool to assist in developing
assigned papers, or simply for your own reference. Even if it is not required, we encourage
you to photocopy and use this page; you will find that reflecting on the articles will greatly
enhance the information from your text.

We Want Your Advice

ANNUAL EDITIONS revisions depend on two major opinion sources: one is our Advisory Board, listed in the front of this volume, which works with us in scanning the thousands of articles published in the public press each year; the other is you—the person actually using the book. Please help us and the users of the next edition by completing the prepaid article rating form on this page and returning it to us. Thank you for your help!

ANNUAL EDITIONS: ARCHAEOLOGY 97/98
Article Rating Form

Here is an opportunity for you to have direct input into the next revision of this volume. We would like you to rate each of the 45 articles listed below, using the following scale:

1. **Excellent: should definitely be retained**
2. **Above average: should probably be retained**
3. **Below average: should probably be deleted**
4. **Poor: should definitely be deleted**

Your ratings will play a vital part in the next revision. So please mail this prepaid form to us just as soon as you complete it.
Thanks for your help!

Rating	Article	Rating	Article
	1. The Quest for the Past		21. Ice Age Lamps
	2. The Enlightened Archaeologist		22. Paleolithic Paint Job
	3. How Archaeology Works		23. Bushmen
	4. The Golden Marshalltown: A Parable for the Archeology of the 1980s		24. The Earth Is Their Witness
			25. Legacy of Fort Mose
	5. Epistemology: How You Know What You Know		26. The Guns of Palo Alto
	6. Archaeology: Integrating the Sciences and the Humanities		27. Living through the Donner Party
			28. Colorful Cotton!
	7. Surrogate Stone		29. Murders from the Past
	8. History Unearthed		30. An Anthropological Culture Shift
	9. Hard Times at Lizard Man		31. The Antiquities Market
	10. Coming to America		32. Who Owns the Spoils of War?
	11. First Americans: Not Mammoth Hunters, But Forest Dwellers?		33. Troy's Prodigious Ruin
			34. Lure of the Deep
	12. Rhinos and Lions and Bears (Oh, My!)		35. 35,000-Year-Old Artifacts Repatriated in Tasmania
	13. Ancient Odysseys		36. Beirut Digs Out
	14. Toward Decolonizing Gender: Female Vision in the Upper Paleolithic		37. The Past as Propaganda
			38. The Preservation of Past
	15. Lithic Technology and the Hunter-Gatherer Sexual Division of Labor		39. Saving Our World's Heritage
			40. Largest Pueblo Ruin to Be Saved
	16. Denizens of the Desert		41. Damming the Past
	17. Find Suggests Weaving Preceded Settled Life		42. Before the Deluge: Dam Construction in Turkey Threatens Invaluable Archaeological Sites
	18. Thailand's Good Mound		
	19. Yes, Wonderful Things		43. Tales from a Peruvian Crypt
	20. Moving the Moai—Transporting the Megaliths of Easter Island: How Did They Do It?		44. Maya Resurrection
			45. The Boom in Volunteer Archaeology

(Continued on next page)

ABOUT YOU

Name _____ Date _____

Are you a teacher? ❑ Or a student? ❑

Your school name _____

Department _____

Address _____

City _____ State _____ Zip _____

School telephone # _____

YOUR COMMENTS ARE IMPORTANT TO US !

Please fill in the following information:

For which course did you use this book? _____

Did you use a text with this *ANNUAL EDITION*? ❑ yes ❑ no

What was the title of the text? _____

What are your general reactions to the *Annual Editions* concept?

Have you read any particular articles recently that you think should be included in the next edition?

Are there any articles you feel should be replaced in the next edition? Why?

Are there other areas of study that you feel would utilize an *ANNUAL EDITION?*

May we contact you for editorial input?

May we quote your comments?

No Postage
Necessary
if Mailed
in the
United States

ANNUAL EDITIONS: ARCHAEOLOGY 97/98